THL HITLER YOUTH

Origins and Development 1922–1945

H. W. KOCH

Cooper Square Press

First Cooper Square Press edition 2000

This Cooper Square Press paperback edition of *The Hitler Youth* is an unabridged republication of the edition first published in New York in 1975.

Printed in the United States of America on acid-free paper.

Published by Cooper Square Press
An Imprint of the Rowman & Littlefield Publishing Group
150 Fifth Avenue, Suite 911
New York, New York 10011

Distributed by National Book Network

Library of Congress Cataloging-in-Publication Data

Koch, H. W. (Hannsjoachim Wolfgang), 1933-
    The Hitler Youth : origins and development 1922-1945—1st Cooper Square Press ed.
        p. cm.
    Originally published: New York : Barnes & Noble Books, 1975.
    Includes bibliographical references and index.
    ISBN 0-8154-1084-0 (alk. paper)
    1. Hitler-Jugend—History. I. Title.
DD253.5 .K6 2000
943.086—dc21
                                                                        00-034617

⊖™ The paper used in this publication meets the minimum requirements of American National Standard for Information Sciences—Permanence of Paper for Printed Library Materials, ANSI/NISO Z39.48-1992.
Manufactured in the United States of America.

*Dem Gedächtnis
meines Bruders
Wolfgang Koch
1924–1944*

Contents

Illustrations

Acknowledgments are due to Bayrisches Haupstaatsarchiv, (BHSA), Bundesarchiv
   Koblenz (BA), Süddeutscher Verlag (SV) and Ullstein (U)

Preface

Personal experience apart, the origins of this book lie in a study begun several years ago and suggested by my friend Professor Gwyn Williams. The study proved both enlightening and depressing, for it revealed how Herder's concept of the *Volk*, which offered an alternative approach to popular democracy from that provided by 'the ideas of the French Revolution', changed – in fact mutated – year by year and decade by decade until it became one of the component strands of National Socialism.

My original intention had been to call this book 'Youth in Bondage', for it ultimately required the cataclysm of the Second World War to break Germans, and especially Germany's youth, from what was the last and strongest perversion of the concept of the *Volk*. This perversion was very much part of the ideological make-up of the Hitler Youth and other German nationalist youth movements. (Whether of course the end of National Socialism has liberated German youth in general from ideological shackles is doubtful, for in our own day the ideological landscape is littered with very much the same elements as is the consumer market: namely substitutes and synthetics.)

No pretence is made here of supplying a definitive history of the Hitler Youth. For one thing the sources are far from satisfactory. Such as there are help us to gain a fairly coherent outline, but although the bureaucratic apparatus of the Hitler Youth was as inflated as that of any other NSDAP organization, its administrative methods, certainly at the regional and local level, left much to be desired. Thus knowledge of what happened in a Hitler Youth *Gebiet* in part depends on how dedicated an administrator its head was. Furthermore much material must have fallen victim of the systematic destruction that took place shortly before the arrival of the Allies. Whether the latter collected all they could of the remainder is doubtful. In the late autumn and winter of 1945–6 I transported home several cartloads of files which were scattered over the administrative premises of the *Gebiet Hochland*. Alas, this action was not carried out in the interests of historical investigation but simply in order to keep the stove going in temperatures of about − 30°C. However, in recent years I have been fortunate in acquiring a number of relevant documents from private sources. These and other materials will in due course be made available to the Bundesarchiv in Koblenz.

I have deliberately omitted any detailed treatment of the relations between the Hitler Youth and other German Youth Leagues. To have done this would have meant writing a different book as well as adding immeasurably to the length of this one. As it happens the entire complex of the *Bündische Jugend* will receive treatment in a different volume.

One major problem concerned the translation of a number of terms. Since many of these proved virtually impossible to translate they have been left in the original. Thus, for example, the significance of Hitler Youth ranks can easily be established by looking at the diagram on page 271 setting out the organizational structure of the Hitler Youth at the *Obergebiets* level and below. A distinction has been made in the use of the terms 'Hitler Youth' and 'HJ', the former applying to all youth organizations within the NSDAP, the latter only to the 'senior branch' of the Hitler Youth, to those aged 14 to 18.

Obviously I am indebted to many people for their help, advice and assistance. First I must express thanks to those friends in Germany's other half who have been kind enough to supply me with relevant materials which otherwise would not have been accessible to me. But it is − for the time being − in their interest and in compliance with their wishes that they shall remain nameless. Herr Dr Bauer, Frau Dr Schlichting and Frau Bayer of the Bayrisches Hauptstaatsarchiv, were helpful to a degree far beyond 'the call of duty', as were Frau Dr Kinder, Herr Dr Haupt and Herr Regler of the Bundesarchiv. I must also express my gratitude to Dr Schwebel of the Staatsarchiv Bremen, Dr Johe of the Forschungsstelle für die Geschichte des Nationalsozialismus in Hamburg and Herrn v. Löwis of the Textarchiv der Süddeutschen Zeitung, Munich. And I doubt whether anyone working in the Institut für Zeitgeschichte has ever come away from a conversation with Herr Dr Anton Hoch without considerable profit. The Bayrische Staatsbibliothek, and the Library of the University of York have also been of considerable assistance. For editorial help I must thank Mr and Mrs Terry Beechey.

Then I must express thanks to my maternal friend Frau Karla Zapf of Munich, whose *Wurstsalat* and *Bierle* kept occasionally flagging energies going. My thanks are also due to the Sailer families of Haag and Kirchdorf who provided the necessary tranquil environment for work; in fact I should extend my thanks to the people of Haag/Obb generally for their hospitality.

I am grateful to Eyre & Spottiswoode (Publishers) Ltd for permission to

Preface

quote from *Nazi Seizure of Power* by W. S. Allen; to Rowohlt Verlag GmbH for the extract from *Die Letzten Tage der Reichskanzlei* by Gerhard Boldt; and to Deutsche Verlagsanstalt GmbH for the quotation from *Fazit* by Melita Maschmann.

Above all I am indebted to my wife and family, including of course my daughter Freya who helped prepare the diagrams.

York/München 1973   H.W. Koch

1 Traditions

It is 10 November 1914, three months after the outbreak of the First World War. On the Western Front the German advance on Paris has been halted at the Marne; the race to the Channel ports has been settled at Ypres; the war of movement is about to end. In a desperate attempt to evade the approaching stalemate the German Fourth Army has been given the task of smashing through the defensive line established by the Allies between Ypres and the Channel. And on this November day the 26th Reserve Corps of the Fourth Army has been sent into battle, ordered to take the village of Langemarck, the heavily-defended core of the British position.

The attempt is doomed from the start. Whoever ordered it is guilty of a military blunder – a crime even. For the task of seizing Langemarck – which would have dampened the spirits of the hardiest veterans – has been entrusted to some of Germany's youngest and least-experienced troops. There are few regular soldiers in the Fourth Army; it is made up largely of regiments of young volunteers, among them apprentices, university students and 40,000 grammar-school pupils who have had part of their last year at school remitted. It is these boys – the flower of German youth: no other way to describe them – who are dying under the guns of Langemarck.

A last desperate assault is called for. The decimated units of the 26th Reserve Corps move forward. It is hopeless, clearly hopeless, everyone can see that. But suddenly, above the battle roar, a young voice breaks into song, and the tune is taken up quickly by his comrades. It is the *Deutschland Lied* – '*Deutschland, Deutschland, über alles*' – not yet Germany's national anthem but famous since the 1840s as a patriotic and nationalist song. Singing now, and with passionate courage, the volunteers attack the British lines time and again. The slaughter continues; the attacks grow weaker; so does the song. By early afternoon it is clear beyond all possible doubt that this battle is lost for the Germans. The landscape around Langemarck has been transformed into an arena of death, littered with corpses and wounded men, with stretcher-bearers and medics doing all they can

1

among the moans and groans and the shouts of '*Kamerad!*'

Yet suddenly, even in that hell of desolation and despair, once again an unknown young soldier intones the *Deutschland Lied*. And *again* it is taken up by his comrades across the battlefield. Groups of drifting soldiers, deprived of their officers, many of them wounded, mostly without helmets, but still clutching their rifles, without orders, acting on irrational compulsion alone, turn back to renew the attack.

To those who watched them advance they must have seemed no longer men or boys but singing maniacs as they rushed futilely once again into the terrible fire of the British machine-guns.

As well as these doomed young men, something else was destroyed at Langemarck and on the other great battlefields – Dixmoiden, Birschoote, Paschendaele, Beclaere, Hollbeke, Messines – that mark the agony of the volunteer German armies of 1914. A generous idealism died there too. In large part German youth had rushed to join the colours in 1914 out of a vague, wild belief that by this war – the supreme act of national will – the old, staid, bourgeois society would be brought crashing down. The war, so many young Germans believed, would sweep away despotism and capitalist plutocracy inside as well as outside Germany. The battle between the forces of materialist civilization and the spirit of culture seemed at last to have been joined, and in the first flush of enthusiasm they had no doubt which side would triumph. But in the carnage of Langemarck they learned that they were mistaken, that the hope of changing the world and their society by one mighty exertion was doomed. The First World War showed its real face, and the armies settled down to the atrocious business of mass-slaughter.

Yet if one myth died at Langemarck, another was being brought into full-blooded life there, one that was of incalculable danger for the future of German youth, exercising its morbid fascination over the younger generation for decades to come. It was the myth of obedience to orders even if their purpose was highly questionable, and of self-sacrifice even unto death in the cause of the German people and the German nation. The myth was not born at Langemarck. It very clearly had its origins in one form or another in the complex cultural, intellectual and political history of Germany over the hundred years and more that preceded 1914 – as indeed did the naïve idealism and optimism that perished in that year – and we now have the task of exploring that history to trace if we can the development of the youth movement and youth outlook that produced such a complicated and fertile mythology. But in the end we shall have to return to the battle-fields. For if the myth of self-sacrifice and unquestioning loyalty was not born there, it was certainly weaned into a lusty maturity on the blood of the singing martyrs of Langemarck. And the whole tragic German epic of death and defeat in the First World War is the great catalyst in the process that saw the patriotic, idealistic, utopian traditions of young Germany in the nineteenth century dwindle away into the excesses and cruelties and fatuities of the Hitler Youth in the third decade of the next.

Though the origins of the organized German youth movements can be traced back as far as the mid-sixteenth century[1], it must be emphasized that 'youth' as a social group, in Germany and elsewhere, was not an organized body or a force in its own right until the end of the nineteenth century. The slow process which in time produced a genuinely autonomous youth movement began with the French Revolution and took its course gradually throughout the following century–though events like the Napoleonic invasions and the revolutionary movements of 1848 supplied short but intense bursts of energy which helped to accelerate the process.

As in so much else, Napoleon is the key figure here. At the end of the eighteenth century young Germany, fired by news of the exciting events in revolutionary Paris, was in revolt against the enlightened rationalism of the day, which, it was contended, was suppressing human spontaneity within its artificial boundaries. In this period of *Sturm und Drang* youth proclaimed its inalienable right to be young; to be themselves, not copies of a fossilized parent-generation which was only the product of a fossilized social system. Where young men had previously joined student organizations which were based on regional loyalties, many of these groups underwent a transformation into 'fraternities' whose common aim was the realization of some future utopia, the precise nature of which remained for the most part rather vague though tending towards the future achievement of universal brotherhood and peace. The words of a young librarian of Mainz, Georg Forster, in 1792 express the typical yearnings of his time and age-group: 'The world is my fatherland, and all men are one people united by one language. And that language is the sight and tears of the people. . . . Is it necessary for mankind in order to be happy to be locked up in states in which everyone is the serf of the other and none free?'[2]

The emergence of Napoleon in France and his triumph as the liquidator of the revolution brought about the rude awakening of German youth from its romantic and utopian day-dreams. When Napoleon's seemingly invincible legions crossed the Rhine and, with powerful blows delivered at Austerlitz, Jena and Auerstädt, Eylau and Friedland, forced their will upon the population of Central Europe, ideas like that which saw the German mission in terms of propagating world citizenship and brotherhood were shattered. The question of individual and national survival now moved to the fore. The factor of power asserted itself, against which the idealism, the art and the poetry of the *Sturm und Drang* period proved very feeble and ineffective weapons. Though the principles of the French Revolution had found favourable reception among German youth, their abuse at the hands of Napoleon and their application in the national interests of the French state caused many young Germans to begin an urgent reappraisal of the intellectual premises they had previously accepted without question.

In fact an ideological weapon that could be used against Napoleon was already at hand. Quite unconscious of the purpose to which it would ultimately be applied the philosopher Johann Gottfried Herder (1744–1803) had already forged it in his concept of the *Volk*.[3] While to the rationalist of the Enlightenment *society* is the sum of its members, to the religiously-inspired romantic the members dissolve in the whole, into the *community*. The community, be it religious, be it national, was considered to constitute a natural organism, and in national terms this organism, in Herder's view, was the *Volk*. Herder argued that the individual can only fully realize his potential within the *Volk*, just as the *Volk* can only fulfil its God-given mission as the equal of other national communities – other *Völker*. Without his *Volk* the individual is nothing, any more than the *Volk* is anything without its state. Hence in Herder's view the realization of the *Volk* could in many instances only be achieved in opposition to the existing state – supposing the state did not correspond with the true interests of the *Volk* – and especially when that state was occupied and dominated by a foreign power. This kind of religiously-inspired patriotism tended to transform all rational aspects of politics into what Hegel later called a 'stew of the heart'.[4] Yet in spite of its inherent emotionalism, the political situation of the German lands during the first decade of the nineteenth century compelled many Germans to give serious thought along the lines proposed by Herder to the structure of the state, once a truly national community had been achieved.

Herder himself strictly opposed the egalitarian tendencies of the Enlightenment which had intrinsically contradicted his organic world view, dominated as it was by its Christian belief in divinely ordained differences in human beings.[5] Following this theme, a nation divided into its several estates, with each capable of being of service to the whole community, corresponded in Herder's view with earthly necessity and divine will. Each estate and all estates are equally necessary for the common good of the national community, though they are not equal with one another. Nevertheless their contribution is equally needed by the community as a whole and they are therefore equal before God. They form one link in the many interconnected links of a whole chain or organic being. If the church is the community of saints, so the nation is the community of service and service to the nation is the duty of all.[6]

Herder also opposed the spokesmen of the Enlightenment in his definition of liberty. His concept is also based on the Christian ethic according to which man can only be completely free in God by subjecting himself unconditionally to His will. Herder interpreted Germany's specific liberty as the liberty of conscience, a concept which the philosopher Kant later took a stage further by defining as the right and ability to dedicate oneself to the fulfilment of duty.

That Herder was not 'nationalist' in the derogatory sense of the term is borne out by the evidence. But he too was susceptible to a more militant patriotism when confronted by the political and territorial ambitions of Napoleon.[7] However, it was a patriotism which had its roots in the old universalist conception of the *Reich* – the 'Holy Roman Empire, the German Nation' – rather than one which envisaged a new German nation. He did accept that in defence blood would have to be sacrificed 'on the altar of the fatherland' for the organism called *Volk* and nation however, not simply for the state, because, once again, in his view the state does not produce the nation, but the nation the state.[8] To Herder the entire rational concept of the state was too mechanistic, devoid of the vigour, the virile impulses generated by the *Volk*. The state represents a herd held together by brute force, while the *Volk* is the natural family, an organism of nature embedded in the mainstream of the divine will.[9] In fact the *state*, as it existed in Herder's time, is the very antithesis of the *Volk*. It is an artificial entity, while the *Volk* is perfectly natural and harmonious. It follows therefore that a state is what a nation desires it to be and that consequently a nation's, or a *Volk's*, major constituent element is its history, which in the final analysis represents an organic process, the unfolding of a divine design. Herder, viewing God as the source of all organic strength, interprets history as one facet of the much larger organic development of the cosmos – an historical view of profound influence upon German historiography in the nineteenth century.[10] If Herder does not view history as the march of human progress, he views it nevertheless as a progression towards human salvation in Christ, Salvation in place of infinite progress, history in place of reason. History not only reveals God's design for the nations but reveals the nucleus of a higher form of life for man, leading towards his salvation.[11]

While history is the nation's major ingredient, the key to its character, its unique manner of expression, is the nation's language. Again, Herder was not the first to place the emphasis on German language and German folklore, an emphasis which was part of Germany's cultural renaissance during the latter half of the eighteenth century. Among others Opitz, Spener, and Francke had endeavoured to revitalize the German language in order to prevent it from declining into obscurity in the face of the dominance of the French language. But to Herder the language of the *Volk* is not merely a means of communication, but also an emotional spectrograph: it communicates factual detail but also conserves the spirit of an epoch. It is the memory of the *Volk*, and like the *Volk* it represents an indigenous organic growth without which there would be neither *Volk* nor fatherland, without which the nation would be deprived of its individuality.[12]

It is important not to overstate Herder's message; it is potent more in its later applications than in itself.

Herder propagated his ideas in an era in which the process of secularization had made immense strides, secularization in which, even so, religion was still a vital part of the German cultural and social fabric. Therefore his emphasis upon national individuality is without any qualitative connotations. The suffering of Christ is still the central event of mankind, Christianity the bond which conciliates and holds together all men. The fulfilment of the individual – that is, the development and full exercise of his faculties – can take place only within the *Volk*, just as each *Volk* can fulfil its divine destiny only in association with other nations. Humanity is still regarded as one entity;[13] Germany's mission is a mission of service, not a mission of domination.[14]

On the eve of the Napoleonic invasions, then, German patriotism was not absent, as Herder and a host of other examples show. What needed clarification and clearer definition was the object of that patriotism. Was it to be the *Reich*, the Empire, which Herder and many of his contemporaries desired to see rejuvenated, and which they hoped would project a cultural universalism? Or was it to be the nation, the *Volk* plain and simple, the concept which Herder had articulated at great length?

The intellectual climate in Germany was changing. At first the propagation of greater human liberties in Germany had received a major impetus from the French Revolution, but the growing resistance to French occupation generated militant German nationalism. Suddenly the realization dawned that it was the absence of a powerful united state which had allowed France to deal with Germany piecemeal; that Germany needed not only unity but an ideological *raison d'être* with which to oppose French revolutionary ideology.[15]

Napoleon crystallized the issues. In the intellectual armoury mustered against the French dictator, Herder's concept of the *Volk* represented the most potent weapon available, because with its help the transition could be achieved from a generation of German intellectuals who had considered themselves 'world citizens' to a generation of fanatical enthusiasts for a German national state. 'To be a *Volk* . . . that is the religion of our time,' wrote Ernst Moritz Arndt (himself not a subject of any of the German dynasties but a Swedish one) in order to raise Germans from their apathy to rise against Napoleon.[16] Arndt was the first who, still unconsciously though, endeavoured to isolate Herder's concept from its amalgam of Christianity and patriotism. But unlike the French Revolution, which in one of its phases deliberately attempted to replace Christian with non-Christian substance, in Germany the evolution of nationalism amounted to gradual dilution of the Christian substance, a gradual process of secularization of which the Germans as a whole were largely unaware. For German nationalism in general this meant that until the first decade of the twentieth century religion and patriotism were apparently concomitants, while in fact by the eve of the First World War the latter had fully replaced the former.

Though ultimately his work was hostile to religion, Arndt himself expressed his patriotism primarily in religious forms. He had travelled through France in 1798 and 1799, at a time when the German part of the left bank of the Rhine had already been annexed by France. He remained impressed by the revolutionary fervour of the French, but was somewhat sceptical about their attempts to bestow its blessings upon other nations, freely or by means of systematic oppression. Conscious of the individuality of nations, a consciousness clearly derived from Herder, he wondered whether the reaction to French policy would not actually produce results ultimately detrimental to French interests. As for Germany, he was certain that, fragmented and divided though she was, any further French inroads would only help her to recover her national consciousness.[17]

In that recovery he himself played a major role as the propagator of a militant national Protestantism, which found a ready response especially among the youth of Germany's Protestant regions. By identifying Luther with 'the German cause' against that of 'Rome' (France) it was ultimately Protestant Prussia which he thought stood for the cause of the German *Volk* against the foreign foe. Because the national language was a main ingredient of the *völkisch* ideology, Luther as the first translator of the Bible into the German vernacular was considered by Arndt as the founder of German literature. If, as Herder had formulated and as Arndt believed, the spirit of the *Volk* is revealed in its language, was not Luther the genius of the German language? In turn, like Luther, so Prussia would become the genius of the German *Volk*, forging it into one organic unity. Exponent of the Romantic movement as Arndt was, his vision of the future Germany was one of the rural past, rather than of the commerce and industry looming on the horizon or already reality in some parts of Prussia. In fact one of the main charges he levied against the concept of liberty as espoused by the French Revolution was that by furthering industrial growth it was destructive of the organism of political, economic and social life.[18]

In Friedrich Ludwig Jahn too we find the combination of religious and *völkisch* thought, and fervent conviction in the resurrection of the German *Volk*.[19] As a Prussian clergyman, the fulfilment of religious and of national duty was for him identical. His personality and his teaching particularly attracted young people. He left his mark on early nineteenth-century German history as an indefatigable propagator of German nationalism, and was particularly influential in the organization of gymnastic associations for training patriotic fighters and in the formation of the military *Freikorps* of German volunteers. After hostilities with France were concluded he continued to imbue student fraternities with nationalistic enthusiasm. He also coined the term *Volkstum*, which essentially connotates an image of an organic community, and thus differentiated between the romantic concept of nation, – the *Volk*, – and the rational concept of nation – 'artificially' combined territories ruled over by a dynasty which Jahn, like Herder, condemned as unnatural. Napoleon's ambition to combine all European nations into one Empire under French supremacy he abhorred; it would be tantamount to the rule of anti-Christ, it would mean the end of the divinely-created organic unity of the *Volk*.

Friedrich Schleiermacher was also a clergyman, and like Jahn he superimposed his religious frame of reference upon a political environment in which the national community represented the only legitimate and divinely-ordained institution. In his sermons Schleiermacher outlined the entire structure of religious and nationalist thought, which on this earth culminated in the '*Volksstaat*', which was man's 'greatest work of art' allowing him to climb to the highest state of humanity.[20] That there was an inherent contradiction in Schleiermacher's view between the state as a 'work of art', and the organic theory of the *Volk* and human institutions, appears to have escaped him. The true patriot is equally at home in church and *Volk*; both are part and parcel of the same organic whole, an organic whole best described by Jahn's term *Volkstum*. The ideal citizen and the fully harmonious and autonomous human being are in fact one and the same. The national community represents the divinely inspired order within which man can fully develop his faculties; outside which, however, his growth must inevitably remain stunted. This of course stands in direct opposition to the rational social contract theory; since society alone makes human existence possible in its sublimest form, the question of whether one obtains value in return for surrendering part of one's inherent rights to society is irrelevant. As in Christian doctrine true man does not exist outside the grace of the Church, so, to those who adapted Herder's ideas to their own purposes, man as such cannot really exist outside his *Volk* group.

Herder's definition of liberty had been one of the liberty of conscience, but a liberty enjoyed 'in the shadow of the throne' in which he could also enjoy the fruits of his labour, his comforts, his friends, his children, 'a moderate liberty which nowadays every patriot desires'.[21]

Kant's definition was much more sophisticated but in essence also described a liberty of conscience in the shadow of the throne, or the liberty to dedicate one's entire abilities towards the common wealth which, when allied with an essentially Christian world view, tended to endow the state with metaphysical qualities similar to those of religion. The natural scientist and philosopher Heinrich Steffens considered the existence of the state as a precondition for individual liberty, because, as to many of his contemporaries, the state appeared to him coterminous with the *Volk*, and the highest liberty of all is to realize the depth of the national spirit to its fullest extent.[22]

It was natural that, in opposition to the Enlightenment and its product the French Revolution, with whose perversions Napoleon was equated, Germans should develop a different concept of liberty. In the absence of a firmly rooted and specifically German-developed political theory, they therefore had to fall back upon the one major tradition left: that of religion. Liberty is thus attainable only within the national community which ideologues, deriving their premises directly from Herder's thought, equated with true Christianity. Service to the national community is indispensable for its life, and is tantamount to fulfilling one's duty as a Christian. But besides the general there was also the need for the particular, namely the need for sacrifice to liberate the national community from the French oppressor. For that reason the war against France in 1813 is in German history distinct in kind from any of the wars of the eighteenth century: it is the first 'popular' war, a 'crusade' against Napoleon, the intensity of which was greatly heightened by the writers and poets of the period, and which in its expressions of blind hatred was equal to that of the Crusades of earlier days.[23]

Looking at the idealistic poetry of men like Körner, Kleist and Rueckert it is quite obvious that one inherent ingredient of the new 'crusade' was a sacrificial ethos which found its expression also in the visual arts, though frequently with much less taste than in literature.[24] The early Herder had already made reference to the theme of sacrifice for the Fatherland, but the poets of the War of Liberation were to outdo him greatly.[25] Particularly Arndt, who during the war officiated in Prussian general Blücher's headquarters as a kind of official propagandist. And like him, others too interpreted death in the crusade for the Fatherland as being akin to the passion of Christ.[26]

History, too, was put in the service of the crusade. A heightened, exaggerated glorification of Germany's national history emphasized the sense of obligation to their homeland that Germans were expected to feel. National history became a revelation of national glory from which to derive new strength for the trials of the present and the plans for the future. But again, it was argued, the understanding of history requires the individual's complete surrender to and immersion in the national identity. Only that would ensure the full understanding of the *Volk* as a unit of historical continuity – the understanding that would equip the individual to serve the national community.[27]

Linguistics too was brought into the struggle against the invader. Herder had emphasized the importance of the language for the character of the *Volk*. Others took his teaching much further. Fichte, in his 'Addresses to the German Nation', seems to have been the first to lift patriotism and the concept of the *Volk* from a religiously influenced context into a mainly secular political one. Above all he stressed time and again the need to preserve the individuality of the German language because only through it did the German *Volk* exist.[28] The German language as opposed to the Romantic languages was, so he argued, largely unadulterated by foreign influences, and that gave it immeasurable depth and a virile force of expression, whereas other Northern European languages, heavily latinized, were capable of expressing the surface of life only. They were dead languages. Hence, he went on, the attempt to compare these languages with German is futile – one cannot compare life with death. Germany, as the sole unique possessor of a living language, represented the original *Volk*, the *Urvolk*, the only one with an original language. It did not matter in this view that the German nation was politically disunited – as long as it maintained the integrity of its language. For sooner or later this common language would resurrect the nation, the German *Volk*, as one political unit.[29]

Such exaggerations of cultural nationalism ignored the warnings and qualifications with which Herder had originally studded his own discourse.[30] For him language was merely one of the indigenous expressions which are part of a diversity through which mankind represented its essential unity.[31] But this mild and universal viewpoint had been overtaken by harder philosophies in the great national emergencies of the War of Liberation. This is best borne out by contrasting Herder, to whom mankind is still one organic entity and whose philosophy envisages the *Volk* as part of a cosmopolitan unity, with Schleiermacher, who rejected the humanism inherent in cosmopolitanism.[32]

Schleiermacher, and with him many of the patriots of 1813, accepted the diversity of mankind but also introduced a qualitative valuation which Herder had explicitly excluded at all times.[33] The younger philosophers taught that as in an organic state all components are required to function in an integrated fashion, so this in turn requires that some lesser functions should be carried out by certain individuals and higher ones by others.[34] This introduces a qualitative differentiation amongst individuals. The same, so it was argued, was the case between nations: some were of greater

value than others, even though lip service might still be paid to the idea of
the entity and equality of the whole of mankind before God.[35] Another
dangerous twist was then added to Herder's message: in the same way as it
is imperative for the individual to realize that the greatest and most important part of him is his membership of the *Volk*, so in the relations between
several national communities the most profound fact is their individual
existence, their life as a *Volk*, and to secure it and to perpetuate it requires
the rejection of any attempt at intermingling or mixing of respective
national communities.[36] Each individual has received from God a distinct
and separate task and so has each nation. Intermixture would therefore
mean interference with divine providence. National separation and definition are the prerequisites for the survival of the national community and
it is this principle which throughout the nineteenth century was to have a
profound influence in the political development of Central Europe.

The task of the preservation of national individuality was of course
widely preached before and during the War of Liberation, and the whole
propaganda of that period is based upon the religious ethos of war for
liberty. It should be noted that in the writings of Schleiermacher, Jahn, and
Arndt wars for the increase of power, which were thought to have been typical of the eighteenth century, were condemned as immoral again and again.
War in fact is only justified in their view if the existence of the national community is threatened.[37]

Even so, there was much potential danger in their teachings. Their full
acceptance of an organic theory and application of it to international relations inevitably led to the belief in an established hierarchy among the
several nations. To accept that each nation had a specific, divinely-ordained
mission could still be harmless; however, to add qualitative distinctions
placing some nations on a higher, others on a lower level, raised more
serious implications. Jahn saw in Germany the founder of eternal peace in
Europe and the 'angel of protection of mankind';[38] together with the
Greeks, they were the holy nations of mankind. Others were even more
explicit in advocating European federation under German auspices and as
this idea had had some political reality during past centuries with Charle-
magne and the Holy Roman Emperors, it held considerable attraction for
many.[39] For Fichte, of course, to be the *Urvolk* and to remain it constituted
the mission itself. To be a German, in his eyes, was not merely an accidental
characteristic but already a sign of perfection – a perfection on behalf of
which Arndt passionately preached the complete and merciless destruction
of the morally inferior foe.[40]

With Fichte, Schleiermacher, Arndt, and Steffens we enter the era of
German political romanticism during which Herder's cultural nationalism
was systematized – forged into a coherent ideology which subsequently was

to be one major element influencing German political thought. Within a span of less than fifty years Germany had made the transition from an essentially universalist cosmopolitan ideology to a specific brand of nationalist ideology. Herder's intention had been to draw attention away from the mechanistically-orientated views of his time to the process of actual growth as expressed in the development of national culture. The 'state' played a small part in his thought, until its tranquillity was disturbed by the foreign invader. Herder's concept, it turned out, was capable of mutating into an ideology directly confronting and countering the libertarian ideas of the French Revolution, on behalf of which Napoleon claimed to march and conquer. It was a shock therapy which created a new perspective, allowing the observation of the evolution of mankind to be transformed into an ideology of national defence. In so doing it changed the early indifference of many who suffered the French invasion into a passionate hatred of the foreigner, making them only too eager to seize any instrument handed them, which would allow them to assert and preserve their identity, and to rediscover in the process the supposed glory of the past which was to be resurrected in the future.

German nationalism of the time was then not the product of the reason of the Enlightenment but of political romanticism. From the outset it was loaded with highly emotional and therefore explosive charges. And perhaps in consequence it made a particularly strong appeal to German youth. This could already be seen during the first decade of the nineteenth century. Students were among the first to believe in – and to act upon – the principle that by drastic action Germany could be liberated from the oppressor. Ludwig Stabs, a student of law at the University of Göttingen, was one of several who in 1808 sacrificed their lives in vain in an attempt to assassinate Napoleon. The poet Heinrich von Kleist, in his drama *Die Hermannsschlacht,* used the example of the slaughter of the Roman legions of Varus at the hands of Arnim the Cheruskan in the Teutoburg forest as an appeal to all Germans to rise against Napoleon and drive him from German soil: '*Schlagt ihn tot, das Weltgericht fragt euch nach den Gründen nicht!*' – 'Kill [Napoleon], the universal court will not ask you for the reason!'[41] A remarkable proportion of German students and journeymen participated under Andreas Hofer in the Tyrolean rising against Napoleon, which twice in 1809 succeeded in driving out his forces from the Tyrol.[42] When in the same year Austria decided to resume arms against Napoleon she did so accompanied by a proclamation to the German *Volk.*[43] The call did not go unheeded. In spite of Prussia's official reluctance to aid Austria, the Prussian Major von Schill took the law into his own hands, hoping that the Prussian crown would follow his example. He led his unit (containing a substantial number of student reservists) to war against the French unaided, hoping that Austria would be blessed with victory. Since they were not, and his monarch publicly disowned him, he failed in his attempt to link up with a popular rising in Westphalia under Colonel von Dörnberg. The simultaneous uprising of the 'Black Band' of the young Duke Frederick William of Brunswick failed for similar reasons. There was nothing left for them but to fight their way out to the ports and find refuge on British ships, which the Duke of Brunswick and Dörnberg succeeded in doing. Schill, however, was killed in ferocious street fighting in the city of Stralsund on the Baltic. Of the eleven officers subsequently shot on Napoleon's explicit orders the oldest was barely 20 years of age.[44]

Four years later the proper time had come. The Prussian General Yorck von der Wartenburg's signature of the Convention of Tauroggen with the Russian forces helped to force his monarch's hand. Napoleon's defeat in Russia provided the opportunity. Frederick William III of Prussia, solidly backed and prompted by the military and civilian members of the Prussian reform movement, declared war on France and simultaneously appealed to the people to rise against the French usurper. The response was overwhelming. The Prussian forces in the twelve months from March 1813 to March 1814 drew more than 50,000 volunteers from all parts of the German lands, and of all occupations.[45] The poet of the War of Liberation, Theodor Körner, was a Saxon occupying a position at the Vienna Hofburg theatre when he heard of the Prussian mobilization. He immediately left his position and made his way to Breslau where, as an ordinary soldier of the light infantry, he entered the *Freikorps* Lützow – one of several units which did not consist of regular soldiers, and which made a point of being a German rather than a purely Prussian unit. The colours of its uniform – black, with red piping and golden buttons – were to provide that tricolour combination which gave the men of 1848 their national colours, black, red, and gold. Körner in many respects was the 'ideal' man of his time, a fighter and poet whose stature attained heroic proportions after his early death in action in August 1813. His poems set to music remained among the favourite songs of Germany's youth for well over a century. They are still sung by the armed forces of the DDR, as are many others which originated in the War of Liberation. Perhaps the line of Körner's poetry that was to become most famous, or rather infamous when it was used by Goebbels 130 years later, to conclude his 'Total War' speech in Berlin's Sportpalast, was 'Now people rise and storm break loose'.

It has been part of German historiographic mythology, right up to the present, to interpret the volunteer movement of 1813–14 as originating mainly in the middle classes and especially among the academic youth. No doubt students played an important part and compared with other occupations were proportionately very highly represented. Nevertheless students and grammar school pupils together amounted to no more than 7% of the volunteers (students 4.9%, pupils 2.1%), while artisans, manual labourers, and peasants represented a total of 59.5% (artisans 41.2%, manual labourers 14.7%, farmers and peasants 3.6%). The areas traditionally under the Prussian crown before the reign of Frederick the Great brought forth 53.7% of the volunteers; the rest, slightly less than half, came from all other parts of Germany including those of the states of the Confederation of the Rhine. In other words it was not simply the educated academic middle class youth which rushed to the colours in the struggle against Napoleon, but Germany's broadly based young generation, its representation cutting across class lines, and geographic borders.[46]

Waterloo put an end to a period that had begun with the fall of the Bastille. Europe's governments were now endeavouring, as much as was possible, to re-establish the *status quo ante bellum*. In Germany's official vocabulary the term German *Volk* quickly disappeared, as did that of the German nation. The ideology of the *Volk* was there though, and the call for a greater political unity than that established at Vienna could not be silenced. For thirty years and longer it was Germany's young generation particularly which kept the glowing embers of German nationalism alive.[47] From within and without they attacked the restoration of the *ancien régime* until they finally clamoured for revolution. Prisons registered an increasing intake of political 'freethinkers'. Youth kept on protesting until finally it went to the barricades. It is in this context that Germany's academic youth gained real prominence. Having fought for the liberation of their country, they now felt that they had also the right to help to determine its political future.

On 12 June, 1815 at the University of Jena, and under the patronage of the liberal Duke Karl August of Weimar, eleven students formally founded the *Burschenschaft*, a students' association that aimed at breaking down the regionally-based student clubs at Germany's universities.[48] At this university, where students from all parts of Germany gathered, the new national consciousness could be combined with the ideas of university reform of Humboldt and the nationalism of Jahn. Of the eleven founder members of the *Burschenschaften*, nine had been members of the *Freikorps* Lützow. In their constitution they announced that at every German university the *Burschenschaft* should represent and further the cause of liberty and the 'independence of the fatherland'. They chose a ceremonial dress based on the uniform of the *Freikorps* Lützow and a year later they showed for the first time their flag, the tricolour of black, red, and gold. From Jena where by 1816–17 500 out of 650 students were already members of the *Burschenschaften*, the movement spread rapidly to other German universities, especially in southern and central Germany. 'We desire among the individual states in Germany a greater responsibility for the common good, a greater unity in their politics, no politics at all to be conducted by the individual states . . . we desire that Germany shall be treated as one country, and the German *Volk* as one *Volk*,' wrote one of its prominent members, Heinrich von Gagern.[49] However, divisions soon became noticeable, such as that caused by the radicals, led by a lecturer of law Karl Follen of the University of Giessen, who demanded unitarian policy and the establishment of a German republic.[50]

For the time being though the liberal-constitutional wing dominated, with its romantic idealism, probably most eloquently expressed at the first meeting of the German *Burschenschaften* at the Wartburg (the Thuringian castle where Martin Luther had once found refuge and time to translate the Bible) on 18 October ·1817, the 300th anniversary of the Reformation and the fourth of the Battle of the Nations at Leipzig. More than 500 students from Berlin, Erlangen, Giessen, Göttingen, Halle, Heidelberg, Jena, Kiel, Leipzig, Marburg, Rostock, Tübingen, and Würzburg assembled at Eisenach and their first meeting was introduced with the words, 'You are not to discuss what shall and shall not happen in the state, you are to consider how you shall act in the state once called upon and how to prepare yourself for this task'.[51] In the evening, however, disappointment was freely aired about the old establishment's misuse of idealism in the cause against Napoleon, and some members went as far as publicly to burn reactionary law treatises as well as the Code Napoleon.[52] Exactly a year later the General German *Burschenschaft* was founded, 'based on the relationship of Germany's youth to the growing unity of the Fatherland'. Soon after, a sensational event turned the movement into an item on the agenda of European politics. Among Follen's radical wing was a student by the name of Karl Ludwig Sand, who on 23 March 1819 assassinated the poet August von Kotzbue, who was an informer in Russian pay and who seemed to Sand to epitomize the reactionary establishment.[53] The ultimate result of that action was the Karlsbad Decrees, which enacted sharp political controls of the universities, prohibited the *Burschenschaften* and introduced 'preventive censorship of the press. The movement towards German unity among Germany's young generation had been contained and it was no longer able to articulate its political aims openly. But it had not been vanquished. In fact, it gained additional support from outside quarters, from other sectors of German society, particularly from the growing German working class, many of whose 'workers' associations' actively supported the aims of the *Burschenschaften*.[54] When, in the wake of the revolutions of the 1830s, members of the *Burschenschaften* as well as journeymen of various crafts met at Hambach – where as an expression of sympathy with Polish national aspirations the Polish colours of white and red fluttered side by side with the German black red and gold – the Diet of the German Confederation renewed the Karlsbad Decrees against the universities, and prohibited all political assemblies.[55] The only political forum left was that which formed itself round 'young Germany' abroad, but all its publications were officially banned soon afterwards. Thus the only opportunity for political expression lay outside Germany. Heinrich Heine wrote in Paris that he foresaw the consequences of a situation when the forces that were now held back had grown stronger than their controllers, and when the moment would come when ambitions frustrated for decades would be suddenly released: 'then a German thunder will reverberate such as the history of the world has never heard before'. Germany's eventual national anthem, '*Deutschland, Deutschland über alles*', was written by Hoffmann von Fallersleben in 1841, when, having been expelled from Prussia because of his political activities, he went to live on Heligoland, then a British possession. In fact, the majority of those who at one time or another had been actively engaged in changing the political face of the German nation now lived in Switzerland, France or Britain.[56]

The events of 1848–49 did little to change that. The wave of revolutions which spread through Europe at the time, driven forward by the political aspirations of the middle classes and the economic grievances of workers and peasants, differed in its effects from country to country. In the states of the German Confederation it produced serious anxiety among the upholders of the political and social *status quo*, but really no more than that. True, the revolution of 1848 also produced the first German parliament, but those honourable men who assembled as the first German parliamentarians in Frankfurt's Paul's Church lacked one important instrument – that of power. Without it the parliament was, however idealistically motivated, reduced to the role of an impotent debating club. If anything, it is a sad epilogue to the high expectations of the reform movement of 1807–15, a movement which was in composition less Prussian than German and found itself in possession of real power, though for fear of emulating the excesses of the French Revolution it proved too reluctant to use it for the purposes of internal change. Many of those who were delegates at Frankfurt had in their youth been the volunteers of the *Freikorps*, but now, with the revolutionary movement all over Europe in decline, they returned with few exceptions to their studies and libraries.[57]

What remained was a tradition, by now almost a century old, of youthful political activism, an unquenched desire for a political unity that was not artifically created but that would be the product of organic growth in the form of the *Volk*, radiating the spirit of German *Kultur*, the true German *Volksgeist*, a *Volk* which in its institution would reflect not the divisive class characteristics of a society, but the integrating forces of a national community. The ideas making up this tradition developed in the course of time into an ideological bondage which for more than a century was to keep the greater part of Germans in spiritual captivity. None more so than her youth.

II Beginnings

After the abortive attempt at revolution in 1848, Germany's youth on the whole reconciled itself for the time being to the existing state in all social and political matters. Presuming itself released from what it had once considered to be its political obligations, it adopted an attitude of mind in which resignation replaced the former political activism. The one important political heritage of 1848, the newly-established political parties, took on the tasks which had once been those of the élite of Germany's political and literary youth, and in the person of Bismarck a unique individual emerged on the German political scene, who virtually alone solved most of the 'national' problems which had been the concern of the German unity movement since shortly after the turn of the century. The post-1848 generation, though deeply attached to the Prussian and German causes, and ultimately to Kaiser, Chancellor and Reich, seemed devoid of the ability to develop political initiatives of its own. 'The state' was the yardstick, the measure of all things; its almost god-like position in the hierarchy of values sapped the very energies which had in previous decades generated much of the political élan of the youth. National celebrations appeared to replace national agitations. Formality and conformity, especially as demonstrated in German student associations (once again regionally grouped and divided), determined the outward appearance of these celebrations. The stages in which Germany was unified between 1862 and 1871 were duly celebrated, and beery jubilation accompanied the increasingly institutionalized annual jubilees: the Reformation jubilees, the jubilee of the Battle of the Nations at Leipzig, the *Burschenschaft* jubilee, the Wartburg Festival jubilee, and the jubilees of the universities.[1] It was a time when the unveiling of monuments to esteemed artistic, literary, political, and military figures became almost a national hobby. In Germany between 1850 and 1900 more public statues were erected and unveiled than in the total of the preceding 1850 years.[2]

National monuments and national celebrations seem somewhat contradictory, at least before 1871 when no national state existed. But the absence of unification does not imply the absence of any national consciousness or any national feeling, particularly at a time when across the Alps a unified Italy was taking shape and providing new impetus to the German national idea. Even the workers' associations, which after 1848 had been temporarily forbidden, but which during the course of the 1850s resumed their activities, followed the nationalist trend as before 1848.[3] It was only a matter of years before the barricades of 1848 seemed almost of mythical substance and no longer part of the nation's real experience – though a mythology nevertheless influential on behalf of the national cause of a unified Germany. The demand for that unity was there among the young generation; opinions diverged only over what form it should take – a socialist, imperialist Caesarism integrating all classes of the nation into the national community, as Ferdinand Lasalle proposed, or a German Socialist republic, or a German Empire in the form of a constitutional parliamentary democracy, or simply a German Empire, irrespective of the form?[4] And even those who spoke of Empire, meaning the *Reich*, were far from unanimous in their interpretation of this term, which ranged from the greater German notion of a German national state embracing all Germans to an updated version of the supranational medieval *Reich*, only now being interpreted as a German-dominated Central Europe. While the debate continued, the armies forged by Roon and commanded by Moltke, and the political course determined by Bismarck provided the solution. Three strong men achieved by 'iron and blood' what national-minded socialists and nationally unitarian liberals had failed to produce: they at least partially unified Germany.[5] However, over the long term one of the most serious legacies of the Bismarckian solution was that it produced neither a proper nation state nor the *Reich* of days gone by. But for the time being there was no more need to argue, let alone fight for the national cause. Bismarck would do it alone. There is a good deal of truth in fact in the argument that the generation after 1848 represents in modern German history the only generation devoid of widespread attitudes of protest against the society in which it lived, devoid of the will to translate its own vision of the world into reality.[6]

Basically it lacked inspiring leadership. The ideas of Marx had not as yet blossomed, let alone borne fruit, and the youthful followers of Lasalle, Bebel, and Liebknecht were too few to have any impact. This in turn reflected the state of Germany's industrial development, which was still in its relative infancy and had yet to produce a class-conscious working class of a size significant enough to make it a decisive political factor.[7] Even German literature of the period reflected this state of political passivity on the one hand and excessive indulgence in patriotic sentimentalism on the other.[8]

The majority of Germany's students of that generation came from the prosperous middle classes. Particularly after 1871 they profited from the general economic boom initiated by their fathers; the industrial revolution was under way in Germany.[9] Yet it was precisely this rapid, thorough-going industrial and technological change that was to be the major factor during the last quarter of the nineteenth century in introducing a new air of unease among youth. Books and pamphlets flooded the market prophesying the doom of civilization as a result of industrialization and its by-products in the social sphere, such as the growing depersonalization of the individual in the organizational structures of corporate industry and commerce.[10] Polemics against 'mass society' became widely read, such as Gustave Le Bon's work *The Psychology of the Masses*, which forecast the gloomy results of a purposefully directed manipulation of the masses. In retrospect, the contemporary observer may be inclined to think that such pessimistic prognoses about the future of Western society were, measured by the historical experience of our own century, not so far off the mark after all.[11] However, in the main the growing wave of arguments against industrial modernity possessed more of the character of an emotional outburst than a rational analysis of the condition of society. And in that emotional reaction against industrial modernity lay, besides much else, the origins of the German Youth Movement, and ultimately, in its most perverted form, of the Hitler Youth.[12]

It is a history easier perhaps for the social psychologist to analyse than for the historian, for its motive forces were predominantly irrational and emotional. It is a history of bold dreams of social liberty and individual independence being ultimately squeezed into the framework of tight and militant organization, a history that leads from extremes of individualism to the extreme of militancy. In many respects it mirrors the history of the Germany of the period, marked by a rapid decrease of reliance on reason and rationality, a history leading from the bold, calculating, but nevertheless cautious policy of Bismarck, through the anachronistic daydreams of the Wilhelmine empire, to the unscrupulousness and criminality of Adolf Hitler. A history leading from illusions to obsession.

The alienation of the individual within the framework of the new organizational structures of industry was, in retrospect, inevitable.[13] In place of the former personal relationship between master and journeyman or apprentice, appeared a relationship in which the worker ultimately knew his employer as little as the private knows his commanding general. But while the new industrial system, dependent upon the unpredictable fluctuations of a world market was full of insecurities for the individual, ironically enough the army was free from such handicaps and therefore more secure. Its inherent inhumanity and forcible depersonalization were more than compensated for by its secure and hierarchic structure. Here everything was as it should be. One could not fail simply by making a wrong decision. The army provided firm and clearly-defined boundaries, a definite yardstick, instruction, order, and discipline. The army represented a community that appeared to contrast well with the 'anarchy' of industrial society. Little wonder therefore that even formidable intellects such as the elder Moltke denigrated the materialism of the new age, considering war as the only God-given instrument that would cleanse the world from the abominations of an industrial society. Consequently to many Germans the antithesis of a liberal free-enterprise economy was the army, a tendency which furthered and accelerated the already existing trend towards the militarization of German society.[14] Others reacted by trying to escape from reality. Repelled by a Germany which was no longer that of the thinkers and the poets, in which Beethoven's Ninth Symphony was drowned by the cacophony of steel mills and forges, they turned to an age gone by, epitomized by the misunderstood and misinterpreted romanticism contained in most of Wagner's operas.[15]

But common to both reactions was the demand and the quest for a firm substance to the form of the Fatherland.[16] And here again it was youth which assumed a significant role. Surrounded in their childhood by the reality or pretence of harmony, they now demanded its further refinement into patriotic substance; they endeavoured to become what Max Weber in one of his early letters described as *'Bismarck sans phrase'* – that is, without the Byzantine trimmings of Wilhelmine Germany.[17] In that period of intense spiritual crisis, Nietzsche, dismissed and ignored during his most creative period, experienced a renaissance; the socially-critical plays of Ibsen and later of Gerhard Hauptmann found an ardent and passionately committed audience, particularly among the younger generation. In Germany one author gained importance who under different circumstances would very likely have been ignored, and whose book might never have found a publisher.[18] Julius Langbehn's *Rembrandt als Erzieher* offered an answer to the question which La Rochefoucauld once asked: 'What is Youth?', to which he himself replied, 'it is eternal intoxication, reason conditioned by high fever'.[19] Langbehn emphasized the role of race and asserted that blood determined men and that inborn qualities were more important than acquired ones. *Sturm und Drang* had been followed by the *Burschenschaften* and *Jung Deutschland*; then came the emergence of the German Youth Movement, which provided a ready readership for Julius Langbehn's book, that 'rhapsody of irrationalism' as it has been described, not without justification.[20] That generation, intoxicated by the rhapsody, carried its enthusiasm like a torch in the last two and a half decades before the First World War. It was an enthusiasm which rejected the rootless objectivism of the intellectual and the matter-of-fact methodology of the natural sciences, since theirs – so it was alleged – was the responsibility for the ugly factory system which had once again reduced the free individual to a state of impersonal servitude, more demoralizing and degrading than the serfdom of the feudal age. Fervently believing this, young people all too readily escaped from the artificial norms of their society into the cult of a *Landschaftskultur*.[21] At weekends or during holidays they left home, school, university, or factory floor, with tent, rucksack and guitar, to hike through Germany, north to south, east to west, discovering for themselves the exquisite beauty of the German countryside which was so much in harmony with Beethoven's 'Pastoral' Symphony and Schiller's *Ode to Joy*, and contrasted so strongly with the tenement flats, the industrial slums and factory chimneys of the urban centres.[22]

More than that, the German Youth Movement protested against the values of the apparently saturated yet never satisfied bourgeoisie of Wilhelmine Germany.[23] It was a protest movement from beginning to end, a protest against a society which had nothing to offer but to live for the present, and which was careless and complacent about the future: 'our glorious Kaiser will look after that'. They derided the bric-à-brac façade of Wilhelmine Germany, a derision which had its equivalents among youth movements throughout the nations of Central and Western Europe. Wilhelmine, as well as late Victorian and Edwardian society, seemed unable to accept the fact that childhood and youth are stages in the development of each human being, each stage representing a step which is itself fully autonomous. The idea that an individual could develop his personality largely under the influence of personal experience and the power of imagination was too radical a notion for a German parent to consider at the turn of the century. Instead the parent, and adults in general, considered themselves – as they had always done – as prototypes worthy of emulation by their own children and by the younger generation generally.

In many respects, on the surface at least, this insistence by the older generation that they were setting the only proper example did have plausibility. Germany had become a satisfied country which could look back to unparalleled recent military successes and the consequent unification of the largest part of the country. Prosperity, even riches, existed among the new empire's middle class and, compared with the standards of other Western countries, the working classes too had little to grumble about, at least from a material point of view. Almost inevitably people thought that the young generation could hardly fare better than by emulating their parents and continuing in the tried-and-tested ways. The same attitude governed the general views of the political and industrial establishment. Late nineteenth-century Germany was an authoritarian and bureaucratic state, a piece of relatively smoothly-running machinery which a large portion of Germans thought could hardly be improved upon. Others, a minority, were provoked to criticize the impersonality of the state in which the people comprising the nation played only a very small part in the political decision-making process. On the whole, though, Wilhelmine society appeared to be reconciled to leaving things as they were, in the hands of experts, be they professional academics, engineers, or part of that vast annual output of German universities: graduates of jurisprudence. The affair of the 'Captain von Köpenick' illustrated the more ludicrous aspects of the system, when Wilhelm Voigt, a shoemaker by trade, tried to twist the arm of fortune by donning a captain's uniform. In this capacity he commandeered some soldiers from their barracks and marched on to the town-hall of Köpenick, a Berlin suburb, hoping to raid the office of the treasury. This abortive attempt at first caused a public outcry in Germany which was quickly followed by universal laughter. The Kaiser himself pardoned the *Hauptmann von Köpenick* – but not before the latter had led the whole military and bureaucratic system of Germany *ad absurdum*.

However, a strong insistence on the preservation of the status quo in all spheres of life was impossible to maintain indefinitely. Influences were at work which challenged the values and assumptions of the older generation and the generations of the past. Social Darwinian currents of thought, originating in Great Britain and the United States, were popularized in Germany by Ernst Haeckel and others and permeated social and political thinking, although many found them repellent at first.[24] Friedrich Nietzsche, especially, appealed to Germany's youth, not so much for his cult of the superman as for the manner in which he mercilessly confronted the German middle and upper classes with the hypocrisy of their cultural pretensions, their worship of Mammon, and their adulation of the 'state' as the omnipotent source of true German happiness.[25] This contempt for the status quo and the classes who upheld it is best summarized by the most brilliantly erratic scholar and moralist of the period in Germany, Paul de Lagarde,[26] who five years before the nineteenth century drew to a close wrote, 'I do not complain that our youth is lacking idealism. I accuse the men, above all the statesmen, incapable of offering ideals to our youth by which means the idealism existing in great measure among our youth could be transformed into ideality. Germany is under the spell of the conviction that the state represents the highest form of human existence. . . . I believe in this youth, I believe in the future of our Fatherland, but I do not believe in the suitability of the present ruling system, in the calling of those men who want to satisfy the desires and the requirements of their sons and grandsons with the trash that has remained in their hands as the remnants of their earlier days, the remnants of the old'.[27]

Lagarde appealed to a generation which even without his gifted pen was attacking those two institutions whose oppression they felt most directly.

Despite the considerable achievements of the German educational system of the nineteenth century it nevertheless displayed glaring defects, the major one being its failure to develop and form independently-thinking personalities.[28] The German school, like the Protestant church, was a state institution whose personnel were primarily civil servants and only secondarily teachers. No doubt they were well-trained specialists in their respective fields, but they also performed the role of purveyors of state piety, of nationalistic and militaristic propaganda. Religious instruction, the one avenue by which these more sinister currents of the age could have been counteracted, had declined into a routine of uncritical Bible reading, the saying of prayers in the fashion of a Tibetan prayer wheel, and the learning by heart of the catechism.[29] Indeed, the two main denominations, which monopolized religious instruction, had themselves become mere state functionaries by their utilization of Christian teaching to cement further the political and social status quo. Those pupils who rebelled openly against this educational system were dismissed as simply rather twisted, maladjusted individuals. And though many even so were prepared to disagree with the system, by the majority it was considered wiser to accept it and get it over with as smoothly as possible.

If the school was felt to be oppressive, so too was the family, with its all-powerful father at the head and docile mother in the background. The emphasis was on children being seen (forever neatly and tidily dressed) but never heard voicing their own opinions, most certainly not any that differed from those of the head of the family. Little wonder then that a generation should emerge which judged the religiosity practised in school and home as mere hypocrisy, which, as passive bystanders, witnessed disapprovingly the unscrupulous and dishonest transactions of industry and commerce, and which dismissed the politics of the day as irrelevant to the needs of the time. The primacy of conformism did not end there. The arts were dominated by patriotic *kitsch* and sentimentality, full of insincere pathos, an intellectual and artistic environment which sooner or later was bound to precipitate a reaction. And that reaction came in the form of the German Youth Movement and had its principal support precisely among that sector of German society which was most exposed to the hypocrisy of Wilhelmine Germany: the German middle class.[30]

Among the major influences at this time upon German youth, especially middle-class youth, must be ranked German idealism, with its roots in the *Sturm und Drang* period.[31] The 'longing for absolute beauty and the charisma of historically or artistically significant individuals' was really a longing for larger-than-life examples on which to model one's own life with the aim of achieving 'the good, the beautiful and the noble'. The idealism expressed, for instance, in the poetry of Theodor Körner was by the end of the nineteenth century no longer so genuine. The examples epitomizing this idealism were drawn in almost equal proportions from an uncritical idealized version of Prusso-German history and from the German classics, particularly Goethe and Schiller. Significantly the German army was idealized in history textbooks and literature as the 'shining armour' and 'Prussia's Glory', and the volunteers of 1914 can be said to have been conditioned by this educational process. In place of the civilizing humanism of an earlier period pupils were subjected to the stifling pedantry of grammar, and discipline rather than education was the watchword and guideline up to matriculation. The living forms of German culture were ignored in favour of the study of a history which stopped at the Franco-German war of 1870–1 and a literature which ended with Goethe, Uhland and Kleist. Similarly in the natural sciences the emphasis lay not on contemporary scientific developments but on the progress achieved yesterday and the day before. The textbooks of the time showed a definite anti-industrial bias.

In this oppressive atmosphere fostered by the educational establishment youth naturally tried to free itself by escaping from adolescence into the pretence of adulthood, for instance, by stowing away or joining the Foreign Legion (Count Luckner and the writer Ernst Jünger are prominent examples of many such runaways), or by way of the youth movement, such as the *Wandervogel*, hoping by such means to create the *Reich* of youth. In the field of the visual arts the German expressionist school can be seen very largely as one form of youthful escapism.

On the whole, however, these characteristics and attitudes applied only to one sector of Germany's pre-1914 youth – the lower and upper middle classes – a youth only vaguely familiar with economic shortage and the misery of slum housing. For working-class children the school-leaving age was fourteen and from then onwards their lives revolved around factory or workshop; the fine arts, literature and the theatre were inaccessible to them, so that their mood was less abstract, more practical and directly political.[32]

The German Youth Movement, in the form of the *Wandervogel*, began to emerge during the last decade of the nineteenth century when a Berlin student, Herman Hoffmann, founded at his grammar school at Berlin-Steglitz a study circle for shorthand, which on occasional weekends went on outings into the surrounding countryside.[33] Steglitz, a Berlin suburb, represented at that time an area of 'social transition'. It was neither genuinely working class nor properly middle class. Men and families aspiring to middle-class status could be found there, on their way up, so to speak. Equally, those on their way down the social ladder would find a home there in their decline, which, if not arrested, would lead them ultimately into working-class districts like Berlin-Wedding or Moabit. Steglitz was referred to as the 'stiff-collar-proletarian suburb'. Hoffmann, without having a firmly-defined programme, had notions about what did and did not represent a reasonable life. He was aware that industry and commerce had come to stay, but he was equally convinced that the individual, instead of passively surrendering to the impersonal and atomizing forces of industrialism, should actively control them. And in order to do this he had to be made aware of his natural environment in the first place. Youth had to rediscover nature, the fields, woods, brooks, lakes, and meadows from which the city dweller had been alienated. Nature, Hoffmann felt, had to be experienced in the raw: the burning scorch of the sun, the whiplash of the rainstorm and the snowstorm. Travelling through sunshine or storm in a protected railway carriage was no substitute for marching on the open country road (if necessary battling with the elements), rucksack on back, uncertain of the comfort of the next night's shelter. A haystack was preferable any time to a well-made bed, fresh air to nicotine, and water to alcohol. Only by an awareness of preindustrial forms of life would man, and then society as a whole, appreciate the good in the past and use it to alleviate the abominations of the present. In order to be free one had to break the existing conventions; in place of the prevailing greeting of a simultaneous bow and clicking of heels, Hoffmann thought it sufficient to raise one's right arm in the ancient form of salute, accompanied by a '*Heil!*' The style of clothes had to fit this way of life. Creased trousers, starched shirts, and ties were hardly suitable attire for cross-country hikes. Instead shorts, dark shirts, a waterproof, and hobnailed boots were indispensable.

Karl Fischer, a contemporary of Hoffmann and for a time his close associate, seems by all accounts to have exercised a considerable charisma over those who followed him. 'Everyone who came into contact with Fischer or enjoyed his friendship felt inevitably that here was someone capable of achieving more than oneself.' And it is really Fischer rather than Hoffmann who was the born leader, capable also of devising the *Wandervogel*'s programme. It was not an ambitious programme at the start. The small group of Berlin youths ventured out first only into the countryside surrounding the capital. But ambitions grew from year to year. In 1897 they hiked through the Harz mountains for two weeks, a year later along the banks of the Rhine, and in 1898 through the Bohemian forest.[34] In order not to be dependent upon parents or relatives they rented a room once a week in which to meet, a place they called their 'nest'. Reviving past traditions that they believed had been abandoned, they sang old folksongs, mainly those collected earlier in the century by Arnim von Brentano and published under the title *Des Knaben Wunderhorn*. The obligatory instruments of piano and violin in the parental home were ignored. Instead they played on the guitar, the mandolin, or the mouth organ. On their hikes they discovered new folklore and folksongs, a friend of Karl Fischer, Hans Breuer, compiling the latter, composing new tunes where necessary, and publishing them under the title *Zupfgeigenhansl* (the *Zupfgeige* being a dialect term for the guitar or the mandolin). This collection has enjoyed great popularity with German youth groups to the present day, bridging classes, parties and denominations. The renaissance of the German folksong in the late nineteenth century was not without its sociological significance either, for it explicitly rejected the growing cult of the 'hit' and the 'pop-song' which had reared its head among the younger age groups of Germany's adults.[35]

At the turn of the century Karl Fischer completely took over the leadership of the *Wandervogel* from Hoffmann and under him it became not merely a movement for escaping the urban and industrial world, but a protest movement too against the inroads of technology into everyday human life, a protest movement that within a matter of a few years had spread from a Berlin suburb throughout Germany and had also found its equivalents elsewhere in Europe.[36] Despite its vagueness and absence of firmly-fixed objectives, it represented an attempt to shake off the artificial veneer of civilization and to return to the panacea of all social ills: a truly German culture, a return to the *Volksgeist*. The idea of a specific *Jugendkultur* (a culture of youth), had already been coined by Gustav Wyneken, one of the most influential reformers of German education. 'A synthesis must be found, a reconciliation of youth with that culture which, as it happens, is preserved and tended by adults. But this kind of synthesis cannot mean the return into the fold of the family, it cannot mean the subjugation of youth by the conventional style of life of the old.'[37] Wyneken, rather like some sociologists of our own day, denied and rejected the all-embracing claims of family life. Youth, as he saw it, should develop among youth, youth should lead youth, with adults providing ultimate guidance as imperceptibly as possible.

The early members of the *Wandervogel* movement liked to consider themselves the pioneers of the youth mission, yet not until November 1901, in the Steglitz town hall cellar, was the *Wandervogel*, as an association, formally created. The origin of the description *Wandervogel* is perhaps symbolic for many of its members, and for many members of other elements in the German Youth Movement, including the Hitler Youth: the name was discovered on a tombstone and means, literally, 'wandering, or migratory, bird'.[38] And truly tombstones were to be young Germany's milestones, from Flanders to the Volga, from the Polar Circle to Africa, from the tombstones of Königsberg and Breslau to those of Berlin.

Fischer and the writer Heinrich Sohnrey drew up the *Wandervögel*'s first constitution and its growth thereafter was very rapid, its dynamism so strong indeed that soon splinter groups made their appearance. But however much these groups proliferated, they differed from one another only very marginally. There were, however, certain questions which cast their dark shadows on the problems of the future: questions such as the admission into the *Wandervögel* of German youths of the Jewish faith. Besides the *Wandervögel*, the *Bündische Jugend* was making its appearance, youth leagues organized for or against diverse causes, for the prohibition of alcohol and nicotine, but also for the cause of nudism, and another burning issue was whether girls should be allowed to join such groups – until the girls took the initiative, forming their own organization and adapting the *Dirndl* (a Bavarian folk costume) as their uniform. But boys and girls did find a means of coming together – as they were inevitably to do in any case – in the revival of folkdancing.[39]

The process of breaking hitherto accepted norms and conventions had other consequences. The escape from parental authority was bound to bring to the fore not simply the rediscovery of the physical beauty of the landscape but logically also the physical beauty of man's body, thus breaking the taboo which had surrounded the entire problem of sexuality. Freud's theories had little to do with this, for Germany's youth was hardly aware of his existence. It needed no scientific theory to recognize what was so patently obvious. The call to the return to nature was bound to produce the ultimate confrontation between the individual and his own sexuality. (The contention, however, that the German youth movement was essentially a homo-erotic movement, or more crudely a club for homosexuals, is blatant nonsense, for which there is no evidence whatsoever.) The German Youth Movement, middle-class as it was in origin, also confronted the task of trying to win other social groups to its cause and for its ideals. For working-class youth the conflict was at first one not so much between generations as between classes. It must be said at the outset that the gulf between middle-class and working-class youth never disappeared, but it could be bridged.[40] Organized socialist youth movements, though apparently wedded to the concept of the class struggle, had their own inter-party struggles as well. Youth reacted against a socialist party which had fossilized into an institution, and which, like the all-powerful, all-embracing state, had degenerated into a way of life which determined the pattern of the lives of its members from cradle to grave. The German Social Democratic Party, the SPD, on the eve of the First World War could look upon four decades of development in which it had increased its vote in the *Reichstag* elections from 124,000 in 1871 to 4,250,000 in 1912, by which time it was also the largest single party in Germany. However, along the way most of its early revolutionary élan was lost, and the SPD had become as bourgeois as the bourgeois parties it opposed. To all practical intents and purposes the rank and file of the party membership had become integrated into the Hohenzollern Empire, illustrated by the example of 1914 when the great majority of SPD deputies in the *Reichstag* voted in support of the Government at the outbreak of war. For Socialist youths there seemed to be little that distinguished their fathers from the rest. The generation problem affected them as much as other German youths. Face to face with their middle-class contemporaries, working-class young people did not feel completely at ease, but it became increasingly apparent that at least both sides were beginning to understand one another's problems.[41]

The proletarian youth, like his middle-class contemporary, hated industrialization, mechanization, and rationalization of all spheres of everyday life. But instead of viewing this as a process of ultimate destruction of all values, working-class young people reacted against the immediate consequences as felt by them on a day-to-day basis. In the long term, so Marxist dogma promised, the dialectical process would culminate in the victory of the disinherited. However, in the truism that in the long term we are all dead, that what matters is not only the distant future but life here and now, a basis of common understanding between all youth was provided, irrespective of class origins. Working-class youths too desired an improvement in the quality of life. Although socialist youth movements and those of the German middle classes had their fundamental differences, for a time it appeared that if they were marching in separate columns, at least they were both going in the same direction up to 1914.[42]

Even the German government found the atmosphere of restlessness among its youth strong enough to merit detailed investigation which resulted in sweeping recommendations for the institution of a youth social welfare programme. Its implementation, however, was cut short by the outbreak of the First World War.[43] The army too thought it a problem worthy of attention and suggested absorbing the excess energy of youth in paramilitary training on the barrack squares of Germany's military garrisons.[44] The churches soon followed suit. In the Catholic Church it had always been a maxim that adolescent boys and girls were in need of guidance, more so than any other group of the population, and that any neglect would yield results very detrimental to the position of the Church. The Catholic youth organizations in their outward appearance differed very little from that of the *Wandervögel* except perhaps that the sexes were more rigidly segregated and that the general supervision always remained in the hands of the church authorities.[45] Soon they too discovered long-forgotten Christian songs of the Middle Ages which found their way into the pages of the *Zupfgeigenhansl*, in company with the anti-clerical songs of the peasant rebellion of the sixteenth century. The Catholic youth groups enjoyed the advantages of international connections – an advantage which was also shared by the youth organizations of the Protestant church, though diminished somewhat by the innate sectarianism of that body.[46]

And in fact sectarianism seemed to become a general feature of the German Youth Movement during the first decade of the twentieth century. The Boy Scout movement spread from Great Britain to the European mainland, indeed entered into direct competition with the *Wandervögel*.[47] Also trade and professional associations directed more attention to the youth within their ranks, creating special youth associations for them. The total picture then appeared as a highly complex mosaic of movements, leagues, and associations, none of which, with the exception of the socialists and the Catholics, had any connections with the existing political parties of Wilhelmine Germany.[48] It is surprising that although government, army, and the churches had realized the importance of drawing youth into their ranks and obtaining its support, most of the established political parties ignored it, leaving the impression that the country was run by old men with little or no understanding of the younger generation in a continuously changing environment. It can be legitimately argued that it was precisely their lack of interest in youth that was one of the major factors leading to the formation of the German Youth Movement in the first place.[49]

Possibly the indifference shown by the politicians owed much to the fact that the Youth Movement's leaders were not particularly good at articulating specific aims, preferring to give vent to a feeling of general discontent, particularly discontent about the older generation, which very often was expressed in the form of escapism. Negation rather than affirmation, elusion rather than conclusion were the characteristic marks of those who in the age-group between twelve and nineteen formed the main body of the Youth Movement. From the lack of a clearly-formulated programme the step into irrationalism was very often all too easily taken. There were instances where members of the Youth Movement never really found their way into the adult world, running around with shorts, hobnailed boots, and lumbershirts well into their fifties, frequently pretending to be and to represent youth.[50]

Organizationally the structure of the various movements was fairly uniform. Youth was led by youth with a group leader being on average three to five years older than the youths he led. He had to be old enough to be able to exert and maintain authority, yet young enough to be capable of identifying himself personally with the group and the concerns of its individuals. A group was about twenty strong at its maximum, though of course where a youth movement was in its early days it could be considerably less. In a city with a varying number of groups these would come under the guidance of an *Ortsgruppe*, a local branch, while the local branches of one particular area were designated a *Gau*. The leader of the *Gau* would be responsible to the head of the movement for the activities of all the local branches. Meetings of group leaders of local branches took place regularly, at least once a month, while *Gau* meetings of all its youths were spread out over two or three occasions per year. However, once a year the movement as a whole met at a place somewhere in Germany at a big camp meeting. Besides the annual camp, the big event of the year – often preliminary to the camp itself – was the *Fahrt*, the big cross-country expedition which took place during school holidays and when weather conditions could be expected to be reasonable for camping in the open. Youth hostels did not exist during the early part of the century, and conditions therefore could occasionally be rough, but in most cases that was half the fun for the participants. Money was scarce, and reports from German consulates in Italy, France, and the Netherlands make frequent mention of virtually destitute German youth groups, usually on their way back home, in some cases openly begging for money, though more frequently singing and playing guitars in public squares and then passing the hat round – something to which native vagrants sometimes objected in no uncertain terms, the more so as local by-laws required a licence which neither the penniless German youths nor the vagrants possessed. Public transport – a sign of modernity – was shunned: *Schusters Rappen*, the cobbler's stallion, in other words one's own pair of feet, was the principal means of transportation.[51]

Between 1910 and 1913 the youth movement also spread into the German-speaking parts of the Austro-Hungarian Empire and into Switzerland, an 'invisible revolution', as it has been described, against the inevitable process of mechanization.[52] But as a 'revolution' the German youth movement achieved nothing. Rather than a crisis it was the symptom of a crisis; neither state, school, family, nor society were reformed. But it was not completely ineffectual even so. By inculcating a more critical attitude towards institutions, values, and ideas that had hitherto found unquestioned acceptance, it paved the way for something new, though what this was to be no one yet knew. In its contempt for political parties that had degenerated into interest groups, in its rejection of a parliament which had become no more than an ineffective debating society, the Youth Movement exemplified an attitude general to German middle-class thought as a whole, namely that politics was a dirty business and better left to those with the capacity for washing dirty linen in public. And, too, while rejecting the political process of the time the Youth Movement equally rejected the patriotic cant so typical of Wilhelmine Germany.

The major occasion for a public rejection of that wave of nationalism which swept Europe in the first years of the twentieth century, came in 1913, the centenary of the Battle of the Nations at Leipzig in which Prussian, Austrian, and other German forces, together with the forces of Russia, decisively defeated Napoleon, and ultimately drove him to retreat to areas beyond Germany's western frontiers. The centenary celebrations were occasions for outbursts of nationalist euphoria.[53] Kaiser Wilhelm II was to unveil a monstrosity of a monument at Leipzig on 18 October 1913, and the leaders of the German Youth Movement considered this an appropriate moment for a demonstration by German youth, whose purpose would not be the negation of sincere national feeling, but to allow national feeling to be put into a true and balanced perspective as well as to enunciate something resembling a programme of the German Youth Movement.[54] The dates chosen for the meeting were 11 and 12 October, and the site was located at the *Hohe Meissner*, a mountain south of Kassel, on which, according to German folklore, Frau Holle, the maker of snow, has her home.

On the evening of 11 October groups of boys and girls, including the Socialists and students from the nearby universities of Marburg, Göttingen and Jena, converged upon the *Hohe Meissner*. Contingents from Austria, the Sudetenland, and Switzerland were present as well. The meeting began in inauspicious circumstances. Rain poured down but when it stopped next morning and the temperature rose so did the spirits of the attending crowd. 'The Festival of Youth' could commence, and with it the speeches: 'Above all things we detest the unfruitful patriotism which immerses itself in words and emotions, which, at the expense of the historical truth, derives its enthusiasm by looking backwards instead of setting out new aims for the future'.[55] Demands were made for the free and untrammelled development of the individual, for truth, honesty, and responsibility. The speaker for the students of Marburg underlined the necessity for youth to be allowed to educate and discipline itself. Others emphasized the need to awaken its social conscience at a time when the division of labour and the factory system had reduced men to the status of 'tools of tools'. Gustav Wyneken, the renowned German educational reformer and ardent supporter of the German Youth Movement, addressed the thirteen or so German Youth Movement groups represented at the festival, warning them not to be hypnotized by nationalist slogans cheaply come by, and emphasizing the cosmopolitan elements inherent in German culture. 'When I look at the glowing valleys of our fatherland spread out at our feet I can wish nothing other than that the day may never come on which we are compelled to carry war into the valleys of a foreign people. . .' He referred to one of the principal members of the Prussian Reform Movement, Neidhardt von Gneisenau, who a hundred years before had written that principles were more important than countries. He warned them to beware of the exaggerated nature of German patriotism, ready to flaunt itself at the slightest provocation. But he also drew attention to a national interest which troubled many liberals too at the time – the deep cleavage running through the

German people which divided Austria's Germans from the Germans of the Reich, and he referred to the distress of German minorities outside Germany. But distress was not solely confined to them, he emphasized: there was plenty of distress among Germans within the Reich. Martial speeches and sabre-rattling would provide no solutions to the problems engulfing Germany, and if war should come Germany and its youth especially should be sure that this would be a righteous war in which Germany would represent the forces of light against those of darkness. Happiness might not be the fate of the present young generation, it might be heroism instead, but if that were the case then the heroism should be productive, it should be for the sake of changing the world permanently and for the better.[56]

In its final resolution the meeting declared: 'The free German youth is determined to shape its own life, to be responsible to itself and to be guided by the innate feeling of truth. To defend this inner liberty they close their ranks . . .'[57]

The *Hohe Meissner* meeting demonstrated that in its basic sentiments the German youth of this period was united; superficial divisions such as those of religious denominations and class persisted, but they were no longer unbridgeable. Though predominantly middle-class in origin, this sector reacted particularly against its own background. This anti-bourgeois stance does not mean of course that it ever completely cleared the obstacles lying between itself and the organized youth movement of the Socialist party. Conversely, within the Socialist youth movement reaction had been stirring for some time against a party which was no longer the party of social revolution, leading the fight against anti-socialist laws, but one which, in spite of some notable exceptions like Rosa Luxemburg, had become bourgeois in its rhetoric – a party which, in spite of occasional lip-service to the contrary, had been effectively absorbed into the political framework of the German Empire, whose members, if not yet quite at the level of the national government, still at the level of regional governments and municipal administrations had become respected fellow-members of German society, tarred with the 'red' brush only by the more extremist conservative circles. To its own socialist youth the party had fossilized into an institution and a way of life.[58]

Sadly, when Germany's youth at last met as a whole, only ten months after the *Hohe Meissner* meeting, it was in the trenches of the First World War. All through the preceding years they had searched for the great and formative 'experience', whether on a hiking tour or around the camp fires. But all that was a poor substitute compared with what confronted them now: war! It would be war which would create the final shape of their new man; out of war would emerge a new spirit and consciousness that would dominate a new time. In an almost incomprehensible wave of enthusiasm and idealism, almost submerged by a jubilant population, they marched to the battlefields in August 1914. All the divisions of the past had now lost their significance and became meaningless petty squabbles. The long-desired national community, the community of fate, appeared to have become reality. Barracks were incapable of coping with the masses of volunteers. From the factory floor, from classrooms and lecture halls they streamed, until during the first few weeks after the outbreak of war even the German army had to put a stop to the numbers of volunteers, for it could no longer cope with them all.

To describe this emotional wave simply as an expression of jingoism on the part of Germany's youth would only touch one aspect of the truth and probably a minor one at that. Not blind hatred and irrational nationalism provided the motive force for most, but the pursuit of a dream. At last the hour seemed to have struck when the corrupt old forces of materialism and international capitalism were to be thrown down by the idealism and true nationalism of a new generation. And it was to this bright prospect that the young German legions marched so blithely away in 1914.

They found instead the graveyard of Langemarck.

III Re-formation

Out of the terror and the cruelty of war arose the first doubts that the war itself would result in the fulfilment of the ambitions of Germany's youth. Death occurred on too vast a scale, in too brutal a fashion, and seemingly without end, to serve any positive purpose or to make any sense. In some, reason reasserted itself, asking why these terrible and apparently pointless things should be.

But war created too its own yardstick – and its own 'society'. The staccato of machine-gun fire and the endless pounding of artillery barrages forged the *aristocrazia trencheresta*, the aristocracy of the trenches, and the trenches proved to be the great levelling force between classes, between officers and men, between the former student and the former worker. Conditions demanded individual self-sacrifice for one's comrades and the whole tenuousness of life created new forms of human relationships, some kind of new order in which the artificial hierarchy of the garrison and barrack square was purified into a more natural hierarchy. Here, in the final analysis obedience was voluntary because he who commanded had first of all to command the respect of men who were not just subordinates, but comrades upon whose every action his own life and that of the unit might depend.

German youths of all political convictions and social backgrounds had reacted against the bourgeois society of Wilhelmine Germany through the entire spectrum of youth movements. The majority of them had entered the war with the conviction that a 'new man' would emerge from it. But those youths of 1914 who survived to crawl out alive from their trenches and dugouts in 1918 had a physiognomy quite different from that heralded by the poets of the youth movement in 1914.[1] They were not preceded by fluttering flags and symbols of victory. Grey in complexion, hollow-cheeked and emaciated, with the soil and the dust of the frontline still clinging to their uniforms, they marched home: a youth many of whom had lost all point of contact with normal life in four years of slaughter, many of whom lacked any comprehension of the defeat inflicted upon Germany.

The revolution in Germany which broke out at the end of the First World War, overthrowing the Kaiser, had not started in the front line. Though eager to return home, there is nothing to indicate that the majority of troops sympathized with this revolution.[2] The 'young republican' was a relatively rare specimen and this feature which could already be seen in November 1918 and in 1919 was to mark the history of the new Weimar Republic: it was the republic of the old and the middle-aged. There was no place in it for its youth. The broad mass of German youths kept their distance from the vast number of new political parties that quickly arose. So far as a desire existed to join youth movements, they joined the *Bündische Jugend*,[3] the youth leagues, and those who accepted political engagement polarized themselves at the political extremes, in conformity with the political attitudes of their elders. Often where the father had returned from the front exhausted and fed up with 'the imperialist-capitalist war-mongers' the sons could be found in the youth organizations of the radical extreme left.[4] On the other hand, in homes where the phrases 'November criminals' and 'stab-in-the-back' had general currency, the youth could be found in right-wing youth organizations.[5]

The Hohenzollern Empire had disappeared and made way for a republic. But it was a republic only by accident. Friedrich Ebert and his colleagues had had in mind to continue a fully parliamentarian constitutional monarchy when they feared that they would be overtaken on the Left by extremists. That fear led to the proclamation of a republic. But the leadership of the SPD did not wish for a revolution, though in Berlin and elsewhere in Germany, notably in Munich, attempts at revolution *were* taking place. The question of how to control them was beyond the SPD, for it did not possess the necessary means, the monopoly of power. That monopoly rested in the German Army High Command, and only in alliance with it could the Social Democrats hope to quell the revolutionary fervour. But the Army High Command too faced serious problems, especially the prospect of being a High Command without an army, for the returning soldiers in the main quickly left their garrisons to return to their homes. The only alternative was to recruit volunteers into government service, the origin of the *Freikorps*. In engagements and actions which in their violence are typical of any civil war, the revolutionary forces of the Left were effectively suppressed. However the legacy of civil war remained throughout the Weimar Republic, one of its expressions being the para-military forces of the Right as well as of the Left, storm-troopers versus Red Front. The political atmosphere remained poisoned by attitudes that allowed no compromise. In the eyes of the Right the Republic had been created by the November criminals, the men who had proclaimed it and who had signed the armistice with the enemy. Indeed they were alleged to have worked for Germany's downfall during the war; by undermining German morale at home they had 'stabbed the German armies in the back'. Extremes such as this, matched by equally radical denunciations on the Left, always came prominently to the fore in days of political and economic crisis. And crisis in general was never far away in the Weimar Republic. This all-pervading sense of stress, the erosion of the economic base of the middle classes, and the political vicissitudes of Germany's parliamentary democracy resurrected among a large part of the electorate suspicions of a multi-party state. Since the Republic appeared unable to master the frequent crises, these suspicions hardened into conviction, and the call was heard to do away with party politics and look for a *Führer* who in place of conflict would create national harmony, a call already heard in the days of the Bismarckian and Wilhelmine Empire. Yet paradoxically enough, although the lack of readiness to compromise was a major reason for the instability of the Republic, compromise itself was a reason for disquiet. After all, the origin of the Republic and its survival during its first four years rested upon the compromise between the democratic parties – the Social Democrats, the liberals, and the Centre – and the established institutions – the army, the civil service, the judiciary, and the economy – thus precluding any possibility of thoroughgoing reform; this compromise structure in effect compromised the entire Republic in a period of political and economic crisis.

However, the immediate post-war period was influenced especially by a certain category of young person who had perhaps been a member of the Youth Movement on the eve of the war but who, by the end of it, too old now for such mild diversions, had joined one of the numerous unofficial right-wing military organizations – the *Freikorps*.[6] And indeed the *Freikorps* on the extreme Right and the *Spartakists* on the extreme Left represented the traditions and the ambitions of the German Youth Movement to the point of excess,[7] but nevertheless more faithfully for the time being than the newly emerging youth leagues. Among them could be found those who were disinclined to assist in the restoration of a society that had failed to withstand the test of war. The activists of both the *Freikorps* and *Spartakus*, though never united, fought what they often considered to be the common foe, the restoration of the bourgeois social *status quo*. What divided the political activists of the Left and Right was the simple fact that the latter were never prepared to destroy their own country in order to destroy capitalism, and the politically more articulate of them picked up the thread left by the German liberal, Friedrich Naumann, and endeavoured to achieve what they thought would have to be a genuine synthesis between nationalism and socialism – the antithesis between an 'unhistoric humanitarian Marxism and a rootless capitalist society'.[8] Some of these young men, realizing that they 'had to lose the war in order to win the nation',[9] were prepared to drive the still-born revolution of 1918 even further and remove by assassination anyone who seemed capable of restoring Germany to its pre-1914 position.[10] Walther Rathenau, the industrialist and writer due to whose efforts Germany had managed to obtain its essential raw materials during the First World War, was their most prominent victim, not because he was a Jew but because he was considered by far the most able of those politicians aiming to return to the *status quo ante bellum*.[11] But he was sacrificed in vain; by 1922 the revolutionary impulse, Left and Right alike, had exhausted itself in Germany. What the public desired was a return to normality.

But youth did not want normality. Once again they founded their multitudes of movements, movements greater in number and membership than they had ever been before the war. 'Young Socialists', 'Young Democrats', 'Young Conservatives', 'Young Protestants' are but few of many autonomous youth organizations that mushroomed in Germany between 1923 and 1933. The cleansing of the German body politic of the abominations of industrialism, the fight against the manifold social injustices of the capitalistic system, the struggle against the *Diktat von Versailles* (the peace settlement forced on Germany by the victorious Allies) were points common to most of them and played their part in the foundation of student associations such as the *Deutscher Hochschulring*, the *Deutsche Studentenschaft*, or the *Kommunistische Freie Proletarische Jugend*.[12] It is self-evident that the vast number of youth organizations and their immense proliferation reflects just how deeply divided Germany was politically. But above and beyond this were such common factors as the explicit rejection of the old, the sense of mission to create a new world for some, a new nation for others. There were also determined attempts to analyse what were thought to be the realities of the time and by direct positive action to influence them, to shape them to their own image, whatever that image may have been. Directly or simply by implication they accepted the maxim coined by the German writer and poet, Walter Flex, 'Whoever swears upon the Prussian flag has nothing any more that belongs to himself'.[13] Youth organizations of all political shades alike sang the song written for the Communist Youth by Herman Claudius – descendant of the German poet Matthias Claudius – who was later to become a National Socialist

> When we march side by side
> And sing the old songs
> That they resound in the woods
> We feel that we shall succeed
> In creating a new time.[14]

The youth of the front-line generation who had learned at an early age to put their lives at risk were prepared to do so again. One of the most articulate exponents of what could be termed 'socialism of the trenches', the writer Ernst von Salomon, described their position in 1928: 'The war had exercised an all-compelling force over them, the war would never release them, they will never be able to return home, never will they belong entirely to us. The front-line experience will forever run through the current of their bloodstream, the sense of the close proximity of death, of preparedness, the horror, intoxication and steel. What now was attempted could never succeed in the first place, the attempt at integration into a peaceful, orderly, bourgeois world. This was a fraudulent transplantation which was bound to fail. The war is over but its warriors are still on the march. And because the masses are standing here in the midst of a German world of ferment, helpless, divided into small desires and great hopes, but of significance because of the weight of their numbers and containing all the elements of nature, because of that the soldiers are marching for a revolution, whether they wish it or not, driven forward by forces that escape definition, dissatisfied when they part company, highly explosive material as long as they stay together.'[15] Their national revolutionary attitude, hardened into conviction by the war, did not allow them even to consider the restoration of the short-lived empire gone by, nor to be convinced by its bourgeois epilogue, the Weimar Republic. Paradoxically, although there seemed no place in the Republic for its youth, during the early period of Weimar the youth that had belonged to the pre-war youth movement represented one of its vital forces. Without it the young Republic would hardly have survived the first six months of its existence. In the *Freikorps* those youths, hardened by the war-time 'Thunder of Steel', secured German frontiers in the east, and they radically suppressed the threat of separatism in the Rhineland and of particularism in Bavaria. After the occupation of the Ruhr by the French and Belgians, both Left and Right, Communist and *Freikorps* combined to fight the occupiers, created conspiracies, blasted separatist movements and railway bridges in the Rhineland.[16] In the Rhineland and in Upper-Silesia alike they created a new prototype of fighter: the urban guerrilla.[17]

Probably the politicians of the Weimar Republic never realized the implications of their failure to attract the Republic's youth after the initial period. A permanent state of crisis existed for the first four years, followed by a period of relative calm in which the Republic became placid, bourgeois and complacent. And again, its last four years were years of crisis in which its democratic politicians signally manifested their incapacity to deal with acute economic and political problems. From its very beginnings it was burdened with too many compromises; it cared too much for party loyalties and the vested interests of its pressure groups to elicit any spark of excitement among its youth.[18]

Given the excess of democracy inherent in the Weimar system of proportional representation which by 1932 had produced a score of parties, Germany's ideological fragmentation was aggravated by political and economic difficulties and by the heritage of the Versailles Treaty. There were numerous reasons which would account for an alienated generation organizing itself not for but against the new Republic. Already in 1919 a proclamation calling for the new organization of the German Youth Movement declared: 'From a thousand wounds our people are bleeding. We are to be deprived of all that made us great . . . Today every German is faced by the question: downfall or recovery – life or death? Therefore to Germany's youth of both sexes and all classes, to those who still attend school and those who have left it already, we appeal to them irrespective of their denominational background. We want to gather that which has been sundered apart. The existing youth movements shall continue in their work; what we want to do is to weld them into one large national youth community. But we also appeal to those hundreds of thousands who are not yet organized. We appeal to the youth of Germany as a whole!'[19]

Little came of that appeal, or of most other appeals which were even remotely suspected of having any connection with any of the 'established' parties. But this appeal of 1919 carries all the characteristics of the extreme political propaganda of a decade or more later. It suggests the existence of only two extreme alternatives; it invokes the German *Volksgemeinschaft*, the national community, above all other divisions, religious, social or otherwise, and claims alone to represent that striving for a spiritually united Germany that would be capable of recovering the lost political strength.

The appeal for unity came perhaps a little too early, and for several years the spectrum of German Youth Movements continued to contain a large number of organizations which appeared to refuse to make common cause with the youth organizations of its extremes. The idea of the *Wandervogel* appeared to experience a renaissance, but also literally hundreds of *Bünde* of youth leagues were created, 'gilds', 'hordes', and youth associations.[20] However, like their elders, their life was marked by a refusal to compromise with other groups, which made greater mergers only of short duration. By comparison with the decade prior to 1914, the picture represented by the German youth leagues is too confusing, contradictory, and even bizarre to allow generalizations. The whole term *Bündische Jugend* is no more than an expression of convenience, rather than a term clearly indicating the nature, character, and aims of the youth movements bracketed by it. Of course they all claimed not to be orientated towards particular political parties, even though individual youths were bound to show and demonstrate their own political beliefs in a period highly charged with explosive political discussion. Moreover the parties themselves tried to make their own bids for youth allegiance and in some specific cases the line dividing the youth leagues and party youth associations became very blurred indeed.[21]

To the outsider, the image projected was one of continuity with the traditions of the past. Youth groups went hiking; their songs as before came from the *Zupfgeigenhansl,* by then enriched with some of the songs brought back from the Great War, as for instance Walter Flex's *Wildgänse rauschen durch die Nacht.* Folksongs, as well as traditional folk dances, were regularly practised and the weekly meetings went on as usual. But while the pre-war Youth Movement had chosen its own garb for mainly functional reasons, the post-war youth leagues tended to uniform themselves along military lines.[22] Whereas previously command was achieved by more or less general consent, military hierarchic structures of leadership gained general currency. A whole series of ranks, differing in terms from league to league, was invented and as one observer commented, 'During a time in which democracy conquered the world, when the masses were thought to be capable of governing themselves, within the Youth Movement the concept of leadership and faithful followers gained new currency.'[23] While the war had helped to bridge the class barriers among the frontline generation, after the war many of the youth leagues deliberately burnt such bridges as existed. The *Wandervögel,* for instance, would admit only grammar-school pupils, thus relegating working-class youths to the youth organizations of those political parties which, like the Social Democrats or the Communists, claimed to represent their interests, or to others who completely ignored the pluralism of classes. Some small youth associations believed themselves to be able to work for the cause of working-class youth without committing themselves to a political party.[24] At a cultural festival of the Working Youth in Weimar in 1920 a resolution was passed which was really a bid by working-class youth for middle-class support: 'In the close community life of both sexes we shall crystallize aristocracy within ourselves to enable us to participate in creating a socialist future until in place of envy, hatred and meanness, love among men and within national and international communities will have conquered. We desire the rejuvenation of the Socialist Movements out of action and example of our youth movement.'[25] The utopian streak made itself noticed again.

The resolution found no reciprocal gesture from the political Left. Classes marched not simply separate from one another but also divided in themselves. In the wake of the overwhelming catastrophe of a lost war, of psychological humiliation, it was quite forgotten that, a century before, German youth had initially begun to organize itself in reaction first against foreign despotism and then against the petty tyrannies at home; the quest for national as well as personal liberty had been their cause. That personal liberty had actually been attained within the framework of a new republic was either not recognized or deliberately ignored. Probably the latter. As before the war little or no attempt was made to come to terms with an industrial society and urban patterns of culture. On the contrary symptoms of alienation multiplied as the so-called 'golden twenties' went their course. They provided ample ammunition to argue the case for the prevalence of Western cultural decadence. The German Youth Movement tried to meet it by artifically fostering all forms of *Volk* art, hallowed by tradition, and in due course became itself highly vulnerable to the arguments of the apostles of a *völkisch* mystique.

In contrast to the youth leagues, the party youth organizations are more clearly defined. Thus the KPD (Communists) and the SPD (Socialists) each had its own youth organization with a combined total of approximately 803,000 members in 1933; the Centre party youth organization claimed more than 35,000 members while the right-wing parties (excluding the Hitler Youth) managed to rally a total of 253,000 members.[26] The effectiveness of the Left was reduced by the deep ideological division between Socialists and Communists, the effectiveness of the Right was neutralized through their fragmentation and petty squabbles. Both Left and Right also shared the trend already observed among the youth leagues, the emphasis on uniforms, military themes, and hierarchic leadership structures. Long before the National Socialists had 'co-ordinated' and 'integrated' the diverse formations of the German Youth Movement into the Hitler Youth, Germany's young minds were permeated by attitudes and convictions which for many made the change of the colour of the uniform a mere formality.

The task of turning these tendencies into valuable political capital was ultimately left to a man who by the standards of the day was of somewhat obscure origins, but who, by comparison with his much more experienced rivals for political power, had from the earliest stages of his political activities moved with much greater subtlety and conveyed much greater conviction to his audience. Adolf Hitler, the lowly corporal who had served in the trenches and not time-served in the *Reichstag*, possessed the ability to simplify, reducing complex problems into tangible slogans. His 'National Socialist' movement met the needs of many who felt that a synthesis between nationalism and socialism was possible. Since he never said what he meant by 'nationalism' or by 'socialism' he could be, at least for a time, all things to all men. His movement, under the impact of political failure and economic crisis, became, from a group of purely local Bavarian significance, the great *Sammelbecken*, the melting-pot of frequently exclusive concepts, personalities, and political aspirations. In this pot, nationalist and socialist ideas, the late nineteenth-century perversions of Herder's originally humanitarian concept of the *Volk*,[27] racism – as exemplified by the writings of Houstan Stewart Chamberlain – Pan-German wish dreams, Catholic corporate ideology and Fascist party leadership principles were all stirred together, along with the old concepts of the *Reich* and the Prussian traditions of sobriety and obedience.[28] Whether these elements would fuse was another matter; for the present they apparently managed to co-exist. But to those sections of the German public to whom Weimar meant little other than royal institutions minus the Kaiser, to those whose economic position had been eroded in the inflation and the Depression while, from their perspective, politicians just stood by doing nothing until the harm had been done, to many who could not see the solution of their country's present problems other than by means of a strong, energetic, and single-minded leadership, Hitler had something new and different to offer.[29]

His storm-troopers and later his SS formations attracted greater numbers of volunteers than any of the other private armies of the Right-wing and Left-wing parties which had flourished throughout the days of the Weimar Republic. One who at that time had not yet become a member of any of the National Socialist organizations wrote:

'We are now ready to create large groups and formations, which with immense strength will pursue one aim only. We are ready to subordinate ourselves to our leaders and we despise those who, typical of yesterday and the day before, care only for the superficiality of the ego, those who think that by obeying an order from outside they are giving something away. This cult of individualism of past generations, this caressing of one's own peculiarity down to the most insignificant matters, we deplore. Therefore we also despise those circles of the present bourgeoisie which are incapable of organizing themselves into forceful movements because they cannot and will not subordinate themselves, in the perpetual fear of losing a minute quantity of their own individuality.'[30]

These are the words of a member of a generation that had learned to sacrifice, to suffer, and to kill. Too young, too involved, and often overwhelmed by the turmoil around them, they did not possess the ability, or perhaps the time, to analyse coolly and to judge fairly. Many of them were the ready-made material for the Pied Pipers of Nuremberg who promised a new Germany, a new *Reich*, and a new society.

All this was not immediately apparent in 1919. But in Germany's second largest state, Bavaria, post-war dislocations of political and economic life produced conditions which were instrumental in Hitler's early rise to prominence. A Soviet Republic had been proclaimed there in 1919 and then bloodily suppressed by the forces of the central government, the *Reichswehr*, and the *Freikorps*. In order to ensure their hold on the Bavarian population the *Reichswehr* staff in Munich had cannily decided to subsidize political activity and agitation among the proletarian masses. And one of the army's agents in this undercover work was the ex-corporal Hitler. It was while carrying out a *Reichswehr* mission, in fact, that Hitler first came into contact with the tiny and insignificant *Deutsche Arbeiter Partei* (German Workers' Party), the germ of the later NS Party. And Hitler's contacts in the *Reichswehr* were to prove enormously helpful when he left the military service in order to devote all his time and talents to the little DAP. In particular, a certain Ernst Röhm, a clever but rebellious young officer in the Munich *Reichswehr*, supplied the nucleus of the future storm-troopers of the SA by delegating Mortar Company 19 to protect Hitler's assemblies and public addresses.

The party that Hitler joined, the DAP, was founded on 5 January 1919 by workers from Munich's railway repair shops who through at least two of its members enjoyed contacts with Munich's old-established middle class. The one surviving attendance list of that period is of a meeting in Munich's *Sterneckerbräu* in the Tal, a thoroughfare connecting Munich's Ludwigsbridge with the Marienplatz and the Munich Town Hall. The meeting was attended by 46 people who recorded their professions in the attendance list. Present were twelve locksmiths, mechanics, and armourers, six soldiers, five students, thirteen independent professions made up of one chemist, one medical general practioner, two shopowners, two merchants, two bankers, one painter, two engineers, one writer, and one daughter of a county court judge. Furthermore there were present four artisans, a shoemaker, a carpenter, a barber and a subcontractor. Five indicated no profession, among them one female member.[31]

It emerges clearly that workers and *petit bourgeoisie* predominated. The oldest complete list of members dates back to January 1920. It shows a total of 190 members with an average age of between thirty and thirty-two, of which ten and a half per cent were women. They comprised:

Skilled workers and artisans	33%
Academics	14.5%
Civil servants and employees	15%
Soldiers and officers	13%
Commercial occupations	12%
Students	7%
Shopkeepers	4%
Unskilled workers	2.5%[32]

Skilled workers and artisans, especially locksmiths and mechanics from Munich's railway repair shops, were still the largest single group. With the exception of eight members, all were born or resided in Munich, and the other eight were all living in Bavaria. Some members, like the later highly-influential manager of the publishing ventures of the NSDAP (*Nationalsozialistische Deutsche Arbeiter Partei*), Hermann Esser, had previously been members of the Social Democratic Party, but had become disillusioned as a result of the SPD's wavering attitude during the post-war crisis.[33]

Founded in January 1919, the DAP was joined by Hitler in September 1919. By July 1921 he had asserted his leadership and the DAP had become the NSDAP. By January 1923 it had become a Bavarian mass movement which posed a serious threat to law and order in Bavaria and which at a moment of crisis in that month compelled the Bavarian government to back down regarding its ban on all public meetings. Hitler could hold his party day in Munich in public and review a march-past of his storm troopers while the public demonstrations of the Social Democrats remained forbidden. It is well worth considering how an insignificant collection of railway workers, members of the lower-middle classes, unemployed, soldiers and intellectuals should within such a short span of time reach such (though still only regional) importance. Obviously the lost war, the revolution, the Versailles Treaty, and the inflation which since 1917 had begun to affect precisely those sectors of German society most prominently represented in the NSDAP, had played their role. It is also true to say that the Hitler movement was a product of the frontline experience and the consequences of the war; but to this one must add the personality of Hitler himself. Without Hitler the DAP or the NSDAP were no doubt possibilities, but as little other than backroom clubs, meeting in a medium-sized Munich restaurant. Hitler made, and in a sense was, the party; without him it was doomed to disintegration.[34] In his political oratory he could be inevitably relied on to touch the chord of an anti-capitalist and anti-industrialist desire and sentiment which had been prominent among the German lower-middle classes ever since the 'founder years' of the 1870s.

The experience of the trenches, the awareness that all sacrifice had been for nothing, caused an emotional upheaval which made it impossible spiritually for a large section of that generation ever to find their way home. Values once cherished unquestioningly had lost their meaning. Home, Fatherland, God, and Family had become mere slogans. True enough, the majority found it nevertheless possible to accommodate themselves within the new state of affairs. But a considerable minority did not. They looked towards the creation of a community with new ideals that would not include class differences, differences of social standing, of property, or of religious faith. Death had been the great leveller on the battlefield. And if social differences did not count in death, they should count even less in life. Apparently deprived of their future by defeat in war, let down by institutions led by royal figures on whose names they had sworn their oath and whose supreme representative had departed for Holland (while a minor one like the King of Bavaria had simply made his way out through the backdoor carrying only a box of his beloved cigars), for them the future looked bleak. The peace settlement confirmed that a world order was to be created within which Germany was to be the pariah. Germans could no longer look to the outside world as a safety valve, where their surplus of energy and idealism could be constructively deployed, and in the absence of this the pent-up energies and frustration unloaded themselves destructively inside Germany. If war is the father of all things, civil war is the mother, giving birth to new forms; and the Weimar Republic throughout its existence, even in its more tranquil periods, was never far away from civil war. Hitler, as much as his contemporaries, was a product of this physical and spiritual upheaval, but he was also one of the very few who could give to those who felt themselves deprived of their rightful heritage, cheated and betrayed, a new sense of purpose. His speeches heard in times of normality fall flat because of their essential coarseness. At the time when they were delivered, however, they embodied the collective sense of frustration of a large part of the German nation – and that is what gave Hitler his quality as an orator. The common denominator which he invoked and deployed to bridge differences of class and religion was the concept of the *Volk*, a concept which by the time Hitler began to use it had been perverted to the extent that it was synonymous with race. Bavaria's capital provided the unique combination of opportunities that facilitated Hitler's rise. A social structure predominantly agrarian-peasantry and middle-class dominated, it felt the threat posed by industrialization and the recent influx of an urban proletariat, a feature common also to cities such as Augsburg and Nuremberg.[35] Political and religious attitudes were determined by a devoutly Roman Catholic tradition. Socialist revolution, the attempt to establish the dictatorship of the proletariat, for a time overtook and paralysed Bavaria's middle class, but patient by nature they were content to wait until events had reached the point of excess, and then reacted with excess themselves. Bavaria simply was not ripe for a Socialist revolution; on the contrary it was more noted for revulsion against it. Little wonder therefore that it should become the haven and refuge of the forces of reaction from all regions of Germany.[36] Bavaria became the 'cell of order' for all anti-Marxist forces in Germany, a position which was complicated and compounded by the traditional conflict between Bavaria and the central government in Berlin, Bavaria insisting upon special privileges within a federal framework, Berlin insisting on reducing these to an absolute minimum.[37] Thus Bavaria concentrated within its boundaries all the forces that personified the traditional antipathy of the South towards the North of Germany. Its government espoused the cause of federalism, of the middle class against the forces of the proletarian atheist revolution from the North whose represen- tatives were apparently set upon a course of centralization. Against the revolution there seemed only one answer – vigorous counter-revolution.

Increasingly, the cutting edge of this Bavarian counter-revolution was provided by the National Socialist party whose tactics and aims in its early phase were determined by former soldiers and *Freikorps* members. The tac- tics of the assault troops provided the model for the early formations of the storm troopers, the principles of an authoritarian military leadership being gradually introduced by Hitler into what was ultimately to be his party: a machine forged from the DAP, Julius Streicher's German Socialist Party, the fighting formations of the *Freikorps Epp, Oberland,* and the naval brigade Ehrhardt, as well as members of local self-defence units and other para-military associations. Once forged, the party was his personal instru- ment to mobilize the masses to achieve his aims. As a party, or rather move- ment, it represented an opaque mixture of idealism of the highest order and the most inhuman brutality; of the power of fanatical, genuine convic- tion, and untrammelled terror. But in its early years – and this with some greater qualifications also holds true of the years 1925 to 1929 – it was not a national but a regional or as some might say a typically Bavarian affair.[38]

Given the composition of his movement, its essential youthfulness, and its incessant appeal for support from Germany's youth, it is rather surpris- ing that the actual initiative for the foundation of the specifically National Socialist youth movement did not come from Hitler himself, or for that matter from any of his direct subordinates. It came from a man who is vir- tually unknown, one Gustav Adolf Lenk, a piano polisher by trade, born in Munich on 15 October, 1903. After the war, during the revolutionary events in Munich in 1919, he joined the German National Youth Movement but gradually took exception to that feature common to most 'national'-minded youth organizations of the time, their middle-class bias.[39]

After listening to a number of speeches which Hitler delivered on the steps of Munich's *Feldherrnhalle,* and at the *Hofbräuhaus,* Lenk became one of the early converts to National Socialism. He immediately tried to join the NSDAP early in December 1921 but because he was as yet not quite eighteen years of age he could not be accepted. Asking whether there was at least a party youth organization and receiving a negative answer he was invited to build one up, though within the party this seems at first to have caused some misgivings. Lenk tried his best to argue his cause by a flood of memoranda.[40]

Hitler did not require much persuasion but Adolf Drexler, one of the fellow founders of the NSDAP, though initially in favour of a youth organization, seems to have had second thoughts primarily because the party was in the process of consolidation which required all the available resources of manpower and finance. To add to the existing burdens, looking after a 'kindergarten' seemed a little extravagant when there were already many national-minded youth associations, one of which, once its position was firmly established, the NSDAP could take over en bloc. But Drexler's hesitance appears to have been overcome because by 25 February 1922 Hitler addressed a circular to all sections and sub-sections of the NSDAP and the SA, in which he stated:

'Because of the increase of inquiries reaching the party leadership asking whether the movement has its own youth section, we have decided to call into existence the necessary organization for the purpose of setting up a youth section.

'The statutes of the party are in no way a hindrance to this, but on the contrary by implication carry provision for this step.

'The organization of the youth section will be conducted by the *Sturmabteilung* which will immediately work out in detail organizational statutes, which upon their completion will be forwarded to the individual *Ortsgruppen* [local party districts].

'Therefore, as from now all correspondence concerning a youth section is to be addressed to the headquarters of the SA (Administration of the NSDAP), Sturmabteilung, Munich 13, Corneliusstrasse 12.'[41]

In this circular it is evident that Hitler was not as yet fully aware of the traditions of the pre-war German Youth Movement, of the emphasis on youth being led by youth, a point that was to be a cause of occasional friction until after 1933. He considered a National Socialist Youth Movement politically useful but only under the wings, so to speak, of the storm troopers.

Hitler's circular was followed by a public proclamation published in the NSDAP's official organ the *Völkischer Beobachter* on 18 March 1922 in which he called for the creation of a youth movement of the NSDAP.[42]

'The party has now called into being a "Youth League of the National Socialist Workers' Party" whose purpose it is to gather all our young supporters who, because of their young age, cannot be accepted into the ranks of the storm troopers. The movement has its own statutes; it will educate its members in the same spirit which characterizes the party. We believe that the name of "League" alone is sufficient guarantee that our youths will receive the best possible training for their difficult task in the future. Upon their shoulders rests the future of our Fatherland. The "Youth League of the NSDAP" will ensure that these shoulders will be strong enough some day to be able to carry this gigantic weight.

'We demand that the National Socialist Youth, and all other young

Germans, irrespective of class or occupation, aged between fourteen and eighteen years of age, whose hearts are affected by the suffering and hardships afflicting the Fatherland, and who later desire to join the ranks of the fighters against the Jewish enemy, the sole originator of our present shame and suffering, enter the "Youth League of the NSDAP". We appeal also to youth organizations which at present are not part of any political movement, to join the German united front against the common enemy by joining us, thus creating a mighty battering ram.

'To enable the poorest young Germans also to enter into our youth league we shall not levy a membership fee. We expect and hope however for generous contributions from party members with greater means at their disposal.'[43]

A few days later this was followed by the publication of the statutes. Point I made the Youth League into an integral part of the National Socialist party. Point II stated the existence of the youth league's own statutes, but emphasized that the spirit pervading them was the same as that of the party. It rejected outright any playing down of the seriousness of Germany's present position 'on the one hand' and the adoption of the parliamentary point of view 'on the other' and instead insisted on a rigorous recognition of the facts as they were. It was to be the League of all those who, upon reaching their eighteenth birthday, wanted to join the storm troopers of the NSDAP.[44]

Point III tried to articulate some of the aims of the Youth League: to reawaken and to treasure those characteristics which had their origin in the Germanic blood, namely 'love of one's country and people, enjoyment of honest open combat and of healthy physical activity, the veneration of ethical and spiritual values, and the rejection of those values originating from Jewry and Mammon'. Point III also stated that the movement ignored differences of class, occupation, or social standing, since these did not correspond with true Germanic nature 'and are contradictory to the ancient concepts of a community of race and blood and of all German people'.[45]

Point IV stipulated that this 'spirit' was to be cultivated by weekly meetings, lectures, hiking trips, and games of all kinds requiring a maximum of physical movement, while Point V limited membership to 'Germans (Aryans) between the age of fourteen and eighteen years. Foreigners and Jews cannot be members.' Point VI emphasized that there was no membership fee, while Point VII explained in greater detail what had already been touched upon in general terms in Point IV. There would be a meeting once a week in which lectures, discussions, and talks would be held. Every second Sunday was to be spent hiking through the countryside, an exercise declared compulsory. To prevent the intrusion of 'trashy literature' the

Youth League would establish its own libraries which were to be continuously enlarged by the voluntary gifts of 'good books' by members of
the Youth League. Point VIII required each member upon reaching his
eighteenth birthday to leave the League. 'It is open to him then to enter the
Sturmabteilungen of the NSDAP.' The last two points, Points IX and X,
were of a purely organizational nature.[46]

Contrary to the hopes and expectations nourished within the NSDAP in
general, and by Lenk in particular, there was no rush to join the National
Socialist Youth League. The proletarian youth would hardly have been
attracted by the youth group of their principal opponent, while for the
middle-class the NSDAP was too proletarian. Moreover, of course, the
National Socialist movement in 1922 was still of primarily local significance, one of the many right-wing groups devoted to the 'suppression of
Bolshevism'. As a result of the 'Soviet experience' in Bavaria, whose leaders
were predominantly Germans or Russians of the Jewish faith, anti-
Semitism had become considerably more vociferous and organized than it
had ever been before; yet its explicit espousal in the party programme and in
the statutes of the Youth League could not be publicly sanctioned in Catholic Bavaria, where the Church still held the allegiance of the majority.
Quite apart from this the churches, Catholic as well as Protestant, had their
own youth groups and were hardly anxious to encourage the growth of
rivals.

It took nearly another two months, until 13 May 1922, before a public
meeting could be announced at which the official foundation of the Youth
League of the NSDAP was proclaimed.[47] The meeting, which took place in
the historic *Bürgerbräukeller* in Munich, was filled to capacity. Nevertheless, the meeting was a disappointment, for among those who attended only
seventeen were youths.[48] The speakers were Hitler, followed by the then
leader of the storm troopers, the former lieutenant and *Freikorps* member
Johann Ulrich Klintzsch, and Gustav Adolf Lenk.[49] Lenk possessed considerable gifts as organizer and administrator, but he was not a good
speaker – something he himself realized, for he kept his public addresses to
a bare minimum, relying rather on his persuasiveness in personal conversations and closer circles than public meetings. At the meeting Lenk was
formally entrusted with the command of the Youth League of the NSDAP.
His immediately superior authority was the SA and the first uniforms worn
by the boys were modelled on those of the SA. Lenk also immediately announced a division in the Youth League of the NSDAP, one catering for
those aged between 14 and 16, the other for those between 16 and 18 years
of age. Particularly for this second group named *Jungsturm Adolf Hitler*,
the uniform was to become something of a problem, since it proved almost
indistinguishable from the uniform of the storm troopers, a point very

much resented by the latter. In fact members of Lenk's organization were listed quite indiscriminately together with SA members, and German newspapers as well as official police reports of the time stress the youthfulness of many members of the SA. For instance, Emil Klein, later to rise to the rank of *Gebietsführer* Munich-Upper Bavaria, was listed as a storm trooper although he had at that time not yet reached the age of sixteen. In a list of Munich storm troopers of 1922, out of 244 members of the Youth League of the NSDAP 94 had refused to indicate a date of birth, 47 were less than eighteen years old and the youngest member was fourteen.[50]

The first official public appearance by the *Jungsturm Adolf Hitler* – a short-lived organization, foreshadowing the *Hitler-Jugend* which came to dominate the lives of so many – was made on 28 January 1923, when Hitler held his first official *Parteitag* (party rally) in Munich.[51] The youths in solemn ceremony were handed their first pennants, white bearing an anchor and swastika in the centre. The pennant was a short-lived symbol; during one of the street battles between the various political factions which were so characteristic of the Weimar Republic in general and of Munich in particular, the *Jungsturm Adolf Hitler* was involved and the Munich police confiscated the pennant.[52]

What Lenk lacked in charisma as speaker he more than compensated for by his qualities of personal and informal leadership and even more so by his ability as a tireless organizer. On his personal initiative small units of the National Socialist Youth League were founded in Nuremberg and outside Bavaria, in Zeitz, Dresden, and Hanau, as well as in the Ruhr area in Dortmund.[53] And Lenk was able to extend his organization to areas outside Germany, especially German Austria. There, he benefited from contacts already established by the NSDAP with a sister party that had been founded independently in Vienna.[54]

Austria's German National Socialist Workers Party was considerably smaller than Hitler's organization but, at least until 1924, one of its leaders – Rudolf Jung – exercised a considerable intellectual influence.[55] On Austrian initiative a joint meeting was suggested for some time in 1920, and finally took place on 7, 8 and 9 August in Salzburg.[56] The main issue at the meeting was the possible fusion of all National Socialist groups and their affiliated youth organizations.[57] Jung in his address to the meeting emphasized the common features, but Hitler, in opposition to Drexler, who supported Jung, declared that a fusion could only take place under German leadership, by which of course Hitler meant himself.[58] Hitler at that point of time was just at the beginning of his political career and was therefore considered a political nonentity compared with Jung and his fellow Austrians. Since Hitler at that stage could not succeed, he endeavoured to maintain the existing status quo by charming his fellow Austrians. In his address he said that he was 'almost ashamed that only today, after so many years, the same movement which had begun in German Austria as early as 1904 is beginning to get a foothold in the German Reich. The system of the bourgeoisie has outlived itself as has that of the proletariat, and thus our party has emerged. We should not reproach one another, because the same thought and the same suffering has led to the rise of the same movement in all corners of the Reich. Naturally we are independent of one another [but] the term "worker" is the ultimate test to decide who is ripe for our movement and who is not. For us only he is suitable who willingly accepts it as a title of honour . . . Every popular movement which has not the backing of millions is without value and devoid of purpose. The national idea will become effective once it is common to the entire people.'[59]

Jung, though he had failed in his attempt to bring about the fusion of all National Socialist movements and had forestalled Hitler's bid for leadership, was nevertheless won over to and by Hitler personally. 'Hitler one day will be the greatest of us all,' he declared to his secretary.[60] Hitler too had forestalled Austrian claims to leadership from which he expected little else but disadvantages. The suspicion with which he had viewed the Hapsburg Empire had not disappeared even after the Empire had disintegrated. To him Austrian leadership, personal reasons apart, would have exposed the party to the introduction of a typical Austrian *Schlamperei*, of which he himself to his last day was never free. What he accepted in Salzburg were commonplaces summarized in a report about the Salzburg meeting a month later in Munich – 'Strictly national, strictly anti-Semitic, strictly socialist'.

Lenk's German associates were also present. Eugen Weese had founded the 'National Socialist Youth Association' in the Sudetenland, while in Austria Walter Gattermeyer and Adolf Bauer had successfully founded the 'National Socialist Workers Youth' with branches in the Tyrol, Salzburg, Carinthia, Vienna, and Lower Austria.[61] What the Salzburg meeting did yield was a greater degree of co-operation between the German National Socialists of Munich, Austria, and the Sudetenland.[62] During the same year Hitler addressed rallies in Vienna, Salzburg, St Pölten, Innsbruck, and Linz. Also, one of the founders of the German Workers Party, its 'economic expert', Gottfried Feder, spoke in Austria. By the same token Austrians like Walter Gattermeyer spoke in Germany within the framework of public rallies of the NSDAP.[63] However, in spite of the growing and close collaboration, Hitler opposed any attempts at fusion other than on his own terms. The furthest he was prepared to go was the creation of the general committee of the National Socialist Parties of Greater Germany. The proclamation announcing this new committee referred to the Salzburg meeting and to the fact that 'the representatives of the NSDAP of Czechoslovakia, the NSP of Upper Silesia (Poland), the NSDAP of Germany (Seat Munich) and the German Socialist Party (Seat Hanover) have declared their fusion into a German National Socialist Party'.[64] However, to water down this somewhat extravagant claim it was added that in tactical questions the parties within their respective states should retain complete independence.[65] Also a list of guiding principles was published which stated that 'the German National Socialist Party aims to lift out and to liberate the working sections of the German people from economic, political, and spiritual suppression and to ensure their complete equality in all areas of national life'. With respect to national political aims the guiding principles stated the main aim to be the creation of a territorially united German state; 'we aim at the concentration of the entire area of German settlement in Europe into a Democratic, socialist German Reich, which will provide effective protection for all territories in which Germans have settled and which is dominated by foreign peoples'.[66]

It is very likely that, even without the NSDAP, collaboration between German and Austro-German nationalists would have been very close, because the *Freikorps*, semi-*Freikorps* associations like *Bund Oberland*, and local self-defence units straddled those artificial frontiers which Bismarck had first erected in 1867 and which were cemented by the Paris Peace Treaties. Although collaboration with Sudeten German National Socialists was equally as close, the frontier was less open and, understandably enough, the Czech authorities were less reluctant to turn back undesirable aliens who might wish to fan the flames of irredentism. Nevertheless in 1921 the NSDAP held a mass rally in Prague in which representatives from Munich were present, and Lenk, for instance, was able frequently to attend legal as well as illegal meetings of the National Socialist Youth Association in Eger. But however intense the degree of co-operation was, Hitler's view prevailed. 'It would be the greatest mistake to believe that the strength of a movement increases with the fusion of this association with other similar ones. Of course every enlargement in this way means for a time an increase in size and, to the eyes of a superficial observer, growth and increase in power. But what actually happens is the transfer of the seed of weakness which only slowly but surely makes itself felt.'[67]

This, in effect, also marked the limits of Lenk's power, but his ability for dynamic organization was soon recognized and as the number of youth groups of the National Socialist Youth League increased Hitler promoted him from a hitherto purely regional position to a 'national' one.[68] He was to build up an administrative and organizational centre for a Youth League for the whole of Germany. Lenk divided the area over which his Youth League operated into provincial units which by the summer of 1923 had risen to nine, and he established and deepened his contacts with National Socialist youth organizations in the Sudetenland and in Austria (led by

Eugen Weese and Walter Guttermeyer respectively). But the reins in Munich were held tight and firm, and being still in a subordinate position to the SA he felt at times constrained and frustrated by the 'narrow-mindedness' of Munich's party headquarters.[69]

In May 1923 he published the first youth magazine for the National Socialist Youth League, entitled the *Nationale Jungsturm*. It proved to be something of a financial fiasco. Evidently there were as yet not enough members to carry the magazine financially, and so it was reduced to the form of a regular supplement of the *Völkischer Beobachter* and renamed *Nationalsozialistische Jugend*.[70]

From May 1923 onwards the NSDAP moved into a period of crisis, and this may have been a further factor accounting for the stagnation of the National Socialist Youth magazine. For more than three years now Hitler had promised revolution, had preached the necessity of the overthrow of the 'November criminals' and the destruction of the 'Jew Republic'. But so far nothing had happened. On the contrary, when in February 1923 the French and the Belgians had marched into the Ruhr, Hitler had opposed the policy of passive resistance and declared that the overthrow of the Berlin government should be the first priority. Yet nothing happened to indicate that Hitler was any nearer to his aim than he had been three years before. Among his storm troopers restiveness increased, especially when the monetary inflation began to gather up renewed speed for a further (but also final) upwards spiral. Hitler was under pressure; he felt that he had to act.[71]

The first of May, 1923, had a double significance in Munich. For the Social Democrats and the Communists it was the international labour day to be celebrated with large public demonstrations. For the parties and political groups of the Right, 1 May was celebrated as the fourth anniversary of the 'liberation from the yoke of the Soviet Republic'. Socialists, Communists, and trade unions alike chose for the route of their public march one which only a fortnight before had been taken by some of Munich's para-military right-wing organizations, who considered the intention of their left-wing opponents, therefore, to be a calculated insult and expected the Bavarian Ministry of Interior to ban the demonstration. Much to their consternation permission was granted, provided no 'Soviet flags' or banners and boards with inscriptions of a political content were carried.[72] Hitler tried to intervene personally and requested the *Reichswehr* commander of the Munich district, General von Lossow, and Munich's head of police, Hans Ritter von Seisser, to withdraw permission.[73] Lossow, in fact, indicated that he would open fire upon anyone causing trouble.[74] But Hitler, bluffing, categorically declared that the Red demonstrations would only take place if the demonstrators marched over his own dead body first.[75] It was of no avail. Tempers were further frayed and the situation aggravated through vicious campaigns carried out in the Socialist and National Socialist press. Violent clashes between Communists and National Socialists increased to such an extent that during the last two weeks before May Day certain districts and streets of Munich were areas in which active civil war raged.[76] The Right began to spread a rumour that the Left was planning a *coup d'état*, a rumour which was highly potent in a city in which memories were freshly scarred.[77] Seisser relented and gave in to Hitler, banning the planned demonstration.[78] Hitler seemed to have won; together with several others, including Hermann Göring, the highly decorated First World War air ace who in February had been appointed Commander of the SA by Hitler, he went to see Bavaria's Prime Minister von Knilling and the Minister of the Interior on 30 April, demanding the invocation of martial law against the Socialists, and that the 'patriotic formations' of the Right, including the storm troopers, should on 1 May be enrolled as 'auxiliary police'. Neither Knilling nor Lossow was prepared to accede to this and they reversed Seisser's decision, which did not stop Hitler from claiming *vis à vis* the police president that the *Reichswehr* had agreed to the ban.[79] Hitler had apparently embarked on a course from which there was no return. Göring's storm troopers, with the aid of Röhm, were armed with hand weapons and machine-guns; so were others of the 'patriotic' paramilitary organizations with which Munich had teemed since 1919.[80] From *Reichswehr* garrisons outside Munich, armoured cars were made available to the storm troopers, who came to Munich from throughout Bavaria.[81] At what was to be the site of the 1972 Olympic Games, the *Oberwiesenfeld*, the SA, the *Freikorps Oberland* and another unit, the *Reichsflagge*, assembled fully armed. Inside Munich, in the *Maximilaneum* on the east bank of the river Isar, the present home of the Bavarian parliament, further armed contingents assembled, while Hitler and his entourage, including the accepted head of all the nationalist groups in Munich, General von Ludendorff, assembled at their Munich headquarters.[82] Hitler tried to get from Lossow a *post facto* legitimization for arming his storm troopers. Lossow refused, which did not prevent Hitler, with Röhm's aid, collecting more weapons from the military barracks, including an artillery-piece.[83]

Socialists, Communists, and trade unionists took equally little notice of the government's ban on their demonstration and assembled on the *Theresienwiese*, the very place from which the Bavarian revolution had begun in 1918.[84] Police moved in carefully but only in order to avoid clashes between Left and Right. Lossow on the other hand, issued orders immediately to disarm the para-military organizations, a task given to none other than Röhm, who with *Reichswehr* and police units had to make his way to the *Oberwiesenfeld* where in the meantime Hitler too had arrived. Protected by a steel helmet and making the final preparations for an attack upon the city interior, Hitler was stopped by Röhm and compelled to return his weapons there and then.[85] *Reichswehr* lorries arrived and the storm troopers and their allies were disarmed on the spot. Members of *Jungsturm Adolf Hitler* who were acting as despatch riders were sent home.[86] Hitler's bluff had been called and the repercussions were serious. The period from 1 May to 8 November 1923 shows not a drastic but a steady decline in the membership of his storm troopers, who tended to join other nationalist para-military formations.[87] Fortune seemed to be against Hitler.

Hitler was not the only man in Munich aiming at revolutionary change. One of the others was Lossow, who instigated consultations with the other formations with a view to emulating Mussolini and marching upon Berlin. Significantly, Hitler and his storm troopers were not consulted. It was assumed that it would be only a matter of time before the bulk of Hitler's main following joined the other factions of the extreme Right.[88] Against that background the events of 8–9 November 1923, the famous Munich Putsch, appear in a different light from that shown in the conventional interpretation. Hitler was aware of what was going on, yet he was isolated from the centre of decision. All that was left to him was the 'escape forwards', to set a parallel course to that of Lossow and his associates. At a series of mass rallies his threat of revolution was more open, more radical, and more direct than it had ever been before.[89] Within a few weeks before 8 November he had rallied once again the entire support of the nationalist extremist wing, and in fact managed to overtake Lossow on the Right, especially since Lossow was having second thoughts about his march on Berlin.[90] Hitler once again had unleashed forces he could no longer control, even when he saw that the result was bound to be a disaster. Unless he was to lose his standing forever, as the *Führer* of the party, he had to act and put himself at the front of his movement giving the appearance of leading what, in fact, he could no longer control. He had recovered his position, his star was once again in the ascendancy – but at a price. Since victory was impossible only disaster and defeat could be the coin with which to pay.

In a dramatic intervention at a nationalist rally in Munich's *Bürgerbräukeller* he announced the formation of a new German government with himself as chancellor and Ludendorff as president, and under pressure obtained the support of the local chiefs of the army, police, and administration. However, as soon as the latter had been allowed to leave the beer cellar they reversed their positions and took immediate precautions to stop Hitler. Short of accepting the kind of defeat he had suffered on 1 May, Hitler felt he could do little else than march with his formations into the heart of Munich. Gambler that he was, he thought that perhaps the situation might change on the way. Led by himself and Ludendorff the storm troopers and other right-wing para-military formations which had assembled in Munich from all parts of Bavaria set off from the *Bürgerbräukeller* during the morning of 9 November. Their march was routed into the Residenzstrasse, a very narrow street at the end of which by the *Feldherrnhalle* a cordon of police supported by the *Reichswehr* closed access to the *Odeonsplatz*. Hitler and his followers were called upon to dissolve their procession. Instead of obeying they began to surge forward, and police opened fire. At the *Feldherrnhalle* sixteen of Hitler's supporters paid the price of the gamble with their lives, one of them a member of the *Jungsturm Adolf Hitler*.[91] Ludendorff, who had marched through the cordon unhurt, was accompanied home; Hitler escaped in the mêlée with an injured arm but a few days later was arrested by the police.

Lenk, who was present at the decisive meeting at *Bürgerbräukeller* the night before, appraised the situation correctly and did his best to make sure that the younger members of the *Jungsturm Adolf Hitler* would be in the safety of their homes or far removed from the centre of activity. Special messenger-tasks were invented for the purpose of keeping the boys occupied in journeys to and from various party storm-trooper centres at the outskirts of the city.[92] But some of the older boys could not be stopped.

The 9 November 1923, besides being the end of the first NSDAP, was also the end of the *Jungsturm Adolf Hitler* and the Youth League of the NSDAP.

iv Birth

Just how essential Hitler was to the continued existence of the NSDAP was amply demonstrated by what happened during his absence from the scene while he was in Landsberg prison serving nine months of the five-year sentence pronounced by the Bavarian court for his part in the Putsch. Under normal circumstances this would have been the end of Hitler's political career, but Hitler was no normal person and nor were the circumstances. Confronted by a court which was obviously embarrassed as well as handicapped by the extent to which it had to cover up the illegal actions of members of the official Bavarian government, Hitler could quickly grasp the initiative and dominate the court room,[1] in order to justify his behaviour and add further to the fame of himself and his party. Hitler's tactics yielded immediate results; five days after the court had delivered judgment, local elections in Munich gave the extreme nationalists the majority vote, while in Bavaria as a whole they obtained 17.1% of the vote. Less than a month later, on 4 May 1924, in the *Reichstag* elections the National Socialist Liberty Movement obtained 1,920,000 votes and thus entered the German parliament with 32 deputies.[2]

This success, however, was of short duration. The National Socialists still lacked a proper national organization, and their base of power still remained in Bavaria. This difficulty might have been overcome had it not been for the outbreak of serious in-fighting which resulted in the movement's division into two major groups, one under Alfred Rosenberg and Julius Streicher, the *Grossdeutsche Volksgemeinschaft* (the Greater German National Community), which unequivocally rejected any participation in the parliamentary process, and the other, the *National-sozialistische Freiheitsbewegung* (the National Socialist Liberty Movement), headed by Gregor Strasser and Ernst Röhm. This group was convinced by Strasser's argument that the avenue of revolution was closed for the foreseeable future and that any party remaining outside the existing political framework would condemn itself to political impotence.[3]

Hitler refused to intervene from his cell at Landsberg and, in the light of the growing confusion in the camp of the nationalist radicals, the conviction grew among many of its members that only Hitler's authority could re-establish a unified National Socialist movement – a conviction shared of course by Hitler himself.[4] He alone was the linch-pin of this movement, the one man who could give it coherence and shape.

During Hitler's absence from the active political scene the disintegration and the disunity of the right-wing radicals was also mirrored in their youth movement. Gerhard Rossbach, one of Hitler's early supporters, the founder and former leader of the *Freikorps Rossbach*, had to go into exile in Austria where he founded the *Schilljugend*, named after Ferdinand von Schill.[5] Gustav Lenk, on the other hand, thought he could resume where he had left off and already in mid-November 1923 he had called into existence the 'Patriotic Youth Association of Greater Germany'.[6] It did not take any great powers of detection for the Bavarian police to realize that this was nothing other than the continuation of the outlawed Youth League of the NSDAP under a different name. They quickly moved in, dissolved the association, and imprisoned Lenk.[7] Hardly had he been released than he founded the 'Greater German Youth Movement' in April 1924 which, although founded in Munich, had the centre of its organization just outside northern Bavaria in the Vogtland – a region which straddles both Thuringia and Saxony.[8] Lenk's decision to move out of Bavaria, taken as a result of the attitude of the Bavarian authorities, was to have consequences hardly foreseen by him at the time, because the removal of the National Socialist Youth organization from the centre of Hitler's power ensured for it over the next few years a relatively autonomous development. For the time being, however, Lenk was soon in trouble with the authorities in Munich again for leading an illegal youth organization.[9] He was committed to the Fortress of Landsberg in November 1924 but released a month later on 20 December 1924 together with Hitler, who was paroled at the same time.[10]

Hitler was determined now to heed the advice given during his trial by the state prosecutor Dr Stenglein, who in his final speech had said: 'I am not blind to the existence of a good core. It is understandable that the enthusiastic youth suffers from impatience. But youth must be disciplined and led in the right direction by mature men. Impatience must be replaced by the ability to work quietly and confidently for the future, waiting with clenched teeth until the hour is ripe.'[11] A police report on Hitler less than two months after his release from Landsberg comments that Hitler had succeeded 'in putting himself above the movement'.[12] After his release he waited two months before stepping back into the Bavarian public limelight as the leader of the National Socialist Party. This time-span allowed him to make the necessary plans for the future without undue haste.

Although apparently above the movement, Hitler left no doubt that he supported the group led by Rosenberg and Streicher against that which followed Gregor Strasser. And this for a simple reason: Rosenberg and Streicher would present no problems as subordinates, let alone pose any claims to leadership in rivalry to his own. Not so the Strasser group which in Hitler's view contained his strongest rival of them all – Ludendorff. The most that group was ready to concede to Hitler was the post of chief propagandist. However, Ludendorff himself was growing noticeably tired of active involvement in politics and refused to be the spearhead in the power struggle against Hitler. When Ludendorff resigned from the National Socialist Liberty Movement in February 1925, Hitler considered the opportunity ripe to announce his decision to found the NSDAP anew.[13] Hitler, by waiting and refusing to take sides openly with any one of the nationalist radical groups, had in this way given them time enough to destroy themselves, and to the ruins and remnants of their organizations he could announce on 27 February 1925: 'The arguments have now come to an end,' and 'Join the ranks of the old movement and leave behind you everything that lies beyond yesterday.'[14] In Bavaria the new founding of the NSDAP, with Hitler as its undisputed leader, led to a quick disintegration of the other groupings of the extreme militant right-wing. Hitler could afford to be generous and refer to Ludendorff as a 'faithful and unselfish friend',[15] since Ludendorff had ceased to exist as the leader of the German national revolution. The only leader of Germany's movement for national regeneration was now Hitler. Hitler's support for Ludendorff's candidature in the presidential elections of 1925, after the sudden death of Ebert, was no more than a gesture which cost nothing; after all there was not the remotest chance that Ludendorff would win against his erstwhile chief, Field Marshal von Hindenburg.[16]

After his release from Landsberg Gustav Adolf Lenk was unsure about the future of the National Socialist movement. For the time being he decided to keep his youth movement ventures outside the existing political groupings until the victor or the dominant group had emerged. In spite of the new founding of the NSDAP, Hitler's position as *Führer* seemed to Lenk not yet sufficiently consolidated to deserve his unreserved commitment. He therefore decided to go it alone and founded the 'German Defence Youth Association' independently of the NSDAP.[17] In an atmosphere still contaminated with recriminations and counter-recriminations among the nationalist groupings, this step proved Lenk's undoing. Branded as a traitor to the cause and convicted on what may well have been a trumped-up charge of petty larceny, Lenk withdrew from the youth movement scene altogether. At first he attempted to make a great public gesture of his departure. He asked the *Völkischer Beobachter* to print an article in which he announced his own resignation. As reasons he gave economic pressure combined with considerable opposition to his own personality from within the party. The article raised a complaint which his successors Gruber and Schirach were later to echo, namely the lack of understanding of the youth movement by the party officials. The party paper did not print the article. However, Lenk did not completely sever his connections.[18] In 1927 he joined the SA again and the NSDAP in 1932. He tried unsuccessfully to make a comeback into the Hitler Youth but failed against the opposition of Baldur von Schirach, who became head of the Hitler Youth in 1931. (In later years the NSDAP Main Archive vindicated his claim that the *Jungsturm Adolf Hitler* had been the precursor of the Hitler Youth.) Nevertheless Lenk was to maintain very cordial contacts with several high-ranking Hitler Youth leaders and at the annual marchpast for the commemoration of the events of 9 November 1923 in Munich, Lenk in 1933 headed the former members of his *Jungsturm*. Thereafter he was not to participate.[19]

Lenk, however, left a very valuable and useful heritage, for one of the groups founded under his guidance was the Greater German Youth Movement at Plauen. Its leader was Kurt Gruber, a student of law who had already joined the NSDAP in May 1923 but had not participated in the Munich Putsch.[20] Lenk had him appointed successor to the youth leader of Thuringia and Saxony, Brettschneider, who had proved rather ineffective as an organizer.[21] Gruber quickly set about consolidating the position of his youth group, which during Hitler's imprisonment frequently changed its name, opting mostly for descriptions that suggested a hiking or athletics association.[22] Gruber, born in 1904, was a typical product of that group of the German post-war generation who saw Germany's future and her restoration to her place among the nations of Europe almost exclusively within the framework of the realization of National Socialism – with the accent on the socialism. It was in no small measure due to his influence that the later Hitler Youth were to maintain socially radical attitudes much longer than most of the other formations of the NSDAP.[23]

Within a matter of three months he had managed to fuse numerous other small right-wing youth associations with his own group and in July 1924 held his own youth rally at Plauen.[24] By the time Hitler and Lenk left Landsberg, Gruber had organized in Saxony alone a youth movement approximately 2,500 strong, had built up the necessary administrative apparatus, and had introduced the first Hitler Youth uniform which included the brown shirt and a swastika-emblazoned armlet distinct from that of the storm troopers.[25] Although this was very largely Gruber's own personal success, one must not underestimate the importance of the financial support given to him by a local textile manufacturer, Martin Mutschmann, who himself had become a member of the NSDAP in 1923 and later was to be one of its *Gauleiters*.* The financial support provided by Mutschmann allowed Gruber to work as full-time leader of his youth movement, to rent office premises in Plauen which were to house his administrative headquarters, and furthermore to publish his own newspaper.[26]

For a short time Gruber's Greater German Youth Movement amalgamated with Röhm's forces and adopted the name *Frontjugend*,[27] but after Hitler's decision to reduce the SA's para-military function and restrict it to a purely propagandist role[28] – which caused the departure of Röhm, for the time being, from the ranks of the NSDAP[29] – Gruber re-adopted the former name for his youth movement.[30] Generally speaking, Gruber's success was mainly due to the high degree of independence which, thanks to his tactical ability as well as his organization's financial independence from the NSDAP, he had preserved for himself. Although the members of his organization swore an oath of allegiance to Hitler and adopted the leadership principle, this was as yet not the same thing as being an integral part of the party apparatus which Hitler was about to rebuild in Munich.[31] Meanwhile Gruber tried to extend his movement beyond Thuringia and Saxony, to open up branches in Franconia, the Rhineland, and the Palatinate. In this he achieved some successes, but similar endeavours in Berlin and Prussia at that time met with complete failure in face of the tight control exercised by the established right-wing parties over their own youth organizations.[32]

In spite of Gruber's success, the support he received from the NSDAP in Munich or from Hitler personally was less than encouraging. His independence caused frowns and suspicions in Munich, where Hitler in accordance with his ideas set out in the recently published first volume of *Mein Kampf* had decided to rebuild the youth movement as an integral part of the NSDAP.[33] Gruber, personally unknown to Hitler, surrounded by an atmosphere of suspicion and intrigue, was at first not Hitler's choice for the leader of the youth movement. Instead he preferred Edmund Heines, a former lieutenant and member of the *Freikorps Rossbach*, who by Hitler's order of 6 May 1925 was instructed to deal with 'all matters relating to the youth movement'.[34] This, of course, was still short of appointing Heines as youth leader. The order reflects Hitler's own uncertainty and his reluctance to commit himself at this stage one way or the other, especially as Heines' position as one of the leaders of the *Schilljugend* was likely to produce conflict within the party and the nationalist youth groups.

Hitler's reluctance was amply justified. Heines' *apparent* appointment immediately produced a conflict which as far as the underlying crucial

---

* The title *Gauleiter* had emerged during 1921–22 and ultimately denoted the head of the NSDAP of a particular *Gau*, which in turn was, at the regional level, the highest administrative unit of the party. All *Gauleiters* were subject directly to the *Reichsleitung*, the Reichsleadership Office of the NSDAP, which was controlled at first by Rudolf Hess and then by his successor Martin Bormann.

issues were concerned remained unresolved throughout the early history of the NSDAP. The reputation of the *Schilljugend* was that of an élitist, predominantly middle-class body which had little time for its working-class brethren.[35] Gruber immediately addressed himself to Hitler, virtually refusing to allow his Greater German Youth Movement to subordinate itself to the *Schilljugend*.[36] Gruber, whose adherents were mainly working-class youths from the industrial districts of Saxony and Thuringia, argued that absorption of his own organization into the *Schilljugend* would inevitably narrow its base of recruitment, for no working-class youth would be likely to join the effete and snobbish *Schilljugend*. Hitler was still not convinced enough to make a final decision and Gruber addressed himself to Rossbach directly suggesting a compromise solution in the form of a federation between the two movements within which each would retain its full autonomy.[37] Rossbach rejected the proposal, stating as his grounds precisely those for which Gruber was unwilling to merge with the *Schilljugend*, namely the importance of preserving his group's élitist character.[38] The opportunity for compromise gone, Hitler at long last tried to appease Gruber, whose strength he could not afford to ignore, by appointing him in October 1925 the 'Leader of the National Socialist Youth Movement for Saxony'. Rossbach, at the time still in exile near Salzburg, could do little to affect the issue except to reiterate his decision to refuse any compromise over the issue. The deadlock was finally broken by Rossbach himself when early in 1926 he was amnestied and could return to Germany. Disenchanted with Hitler but even more confident about his own political future, he refused any position subordinate to Hitler and any suggestion of affiliating the *Schilljugend* with the NSDAP. The door which Rossbach closed precluded the possibility of any kind of political activity of his own or of his *Schilljugend*, which ultimately, because of its lack of mass appeal, disintegrated.

Rossbach's failure provided Gruber's opportunity. Hitler, who since May 1925 had kept a close eye on Gruber, did not fail to be impressed by the organizational talent of the 21-year-old young man, in spite of the suspicions of NSDAP headquarters. Gradually the 'Greater German Youth Movement' grew into the role of the official youth organization of the NSDAP. From the point of view of ideological orthodoxy there was nothing that Hitler had to fear from Gruber. Ideologically, Gruber was a simpleton. He took Hitler's programme as he found it, apparently completely unaware of its inherent ambiguities and interpreting the more radical and uncompromising statements, especially those of an anti-semitic character, as the veneer of the times, the implications of which would soon wear off once their propagandist effect had been achieved. Hitler's ultimate support of Gruber's position against the *Schilljugend* seemed to confirm his own assessment of Hitler as a sincere social revolutionary, and as long as he retained that conviction Gruber was ready to obey Hitler's every command. From Hitler's point of view, an uncritical idealist like Gruber could be handled much more easily than the representatives of the former frontline officers, men like Ernst Röhm, Walter Stennes, or Gerhard Rossbach.

The year 1925 was for Hitler essentially one of party reconstruction, and given the multiplicity of rivalries and the numerous direct as well as indirect challenges within the NSDAP to his own position,[39] it was inevitable that the problem of the National Socialist youth organization was not of the first priority. Nevertheless, it was among the priorities and the opportunity to rely unreservedly on a man like Gruber allowed Hitler to concentrate on his immediate task, that of establishing once and for all his own *Führer* position not only in Bavaria but throughout the party in Germany.[40] Once Hitler had cleared the air, at least for the time being, regarding his own claims to unquestioned obedience by his *Gauleiters* he could go ahead and call his first new party rally, this time at Weimar.[41] The choice was determined by the fact that Thuringia was one of the few states in which Hitler was allowed to speak in public. Whereas most previous party rallies had been organized as joint meetings of various extreme right-wing groups, including the NSDAP, the rally at Weimar followed the pattern established at Munich in 1923 by being exclusively National Socialist and was thus a forerunner of the many which – with one exception – year after year up to 1938 were to be staged at Nuremberg. On 3 and 4 July 1926 the party formations met, and Hitler in his main speech particularly emphasized the importance of the task of winning over the German youth to the National Socialist cause.[42] Towards the end of the month Hitler mentioned his intention of appointing a new SA leader to succeed Röhm and also that the youth organization would be subordinated to the SA.[43]

Actually Hitler's intention coincided with the pressure exercised during 1925 and the early months of 1926 by small but nevertheless growing National Socialist groups in northern and north-western Germany who wanted their man represented at the party's headquarters in Munich.[44] Their choice fell upon Captain Franz Felix Pfeffer von Salomon, a renowned former *Freikorps* leader from Westphalia of Huguenot descent and the first *Gauleiter* of the Ruhr.[45] With his military background Pfeffer seemed to Hitler to be the man most suited to carry out the reorganization of the SA while at the same time meeting the demand of the north to be adequately represented in Munich.[46] Pfeffer assumed his office on 1 November 1926. In the guidelines issued by Hitler to Pfeffer it was explicitly stated that the organization of the SA should not be modelled on the old army.[47] Instead it should be a party formation, an instrument for party political use, whose immediate task must be to turn the NSDAP into a mass movement.[48] This instruction also determined the pattern of the development of the Hitler Youth for the next six years.[49] Already at the party rally at Weimar on Sunday 4 July 1926, at the suggestion of the notorious Jew-baiter Julius Streicher, *Gauleiter* of Franconia, Gruber's Greater German Youth Association was renamed *Hitler-Jugend, Bund der deutschen Arbeiterjugend.*[50] The Hitler Youth was born, and Gruber, from regional head of the youth movement of the NSDAP, was promoted to the position of first *Reichsführer* of the Hitler Youth, as well as adviser for youth questions in the party headquarters in Munich.[51] It speaks much for Gruber's political sense that having achieved his ambition of seeing his youth organization established as the Hitler Youth, with himself as its leader, he refused to take the bait and establish himself at the office awaiting him in Munich. Instead he maintained the Hitler Youth headquarters in Plauen and thus, as much as possible, his distance from the centralizing tendencies at work in the Bavarian capital.

Over the long term, however, these tendencies were inescapable, because the Hitler Youth was now *de jure* integrated into the party apparatus and Gruber's own position that of a party official. It was certainly no longer that of an independent youth leader who could take such initiatives as he desired. For the immediate future, nevertheless, the advantages outweighed the disadvantages for Gruber. There had been various groupings – mainly of a minor character – of National Socialist youth associations which had previously declined to join Gruber. The most important as well as the most populous was the National Socialist Workers Youth of Austria which had existed since 1923.[52] As a result of Hitler's decision they now accepted full integration into the Hitler Youth and consequently Gruber's field of activity was no longer restricted to Saxony but included the whole of Germany and Austria. Never a man given to forceful demonstrations of his own power, but rather relying on his ability to persuade on a man-to-man basis, he was highly successful in accomplishing his immediate task of integrating new organizations into the Hitler Youth as smoothly as possible.

In Plauen he established the HJ *Reichsführung*, divided into some fourteen separate departments including one each for education, welfare, military sport, propaganda, and film.[53] The latter made no films – this was something which on any significant scale did not begin before 1933 – but acted as a distribution service of 'approved films' for local Hitler Youth units. A distinct novelty were two departments, one dealing with Hitler Youth groups for those under fourteen years of age, and the other run by two girls for female members.[54] Furthermore, the Hitler Youth now began to adopt organizational divisions identical to those of the NSDAP, into *Gaue, Kreise,* and *Ortsgruppen,*[55] a process which was not completed until the early years of the Second World War when a *Gebiet* coincided with an NSDAP *Gau.* Out of isolated units scattered across the whole of Germany there now emerged one youth organization. More difficult, as the following years were to show, was the complete integration of the Hitler Youth into the party apparatus of the NSDAP. Upon his appointment, Pfeffer von Salomon immediately set about implementing Hitler's demand to subordinate the Hitler Youth to the SA.[56] This caused Gruber to become suspicious. He called the first meeting of the leaders of the Hitler Youth at Weimar for December 1926 and an invitation was – somewhat reluctantly – extended to Pfeffer von Salomon.[57] Pfeffer accepted. Exercising considerable tact and an approach which radiated paternal friendship Pfeffer quickly managed to calm all Gruber's suspicions and turn him into a ready collaborator. The practical result was that Gruber now publicly acknowledged the decree of the party headquarters in which Gruber as *Reichsführer* was made personally answerable to the SA Supreme Commander.[58]

Also at the meeting guidelines were drawn up concerning the relationship between the NSDAP and the Hitler Youth. In essence these reaffirmed the main provisions of the statutes of 1922, which of course had lapsed in the meantime.[59] There were also important additions such as, for instance, that any Hitler Youth member above the age of eighteen had to be a party member, and that the loss of party membership automatically included the loss of Hitler Youth membership as well.[60] This meant that higher functionaries of the Hitler Youth had to be party members, certainly a measure which would allow the party to control the composition of the upper echelons of the Hitler Youth leaders. The organizational framework of the Hitler Youth was fitted into the structure of that already existing for the NSDAP, a step which Gruber with his own measures in this area had already anticipated. All appointments to the higher ranks of the Hitler Youth required the agreement of the NSDAP as did any one of the Hitler Youth public appearances.[61] The Hitler Youth was to obey any command issued by a party leader, and quarterly meetings of its leadership were to be held under NSDAP guidance. For the first time a membership fee of four *Pfennigs* per month was to be levied.[62] Uniforms were to be standardized, with special emphasis on the avoidance of any confusion with the uniform of the storm troopers. This confusion had been a source of annoyance to both sides for some time. The early similarity of some NSDAP youth formations with the SA had caused them to be described as *Jung-SA*, and Pfeffer von Salomon as well as Gruber was determined to introduce a greater degree of differentiation.

The co-operation between Pfeffer von Salomon and Gruber was always good and relations between them very cordial; at a lower level, however, attempts by the NSDAP to encroach upon the Hitler Youth were frequent.[63] Between 1926 and 1933 the major preoccupation of the Hitler Youth appears to have been to assert its own position within the NSDAP where some members tended to consider the youth organization as no more than an appendix of the SA and others as Boy Scouts of a National Socialist vintage. Within the Hitler Youth the threat of a tendency towards being commanded by members of an older generation gave cause for anxiety, since it offended the fundamental maxim of the time – that youth must be led by youth. It also made the Hitler Youth vulnerable to the criticism of other youth movements, as well as to the charge that as far as subordination to the party was concerned there was little to choose between the youth organization of the Communist Party and that of the National Socialists – a charge which seemed to receive further substantiation when towards the end of 1927 an NSDAP order decreed that all members of the Hitler Youth upon attaining the age of eighteen had to transfer to the storm troopers.[64]

This development, or rather the fears regarding the course which this development of the Hitler Youth was likely to follow, was the reason for the first major crisis which Gruber had to face early in 1927. The Hitler Youth of the *Gau* Berlin-Brandenburg, Hamburg, Hannover-Braunschweig, Anhalt-Sachsen, Nord and Ruhr – the very areas from which Hitler the year before had met major opposition, led by Otto Strasser, who claimed sole leadership of the NSDAP – dropped its name and adopted a new one, *Bund Deutscher Arbeiterjugend* (BDAJ).[65] In the local NSDAP press which appears to have condoned the action, a BDAJ appeal was published informing the public of the change of name, without, however, giving any reasons, but asking the organizations of the NSDAP to support the BDAJ: 'We appeal to all activist revolutionary elements of the German youth to liberate themselves at long last from tutelage by reactionary and Marxist organizations. Your place is in the ranks of those who are engaged in a passionate struggle for the reformation of the German people and state in a national and socialist spirit. Break the chains of bourgeois cowardice and Marxist lies! Join the ranks of the BDAJ.'[66]

Gruber, who by the end of 1926 had just established nine further branches of the Hitler Youth, eight of them in northern and north-western Germany, with an estimated total membership of between 700 and 1000 boys,[67] at first regarded this secession as a major set-back. A few months later, though, it became evident that if Gruber's relatively well-organized Hitler Youth had initial difficulties in attracting a mass membership, these difficulties were even greater for the BDAJ, which soon ceased to exercise any attraction at all. Its last leader, Günther Orsoleck, finally joined the Social Democrats in 1930.[68] The loss sustained by the secession was also made good by the addition of a new group of members, this time from the conservative nationalist camp. The *Deutsche Jugend*, led by Herman Lauterbacher, later to be one of Baldur von Schirach's closest associates as well as his deputy, joined the Hitler youth as a body.[69]

A problem which seriously affected the growth of the Hitler Youth was its lack of trained leaders, because as soon as they emerged they were old enough to be taken over by the SA immediately.[70] To introduce greater co-ordination of Hitler Youth affairs with those of the NSDAP, a Youth Committee of the NSDAP was founded on 27 October 1927 which was chaired by Pfeffer von Salomon.[71] The lack of trained leadership of the Hitler Youth was one of the problems discussed at its first meeting, and Pfeffer von Salomon sympathized with Gruber's complaints and accepted their validity. As a result, an informal arrangement was agreed upon according to which the Hitler Youth could retain those members in its ranks who, although having reached the age of eighteen, would be further required for Hitler Youth service.[72] A little more than a year later the Youth Committee was expanded into a full Youth Office within the NSDAP headquarters. It was to co-ordinate all youth activities of the NSDAP including student affairs and to ensure that party orders were obeyed. But in place of bringing about greater co-ordination the Youth Office served as a stage on which the various conflicts between Hitler Youth and SA leadership, petty as well as substantial, were carried out. Whether this was one example of Hitler's policy of 'divide and rule' by keeping respective competencies ill-defined is doubtful because such an assumption would be based on an overestimation of the importance of the Hitler Youth within the NSDAP at the time. Moreover, on the whole, conflicts usually ended in favour of the Youth Office and Hitler Youth. In this Gruber was greatly assisted by the head of the Youth Office, Walter Buch, a former Major and *Freikorps* member who had joined the SA and become the chairman of the party investigation and arbitration committee. Once himself a member of the German pre-war youth movement he had a ready ear for complaints concerning unwarranted party interference into youth affairs.[73]

If trained leadership for the upper echelons of the Hitler Youth was one problem Gruber had to overcome, the problem of finance was another.[74] The resources of a private individual helped the expansion of the Hitler Youth in Saxony; however they were insufficient for expansion on a national basis and incapable of sustaining the Hitler Youth branches established by the end of 1927 in twenty *Gaue*. The newly introduced membership fee at the best of times could only be a partial answer.[75] The supply from party funds was limited, financial resources in 1927 being considerably scarcer than three or, for that matter, six years later.[76] One way of raising money, though of doubtful legality, was by direct public collection in the wake of propaganda marches. Public marches were cheap to organize and achieved maximum effect,[77] but with the growing militant opposition from that other party which laid claim 'to rule the street', the Communists, they became increasingly dangerous.

The first such major public demonstration was made on Labour Day, 1 May 1927, when Gruber, together with the SA and SS, staged a major rally with his Hitler Youth at Plauen, which, as some observers noted, differed markedly in matters of discipline from the traditional and Socialist processions.[78] But the crowning point of Gruber's endeavours for 1927 was represented by the participation of the Hitler Youth in the party rally at Nuremberg between 19 and 21 August 1927.[79] For the first time 300 Hitler Youth participated. Hitler, who since May 1927 had again been allowed to speak in public in Bavaria, paid tribute to the patriotism and unselfishness of his young followers, many of whom had had to make the journey on foot, while the other party formations had arrived in forty-seven special trains laid on for the event.[80] The Hitler Youths represented only one per cent of the 30,000 storm troopers who attended, but Gruber felt that a beginning had been made and that his labours were showing results.

Also assured now of his own leadership corps he believed that the way was clear, that the state of dependancy on the SA had been eliminated, allowing the Hitler Youth to develop its own character and traditions, or, as he himself later wrote about this period, 'At this time organization as an end in itself ceased. The idea began to be effective. Young men worked and managed to give the Hitler Youth a face of its own. Soon one could see the results and successes of this untiring tough work; signs of its own life became evident in the Hitler Youth. The continuous participation with the SA and the party ceased. The boys started "to go on their own hikes", to hold their own meetings and gatherings – in their own fashion.'[81]

Of course, the absence of traditions of its own was often felt among the rank and file who did not even have their own youth movement songs and therefore had to sing those of its 'bourgeois-nationalist' rivals or not sing at all.[82] The alternative was simply to put new words to old songs and here the NSDAP and the Hitler Youth were not over-scrupulous as to where their tunes came from; even Communist ones were 'borrowed' as long as they were rousing enough, especially for public demonstrations.[83]

During 1928 the major portion of Gruber's financial support still came from private sources as well as from members rather than from the party itself. This enabled him to move into larger premises in Plauen, the 'Reichs Administrative Office of the Hitler Youth'.[84] All the staff there worked on a voluntary unpaid basis. Gruber could even extend the activities of his office by establishing a separate department for the 'frontier regions'.[85] This department resumed the old contacts and tied anew the connections first established by Lenk with the Sudeten German groups in Czechoslovakia and also some of the German minority groups in Poland.[86] To help to increase an awareness of 'inner solidarity', a sense of belonging to a truly nation-

Gustav Adolf Lenk leads former members of the original *Jungsturm Adolf Hitler* in the march
commemorating the tenth anniversary of Hitler's *putsch* in 1923. This photograph was taken at the
spot in Munich's Residenzstrasse where Hitler's formation was fired on and stopped

Above One of the rare surviving
pictures of Kurt Gruber, first
Reichsführer of the Hitler Youth

Below Members of the *Jungsturm
Adolf Hitler* during an outing near
Munich in the autumn of 1922

Above Rudolf Schroeder, a Hitler
Youth member killed by political
opponents in Leipzig in 1931

Right Baldur von Schirach, *Reichsjugendführer*,
photographed in 1938

Left The Pied Piper and the trumpeter at a Hitler Youth rally in Nuremberg in 1933

Below Arthur Axmann, who succeeded Schirach as *Reichsjugendführer* in 1940, seen with Hitler Youth members specially decorated for valour in the face of Allied air attacks, 1943

wide youth community, and as such to the German national community, Gruber on 18 November 1928 introduced the *Reichsappell*, which meant that special days of the year were allocated on which at the same time throughout Germany all Hitler Youth units were to rally publicly to listen to a special order of the day or a policy declaration.[87] Hitler Youth mass-demonstration marches were continued on an increasingly wider scale, though the financial returns at least seemed somewhat meagre. But this did not apply only to the Hitler Youth, it reflected the general development of the National Socialist movement at the time. The May elections of 1928 had brought the NSDAP only twelve seats in the *Reichstag*. The extremes of both ends of the political spectrum of the Weimar Republic were suffering. It looked as though the German electorate was rallying behind a Republic which, though not loved, appeared to be consolidating its position at home and abroad. The chaos of the first four years of its existence seemed to have been overcome. This picture was deceptive; the combined anti-republican vote, that is to say the extreme Right and Left, still amounted to 27%.[88] The NSDAP, although it did not grow in leaps and bounds, nevertheless grew steadily, as did its youth organization. At the end of 1928 Hitler had behind him a movement which in the past four years had grown from 27,000 to 108,000 members, and membership was now no longer restricted to Bavaria but reached out into all parts of Germany.[89]

For the end of the year 1928 Gruber convened a meeting of the entire Hitler Youth leadership at Plauen.[90] Leaders of almost all the NSDAP *Gaue* attended.[91] The exceptions were the Rhineland, where Gruber had yet to assert his position over the BDAJ, and East Prussia, where both financial as well as organizational problems appear to have been responsible for the absence. After Gruber had received a vote of confidence and been confirmed as *Reichsführer*, three major problems were discussed at the meeting. First came the setting up of *Jungmannschaften*, junior groups for the ages ten to fourteen, which were later to become the *Jungvolk*.[92] Secondly, while a separate department for girls had been established in the *Reichsleitung*, no specific organization for girls within the Hitler Youth had been established. This was to be remedied by setting up *Schwesternschaften*, which later were to become the *Bund Deutscher Mädel* (BDM – the League of German Girls).[93] Thirdly, Gruber thought it necessary to establish once again the principles which clearly defined the separateness of the Hitler Youth from other nationalist groups.[94] He insisted that the Hitler Youth should be compared as little with any other existing youth groups as the NSDAP with any other party. It was, so he argued, neither a political para-military association, nor an association of 'anti-semitic Boy Scouts', nor for that matter part of any of the bodies of the existing fossilized youth movement. It was a 'new youth movement of young social-revolutionary-minded Germans'[95] who felt themselves deeply involved with the fate of their nation.

Its major aim was to train the individual personality to face and master existing circumstances. This did not simply mean to find out about and experience one's country, but to fight for it, putting at stake one's own life to liberate it from 'the shackles of capitalists and the enemies of the German race'. It therefore followed that the new socialist national community of Hitler's conception could be created only over the dead bodies of capitalism and Marxism. Gruber vigorously denounced the sectarianism of other youth movements and prophesied that they would be superseded by an all-embracing Hitler Youth.[96]

Finally the creation of new departments within the *Reichsführung* was discussed and announced. A Hitler Youth news service was set up to aid the National Socialist endeavour of breaking 'the Jewish monopoly of news',[97] a special department, the *Landjugendamt*, was to concern itself with the youth from agricultural regions, and another, the *Grenzlandamt*, was to co-ordinate Hitler Youth activities in the border regions as well as supervise the Hitler Youth groups among those of the German race who lived outside Germany, especially in Czechoslovakia and Poland.[98]

Gruber's renewed emphasis on the separateness of the Hitler Youth from other nationalist youth groups was not merely based on what he considered should be general policy, but stemmed also from his personal fears regarding a certain potentially dangerous development. Apart from the Hitler Youth, the National Socialist Student Movement had been founded, which by late 1928 was led by Baldur von Schirach who used this student organization as the lever of power with which he hoped to bring about the fusion, under his own leadership, of al! nationalist youth groups.[99] Naturally enough Gruber considered this not only a challenge to his own personal position but also to his own conception of the Hitler Youth.

Schirach, born in 1907, was the son of a former captain of the Prussian army who after retirement became administrator of the Court Theatre at Weimar. Schirach's mother was American, as was his paternal grandmother. All the children of the Schirach family were sent to highly exclusive schools – an education which was interrupted by Germany's defeat in 1918. Baldur von Schirach's older brother committed suicide because he did not wish to survive Germany's humiliation. The other children had to transfer to local grammar schools. In 1925, while still a grammar-school pupil, he heard Hitler speak for the first time and as a result at barely eighteen years of age he became a member of the NSDAP. Prompted by Hitler personally he entered the university in Munich to read German and the History of Art. Hitler himself, always flattered whenever members of what he took to be the upper levels of German society paid their respects to him, welcomed

Schirach with open arms. By 1925 he had already paid his first social call on the family, and the father soon followed the son's example and joined the party.[100]

In Munich young Schirach became a storm trooper, though he experienced frequent ridicule because of his schoolboy image, one that he was to retain until the last days of the Third *Reich*. He also joined the National Socialist Student Association, then led by a sincere national socialist revolutionary, Wilhelm Tempel. Schirach, who had never had to earn his own living, was totally out of touch with the working classes and hence became increasingly recognized as the spokesman of the upper-middle-class element within the Student Association. Thanks to Hitler's direct support, he became the leader of the NS Student Association on 20 July 1928 when he replaced Wilhelm Tempel as *Reichsführer* and adviser for student affairs in the party headquarters. He was now intent upon obtaining the leadership of the entire Hitler Youth.[101]

Schirach provides another example of the almost total colourlessness which is so typical of most of the leadership of the NSDAP. One is reminded of Hannah Ahrendt's brilliant phrase, the 'banality of evil', except that Schirach was not really evil so much as stupid, and, given the coincidence of time and circumstance, a stupid man can be as dangerous as an evil one. He was not only stupid but also ambitious, ambitions over which he draped the cloak of nationalistic pathos, which he chose to call youthful idealism. It may be true that we have the leaders we deserve but the Hitler Youth is then an exception, for in spite of all reservations it did deserve better.

Without the knowledge of either Hitler or Gruber, Schirach sent out circular letters to other nationalist youth groups.[102] Although meant to be confidential, news of Schirach's endeavours soon became public, much to the relish of other nationalist youth groups who believed that this was the first sign of a serious split in the Hitler Youth. Gruber did his utmost to prevent this development spreading, and personally visiting every leading Hitler Youth subordinate he used all the powers of persuasion he could command to convince them of his own point of view.[103] He correctly suggested that the danger inherent in Schirach's ideas was that the social revolutionary content of the Hitler Youth would be diluted into insignificance.[104]

In order to create a favourable impression on Hitler Gruber rapidly expanded the press activity of the Hitler Youth which by the spring of 1929 could boast two monthlies – *Die Junge Front*, intended for the Hitler Youth leadership, and the *Hitler-Jugend-Zeitung* for the rank and file.[105] Furthermore there was a bi-weekly, the *Deutsche Jugendnachrichten*. Reliable circulation figures cannot be obtained, and claims such as 15,000 for *Hitler-Jugend-Zeitung* for example are exaggerated because they refer to the number of issues printed only.[106] Since by far the largest part of the printed propaganda output of the NSDAP was distributed free there is no reason to assume that matters were radically different in the Hitler Youth. Apart from his personal visits to other Hitler Youth leaders Gruber organized a speaking tour in which during March and April 1929 he addressed thirty-two Hitler Youth rallies throughout Germany.[107]

These efforts seemed not merely to secure Gruber's own position *vis à vis* Schirach but also infused further self-confidence into the rank and file of the Hitler Youth, 2,000 of whom, to enthusiastic applause, marched past Hitler at the 1929 Party Rally at Nuremberg, the 'Party Day of Composure'.[108] Almost half of them are said to have come from Austria, the strongest delegations from within Germany coming from Saxony and Berlin Brandenburg.[109] The Berlin contingent created a precedent: it had marched by foot the entire distance from Berlin to Nuremberg – some 400 miles. The march was to be repeated every year as the *Adolf-Hitler-Marsch*.[110] Events at the rally tended further to consolidate the sense of identity of the youths – not so much the handing over of new Hitler Youth banners (depicting an eagle holding a black crossed hammer and sword on a red background), but rather the attending threats and violence. One storm trooper was killed by a sniper, another knifed to death.[111]

Schirach in spite of his previous setback remained active at the rally. Supported by Alfred Rosenberg, the party ideologue, he invited leaders of other German youth leagues to a meeting at Nuremberg on 3 August.[112] Gruber was not prepared to attend personally; instead he sent one of his subordinates, Robert Gadewoltz, the *Gauführer* of Berlin.[113] Gadewoltz represented Gruber's attitude clearly and rejected any fusion with youth movements organized along élitist principles.[114] Instead the basis of any fusion would have to be the acceptance of the fact that fusion would mean submergence into the Hitler Youth, something which of course the other youth leaders rejected outright.[115] Gruber also obtained the support of Pfeffer von Salomon who issued a directive to both Schirach and Rosenberg stating that now and in future the only National Socialist Youth movement could and would be the Hitler Youth.[116] When Hitler personally visited the tents of the Hitler Youth camp shortly before the end of the party rally, Gruber believed himself to have won in the struggle against Schirach.[117] His achievement was, in fact, formidable. From 80 branches in 1926 he had expanded the Hitler Youth by 1929 to approximately 450 branches and membership had risen from 700 in 1926 to 13,000 in 1929.[118] Certainly this growth of the Hitler Youth was unspectacular when one bears in mind that the youth movements represented in the Reichs Committee of German Youth Associations totalled a membership of 4,338,850 boys and girls.[119] Nevertheless, against the background of the Depression whose first effects were to reach Germany during late 1929 and which was to radicalize the political atmosphere of the Weimar Republic almost as thoroughly as had been the case between 1918 and 1924, the existence of a tightly knit cadre both at party and Hitler Youth level was to prove invaluable to Hitler.

In the autumn of 1929, after several vain attempts, Gruber again applied for membership of the Reichs Committee of German Youth Associations.[120] This application, as previously, was rejected mainly on the grounds that on the basis of its statutes the Hitler Youth had refused to co-operate with other youth associations and also was politically opposed to the existing state.[121] Membership and rejection mattered to Gruber and to some of his members who were associated with the Hitler Youth for prestige as well as practical reasons, which included privileges such as reduced railway fares and youth hostel facilities. To the rest of the NSDAP leadership it did not matter at all. Although since 1926 the NSDAP had been able to exercise tight control over all its organizations, this was rarely put into practise. Gruber hardly minded because the exercise of practical independence was to him of greater concern than the letter of the statutes. His and the *Reichsleitung*'s geographic location at Plauen was still remote from Munich, and Munich at least up to 1931 had never responded to any of Gruber's requests for financial aid.[122] This failure of party headquarters left Gruber to his own devices and Munich was not anxious to change the position since it would inevitably affect the party treasury adversely. For this very reason several NSDAP branches had refused to establish Hitler Youth branches on their own initiative.[123] The rank and file of the party members saw in the Hitler Youth little more than a club for adolescents. As one Bavarian police report put it in 1927, 'In so far as can be observed, there is so far no particular enthusiasm in National Socialist circles for the youth organization.'[124] Pfeffer's concession of late 1927 which made it no longer obligatory for 18-year-old Hitler Youths to transfer to the SA began to have its effects, making for greater independence. All the same, the basic role of the Hitler Youth within the NSDAP remained what it had been, that of a propaganda unit.

As such, in November 1929 the first great Hitler Youth exhibition was launched in Munich, under the auspices also of the SA.[125] Although there existed no formal obligation on the part of Hitler Youths or their leaders to attend SA rallies, upon request Hitler Youth units had to participate in SA propaganda marches, and high-ranking SA leaders had the right to supervise all public appearances of the Hitler Youth. The precise relationships between Hitler Youth and NSDAP and Hitler Youth and SA were defined anew in the directive of 23 April 1929 though nothing in the directive was fundamentally new.[126] It was in the main a reaffirmation of the existing relationships. The fact that the Hitler Youth became its own independent registered association before the law did not change its position within the structure of the NSDAP. But the *practical* independence of the Hitler Youth was as much due to the personal friendship between Gruber and Pfeffer von Salomon as to Pfeffer's own preoccupation with the organization of the SA which allowed him little time to exercise his supervisory function over Gruber's organization.[127] In addition, a few months prior to the *Reichstag* elections of 1930 discontent began to show itself in the party and the SA. Many members had failed to discern the significance of the slow but steady growth of the NSDAP over the past few years.[128] Instead they pointed to what at the time was undoubtedly a fact, namely that in terms of effective political importance the NSDAP was still in its infancy. Of course, widespread unemployment frayed the tempers of the rank and file even more, and discontent simmered. It culminated in Otto Strasser's departure from the party and finally in March 1931 in the Stennes revolt against Hitler's leadership in Berlin.[129] As so often before, Hitler managed to overcome the crisis by the sheer force of his own personality. However, Pfeffer von Salomon too in the light of the events felt that he ought to offer his resignation, which Hitler accepted.[130] The Führer himself assumed supreme command of the SA until he had persuaded Röhm, who at the time was acting as an instructor to the Bolivian army, to return and take over from him as SA Chief of Staff – though no longer as Supreme Commander.[131] Under Röhm, who had not changed his ideas about the nature and the character of the SA, the storm troopers reverted to their para-military role which appears to have been attractive enough for many Hitler Youths to join them even before their eighteenth birthday.[132] It was now Gruber's turn to emphasize the Hitler Youth's scrupulous adherence to the regulations governing Hitler Youth and SA relations. At one stage even the SA Supreme Command had to intervene to stop the acceptance of SA recruits who were only sixteen and seventeen years old.[133]

In the meantime Gruber continued his public activities. On 20 March 1930 the Hitler Youth was called to Berlin to its first major mass rally to be conducted under the motto 'From Resistance to Attack'. Main speakers were the *Gauleiter* of Berlin Dr Joseph Goebbels, Dr Adrian von Renteln, a Baltic German who had organized the National Socialist Pupils Association, the NSS, and Kurt Gruber himself.[134]

Organizationally, the Hitler Youth now practically implemented what had been in the directives since 1926 by dividing its movement into thirty-five *Gaue* comprising nearly 18,000 German youths and nearly 3,000 Austrians. The latter were organized in six separate *Gaue*.[135] This division corresponded largely with the needs of the NSDAP's electoral campaigning and was therefore not always of direct relevance to the needs of the Hitler Youth.[136] In order to secure the more rapid growth of the Hitler Youth press, Gruber founded his own publishing house in Plauen, the *Jungfront-Verlag*.[137] However, it was a general characteristic of the Hitler Youth throughout its history that with very few exceptions its publications failed to elicit a wide response and Gruber's own publishing venture did little to change this. Gruber even made HJ-leadership appointments conditional on the ability of the appointee to sell a fixed number of Hitler Youth publications per month. It was of no avail; the Hitler Youth leadership had occasion time and again to observe that not enough HJ publications were read by members and that this state of affairs was now catastrophic.[138]

The increased public party political activity of the Hitler Youth soon provoked reactions from the public authorities, who banned marches and prohibited schoolboys from being members.[139] Years later Schirach supplied a vivid picture of the persecution of these days which in many respects was highly exaggerated.[140] However, it is of little importance how we view conditions in retrospect; what is more significant is the degree to which Hitler Youths felt themselves to be endangered by their opponents in the street or by the official bureaucracy. The growing radicalization of the politics of the Weimar Republic was of course most blatant at the extremes of the political spectrum. Within less than twelve months from the onset of the Depression the atmosphere of latent and open civil war of the early days of the Republic had returned. At first the government did its best to curb the growing extremism. The first anti-NS youth reaction came on 16 January 1930 from the *Oberpräsident* of Hanover, Gustav Noske, the former *Reichswehr* Minister of the Weimar Republic, who prohibited all pupils of secondary schools as well as those of trades schools from joining the Hitler Youth.[141] Prussia followed suit on 22 May 1930 by issuing a circular which announced that all National Socialist and Communist youth organizations were excluded from state-supported youth welfare.[142] Since neither Hitler Youth nor the Communists had gained anything from the authorities before, this exclusion meant very little to them in practical terms. The Prussian government believed rightly that it was acting on established precedent; Bavaria had acted in this way in 1924, and the Württemberg government in 1921.[143] Although in Bavaria the laws affecting the National Socialists had been generally relaxed since late 1925, the ban on political activity by schoolboys had continued.[144] Indeed in 1930 the Bavarian police informed the Hitler Youth in Munich of the existence of this ban, in the light of the impending *Reichstag* elections.[145] Other regional governments in Germany followed the example of Prussia and that given by Noske. But proscription could not stamp out the Hitler Youth. On the contrary the Hitler Youth turned government proscription into a propaganda asset in its recruiting campaigns, and the pupils expelled and fined for membership naturally felt they had been persecuted for what in their view were not simply party-political reasons but because of their patriotism. When a Hitler Youth group had been banned it emerged the next day under an innocuous-sounding name; and there was an infinite range of names to choose from, such as the 'Friends of Nature' or 'Young Folk Philatelists'.[146] Those who went to prison or were heavily fined returned as martyrs to the cause.

In spite of these hindrances, the public activity of the Hitler Youth continued. In 1930 the two most important occasions were the anti-Young Plan demonstrations and the *Reichstag* elections. The Young Plan, which was to revise German reparation payments, caused violent opposition from the Right, which pointed out that the Plan meant the continuation of reparation payments until well into the 1980s, thus 'enslaving generations as yet unborn'.[147] This brought about a temporary alliance between National Socialists and Nationalists and therefore between Hitler Youth and other nationalist youth groups.[148] The anti-Young Plan campaign failed in its objective of obtaining a majority in the national referendum on the issue. However, protests continued. Other issues too caused militant protests. In Berlin as well as in Vienna the Hitler Youth disturbed the first performance of the film *All Quiet on the Western Front* so methodically and thoroughly that the government was compelled to have the film withdrawn from general circulation in Germany.[149]

However the most important event of the year was, of course, the election. The NSDAP campaigned on the issue of 'National Socialism' and in its electoral propaganda separated the two terms, defining Nationalism as liberation from the shackles of Versailles and Socialism as the right to employment for every German. The elections had been precipitated by the Social Democrats who misread the result of the Young Plan plebiscite, thinking that elections held now might produce a Social-Democrat-dominated 'small' coalition, instead of the intractable great coalition in which the Social Democrats provided the chancellor. Under the pretext of differences over the method of financing unemployment insurance the Social Democrats left the government benches and voted against the government they headed. Thus on 27 March 1930 the last representative democratic government of the Weimar Republic resigned.[150] The elections resulted in an unpleasant shock. Though the SPD still remained the largest party, the NSDAP took second place with 107 seats in the *Reichstag*, compared with the twelve obtained in the elections of 1928. Its share of the poll had increased from 2.6% in 1928 to 18.3% in 1932.[151]

Proscription or no proscription, within its inherent limitations the Hitler Youth contributed as much as any other party formation. By organizing Hitler Youth rallies, publicity meetings, propaganda marches, and parents' evenings they helped to keep up the dynamics of electioneering. Like the storm troopers, in rural regions they motored through the countryside in hired lorries crammed with youngsters with banners flying, chanting their battle songs or election slogans.[152] The level of activity was so intense that irrespective of the result everyone who participated could come away with the feeling that his own and his group's participation mattered, and the election result was as much a boost to the morale of the Hitler Youth as it was to the NSDAP.[153]

However, Kurt Gruber failed to obtain his due reward for his organization's contribution in the election. This was, in the final analysis, due to Schirach's intrigues and the return of Ernst Röhm from Bolivia to lead the SA. Röhm had his own candidate for the leadership of the Hitler Youth, Joachim Haupt, whom initially also Hitler would have liked as a replacement for Gruber. Schirach did not cherish the prospect of a rival, especially since Haupt had crossed him before when he was the favourite candidate to head the NS students' league. Fortunately for Schirach Hitler backed him against the students' choice and Haupt also turned down twice in succession the offer to lead the Hitler Youth.[154]

More serious than actual proscriptions of the Hitler Youth was the banning of Hitler Youth publications, since these together with the proscription of NSDAP publications threatened an enforced idleness on the party-owned printing presses. Given the infancy of party as well as of Hitler Youth journals and newspapers, their frequent proscription by regional governments as well as by the Berlin government involved heavy financial losses. Schirach used these difficulties of the Hitler Youth press as illustrations of Gruber's shortcomings as *Reichsführer* Hitler Youth. He was, so ran Schirach's argument, suitable and effective only as long as the Hitler Youth operated within a strictly provincial framework. Now, on a national level, he was showing signs of lacking vision and organizing ability, and it was his stubbornness alone which prevented the closing of the ranks of all nationalist youth movements.[155] Pressures were also mounting in Munich to bring about a reorganization of the Hitler Youth. Röhm upon his return from Bolivia was not prepared to accept the semi-independence of the Hitler Youth, and immediately urged for a redefinition of the relationship between SA and Hitler Youth. On 27 April 1931 Hitler issued a directive which made Gruber directly subordinate to the Chief of Staff of the SA, that is to say to Röhm, who could also exercise direct command.[156] All Hitler Youth groups were made subordinate to their respective regional SA commanders but not to other SA branches of offices. However, the SA's guidance of the Hitler Youth was restricted to public marches or any other public demonstrations, supervision of its general outside appearance, and the right to oppose a Hitler Youth appointment at the upper levels. Each regional SA headquarters was to have its own Hitler Youth adviser, while the *Reichsführer* Hitler Youth was to act in this capacity in the central headquarters of the NSDAP and SA in Munich. This directive brought the Hitler Youth once again under direct SA control, especially of course its upper echelons which were integrated into the organizational structure of the SA.[157] The removal of the Hitler Youth headquarters from Plauen to Munich put an end to such independence as Gruber had so far managed to preserve for himself. He distinctly felt that his position was in jeopardy and that he was powerless against the apparent conspiracy of Schirach with Röhm. Never an easy-tempered man, he began to quarrel more frequently with his subordinates, many of whom were aware of the situation and began to change sides accordingly.[158] Röhm pointed to the slow growth of the Hitler Youth since the September elections of 1930, compared with the growth of the NSDAP. Gruber responded by a rash promise to double Hitler Youth membership to 50,000 by the end of 1931, a promise virtually impossible to keep.[159]

The second half of 1931 was one of feverish propaganda activity directed mainly against the youth organizations of the SPD and the KPD. While in a general sense augmenting and benefiting the NSDAP propaganda effort as a whole, for the Hitler Youth the campaign did not produce the new members promised.[160] Although the Hitler Youth strongly participated in one of the major rallies of the year held on the weekend of 17 and 18 October 1931 in Brunswick,[161] at which Röhm personally acknowledged and applauded the contribution of the Hitler Youth,[162] Gruber could no longer save his position. Less than a fortnight later the party headquarters in Munich announced that it had accepted Gruber's resignation – which he had never submitted. Reasons were never made public. Gruber himself seems to have learnt of his departure from the morning papers and even the German police expressed surprise since he had worked for the Hitler Youth so intensively.[163] No doubt Schirach's explanation that Gruber had worked himself to a standstill is true,[164] but this was not the real reason or the whole of it. Schirach's alliance with Röhm, which caused a fair amount of unsavoury and malicious gossip, had its reward. After three years Gruber had at long last been overthrown, and with his departure went the last *Reichsführer* Hitler Youth, a man who had sacrificed his entire personal life to what he considered to be the cause of his country. His successor was neither a social revolutionary nor a dynamic youth leader as he had been, but in the main a chair-born administrator who was soon corrupted by the perks of office holding.

Partly to obscure the sordid background of the affair Hitler on 30 October 1931 issued a new directive which ran as follows:

1. Within the framework of the Supreme SA Command a new office *Reichsjugendführer* has been created.

2. The *Reichsjugendführer* is directly responsible to the Chief of Staff (*of the SA*). To the post of *Reichsjugendführer* I appoint party member von Schirach.

3. The sphere of administration of the *Reichsjugendführer* comprises

    (a)   The National Socialist Student Association (*Reichsführer* von Schirach)

    (b)   The Hitler Youth (to the leadership of which party member von Renteln has been appointed).

    (c)   The National Socialist Pupils Association (*Reichsführer* von Renteln).

4. The *Reichsjugendführer* is adviser for all organizations listed under Point 3 and in the staff of the Supreme SA Command administers all youth affairs. He keeps the Chief of Staff informed about all organizational problems of the youth formations with special emphasis on those affairs which involve the SA. His rank is that of a *Gruppenführer*, his uniform has yet to be determined.[165]

In effect the Hitler Youth was now a unit of the SA under the direct control of Ernst Röhm. Since Schirach got on extremely well with him, the relationships between SA and Hitler Youth remained smooth, and as Schirach in his early phase proved also an able organizer as well as an efficient administrator he continued to enjoy Röhm's support. Within the Hitler Youth his standing was largely established by the party backing he enjoyed, not by his personal qualities as a youth leader; for his main problem among Hitler Youths was and remained throughout his career that of not being taken seriously. Gruber faded into obscurity, a minor post was found for him as an economic adviser, and some tribute – then, as well as later – was paid to his work.[166]

The Hitler Youth as an organization now acquired the National Socialist Pupils' League, which had been founded in Hamburg in 1929.[167] Essentially middle class, it comprised pupils of secondary schools, who with a considerable degree of snobbery looked down on their proletarian brethren from the Hitler Youth. Up to 1931 they had enjoyed greater political independence from the NSDAP than the Hitler Youth itself, and had acquired notoriety for their anti-semitism; Jewish teachers and heads of schools found them increasingly not merely a nuisance but a definite danger. Some of its members did not refrain from physically as well as verbally attacking teachers whose race or political convictions they disapproved of, thus supplying ample ammunition to those who proposed drastic steps against the menace of Hitler and his movement.[168] As it happened the 'drastic steps' were never taken; banning and proscription merely acted as pin-pricks which ultimately caused even greater and more violent reactions.

What is noticeable in Hitler's directive of 30 October is the complete absence of any reference to the girls' association of the Hitler Youth – the

BDM. Its precursor had been a girls' association in 1922–23 and the *Völkischer Mädchenbund* founded on 1 May 1925 by the former *Freikorps* leader Gerhard Rossbach in association with Lenk. A girls' section of the Hitler Youth was first created in 1927 in Plauen, but it vegetated in relative obscurity until July 1930 when it was formally named *Bund Deutscher Mädchen* (BDM), but it was to take another two years before directives were issued making it an integral part of the Hitler Youth and the sole girls' organization of the NSDAP. Apparently the Women's League of NSDAP, the *NS-Frauenschaft*, had been making a bid for control of the girls, and this precipitated the formal integration of the BDM into the Hitler Youth.[169]

The BDM was characterized by its remarkable growth. At the *Reichs* Youth Rally at Potsdam on 1–2 October 1932, of approximately 70,000 participants, 15,000 were girls.[170]

Another youth organization which had joined the Hitler Youth, the *Deutsches Jungvolk*,[171] was not founded in Germany at all but had its roots in German-Austria and the Sudetenland of Czechoslovakia. It still maintained many of the traditions of the pre-war German youth movement.[172] Its slogans contained much from which social revolutionary tendencies could be inferred. It was not affiliated to any political party but nevertheless exhibited a strong right-wing bias. In Vienna it became notorious for the part it played in the demonstrations against the film *All Quiet on the Western Front*. From 1930 onwards, the *Jungvolk* groups inside Germany began to join the Hitler Youth, not as an integral part but as a separate body within it.[173] The legacy of the painstaking work of both Lenk and Gruber was now paying dividends, though Schirach of course used it at first as a demonstration of his own ability that within the Hitler Youth the traditions of the German youth movement were maintained and further developed. In more practical terms he considered the *Jungvolk* as an ideal unit which could cater for the age group up to fourteen, and in which the romanticism of the camp fires and ballad singing would find good response. Out of the total number of youth organizations absorbed into the Hitler Youth, the *Jungvolk* was the only one which was allowed to retain its original colours: a black cloth centred by one victory rune. But as the flow of units of the *Jungvolk* continued to stream into the Hitler Youth, membership of the former was forbidden in many parts of Germany by provincial governments[174] until, between 13 April and 13 June 1932, together with all other uniformed branches of the NSDAP, it was completely banned by the Brüning government in order to counteract the increasing radicalization of the political scene.[175]

The direct subordination of the Hitler Youth to the SA again raised the problem of finance. During Gruber's leadership private sources had contributed the main part of the Hitler Youth's income.[176] Gruber's departure meant more than just the change of an individual; at the apex of the Hitler Youth it meant the end of unpaid voluntary work. All successors and office holders in the *Reichsjugendführung* now became full-time officials who had to be paid – at a time of rapidly-rising unemployment. Schirach had inherited a debt of approximately £100 at 1931 value.[177] During the early months the NSDAP paid a monthly subsidy of approximately £5 which covered the administrative expenses of the Hitler Youth leadership but not expenses incurred for propaganda activities.[178] Furthermore monthly allowances of approximately £1.50 per month were paid to leaders of the rank *Gruppenführer* and *Gauführer*.[179] Revenue was intended to be obtained from membership fees introduced at the end of 1926, but in view of the growing influx of youths who were unemployed or from families where the wage-earner was out of work, this was a rather uncertain source, and with two *Reichstag* elections and two Presidential elections in 1932 the NSDAP began to run into serious financial difficulties.[180] This inevitably affected the Hitler Youth and many regions had to find means of self-help such as lotteries.[181] The only ones who continued to receive their salaries were the staff of the *Reichsjugendführung*.[182] In addition to the economic state of the country, the government banning of the Hitler Youth seriously restricted personal initiatives for fund raising. Even Schirach felt he had to respond and at the Potsdam rally he mentioned that the Hitler Youth treasury was down to £10 and that the NSDAP was unable to lend any money.[183]

But increasingly active involvement in the bitter and violent party political struggle cost more than money. The price of the Hitler Youth's active political engagement, particularly in the years between 1931 and 1933, was the loss of twenty-three lives.[184]

> *Wir marschieren für Hitler*
> *Durch Nacht und durch Not*
> *Mit der Fahne für Freiheit und Brot*
> . . . .
> *Unsere Fahne ist mehr für uns als der Tod*
>
> We march for Hitler through night and suffering
> With the banner of freedom and bread
> . . . .
> Our banner means more to us than death

The words of the Hitler Youth anthem, the *Fahnenlied*, written by Schirach and set to a stirring tune, became reality for many as the political struggle moved away from an impotent *Reichstag* into the streets, where members of the Red Front and the storm troopers faced one another in bitter enmity. The sentiments of the civil war atmosphere of the early 1920s were quick to surface again. The brutality and ferocity of the struggle are features which cannot be attributed to one political party only. The Prussian Ministry of the Interior compiled statistics of political acts of terror in Prussia (but exclusive of Berlin) which occurred between 1 June and 20 July 1932. During this period 322 acts of terror were recorded causing 72 dead and 497 seriously injured. In 203 cases the attackers were identified as Communists, in 72 cases they were National Socialists, and in 21 cases members of the *Reichsbanner* Black, Red, and Gold, the para-military organization of the Social Democrats. In the remaining 26 cases the question of guilt could not be established.[185] The peak, for 1932 at least, was reached with the bloody Sunday of Hamburg-Altona on 17 July, when Communists opened fire from roofs and windows on an SA propaganda march.[186] The values, the vocabulary, and the attitudes of the world war had persisted, further radicalized by economic deprivation and political polarization. The lower-middle and the working classes, hardest hit by their economic and political environment, furnished the street fighters of Left and Right.

The most prominent Hitler Youth victim – prominent because of the propaganda Goebbels made of the incident and the film based on his life made after 1933 – was Herbert Norkus. The son of a Berlin taxi driver who, seriously affected by the Depression, had joined the SA himself, Herbert Norkus was twelve years old when as a Hitler Youth member he was sent out on the morning of Sunday 26 January 1932 to post bills advertising an NSDAP meeting. At this meeting, to be held four days later, prominent Hitler Youth leaders were to speak on such topics as 'Swastika or Soviet Star' and 'What we want'. Norkus lived in the district of Wedding in Berlin, 'Red Wedding' as it was generally known, and on that cold January morning at five o'clock he was with a troop of Hitler Youths bill-posting in the streets of his home district. A motor cyclist passed them, returned, passed again, and then disappeared into the dark. Then suddenly the bill-posters were confronted by a troop of Communists and the boys scattered in all directions. Norkus was caught and stabbed twice; he had enough strength to make another run for a house, but its owner shut the door in his face. He was stabbed again but tried to pull himself up, leaving a trail of bloody hand-prints as he groped for support along the wall of a house. His assassins dragged him along the corridor of Zwinglistrasse 4 and left him there to die. At Moabit hospital the autopsy revealed five stabs in the back, two in the chest; the face had been mutilated beyond recognition with the upper lip completely missing. Of all the Hitler Youths killed up to 1933 the oldest was eighteen, the youngest twelve years old.[187]

Such were the politics of the pluralist consensus during the last days of the Weimar Republic. In Berlin alone six Hitler Youths were killed, three of whom came from the 'Red Wedding' district.[188] No doubt the militant opponents of the National Socialists fared little better in those days, but in view of the sacrifices made by ideologically misguided but nevertheless idealistic young people, it does little justice to either party involved if one is described as containing Socialist heroes and the other as containing Fascist beasts. Equally tragic is the fact that examples like Herbert Norkus were further grist to Goebbels' propaganda mill, which directed the orientation and outlook of young Germans yet to be born.[189]

V Dominance

1932 brought considerable increases to the membership of the Hitler Youth and to the NSDAP generally. Whether the rise in Hitler Youth membership can be attributed solely to Schirach's activity appears doubtful. The successes at the polls in 1932 which made the NSDAP the largest single party in the *Reichstag*, the continued deterioration of the economic situation, the incapacity of the government to provide a solution (and which as long as Brüning, the Catholic Centre Party Chancellor, lasted attempted to cure deflation by further deflationary measures), and the seeming lack of an alternative other than one of the two extremes all contributed to the National Socialists' popularity. And the fact that their party won more votes than did the other end of the political spectrum showed that more Germans preferred the nationalist 'brown' evil to the international 'red' one. At the level of youth organizations this meant that while the Socialists and the Catholic Centre retained their numbers, the youth groups of the non-Nazi right-wing parties lost membership to the Hitler Youth.[1] However, to obtain correct figures for the strength of the Hitler Youth at any time before 1936, and especially for the years between 1930 and 1933, is still impossible, since, for example, few figures exist showing membership of youth organizations such as the *Jungvolk* which up to 1933 led an almost independent existence within the framework of the Hitler Youth.[2] To use membership fees, for instance, as an indicator of the size of the Hitler Youth would produce a completely false picture. The vast unemployment of the day heavily affected school-leavers (then in the age-groups between fourteen and eighteen) and Hitler Youths without employment paid no fees at all.[3] In 1931 there were an estimated 20,000 paid-up members out of an approximate total of 28,800. Berlin, for example, which on a numerical basis had one of the largest Hitler Youth groups, showed less than 1,000 fee-paying members,[4] and this was certainly not because of lack of organization. Under Joachim Walter, Elmar Warning, and Alfred Loose (the latter originating from the Berlin-Wedding district) the Hitler Youth there was

84

one of the best organized units in Germany[5]. More likely the reason for the low figure of fee-paying members was unemployment. By 1 January 1932 Hitler Youth reports claimed an increase to over 37,000,[6] but how reliable these reports are is anybody's guess especially in the light of the claim on 1 March 1932 to have increased to 72,821 members. The fact that they were mainly secret reports to the NSDAP headquarters would at first sight suggest that they would be accurate, but there are indications that point to inflated figures being used in order to pressure the NSDAP treasury into giving larger subsidies to the Hitler Youth.[7] Very often a youth who merely attended a local branch meeting out of curiosity was counted as a 'member' to increase the recruitment figures.[8] Nevertheless, whatever the exact figures may be, the general trend was in an upward direction with the majority of recruits coming from the leagues of the German youth movements, but also substantial numbers coming from the Communists.[9] The 'conversion' of Communists seems surprising, especially since the KPD represented the other extreme that was gaining at the polls during this time, though substantially less so than the NSDAP. However, this phenomenon existed, especially in large urban centres where it not only affected Hitler Youth recruitment but that of the SA as well. Not without reason were Berlin's storm troopers referred to as 'beefsteak Nazis': brown on the outside and red inside.[10] In the regional distribution of the Hitler Youth in 1932, the strongest areas were Northern Germany, Eastern Germany (comprising Silesia as well as East Prussia), and Central Germany, while areas such as Bavaria and Upper Palatinate, Swabia, and northern Franconia, the very areas from which Hitler's movement had originated, remained the weakest.[11] In these areas youth organizations were predominantly Roman Catholic and until 1936 the Roman Catholic Church could maintain its hold over the membership of its Youth groups.

Equally difficult to determine during that period are the social origins of Hitler Youth members. 1930 figures show the recruitment of 2,800 fee-paying members for the Hitler Youth which at that time, however, meant only the HJ and did not include the National Socialist Pupils' League, the *Jungvolk*, or the BDM.[12] Of these, approximately 1,000 are described as being of working-class origin, over 500 as pupils of various institutes of secondary education[13] – who because secondary education had to be paid for at the time are not likely to have included any significant number of working-class children and can therefore be taken as middle-class – 400 recruits from other youth movements (which allows of course no firm conclusion as to their social background) and 900 'others'. Another sample – *Gau* Munich-Upper Bavaria – puts forward these claims of the social composition: 71% manual workers, 11% professional and commercial, and 16% pupils.[14] For 1931–32 more detailed (but no more verifiable) figures are supplied – 69% workers, 10% engaged in trade and commerce (which in Germany at the time would indicate that they were apprentices), and 12% pupils.[15] The remainder has not been clearly determined, but it is obvious that many of them were unemployed.

The Depression which had helped to bring about a landslide vote for Hitler in 1932 also caused a renewed emphasis within the Hitler Youth upon the 'socialist' component and style of its agitation, particularly in urban working-class areas. Berlin-Wedding was one example; Kiel, the city and harbour from which the revolution of 1918 had spread through Germany, was another.[16] There the Hitler Youth was largely ignored by the local NSDAP branch and had to stand on its own feet, members organizing their own discussions and public speeches and protecting their own meetings. The local party organization thought of them only when it was in need of bill-stickers.[17] As in other German cities, so in Kiel, the Hitler Youth organized the systematic disruption of the film *All Quiet on the Western Front*.[18] Street battles with the organized Communist Youth Association, or for that matter with the Communist Party's own para-military formation *Rotfront*, were a regular occurrence. For both sides fists, sticks, and truncheons were no longer enough; the use of fire-arms increased, particularly during 1932.[19]

When in order to curb the growing radicalization of the public scene the NSDAP's para-military formations were forbidden on 13 April 1932, which in practice meant that they could not wear their uniforms, those Hitler Youth members in Kiel who were butcher's apprentices simply wore their working garb, a blood-stained white apron which gave them an even more ferocious appearance than did their uniform.[20] Even adult members of *Rotfront* were apparently reluctant to tangle with this particular Hitler Youth group. In Kiel, as elsewhere, the prime targets as well as the main antagonists of the Hitler Youth agitation were the Communists. In a leaflet from the summer of 1932 the Kiel HJ made the following appeal:

'Fellow youths. We shall overthrow the old system. We are not begging for your votes in the *Reichstag* election, what we want is you. The German revolution begins on the day of the National Socialist seizure of power. Then the young socialist forces from all camps must be united to face the forces of reaction. Our banners do not carry the slogans of 'Moscow' or 'Internationalism' or 'Pacifism'. The only name they carry is that of 'Germany' and nothing but 'Germany'.
With your banners flying, come to us, the German Workers' Youth, fight with us against the old system, against the old order, against the old generation. We are the last fighters for liberty, fight with us for Socialism, for freedom and for bread!
Join the German Workers' Youth, Kiel'.[21]

Propaganda marches were organized through the towns and villages of Schleswig-Holstein, a region which had already been radicalized as a result of widespread mortgage foreclosures and the forced auctions of farms and livestock of farmers no longer able to pay their taxes.[22] They had organized themselves into self-defence units which first prevented the bailiffs from driving away stock or taking possession of farms, and ultimately led to the blowing up of local inland revenue offices.[23] In Schleswig-Holstein the Kiel Hitler Youth can be said to have contributed more to turn votes into account for the NSDAP than the party's own local apparatus.[24] Yet, curiously enough, the complex situation there produced something of a paradox, a tacit alliance between the NSDAP and the Communists who also supported the farmers' actions.[25] But in the cities of Schleswig-Holstein the situation was different. There the degree of violence reached such proportions that at school or at his place of employment any member of the Hitler Youth became suspect. Parents naturally worried about the safety of their children and tried to discourage or even oppose their political activities, usually in vain. The local schools administration asked teachers to compile lists of 'Nazis' in their forms. However this was not by any means a novelty. For example, the Bavarian government had since 1919 endeavoured to enforce a decree which made it an offence for any school pupil to be a member of any political party or attend any political meeting. At least since 1928 the headmasters of all Bavarian schools were required to submit detailed reports on pupils who were suspected of being members of the Hitler Youth as well as of any other political organization.[26]

The examples of Kiel and Schleswig-Holstein have their analogies throughout Germany, the variables being in the main of an economic but also of a religious nature. Thus, as demonstrated in the regional distribution of the Hitler Youth, the attitude of the Roman Catholic Church could seriously affect the growth of, as well as the popular attitude to, the Hitler Youth. The Roman Catholic Church opposed Hitler Youth membership among the younger members of its congregation in pastoral letters and various other directives, as well as by the strict control of its own youth organizations.[27] The obscene racial anti-Semitism of a Julius Streicher and the muddled but clearly anti-Christian philosophy of Alfred Rosenberg, expounded in his book *Der Mythos des 20. Jahrhunderts*, provided vulnerable points at which the NSDAP and its affiliated organizations could be damagingly attacked.[28]

On the other hand, however, the nationalist component of Hitler's programme was impossible to condemn. In their desire to liberate themselves from 'the shackles of Versailles' and to create a new Germany, and in their recognition of the all-too obvious impotence of the Weimar Republic, denominational youth organizations and the Hitler Youth were at one. One of the principal aims was the creation of *Grossdeutschland*, a Germany which would include German-Austria. For many Catholics and Protestants alike the crisis of the democratic system of Weimar was reduced to the generalization that the Western form of democracy, the politics of a pluralist consensus, was unsuited and alien to the German political tradition.[29] Instead many favoured the establishment of some form of corporate state. It was by no means an accident that the most outstanding German theoreticians of the corporate state, such as Othmar Spann, were also devout Roman Catholics.[30]

In defence against the charges levied by the Church, the NSDAP and its youth movements pointed to the Italian example, where Mussolini had been able to obtain the support of the Vatican and thus establish a workable church-state relationship. They argued that all they desired was what church and state had managed to establish in Italy. No doubt many members of the NSDAP wanted no more than that. But this, as do many other factors, points to the heterogeneity of the forces contained within the NSDAP whose common denominator ultimately was not Germany, but one man – Adolf Hitler.[31] For many other National Socialists clearly had much more radical designs on the future of the Catholic Church in Germany.

Finally, the elements which the denominational youth organizations had in common with the Hitler Youth led to the former adapting Hitler Youth practices, in order to forestall defections. In many Catholic Youth groups para-military field exercises were introduced, as well as practice with ·22 rifles.[32] The Catholic hierarchy did issue circulars stating that the gospel and rifle practice were hardly compatible with one another, but did nothing to enforce its views on the matter.[33] One of the most widely sung and most notorious Hitler Youth songs was written and composed by a youth who at the time of its composition was still a member of the Catholic Youth Movement.[34] The song – *Es zittern die morschen Knochen* – ended with the well-known refrain usually quoted as '*denn heute gehört uns Deutschland und morgen die ganze Welt*' ('because today Germany belongs to us and tomorrow the whole world'). In fact, in youthful exuberance and aggressiveness the refrain was often sung as quoted, but its actual words were – '*denn heute da hört uns Deutschland und morgen die ganze Welt*' ('because today Germany listens to us [*our warning against the red menace*] and tomorrow the whole world').[35]

The Protestant youth movements were easier to infiltrate than were those of the Catholics. For one thing they were much more fragmented in organization as well as in their ideological and party political orientation; the composition of their membership ranged from ultra-German national Conservatives to supporters of the Liberals.[36] Some of the youth groups carried as their banner not the colours of the Republic but those of the

Empire: black, white, and red.[37] At this point it is also important to make a distinction between the leadership of the Protestant youth movements and their membership. While the former largely retained an attitude either of reserve or even of outspoken hostility to the NSDAP, the membership was much more receptive to Hitler Youth propaganda. They, as one of their leaders put it, 'were pervaded by something irrational, infectious, which brings the blood into motion and induces the feeling that something really great was about to happen, a forceful current of which one wants to be part. . . .'[38] This undoubtedly applies to members of Catholic and Protestant youth organizations alike; though the former were both better led as well as more firmly controlled. However, in both cases, the Hitler Youth was not able to benefit fully from the seeds of political radicalization until after January 1933.

The year 1932 had brought considerable gains in membership, the total at the end of the year standing at 107,956 members.[39] The Brüning government's prohibition of the NSDAP's uniformed branches then caused the Hitler Youth to be temporarily renamed the 'National Socialist Youth Movement' – to escape any general prohibition of the NSDAP as a whole.[40] For the Hitler Youth the prohibition actually produced a double advantage. From the point of view of recruitment the lure of 'illegality' (which in fact as a consequence of the change of name, no longer existed) exercised considerable magnetism. Secondly the change of name required the dissolution of the ties existing between the SA and the Hitler Youth. On 13 May 1932 Hitler issued a decree which freed Schirach from his subordination to the SA and made him an official of the party headquarters in his own right.[41] From now on he was only answerable directly to Hitler.[42] Also in matters of appointments the Hitler Youth was given full autonomy.[43] How far SA leader Röhm's homosexuality too affected Hitler's decision is difficult to say.[44] It seems plausible that it did, but the only evidence on this point comes from Schirach himself who more than thirty years after the event stated that compromising correspondence of Röhm's had been intercepted by the SPD (Socialists) in April 1932.[45] Hitler feared a political scandal which would inevitably result in serious repercussions for the Hitler Youth, and the work of years would be undone in a matter of days.[46] As it happened no scandal materialized and one is left wondering how reliable Schirach is on this point (and many others) since it is hard to believe that the SPD would not have used correspondence of this nature to embarrass Hitler and the NSDAP. Be that as it may, the May decree ushered in a short period of relative independence of the Hitler Youth from the SA and the NSDAP apparatus, which the latter did not mind since funds were required for the presidential elections of March and April, and the *Reichstag* elections of July and November.

While Brüning was still Chancellor, though governing by presidential decree and in a deadlocked *Reichstag* in which the combined majority of
NSDAP and KPD blocked any parliamentary consent, the republic was still
strong enough to ward off the extremes of both Left and Right. Wilhelm
Gröner, once Ludendorff's successor and in March 1932 Brüning's Minister of the Interior as well as War Minister, did not hesitate to threaten to
ban a large Hitler Youth gathering in Braunschweig.[47] Instead, a closed
meeting of Hitler Youth leaders took place at which colours for individual
Hitler Youth units were handed over with the words 'We dedicate our flags
in the sign of resurrection. May God bless our banners, for the final victory
we fight ourselves.'[48]

When Brüning was ousted in June 1932 and replaced by Papen, one of
the latter's first actions was to revoke the decrees forbidding the uniformed
appearance of the para-military formations of the NSDAP – including of
course the Hitler Youth. He hoped, by means of 'an opening to the Right',
to obtain the support of the NSDAP in the *Reichstag* and with it a stable
parliamentary majority. Hitler was not to be tempted; he rejected the idea
of a vice-chancellorship in a Papen government, took the concessions, and
interpreted them correctly for what they were: a sign of weakness.[49]

Papen's concessions also affected a different aspect of the Hitler Youth
activity. Since the late 1920s the *Reichswehr* had given active support to
para-military training of Right-wing youth organizations, a support extended also to the Hitler Youth but withdrawn under Gröner.[50] He endeavoured to fuse into one body, directly under the control of the *Reichswehr*
and the Ministry of the Interior, para-military associations of all centre-to-
right-wing parties, as well as those of ex-servicemen's organizations.[51]
Hitler, for obvious reasons, was not prepared to put his storm troopers
and the Hitler Youth under any such control, preferring prohibition.
With its revocation in June 1932 co-operation between the Hitler Youth
and the *Reichswehr* was resumed, though of course this concession was of
less importance to the NSDAP than its being able once again to march in
uniformed formations through the cities and the countryside of Germany. Nevertheless it highlights the activities of the *Reichswehr* significantly which already in 1932 and before was supplying officers for the
para-military training of the Hitler Youth, mainly in Berlin and surrounding areas.[52]

Papen's government also proved helpful in the matter of entry to the
'Reichs Committee of German Youth Associations', which on several occasions previously had turned down the Hitler Youth's application for
membership. Schirach's ultimate intention was to turn the committee
into an instrument of the Hitler Youth.[53] For the time being, however, he
was content to don the mantle of legality by founding the *Deutsches*

Jugendwerk e.V. whose statutes were allegedly different from those of the Hitler Youth although it comprised the HJ, the National Socialist Pupils' Association, the BDM, and the National Socialist Students League.[54] In his application Schirach claimed their total membership to be 120,000, of which 70,000 were Hitler Youth members. It seems likely that the figure was exaggerated but the application was accepted on 6 October 1932 and by the end of the year all restrictions in force against the Hitler Youth at national as well as local level had been lifted. The stigma of collaborating with an institution of the 'Weimar system' seems to have caused as little trouble as did representation in the *Reichstag*.

The major events of the year were of course the elections. In the presidential elections the contest was mainly between Hindenburg and Hitler. The latter's strength is indicated by the fact that it took two polls to establish the overall majority of Hindenburg. The holding of parliamentary elections in July 1932 was another concession wrested by Hitler from Papen. Held on 31 July 1932 they resulted in a resounding victory for the NSDAP which had polled 13,745,000 votes and obtained 230 seats in the *Reichstag*, which made it numerically the strongest party there.[55] Hitler paid tribute to the efforts of the Hitler Youth which had made a major contribution in distributing a hitherto unprecedented amount of election propaganda, some twenty million pamphlets and newspapers.[56] Schirach had also campaigned for a *Reichstag* seat and obtained one. Apart from a monthly salary of £40, *Reichstag* deputies enjoyed free travel on all public transport. Schirach could now travel at the state's expense, a state which he was dedicated to destroy.[57]

Despite the National Socialists success, however, electioneering had proved very expensive; the coffers of the party were nearly exhausted.[58] But to show off the new-won strength of the Hitler Youth, in spite of the late prohibition, Schirach called the *Reichsjugendtag der NSDAP* at Potsdam, a rally of all German Hitler Youths. For Schirach and the Hitler Youth it proved a tremendous success, especially since earlier Hitler had been somewhat sceptical about it.[59] Papen, in face of the intractability of the *Reichstag*, had dissolved it again, calling for new elections on 6 November 1932. Because of the shortage of Hitler Youth funds Hitler thought that a national mass rally of this order was running the risk of failure which, he felt, would be bound to affect adversely the chances of the NSDAP at the polls.[60]

Hitler need not have worried. The expected number of participants had been calculated at around 20,000, but when they arrived there were nearly 100,000 boys and girls.[61] Although the preparations were considered by Hitler Youth standards to be on a gigantic scale, they were not gigantic enough.[62] Travel facilities were inadequate and most Hitler Youth units were left to develop their own initiatives and to find their own resources.[63] One Munich Hitler Youth group simply boarded a bus in the suburb and talked its young driver into taking them to Berlin in return for the cost of the petrol. Thus a wayward bus from Munich's municipal transport could be seen at Potsdam. Its driver incidentally was fired after the event, but he was reinstated with an honorary Hitler Youth rank after Hitler became chancellor in January 1933.[64] At Potsdam only fifty large tents were available, and nearby empty factories provided additional sleeping space.[65] By rail, bus, and on foot the youths converged on Potsdam, banners being unfurled whenever they entered a hamlet, village, or town, bugle signals ringing out aggressively, and the cobbled streets resounding with the sombre tread of hobnailed hiking boots and the strains of young voices singing marching songs. None but those devoid of any feeling for the enthusiasm of which youth is capable could fail to respect the idealism and the élan of the brown-shirted youths.

The first evening camp rally took place on 1 October. As the log fires slowly burnt down, tens of thousands of voices broke out into the moving tune of *Gute Nacht Kameraden*. Reveille was at five o'clock next morning.[66] Later Baldur von Schirach laid a wreath at the steps of the Garrison Church of Potsdam, the shrine of Prussia, which held the coffins of its two greatest kings, Frederick William I and Frederick the Great, the architectural symbol of Prussian sobriety, dedication to duty, patriotism, and idealism. While the girls' contingent had assembled at the great Potsdam parade ground, the march past of the boys began, lasting from eleven o'clock in the morning until six o'clock at night.[67] Hitler, who so far had been very doubtful about the rally, unexpectedly turned up and stood on the review stand saluting *his* youth, according to some observers with tears in his eyes.[68] Even observers from other youth organizations were impressed. 'This was more than just a party youth movement which we saw marching in Potsdam . . . The NSDAP has succeeded in attracting to a large measure the best blood of the young generation and infused it with a sacred flame of faith and enthusiasm.'[69]

'They', as the Hitler Youth press chief Willi Körber put it, 'wanted to march in recognition of their Socialism against every form of reaction. Because we are young we cannot desire reaction, and because we are young, we are Socialists.'[70] Hitler addressed the boys and girls personally; it was the high point of the meeting.[71] In his speech he stressed that Germans had once again to learn to stand above their social status, their professional and denominational divisions, and to attach primary importance to their role within the national community. Germany had fallen because Germans had forgotten this elementary rule, and it was up to Germany's youth to become again brothers and sisters of one nation.[72] If the Hitler Youth remained true to the maxims postulated by Hitler at Potsdam, the above-quoted observer concluded, 'the Germany of tomorrow will be a Socialist one'.[73] Schirach in his own speech emphasized the symbolism and the significance of the youth rally. The individual Hitler Youth 'is no longer alone. Wherever the banners of the Hitler Youth fly he has comrades, his brothers and sisters, united with him in one faith, one ideology, all fused in one organization. It is a marvellous and tremendous experience in which Germany's youth participates.'[74]

The rally was subjected to severe criticism by the Socialists for its alleged organizational shortcomings.[75] The SPD press reported that 120 members of the Hitler Youth had collapsed because of exhaustion and had to be taken to Berlin hospitals. The Hitler Youth could immediately refute this statement and point to the fact that only five Hitler Youths were hospitalized, all being cases of appendicitis; two others had been injured in traffic accidents. Perhaps the SPD criticism was a case of sour grapes because the Socialist Youth Rally of May 1932 had attracted barely 15,000 members.[76] The psychological impact of the mass rally upon its participants cannot be overstated. Small groups of Hitler Youths operating for months, even years, in a state of semi-isolation in working-class districts, facing hostile parents, teachers, or workmates, suddenly had the experience of being part of one whole, of knowing that beside themselves there were thousands of others in Germany all fighting for the same cause with the same aim.

If the psychological impact was great on the participants, the youth rally cannot be said to have left any great impression upon the electorate at large, for in the Reichstag elections on 6 November 1932 the NSDAP lost two million votes and 34 seats in parliament.[77] This still left it the largest party, but was a shock nevertheless, and the opinion of many pundits was that the NSDAP had reached the peak of popularity and was now on the decline.

General von Schleicher, who succeeded Papen as Chancellor on 2 December 1932, also thought he could explore an opening to the Right by splitting the NSDAP and offering Gregor Strasser the vice-chancellorship.[78] Strasser, though initially interested, lost his nerve and backed out, resigning all his party offices at the same time and taking a holiday, while Hitler fully reasserted his own position.[79] Schleicher, now exploring an 'opening to the Left', alarmed all the Conservative and Centre groupings, most of which, including the Catholic Centre party, pressed Hindenburg to abandon government by presidential decree and instead return to parliamentary government through a parliamentary majority by forming a government which would enjoy the majority support of the *Reichstag*, even if this meant not simply the inclusion of the National Socialists but the appointment of Adolf Hitler as Chancellor.[80] The aged President after many misgivings and believing he had made sure of keeping

Hitler's hands off the *Reichswehr* by appointing a 'solid conservative man', General von Blomberg, as *Reichswehr* Minister, called Hitler to form a coalition cabinet.[81]

It is difficult, almost impossible, to offer an adequate assessment of the impact of the Hitler Youth upon Germany's youth as a whole during this period; certainly before 30 January 1933 the Hitler Youth had failed to win over in any significant numbers youth groups associated to other political parties. Within the Reichs Committee of German Youth Associations they represented no more than one per cent of its total membership, though probably by far its most active one. But their indirect influence was sufficiently strong for many of these youth organizations, especially those of religious denominations and of other right-wing parties, to adapt their style and their slogans to those of the Hitler Youth.

The difficult years for Hitler's movement between 1926 and 1933 were aptly summarized by Sir Winston Churchill when he wrote: 'The story of that struggle cannot be read without admiration for the courage, the perseverance and the vital force which enabled [Hitler] to challenge, defy, conciliate, or overcome, all the authorities or resistances which barred his path. He and the ever increasing legions who worked with him, certainly at this time, in their patriotic ardour and love of their country, showed that there was nothing that they would not do or dare, no sacrifice of life, limb or liberty that they would not make themselves or inflict upon their opponents.'[82]

However, whether the majority of the Hitler Youth members had clear-cut ideological concepts rather than patriotic ardour and a vague notion of 'German socialism', is more than doubtful. W. S. Allen in his excellent study *The Nazi Seizure of Power* quotes a former Hitler Youth member whose testimony may well apply to many if not the majority of members:

'There was no pressure put on me by my father or anyone else to join the Hitler Youth – I decided to join independently simply because I wanted to be in a boys' club where I could strive towards a nationalistic ideal. The Hitler Youth had camping hikes and group meetings. I was number nine in the Thalburg group when I joined in 1930. There were boys from all classes of families, though mainly middle class and workers. There were no social or class distinctions, which I approved of very much. There was no direct or obvious political indoctrination until later – after Hitler came to power. Without really trying to get new members, the Thalburg Hitler Youth grew rapidly. I think most of the boys joined for the same reason that I did. They were looking for a place where they could get together with other boys in exciting activities. It was also a depression time and there were many evil influences abroad from which decent boys wished to escape. In any event, I don't think the political factor was the main reason boys joined. We did march in parades and hated the SPD, but that was all general, not specific – it was all part of it. We weren't fully conscious of what we were doing, but we enjoyed ourselves and also felt important.'[83]

Or as one BDM member said who during the war was to reach a leading position in the *Reichsjugendführung*:

'When I search myself for the motives which tempted me to enter the Hitler Youth then I find also this one: I wanted to break out from my childish, narrow life and attach it to something that was great and essential. This desire was shared by countless contemporaries.

'It is more difficult to explain that I managed to keep up this initiative over twelve years until 1945. That I remained attached to the cause of National Socialism for so long is connected with my early childhood experiences. It is remarkable, it was the "socialist" tendency, which was expressed in the name of this "movement", which attracted me, because it strengthened my opposition against my parental home. On the other hand, the nationalist component was significant for me, because it corresponded with the spirit which permeated me from earliest childhood onwards . . . my childhood experiences correspond with the experience of a whole generation, which grew up among a bourgeoisie fundamentally inclined towards the Right and from which later so many young leaders of the National Socialist "movement" and the Wehrmacht of the "Third *Reich*" were to emerge.'[84]

The loss of the war, the 'Diktat' of Versailles, the economy suffering under reparations payments, the 'alien' influences on German culture, general political instability, all these led many to a situation in which, talking from a personal point of view, it could be said that 'long before I could analyse all the casual connections, even before I understood the significance of the term "Germany", I loved it as something mysteriously surrounded by mourning, as something infinitely dear and threatened'.[85]

The striving towards a nationalistic ideal, not necessarily one distilled from the pages of *Mein Kampf*, and a novel feeling of importance were, as we shall see, two elements common to those who joined the Hitler Youth before 1933 or after 1939. Both groups were aware of a sense of national crisis, whether created initially by the aftermath of Versailles or later by the fact that the country was at war. The party as well as the actual situation engendered the feeling among youths that what they were doing was not just playing games but, to use the vocabulary of the period, actively participating in the struggle to restore to Germany its honour and its former position in the world.

The Hitler Youths could feel they had made a real contribution to Hitler's coming to power. If the brutality of the adults in the political struggle alarmed and alienated many observers, it was the unselfish impulse of sacrifice, the sheer dynamic idealism of the Hitler Youth which provided a redeeming, even an inspiring, feature. The Hitler Youth had provided proof of its worth both as a youth organization and as a National Socialist propaganda vehicle. 'The police which yesterday persecuted us now saluted us with raised arm. It was a unique fraternization,' Schirach was to observe.[86]

Few of the Hitler Youths who on 30 January 1933 marched past Hindenburg and Hitler on the evening of his appointment as chancellor had the remotest idea where their 'nationalistic ideals' and their feeling of importance would lead them within the short span of twelve years; few would even suspect to what extent their idealism and readiness for sacrifice would be exploited and to what ends. The torchlight processions of 30 January marking the beginning of Germany's 'national revolution', seemed to demonstrate, at least to younger Germans, that at long last the young generation had come in to its own. 'Social despair, nationalistic Romanticism, and the generation conflict produced an almost classic synthesis.'[87] Gregor Strasser in the 1920s had exclaimed 'Make way you old ones'[88] and Baldur von Schirach had summarized it with the sentence: 'The NSDAP is the party of youth.'[89]

The new spirit affected some even of those who were ultimately to become National Socialism's most tragic victims – the German Jews. Jewish German students addressed themselves to Hitler and tried to convince him of their sincere German patriotism.[90] When the liberal politician Theodor Heuss – in 1949 to become the Federal Republic's first president – returned late in February 1933 from a meeting at which he had addressed German Jewish students, he recorded in his diary his disillusioned impression that he had spoken 'to prevented Nazis'.[91]

Though Hitler's government was initially a coalition government, after the passing of the Enabling Act in March 1933 which in effect gave Hitler dictatorial powers for a period of four years – the Act was subsequently renewed by the *Reichstag* in 1937 and in 1941 – he had a clear path, which the leadership of the Hitler Youth was naturally to take as much advantage of as any other party formation. With the entire executive power of the state on their side, the Hitler Youth could now set about preparing its quest for the monopoly position, gradually introducing into the field of youth activities the process of *Gleichschaltung* – gradually 'co-ordinating' and 'integrating' all other youth movements into the Hitler Youth and forbidding other organized youth activity to be carried on outside it. As in all sectors of National Socialist Germany, total control of all Germans was the ultimate aim of the government, which logically required in the first place the reduction and eventual elimination of the individual's private sphere and his total public commitment to the 'National community'.[92]

Traditional social structures and ideological influences such as family and church were of course the most serious obstacles in the achievement of this aim, and at this early stage too formidable to allow a direct frontal attack.[93] Consequently the immediate task in hand for the Hitler Youth in 1933 was threefold: first, to eliminate – with the exception of the Catholic Youth Movement – all other competing youth leagues and youth organizations; secondly, to assume as many functions of youth work as possible ranging from sports and the arts to social youth work and youth jurisdiction; and thirdly, to draw as many age groups as possible into the various organizations of the Hitler Youth, thus establishing a monopoly by the sheer weight of numbers.[94]

'In the same way as the NSDAP is the only party, so the Hitler Youth must be the only youth organization' . . . The Hitler Youth desires to embrace youth in its entirety as well as all spheres of its activities.'[95] However radical these pronouncements, it is important to bear in mind that they were made at a time when the Hitler Youth had very nearly or already established its monopoly position. Up to 1935 public statements were couched in softer, more conciliatory terms, but the action was uncompromising from the very start, with regional variations only in the methods. Very often the potential threat of physical and psychological intimidation brought to a local Hitler Youth leader the spoils which elsewhere could only be obtained by recourse to violence. And even in places where real 'violence' was used, the wielders of this weapon did not feel quite comfortable in their role. A case in point is the occasion when on 3 April 1933 Schirach had the offices of the Reichs Committee of German Youth Associations occupied.[96] The fifty Hitler Youths who were carrying out this operation under the leadership of *Obergebietsführer* Karl Nabersberg (actually the deputy chairman of the committee and Schirach's close confidant) forced their way into the committee's offices in Berlin's *Alsenstrasse*, but apart from the office staff they could find none of its officials. Hermann Maass, who came from the youth movement of the Social Democratic Party and was the business manager of the Committee, had to be called from another part of Berlin only to be insulted by Nabersberg and to be told to pack up his things, go home, and never come back. Meanwhile, the other Hitler Youths searched, bundled, and sealed the files. One of them was put in charge of the office staff, but still rather unaccustomed to his 'authoritarian' role *vis à vis* people of an age group very much the same as his parents, he politely asked one of the clerks whether he could use their waste-paper baskets to dispose of his sandwich papers.[97]

Without putting up other than verbal resistance Maass left his office, which Nabersberg then occupied. The latter demanded that all employees continue their work under his direction. The operation put Schirach in control of the body which represented approximately 6 million young Germans organized in various youth movements. Moreover, the files of the Committee provided ample material and information on the opponents of the Hitler Youth.[98] It was the beginning of *Gleichschaltung* of Germany's youth, accompanied by appeals to end once and for all Germany's division at its root source, among the youth of the country. The implied corollary of this appeal was that any refusal to merge with the Hitler Youth was unpatriotic, indeed un-German.

The first of the youth movements to be affected were those associated with the political parties of the Weimar Republic as well as Jewish youth associations. Already the *Reichstag* fire of February 1933 had provided the necessary lever to proscribe the Communist party and its affiliated associations.[99] Actually, on the evening of the fire leaders of radical youth movements, including members of the Hitler Youth, had met in a restaurant near Berlin's Stettiner railway station.[100] Apparently they had previously agreed on their common social revolutionary aims and approximately 200 young men representing the revolutionary wing of the Hitler Youth, the Socialist Youth, Young Communists, Red Boy Scouts, National Revolutionaries, and Otto Strasser's Black Front promised to co-operate with one another.[101] Among those attending were Heinz Gruber (no relation to K-Gruber but a leading figure in the Youth League) and also Harro Schulze-Boysen, later to be the leader of the Communist spy network, the *Rote Kapelle*.[102] Hitler's coalition with the conservative forces of the Weimar Republic had come to many Hitler Youths as a shock, while many of their opponents began to see the NSDAP in a different light, as a movement of the proportions of an avalanche which was sweeping away the barriers between the middle class and the proletariat. A previously vociferous opponent of the Hitler Youth wrote in a periodical at the time: 'The trenches of the Right against the Left and those of the Left against the Right are false positions, comrades! It was a disastrous remark of the Chancellor of the Centre party when he stated, 'The enemy stands to the Right.' As disastrous as the contention that the enemy stands at the Left. We oppose any attempt to tear our nation apart irrespective of whether it comes from either 'Left' or 'Right'. . . . We call for action against the alien influences in our nation, not merely action against 'marxism'.[103] The echoes of Karl Radek's speech of ten years earlier still seemed to be reverberating.

It seems reasonable to assume that the sudden attempts at *rapprochement* with the Hitler Youth by the left-of-centre youth groups were very largely dictated by the changed circumstances and the fear of the demise of their own youth organizations; nevertheless there were many who believed in the validity of the forces of youth co-operating towards a common end.[104] The *Reichstag* fire however nipped these attempts at *rapprochement* in the bud. Next to the Communists, those most endangered were the 'Socialist Workers' Youth of the SPD.[105] It is typical of the awareness of a general policy line that in the absence of detailed instructions from either NSDAP or the *Reichsjugendführung*, individual Hitler Youth units in some areas either anticipated or even precipitated events. Local headquarters of the SPD's youth movement were raided by the Hitler Youth and the files removed and while police intervention temporarily put an end to acts of this kind, local NSDAP leaders used them as a pretext to press for the closure of local headquarters of their opponents.[106]

The youth groups of Hitler's conservative allies, such as the *Bismarck-Jugend* and some organizations of the *Bündische Jugend, Hindenburg-Jugend*, and the *Scharnhorst-Jugend* lasted little longer. The politically uncommitted youth leagues tried at first to create a common front by founding the Greater German League led by Admiral von Trotha, and to adopt a wait-and-see attitude.[107] Trotha, who had retired from the German Navy some time before, still enjoyed valuable contacts with the *Reichswehr* where he commanded the support of General Edwin von Stülpnagel particularly, who was responsible for the *Reichswehr*'s assistance in para-military training of German nationalist youth organizations.[108] Trotha's league quickly followed Schirach's example by explicitly excluding German Jews from its ranks. Others excluded from membership were 'Democrats' and Socialists.[109] It issued a proclamation expressing loyalty to Hitler and the National Socialist state, and for a short time managed to convey the impression that it was able to overtake the Hitler Youth on the Right.[110] The March elections of 1933 combined with the Enabling Act were signs Hitler's coalition partners could not fail to observe. They immediately joined the party and took steps to fuse their own para-military associations and youth movements with those of the NSDAP.[111] This in essence was the end of the Greater German League although it was allowed to linger on for a few more months. By controlling the Reichs Committee of German Youth Associations, the Hitler Youth indirectly as well as directly controlled the whole of Germany's organized youth, and those who, like their elders, could read the signs of the times joined its ranks. Within Trotha's League itself suggestions were made of joining the Hitler Youth *en bloc*. Both Schirach and Hitler opposed this suggestion for tactical reasons, for it would have meant that all the other previously non-NSDAP youth movements would have joined together with their leaders and the development of a serious body of opposition to the established Hitler Youth leadership would have been virtually inevitable.[112] At Whitsun 1933 the League held its last camp meeting.[113] Members arrived late on Saturday, celebrated on Sunday, and on Monday morning were suddenly confronted by police and storm trooper contingents who dissolved the meeting and sent its members home for causing a 'public nuisance'.[114] A month later the League 'officially' dissolved itself, which did not prevent Trotha from raising an official protest and carrying it as far as President Hindenburg. But nothing came of the protest except that Hindenburg raised the matter with Hitler, which caused the latter to express his regrets and Schirach to write an apology to Trotha.[115] The Admiral appears to have reconciled himself with the powers that be, for he accepted from Schirach an appointment as 'Honorary Leader of the Marine Hitler Youth'.[116] Within less than five months after Hitler was appointed Chancellor, the Hitler Youth had absorbed or eliminated the youth organizations of their coalition partners and the politically non-committed *Bündische Jugend* under Trotha. With the exception of the *Bund der Artamanen*, of which prominent National Socialists like Himmler and Darré were members,[117] Hitler's own maxim had triumphed: 'He who is not prepared to bear my name will therefore not be regarded as a friend of National Socialism.'[118] Other politically neutral youth organizations and institutions, such as those catering for industrial apprentices or youthful athletes, posed no problems. Valuable institutions gained were the German Youth Hostel Association and the European Youth Exchange Service which operated in conjunction with the *Volksbund für das im Ausland*,[119] organizing youth exchanges among European youth groups as well as supporting youth work among German minority groups outside Germany. An important step in the process of *Gleichschaltung* was Hitler's decree of 17 June 1933 which changed Schirach's title from *Reichsjugendführer* of the NSDAP to *Jugendführer des Deutschen Reiches* or simply Youth Leader of Germany.[120] In that capacity Schirach's office exercised a supervisory function over all youth activities in Germany, including activities operated by adults. Any foundation of a new youth organization required Schirach's consent. Needless to say, it was not given.[121] Schirach's new appointment, however, did not give him entire control of youth affairs in Germany. The Ministry of the Interior under Frick, as well as the Ministry of Justice and the newly created Ministry for Science and Education, all participated through their own administrative agencies in deciding youth policy.[122] The net result was a proliferation of responsibility.[123] Schirach also had to contend with the rivalling influences of such personalities as General von Reichenau, who as Chief of the *Reichswehr* Ministry hoped to bring Germany's youth organizations under his control, and party leaders like Röhm, Goebbels, and Hess continued for some time to argue in favour of the appointment of a senior party official as an overall controller of youth affairs.[124] The only certainty inherent in the system was a continuous conflict of temperament and authority which was to lead directly to the assumption of power by the strongest single element: Adolf Hitler.

Above Military-style marching formed one of the standard exercises of the Hitler Youth: *Jungvolk* on a cross-country march
Below 'The drummers of the nation': *Jungvolk* at a rally in Berlin in 1933

Above (left) Instruments and their players at rest; *(right)* flagbearers of the HJ in formal pre-war attire
Below A *Jungvolk* camp in 1934

BDM javelin throwers: theirs was a sport highly popular in all branches of the Hitler Youth

Left and above The led – and their leaders

Above A Hitler Youth hostel in Austria. The centre section of the mural depicts the evolution of the Hitler Youth into the political soldier

One of Schirach's first official actions in his new office was to order the dissolution of the Greater German League; the Reichs Committee of German Youth Associations too had served its purpose and was dissolved on 8 July 1933,[125] shortly after Schirach had passed new measures for the regional organization of the Hitler Youth, as well as the introduction of a structure based on age groups which was to remain in force until 1945. The Hitler Youth was now divided into the following groups:

Male:
Jungvolk (10–14 years of age)
HJ   (14–18 ,, ,, ,,)

Female:
Jungmädel (10–14 years of age)
BDM   (14–18 ,, ,, ,,)[126]

In place of the Reichs Committee, Schirach founded a German Youth Leaders' Council composed of the leaders of the German Youth Movement, but since within less than twelve months, apart from the denominational youth groups, there were no youth movements except the Hitler Youth there never was any role for the Council to play.[127] By the end of 1933, in addition to the youth organizations affiliated to political parties which had been proscribed within the first few months of the Third Reich, twenty youth leagues had dissolved themselves and by and large transferred their members into the Hitler Youth.[128] It was this vast influx of new members increasing the Hitler Youth membership from 107,956 at the end of 1932 to 3,577,565 which had made the structural reorganization necessary.[129] It was bedevilled by the fact that the NSDAP headquarters was in Munich while the capital was Berlin. Schirach solved the problem in his own way; while nominally the *Reichsjugendführung* remained in Munich, Schirach's own office of *Jugendführer* was established in Berlin. Hitler had refused the allocation of funds for the establishment of a large office in a villa on Berlin's well-to-do *Kronprinzenufer*, but private financial support enabled Schirach to make the purchase.[130]

Once established, he could set about reorganizing the Hitler Youth. In his position as *Reichsjugendführer der NSDAP* Schirach was directly responsible to Hitler.[131] In that of *Jugendführung des Deutschen Reiches* his immediate superiors were the Minister of the Interior Wilhelm Frick and the Minister of Justice Franz Gürtner.[132] The *Reichsjugendführung*, until that time a major department with small sub-departments within the NSDAP *Reichsleitung* in Munich, now rapidly expanded into a vast bureaucratic body, whose involvement in numerous additional spheres of

activity did not necessarily make for greater efficiency. Even before the outbreak of war complaints at local level increased about the difficulties encountered with the Hitler Youth bureaucracy in Berlin.[133] The otherwise
very sympathetic SS-journal *Das Schwarze Korps* had occasion to pen puns
on the *Reichsjugendführung*.[134] Important new departments such as one
for radio under Carl Cerff and Press and Propaganda under Gustav Staebe
were called into being. The *Reichsjugendführung* stood at the apex of an
organizational pyramid made up of five regional *Obergebiete*-North,
South, East, West, and Middle.[135] Beneath the *Obergebiete* were twenty-
one *Gebiete* each of which was subdivided into *Oberbanne, Banne, Unterbanne, Gefolgschaften, Scharen* and *Kameradschaften*.[136] Into these sub-
divisions of the HJ those of the *Jungvolk*, the BDM and the *Jungmädel*
were integrated with variations only in the nomenclature. The maximum
number of *Gebiete* each *Obergebiet* was to contain was five, with an approximate total of 375,000 Hitler Youths male and female.[137] Austria was
organized as an independent *Gebiet*, the Saar was added in 1935 as a result
of the plebiscite, and by 1942 there were a total of six *Obergebiete* and
forty-two *Gebiete*.[138] Administration operated through strictly hierarchical
vertical channels; moreover duplicate offices of the *Reichsjugendführung*
were established at both *Obergebiets* and *Gebiets* levels, thus inflating the
administration even more.[139] But irrespective of the growing unwieldiness
of the Hitler Youth's administration the original aim had been attained by
1934 – to achieve a position which would make the accomplishment of its
claims towards exclusive representation of Germany's youth inevitable.
True, inter-party rivalries within the NSDAP still continued to affect the
Hitler Youth. The *Reichssport* leader, Hans von Tschammer und Osten,
was reluctant to hand over control of his *Sportsjugend*;[140] Robert Ley, the
leader of the *Deutsche Arbeitsfront*, the NSDAP substitute for the dissolved
trade unions, pursued much the same aims with the working youth who
automatically upon entering employment had to become members of the
DAF.[141] Tschammer had ultimately to concede to overwhelming pressure,
while Ley found it useful to make an ally of Schirach against the claims of
Bernhard Rust, the Minister of Science and Education.[142] These rivalries
were by no means the only ones. The *Reichswehr*, renamed in 1935 the
Wehrmacht, continued in its endeavour to exercise a controlling influence
upon the Hitler Youth, an attempt which (though only in order to appease
the conservative forces) Hitler for a time was ready to support.[143] This influence was rivalled in the two years before the war, and increasingly and
more successfully during it, by that of the SS, especially the
SS-*Vefügungstruppen*, later to be known as the *Waffen-SS*.[144]

The vast influx of new members could not simply be overcome by
increased organization and centralization; it confronted the Hitler Youth

with a problem which only time could solve: the lack of trained and experienced leadership. One way of ameliorating the problem was by a burst of promotions from the *Reichsjugendführung* down to *Bann* level.[145] Of course a sizeable reservoir of leadership potential existed among the great number of leaders from the proscribed youth leagues which had joined the Hitler Youth. But Schirach considered them politically unreliable and preferred his own small band of 'old fighters' – men like Ammerlahn, Schnaedter, and Lauterbacher who were *Obergebiets* leaders.[146] The same applied to the leaders of the *Gebiete, Oberbann* and *Bann*. The new faces that appeared there did not come from the youth movement, hence they were preciously few. Youth leaders from other youth organizations found promotion only at the lower level, in ranks usually very much lower than those they had originally enjoyed, and there too they were surrounded by endemic suspicion.[147] Several of them were associated, rightly or wrongly, with Röhm and during the purge of 1934 were arrested and dismissed.[148] Schirach tried also to draw on the experience of well-known adults like Karl Walter Kondeyne, who established the Hitler Youth health facilities and the medical division of the *Reichsjugendführung*,[149] or Ritter von Schleich, an air ace of the First World War.[150] But all these were merely attempts to meet the leadership problem – they did not actually solve it.

The need to tackle the problem directly acquired immediate urgency through an incident in Hesse where it was discovered that former trade union leaders and socialists who had become Hitler Youth leaders had endeavoured to keep together a cadre of the youths they had led before 1933.[151]

To produce leaders trained along National Socialist principles and in sufficient quantity, leadership schools were established throughout Germany providing systematic and methodical training for future Hitler Youth leaders.[152] The first of these *Reichsführer* schools to be established was at Potsdam in 1933. It provided an example to be emulated in every other German province. By early 1934 the nuclei of twenty-two such schools existed, offering as an emergency measure three-week courses.[153] Besides leadership training the syllabus included physical training, .22 rifle shooting, instruction on racial principles and German history.[154] The *Reichsjugendführung* claimed that by means of these cramming courses 7,000 Hitler Youth leaders had been turned out by the end of 1933,[155] a somewhat doubtful claim but understandable because Schirach, still enmeshed in the intrigues of internal rivalries within the NSDAP, realized that note would be made of every shortcoming of the organization under his command, and that his own position very much depended on the quality of the leadership of the rank and file. He therefore bombarded with memoranda, directives, telephone calls, and personal harangues the two men in the *Reichsjugendführung* directly responsible for the *Reichsführer* school; *Obergebietsführer* Stellrecht, head of physical training, and *Gebietsführer* Usadel, head of the leadership schools.[156]

In 1934 Schirach created the precedent which was to be followed every subsequent year up to 1944, that of putting each year's activities under a particular heading which then became the annual slogan.[157] 1934 was named 'The Year of Training', in which Hitler youth leaders were to be produced *en masse*. The year was dedicated to providing the leaders with 'sound historic, political, and racial knowledge as well as extensive physical training'. Schirach, in an open address, emphasized that 'the Hitler Youth is a community of ideological education. Whoever marches in the Hitler Youth is not a number among millions but the soldier of an idea. The individual member's value to the whole is determined by the degree with which he is permeated by the idea. The best Hitler Youth, irrespective of rank and office, is he who completely surrenders himself to the National Socialist *Weltanschauung*.'[158]

On 24 January 1934, the anniversary of the birthday of Frederick the Great and the death of Herbert Norkus, a mass rally took place in Potsdam.[159] 342 Hitler Youth colours were handed over to Hitler Youth units. By the end of February Schirach had made his peace with Ley and both called for a *Reichsberufwettkampf*,[160] the National Vocational competition, to be held annually, in which the best performances of Hitler Youths in their respective occupations were assessed and rewarded.[161] The winners were personally received by Hitler. In 1934 500,000 boys and girls participated in it; by 1939 the figure had risen to 3,500,000.[162] The competition was of considerable value because it provided insight into general training standards of the trades and professions, as well as revealing any gaps to be closed in the interest of the national economy.[163] The *Reichssportwettkampf*, introduced in 1935, the sports competition of the Hitler Youth, was the other major annual event for the age groups between ten and eighteen. It required the meeting of very specific standards in athletics which if attained would be rewarded with a special medal.[164] In the summer of each year one day was to be the 'Day of the State Youth', another holiday in a calendar in which gradually the religious holidays began to disappear, to be replaced by National Socialist ones.[165] For Hitler Youths still at school Saturday lessons were cancelled to allow the whole day to be used for either physical training or para-military field games.[166]

For the girls a total of twenty-seven leadership schools were founded during the first half of 1934,[167] but most of them bore the hallmarks of improvisation. Much the same, of course, applied to their male equivalents. However, in August 1934 Schirach could submit an official report claiming to have produced in 287 three-week courses 12, 727 HJ leaders and 24,660

Jungvolk leaders.[168] Furthermore, 15,000 Hitler Youth leaders had passed special physical exercise training courses.[169] Indeed, it was a proud day for many of the youngsters – to which the particular sequence in Leni Riefenstahl's film *Triumph des Willens* (*Triumph of the Will*) bears eloquent witness – when Hitler, flanked by Schirach and Goebbels, addressed the Hitler Youth on the 'Party Day of Unity' at the 1934 Nuremberg rally.[170] Foreign correspondents reported that the youth rally was by far the most enthusiastic.[171] Hitler praised the Hitler Youth for past achievement and for attaining an important goal – discipline;[172] because only discipline and obedience would make them fit to issue orders later in life. He concluded by saying: 'We want to be a peace-loving people, but at the same time courageous. That is why you must be peaceful and courageous at the same time. We want our people to be honour-loving; to that end you must from earliest childhood learn the conception of honour. We want to be a proud people, and you must be proud; proud to be the youthful members of the greatest nation. We want an obedient people, and you must learn to practise obedience. We want a people that is not soft but hard as flint, and we want you from early youth to learn to overcome hardships and privations. There must be no classes or class distinctions among our people, and you must never let the idea of class distinctions take root among you. All we expect of the Germany of the future, we expect of you. We shall pass on, but Germany will live in you.'[173]

Hitler was frequently interrupted by enthusiastic cheers, and at the end of the meeting, to the strains of the Hitler Youth Anthem, the Führer shook hands with Hitler Youths and was then driven once round the stadium, so that everyone could see him.

A previously unknown range of opportunities was now offering itself to those willing and capable of taking them. Within the Hitler Youth the top grade was reached within the 'Leadership corps of the Hitler Youth' and the *Reichsjugendführung*.[174] The leadership corps included all ranks from *Bannführer* (HJ) and *Jungbannführer* (*Jungvolk*) and *Untergauführerin* (BDM). Unpaid part-time posts, they gradually developed into full-time salaried official positions.[175] In 1939 out of 765,000 Hitler Youth leaders, 8,017 were full-time officials, which at the current rate of membership was one full-time Hitler Youth official to 1,450 youths.[176] In a directive issued on 23 February 1938 a training scheme for the full-time officials of the leadership was introduced:[177]

The great tasks which the *Führer* has put to his youth require a leadership corps which in character and achievement fulfil the highest requirements. The training of this leadership corps is carried out by the Youth Academy of the (*Reichs*) Youth Leadership in Braunschweig [the school originally set up in 1932 by Hartmann Lanterbacher]. Every Hitler Youth can be called to the academy under the following conditions:

1. Proof of German-blooded descent.
2. Unobjectionable medical condition and no traces of inheritable illness.
3. Unobjectionable National Socialist attitudes and high physical and intellectual capacity.
4. Completed professional training or university matriculation.

Candidates will participate in a selection course, the purpose of which is to decide the suitability of the candidate. After successful conclusion of labour service and military service the leadership candidate will be required to complete the following tasks:

1. Service in a *Gebietsführung* for a period of four months.
2. Completion of an eight-week course at the *Reichsführer* school at Potsdam.
3. Study at the Academy of Youth Leadership in *Braunschweig* for one year.
4. Three-week training in industry at home and six-months training abroad.
5. Final examination.

By being called to the academy the candidate entered a minimal obligation of twelve years of service. After passing the final examination the leadership candidate received the diploma of a Youth Leader of the German *Reich* and the simultaneous appointment as *Stammführer*, admitting him to the leadership corps of the Hitler Youth.[178] Taking into account his labour service and military service the candidate would have completed his course at the age of approximately twenty-four

However, in spite of this decree, the onset of the war ensured that Hitler Youth leadership training remained a patchy and rather improvised affair. One cannot speak of an 'ideologically homogeneous' Hitler Youth leadership, though homogeneity did develop in a certain aspect, namely its social composition. Making Hitler Youth membership compulsory brought in a much larger sector of the middle-class German youth than had been the case before 1933.[179] And it was the youth of middle-class origins which began to dominate the Hitler Youth leadership. Whereas before 1933 less than ten per cent of the entire Hitler Youth leaders had attained matriculation level and had a university education, six years later this had increased to nearly twenty-four per cent.[180] The professional composition of the entire Hitler Youth leadership for 1939 is made up of 16.4% pupils, 5.9% students, 25.5% trade and commerce, 5.4% teachers, 8.7% engineering trades, 20.9% workers, 3.4% agricultural trades, 11.3% 'others' and 2.5% without profession.[181] Whilst the representation of the workers was still strong, pupils (since this almost exclusively refers to grammar-school pupils which then as now were mostly middle-class), students, trade and commerce, the teaching profession and the engineering trades (which in Germany by definition represent highly skilled occupations with a relatively high income bracket and would therefore not qualify for the 'working class' label) total

62.3%, so that more than half of the Hitler Youth leadership came from middle-class backgrounds. Middle-class domination was even stronger in the leadership of some of the special formations of the Hitler Youth (see below).

These figures, like most concerning the social background of the Hitler Youth in general before 1933 and that of its leadership thereafter, are not reliable and to this date not verifiable.[182] Since, however, they represent official Hitler Youth and NSDAP figures, probably biased to show that the Hitler Youth and its leadership represented a true cross-section of the German national community, the middle-class figures if anything are too low, and those of the working class too high. But this is subject to speculation.

Irrespective of this, they do indicate a transformation of the Hitler Youth after 1936, if not before. Whereas before 1936 the main officials of the Hitler Youth were workers, peasants, and students who had to take full-time industrial and menial employment to earn their keep, these virtually disappeared after 1936, being mainly shunted onto sidelines in the Hitler Youth leadership or absorbed into party offices. Of those who replaced them in the leadership corps of Hitler Youth officials, approximately 66.5% possessed grammar-school and/or university backgrounds, while at the level of *Bannführer* and *Jungbannführer* this type of person provided more than half of the leaders.[183] By the middle or late 1930s the office of the Hitler Youth leader had become 'socially acceptable'. It was no longer the risky, proletarian rough and tumble of the years before 1933. Middle-class background was particularly pronounced in the *Jungvolk*, which shared much less the 'social-revolutionary' traditions of the HJ.[184]

With the increase in numbers and the extent of its claims to authority, the *Reichjugendführung* in Berlin under Schirach and his deputy Lauter-bacher developed into a vast administration comparable in size to that of a ministry, characterized also by some of the worst features of bureaucracy – the juggling for positions and continuous in-fighting and intrigues.[185]

The Hitler Youth also obtained its own broadcasting time over the *Deutschlandsender* and a special Hitler Youth Institute was created to train Hitler Youth radio speakers.[186] In one of the very first broadcasts in 1934 the still existing class distinctions in German education were attacked, particularly the habit of wearing *Schülermützen* or school caps which set grammar-school pupils apart from those of other schools. The result was a nationwide public ceremony in which the caps were banned from all German schools and publicly burnt.[187] Also schoolteachers judged to be supporters of the new classless state were publicly honoured and schools in which ninety per cent of the pupils were Hitler Youth members were awarded a Hitler Youth banner.[188]

While the political integration or suppression of youth movements of a party political or politically non-committed character had been achieved relatively easily, the organized youth movements of the Protestant and Roman Catholic denominations appeared at first to present a formidable problem. Again, among these, it was the Protestant Youth movements that were most easily won over. The appeal made to them was simple and effective and the response matched the occasion. 'A new hour in Germany's history is striking. In the last second Germany has been pulled back from the abyss of Bolshevism. A strong government calls upon all Germans to realize their responsibility. A new movement breaks ground which promises to bridge the differences between classes, estates and ethnic groups. . . . In this hour Germany's evangelical Youth ought to know that its leaders answer a joyous "Yes" to the rising of the nation. In the recognition that that which is at stake is the rejuvenation of the foundations of the life of the entire race and that this lies at the very core of the historical mission of the evangelic youth, it calls for the ready sacrifice of earthly goods and of blood.'[189] With these words, which in content are no different to similar diatribes by National Socialist atheists, one of the leading Protestant Youth leaders, Erich Stange, had saluted the Third Reich. Of course, paying lip service to the new era was hardly enough to keep the Protestant youth organizations out of conflict. One cannot speak of concerted Hitler Youth action against denominational youth groups, but rather that action or inaction depended on the regional NSDAP leadership and, frequently as before, local Hitler Youth leaders tended to take the law into their own hands by issuing decrees forbidding public youth assemblies other than those of the Hitler Youth. Because of the extent of the liberties taken, Schirach had been compelled to issue the following order on 5 July 1933: 'I hereby forbid any interference of the Hitler Youth with other Youth Associations. If the behaviour of members of other youth associations gives cause for complaint then the complaint is to be directed to me through the proper official channels. Insofar as complaints necessitate further action I shall initiate the necessary steps through the appropriate state institutions. Individual actions will be punished.'[190]

In the hope of preserving their autonomy, various Protestant Youth groups were prepared to co-operate with the Hitler Youth at regional level by joint meetings, participation in public rallies, and leadership gatherings.[191] But the bridge thus built carried only one-way traffic to the Hitler Youth. Moreover, the rank and file of the members were betrayed by their own leaders when they accepted the subordination of the Protestant Youth Movements under *Reichsbischof* Ludwig Müller the head of the new NS-inspired Protestant sect, the German Christians.[192] Müller had been a divisional chaplain in the Dardanelles during the First World War and afterwards the army district of East Prussia was under his 'spiritual' care. An early convert to Hitler's cause, he was responsible for the conversion of the then Colonel von Reichenau, Chief of Staff of the 1st Infantry Division, and through him of Reichenau's chief, General von Blomberg, commander of the garrisons in East Prussia. Both had met Hitler in Müller's house. After 30 January 1933 Hitler had appointed Müller 'plenipotentiary of the Chancellor on Questions of the Evangelical Church' and through him Hitler hoped to create an indigenous 'German Church for German Christians'.[193]

Müller, of course, was in favour of fusing the youth movements of his church with the Hitler Youth, but encountered strong opposition from his colleagues, such as Pastor Martin Niemöller, ex-U-boat commander who was to develop into an uncompromising enemy of Hitler.[194] Opposition was also encountered from Protestant Youth leaders. But Müller could point to the example provided by Danzig where the Protestant Youth had joined the Hitler Youth on its own initiative, and also to the simple fact that the Protestant Youth was not gaining members but losing them to the Hitler Youth.[195]

Divided internally, the Protestant church was ultimately forced to give way to the concerted pressure of the Hitler Youth and the NSDAP and on 19 December 1933 an agreement was signed according to which the Protestant Youth movements accepted uniform political instruction by the National Socialist state and the Hitler Youth.[196] All members under the age of eighteen were to be integrated into Hitler Youth formations. The only concession made to the Protestant Youth was that two afternoons a week should remain free for the educational activity of the church, a concession quickly eroded by excessive HJ demands on the boys and girls which took up their entire time and limited religious instructions exclusively to the home and to one hour per week in the schools.[197] The agreement met with considerable protest, but the protesters were powerless to reverse what had already been accomplished.[198]

Within the Catholic Youth movement, developments took a slightly different turn. In his government proclamation on 23 March 1933 Hitler had promised his support for the Christian churches and the continuation of the Concordat which individual German lands had concluded with the Vatican during and before the days of the Weimar Republic.[199] The process of coordination and the abolition of the German states required a new national Concordat.[200] The news was soon leaked that the German government had sent Vice-chancellor von Papen to Rome to negotiate a new Concordat for the whole of Germany.[201] This was successfully concluded and what Hitler did not obtain through the front door he managed to get through the back. The Roman Catholic hierarchy withdrew its traditional support for the

Centre party, at a time when any such support was pointless anyway.[202] But the unreserved adulation which Hitler received from the Protestant Youth community was not shown by the majority of the Catholics. Their youth movement totalling 1.5 million members felt the threat of the Hitler Youth, but as a result of the Concordat they felt that they had been given a new lease of life, which their bishops defended with vigilance.[203] Hitler for his part had achieved the elimination of the Catholic Church as an effective force in Germany's political life.

However, Roman Catholics and National Socialists – and it must not be forgotten that many an NSDAP member was also a practising Catholic – shared a good deal besides opposition to Versailles and a belief in *Grossdeutschland*. Both felt revulsion against the divisions of the 'party-state' of Weimar,[204] both rejected the principles of liberalism and believed in an 'organically developed' German nation state based on the principle of the corporate state.[205]

The *Reichs* Concordat concluded between the Vatican and the German Reich on 20 July 1933 gave the Catholic Youth movements a little more breathing space.[206] But one of its provisions left a loophole which the NSDAP was quick to exploit. Article 31 stated that those Catholic organizations and associations whose purpose was exclusively religious and cultural would enjoy the full protection of their establishments and activities.[207] But this was followed by a limiting clause stating that the determination of which organizations and associations were affected by this article would be subject to bilateral agreement between the government of the *Reich* and the Roman Catholic Episcopacy.[208]

Years of negotiations ensued between party and Hitler Youth leaders on the one hand and Catholic bishops on the other precisely to determine this, during which each negotiating party accused the other of trying to break the Concordat.[209] Of course, it is blatantly obvious that the National Socialist state, determined to be the sole educator of its youth, was bent upon breaking the Concordat before it was even signed. The defensive position of the Roman Catholic Church was stronger only because it was, after all, a universal organization with a strongly hierarchical structure which did not allow dissenting opinions within its ranks to affect its attitude towards the world without.

Cardinal Bertram, the Bishop of Breslau, first asked the question publicly, 'Which functions could the Catholic Church and its youth organizations hand over to the National Socialist state?' His conclusion was essentially negative: hiking, sports, and similar activities as modern means of education were, he argued, as important for practical Christianity as were the rosary and other purely religious exercises. Conflict was thus inevitable.[210]

The anti-clerical wing of the NSDAP represented by Alfred Rosenberg,

Julius Streicher, and numerous *Gauleiters* like Adolf Wagner of Upper Bavaria, looked on Christianity in general and Roman Catholicism in particular as another form of the Judaic conspiracy against the German *Volk*, whose most dangerous executive organ was the Jesuit order.[211] On a purely legal level the fight was conducted by the NSDAP on the basis of pretexts. Catholic journals were compelled to cease publication because they had allegedly printed subversive articles.[212] Youth organizations were closed down because of infringement of the currency laws. Public rallies of the Catholic Youth were forbidden, and when a member of the Hitler Youth committed suicide a press campaign was mounted arguing that he had been driven to take this drastic step by a Catholic conspiracy.[213] Like many of the Protestant youth leaders, some of the Catholics too were at first under the illusion that the persecution was simply the result of a serious misunderstanding which could be cleared up by co-operation with the Hitler Youth. But they were never meant to be given a chance and they certainly had none. No agreement such as that between the Hitler Youth and the Protestant Youth came about, while the law enacted in 1936 making service in the Hitler Youth compulsory also effectively put an end to the organized Catholic Youth.

The Röhm purge was not without repercussions on the Hitler Youth. The *Unterbannführer* Ernst Lämmermann was executed for reasons no longer ascertainable. For years afterwards there was conducted an extensive correspondence with the Ministry of Justice to have him posthumously rehabilitated. But on the whole these repercussions were more favourable for the Hitler Youth.[214] For instance, having already gained its autonomy from the SA, 9 November 1934 was the first occasion when none of the annual transfers from Hitler Youth to the storm troopers took place.[215] Instead they became members of the NSDAP. On 29 March 1935 this change of procedure and the autonomy of the Hitler Youth were legally registered by an executive order which listed the Hitler Youth next to the SA and the SS and other organizations as a subordinate branch of the NSDAP.[216]

The year 1934 saw also the introduction into the Hitler Youth of a body exercising policing functions – the *HJ-Streifendienst* – comparable in its context perhaps to the military police. Its function was to see that law and order were upheld within the ranks and to combat any illegal opposition. Actually in legal terms the *Streifendienst* was not to possess the function of any type of police, but in practice policing powers were assumed.[217] In its operations the *Streifendienst* closely co-operated with the SS and the Gestapo, a relationship formalized four years later between Himmler and Schirach in an agreement which described the functions of the *Streifendienst* and its responsibilities within the Hitler Youth as being identical with those which the SS carried for the whole of the *Reich*.[218] The *Streifendienst* was also to serve as a special reservoir for SS recruits, the *SS-Totenkopfverbände* (the SS units responsible for the guarding of the concentration camps), and the *Junkerschulen*, the SS officer schools.[219] The highly confidential *Informations Dienst*, a news bulletin distributed among the upper ranks of the Hitler Youth during the pre-war years, shows not merely that the *Streifendienst* was a highly effective organization in its detection of opposition within the Hitler Youth, but also that in spite of suppression and *Gleichschaltung*, opposition in the Hitler Youth to official policy occurred time and again.[220]

While 1935 had been the year dedicated to physical training, the year 1936 was the 'Year of the German *Jungvolk*', dedicated to those between ten and fourteen years of age.[221] A vast campaign was initiated to recruit as many boys as possible. The aim was that the entire age group born in 1926, boys as well as girls, should 'volunteer' to join the *Jungvolk* and the *Jungmädel* by 20 April as a birthday present for Hitler's 47th birthday.[222] In order to carry out the recruitment drive as successfully as possible, the Hitler Youth adapted itself to the NSDAP district division (*Ortsgruppe*) which came after the cell and block division. Within one such district approximately 150 ten to fourteen-year-old boys lived, organized into a *Fähnlein*, or of company strength. Girls were organized according to the same pattern. These units within their district carried out extensive recruitment campaigns, marches, evenings of choir singing, and parents' evenings. Teachers in primary and secondary schools, who by that time in order to stay in their positions had been compelled to join if not the party then at least the NS Teacher's League, were persuaded to exert pressure on their pupils to join the *Jungvolk*. The recruitment drive reached its highest pitch during the last four weeks before Hitler's birthday.[223]

The place for the official celebration was the Marienburg, the ancient castle of the Teutonic order, which was chosen as the political example worth the emulation of every Hitler Youth.[224] There in the Gothic main hall among the sombre light of candles and torchlights, new members of the *Jungvolk* swore the oath that was to be repeated every 20 April, including that of 1945:

> 'I promise
> In the Hitler Youth
> To do my duty
> At all times
> In love and faithfulness
> To help the Führer
> So help me God.'[225]

And then followed fifes, drums, and fanfares and '*Vorwärts, vorwärts schmettern die hellen Fanfaren* . . . ('Forward, forward, call the fanfares.')

From then on boys and girls were on probation for between two to six months. This period was concluded by a special test, combining sport, close combat, and questions of an 'ideological' nature (mainly on the history of the NSDAP), culminating in a *Mutprobe*, a courage test which could take the form of having to jump in full battle-dress and boots from the window of the first floor of a block of flats. After passing the test, the *Jungvolk* member was entitled to wear the scout knife, a knife shaped similarly to the bayonet of the German army, the shoulder strap, and the *Jungvolk* insignias on the brown shirt.[226] Every *Ortsgruppe*, every district had now one *Fähnlein* of each HJ, *Jungvolk*, BDM and *Jungmädel*. The ultimate conclusion of the development came less than six months later on 1 December 1936 with the promulgation of the 'Law concerning the Hitler Youth'.[227] According to this law the entire 'physical, spiritual and ethical' education of the German youth was, next to the influences of school and home, the concern of the Hitler Youth.[228] Membership of the Hitler Youth now became compulsory from the age of ten onwards, and the task of 'educating the entire German youth in the Hitler Youth' was given to the *Reichsjugendführer* of the NSDAP, Baldur von Schirach. His position, from being that of a party official, was now defined as a governmental one, with its centre in Berlin and responsible directly to the *Führer*. With parental and school education, the Hitler Youth had now become the third important legal force shaping and moulding the character of Germany's youth.

If this was Schirach's personal success, and perhaps also that of some of his 'old fighters', the years up to the outbreak of the Second World War were for the Hitler Youth as a whole something of an anti-climax. The decade between 1925 and 1935 had been years of struggle and immense personal sacrifice for most Hitler Youth members who believed in dedicating their whole beings to a task that to them seemed worthwhile achieving. Now the Hitler Youth for the majority of members became institutionalized, with routine duties and a repetitiveness which continued for no other reason than that of compulsion. Artificial activity for activity's sake often led in very unsavoury directions.

The participation of the HJ in anti-Semitic outrages, especially in the anti-Semitic pogrom of 8 November 1938, in various German regions was not centrally directed but either instigated by the local SA leadership or, as in Berlin, purely voluntary.[229] When news of the HJ activities reached the *Reichsjugendführung* Schirach immediately convened a meeting of all *Obergebiets* and *Gebiets* leaders at which he explicitly condemned the 'criminal actions' and expressly forbade any Hitler Youth participation in them.[230]

The *Anschluss* of Austria and the annexation of the Sudetenland brought a new wave of membership into the Hitler Youth which by the end

The Regional Organisation of
the Hitler Youth on
1 January 1939

of 1938 reached a total figure of 8,700,000 youngsters, about half of them girls.[231] This year also marked an increased emphasis upon para-military training. Already in 1935 *Obergebietsführer* Stellrecht had remarked 'that it was a remarkable attitude for a nation to spend, out of a number of years, hours in perfecting handwriting and spelling, when not a single hour is available for shooting'.[232] According to his view it was the Hitler Youth's task to ensure that the rifle would rest as competently in the hand of the German youth as did the pen.[233] By 1937 an HJ rifle school existed and in 1938 1.5 million Hitler Youths were trained in rifle shooting. From early 1939 onwards the OKW, the High Command of the Armed Forces, involved itself closer with the *Reichsjugendführung*, supervising both the Hitler Youth shooting and the field exercises.[234]

A new government decree issued on 25 March 1939 concerning the Hitler Youth recapitulated once again the contents of the law promulgated on 1 December 1936,[235] but apart from the principles contained in the latter, the new decree contained further detailed provisions of how the law was to be applied.[236] In particular it decreed that all sixteen- to eighteen-year-old Hitler Youths were to perform annual public services; boys were particularly directed to agriculture at harvest time and girls to families where there were several children. For this reason it came to be called the *Jugend-Dienst-Gesetz*, the Youth Service Law. Actually the practice had existed since 1933 but it lacked a legal basis. From 1939 onwards 'youth service' was as compulsory as that in the labour service and the army.[237] The Hitler Youth had completed the Trinity – *Hitlerjugend* – *Reichsarbeitsdienst* – *Wehrmacht* – which would process every young German from his tenth birthday onwards.

VI Ideology

'Racial teaching is the point of departure of all National Socialist teaching; from it the consequences of National Socialist youth education derive. Corresponding with the will of the *Führer* the strengthening and toughening of one's physical capacity is the first as well as the highest duty of the young generation. In order to acquire physical strength, continuous struggle is required, a struggle which alone will produce those racially fittest to survive. Self-confidence obtained through struggle and victory must be acquired by every member of the *Germanic* racial community from the earliest days of his childhood. His entire education must be planned with the aim of giving him the conviction of superiority over others. The young must accustom themselves at an early stage to acknowledge the superiority of the stronger and to subordinate themselves to him.'[1]

This dubious intellectual precipitate, contained in a PhD thesis of 1940, regurgitated in slightly different words what Hitler had already said about the educational aims of National Socialism, namely of infusing youth with his 'ideology', the fusion of a vulgar version of Social Darwinism with racialism. Although this excerpt reflects adequately what in some quarters of the Hitler Youth and in much of the NSDAP leadership was described as 'ideology', it nevertheless raises the question as to what extent it was actually possible within the space of twelve years (only seven of which fully embraced the entire young German population within the ranks of the Hitler Youth) for this 'ideology' to penetrate the minds of all the members.

Given the circumstance that as an ideology National Socialism as propounded by Hitler was a hotch-potch in no way comparable with the systematic theoretical structure of Marxist-Leninism, one is bound to look for elements other than those refashioned by Hitler which would be particularly attractive to a substantial section of the young generation. From Hitler's as well as Himmler's point of view the one 'ideological tenet' in which National Socialism was consistent from the moment of its inception to that of its demise was its anti-Semitism. However, this was not a tenet around which it would have been possible to rally a mass party, only at most a lunatic fringe movement. Consequently, to popularize anti-Semitism as a political cause it had to be identified with the political and economic ills of the time – in itself nothing highly original, the precedents for this procedure reaching far back into the Middle Ages and beyond.[2] The prominence of some Jewish intellectuals in the Bolshevik revolution and subsequently in Soviet Russia, or in the Communist or Socialist parties especially of Germany, lent itself to the creation of a conspiracy theory whereby 'international Jewry' was about to enslave the German people through Soviet tyranny. But even more effective at this time of economic depression, only six years after the end of the inflation which had practically brought the German middle classes near to a state of proletarization, was the appeal to an economically motivated anti-Semitism, which was inevitably bound to create a greater response than its abstract racial formulation. The 'money power of the banks', the impact of industrialization favouring big business and pushing the artisan and the small trader against the wall, the depersonalization of an industrial society – all that could be blamed on 'international financiers': and the fact that some of them were indeed Jews meant that to minds incapable of understanding and accounting for the complexity of socio-economic changes and the consequences involved in them an 'international Jewish conspiracy' provided a plausible enough explanation.[3] Anti-Semitism then, based on economic grievances rather than racial grounds, was one aspect of Hitler's platform to which the masses responded. But the 'masses' is a rather ambiguous term; it may, with some caution, perhaps be used to describe that section of the German electorate that supported Hitler at the polls. But by definition this would exclude the largest part, who in Hitler's words were 'the guarantors of Germany's future', the Hitler Youth.

After all, the routinized state youth of 1936 to 1945 was not the same as the Hitler Youth before 1933. Its *de jure* existence as a subordinate organ of the NSDAP and for a time of the SA must not obscure the fact that from its inception to Hitler's accession to power it led *de facto* a life of considerable independence and that there was room therefore to develop its own ideological trend, a trend which could borrow freely from intellectual fountains that reached deeply into the sub-soil not solely of the German Youth Movement but also of the German political tradition, refashioned by the impact of defeat in the First World War and the political and economic instability of the Weimar Republic.

Directly from the tradition of the German Youth Movement came the fervently held belief in a philosophy of life, ambiguous and highly emotional, life dynamic and primitive whose only guardian was youth, which alone could work towards constructive ends, unadulterated by the degenerating forces of what was taken to be bourgeois decadence.[4] Much has been written to illustrate and prove that the father of this philosophy was Friedrich Nietzsche, a thesis tenable only if one's sources are those of the distortions of Nietzsche's sister and her husband.[5] On the contrary the source of this philosophy was the German Romantic movement, with its utter conviction in the creative vitality of the original and primitive, its reaction against the artificialities of the Rococo, of the facile Enlightenment and of questionable rationalism, which found its *ultima ratio* on the scaffold, and in the enslavement of many of the nations of Europe.[6] As we have seen, the Romantic search for the creative forces in life had already led to the rejection of the rational model of the state and instead expressed its preference for the 'organically' grown unit since it was in itself a product of natural life forces. The 'national community' rather than the artificial 'state', the *Volk* rather than *der Staat*, was the aim, for the *Volk* is the womb which is the bearer of the great achievements of the intellect, of the arts, of religion.[7]

The Youth Movement had followed these ideas as faithfully as it could. But by the turn of the 20th century the concept of the *Volk* was no longer what it had been to Herder. The historians of Bismarckian and Wilhelmine Germany and the growing influence of Social Darwinian conceptions as expounded in Germany by Gumplowiez, Schemann, Woltmann, and others had transformed Herder's idea into something which consciously and subconsciously identified the *Volk* with race, and explicitly defined qualitative differences between the races.[8] In Heinrich von Treitschke's hands history was misused in the sense that it was presumed to be an empirical science which explained to the German people not only the development which had at last led to the accomplishment of national unity, but which also contained all the lessons for the future, a lesson whose quintessence Treitschke summarized by saying that the main striving of the state is 'in the first place power, in the second place power, and in the third place, again, power'.[9]

To the majority of German youths after 1918 the events that led to the defeat and the collapse of the Second *Reich* seemed to bear out lessons such as these. And among those who had participated in the mass slaughter on the battlefields of the West, the lesson was deduced 'First the new man, then the new state', a lesson which soon became a slogan which with minor variations could be heard being chanted by all youth movements from the Left to the Right.[10] But particularly among the Right the cultural pessimism of pre-war vintage as expressed by Lagarde and Langbehn was further deepened into a specifically anti-Western attitude, one directed against Western civilization, against the yoke of an incompetent democracy, against the parliamentarianism of the 'multiparty state.' In place of the affirmation of a pluralist society came the renewed emphasis on organic unity. And, it was believed, the only man-made institution which appeared to reflect this natural unity was the army. Hence on the Right, and not only among National Socialists, there was an emphasis on the need to subordinate oneself within the ranks of the national community, and on the glorification of the leadership principle – a principle which was believed to have been modified in the war-time 'storms of steel' where the true leader (as opposed to one produced by a strictly hierarchic society) had emerged and was accepted as leader because of the example he had provided to others. The concept of 'the soldier' became the yardstick of German post-war youth movements, as did military forms of organization.[12] The literature of the period from Ernst Jünger to Franz Schauwecker and Hans Zöberlein were the fountains from which most German youths satisfied their spiritual needs – but not the only ones.[13] After all, the pre-war youth movements had already indulged in their cult of the ancient Germanic past. Now attention was concentrated on examples of groups, be they Ostrogoths at Mount Vesuvius or *Landsknechte* at Pavia, who fought to the last and died for a lost cause, a mental attitude summarized soon after in the motto *'Meine Ehre heisst Treue'* ('My honour is loyalty'). Faithfulness and loyalty irrespective of the consequences were an article of faith shared among wide sections of Germany's youth. The saga of Nibelungen, Hagen's example in his fight against the scheming Krimhild who was set upon avenging the death of her husband Siegfried, is invoked time and again in the literature and the youth songs of the period glorifying sacrifice:

> *Lasst den verlor'nen Haufen*
> *Vorwärts zum Sturme laufen*
> *Falle wer fallen mag . . .*

> (Let the lost horde
> Storm ahead in the assault
> Let fall who falls . . .)

It would be a naïve interpretation to argue that the German youth fell under the spell of political radicalism because of the demagogic skill of the agitators of the radical parties. The situation is aptly summarized by the American scholar John H. E. Fried, who points out that, apart from the fact that these sentiments were part and parcel of the youth organizations of the not-so-radical parties as well:

'There was a fateful overflow of military concepts, in fact of a war mentality, into civilian life. In war there can be little tolerance for the enemy, but in peace-time a normal society does not look on nonconformists as outlaws. Fascism did this characteristically. With people who have different opinions one can shake hands, but not if they are stamped as enemies and traitors. Disapproval was sharpened into ostracism. . . . There was a constant trend away from diversity, towards an ever sharpening polarisation into either ally or enemy.'[14]

Perhaps all that needs to be added is that this lack of tolerance characterized not solely the parties of the Right, the NSDAP especially, but also those of the extreme Left. Where the one used the term *Landesverräter* (traitors of one's country) the other used that of *Klassenverräter* (traitors of one's class). Moreover, it must be constantly borne in mind that the Weimar Republic was never throughout its existence a normal society in 'peacetime' but an abnormal one in a continuous state of civil war, never allowing normal attitudes to develop and prevail among its youth. 'War is the axis around which our life rotates.'[15] This observation by Ernst Jünger does not solely apply to the generation that had fought in the war, but also to those whose thought and actions were influenced by it and its aftermath. Or as Schirach was to put it, 'We want to proclaim the purpose of our existence: the war has spared us for war.'[16]

One influence that affected the Hitler Youth profoundly was socialism, or at least what it took to be the meaning of socialism, a kind of comradely socialism of the trenches, which, however, as indicated, had its antecedents in the decades before the war but reached the heights of popularity during the Weimar Republic among the parties and youth organizations of the extreme Right. To the early Hitler Youth it was an article of faith.[17] This 'socialism', as we have seen, was one of the fundamental factors which divided the Hitler Youth, especially during Gruber's leadership, from the élitist middle-class youth leagues.[18] It took its National Socialism very seriously and even the name 'Hitler Youth, League of the German Workers' Youth' is indicative of its attitude, which rejected the class-divisions and the class-consciousness of the Weimar Republic. That aspect of its 'socialism' was present in the Hitler Youth throughout its history, which ranged from the negation of the class conflict to the attempt to build bridges between the classes.[19]

Of course, at no time was the concept of the 'class conflict' subjected to theoretical analysis or opened up for general discussion; instead it was dismissed as one of the excesses of a degenerate liberal democracy. The determining factor of the structure of German society was to be the 'leadership principle'; workers and employers marched behind the same flag in the same uniform with the same aim: the common good of the national community. And within the ranks of the Hitler Youth genuine and successful attempts were made to break down social barriers; the entire educational system was geared to further a particular brand of egalitarianism, in which wealth did not predetermine the availability of equal opportunities.[20] Schools designed to produce an élite did exist, but these were not private schools but National Socialist state schools in which the cost was relatively low, and free for those whose parents could not afford the fee. Figures which indicate the continued predominance at this educational level of the middle classes prove essentially very little, except that working-class and peasant participation was considerably greater than in the *Kadetten-Vorschulen und Hauptanstalten* – the Imperial Cadet Schools before the Great War – let alone the private boarding school, like Salem. In addition, the aim of bringing about equal opportunities for all young members of the German national community was not something that could ever have been achieved in a mere twelve years. Naturally, even at the lowest level of a Hitler Youth unit, problems and resistance were encountered at times, for instance when boys from an upper-middle-class district in Munich formed their own little clique within a Hitler Youth unit, endeavouring to keep aloof from those of their comrades who lived in a working-class district or who did not attend the grammar school. When the *Cliquenwirtschaft*, or the clique system, in this particular Hitler Youth unit became generally known, the intervention of local Hitler Youth leadership was as drastic as it was effective. The middle-class boys concerned were 'sent to Coventry' and for three months had to devote their entire spare time, weekends included, to carrying out chores for working-class families where the father was a soldier. After three months the cure had proved its value and within the unit concerned everything returned to normal as though nothing had happened.[21] Also the events of the war, such as the Allied bombing offensive, forced individuals together, with the realization of the practical need of *Kameradschaft*, the unhesitating reliability upon one another.

In the early years of the Hitler Youth frequent attempts were made to expound the specifically National Socialist meaning of 'socialism', especially since this was the point on which NSDAP and Hitler Youth were most frequently challenged.[22] But when pinned down in cold print all that was left was a collection of anti-bourgeois sentiments and the assertion of a proletarian character combined with the aim of creating a German national community. With the invocation of a proletarian nationalism the Hitler Youth tried to drive home its own social revolutionary message and win converts among working-class youths. But even its slogans were not particularly original; 'through Socialism to the Nation' could be found among the early *Freikorps*[23]; 'the common good before individual profit' is the adaptation of a German saying with an ancestry of centuries; and 'Freedom and Bread' could be heard from the columns of demonstrating Socialists in Bismarck's Germany. However, in spite of the lack of originality in the slogans, they indicate at least the basic attitude of the Hitler Youth before 1933.

Against the background of growing unemployment and social unrest, the Hitler Youth's first leader Kurt Gruber tried to articulate the anti-capitalist and socialist sentiment of his organization when he said: 'The Hitler Youth is the new Youth movement of social revolutionary people of a *German kind* [author's italics] . . . who are chained to the destiny of the nation . . . in order to emancipate the state and the economy from the shackles of capitalist, anti-national powers. Thereafter the new *Volksstaat* of Adolf Hitler will follow.'[24]

In the Hitler Youth agitation against the Versailles treaty, its economic provisions were particularly subjected to the venom of Hitler Youth propaganda as expressed in the demonstration against the Young Plan, 'this devious scheme under the guise of which the Jewish Capitalist World conspiracy endeavours to reduce our German people to a state of servitude for generations and thus sap the life-blood of the German national community until it has ceased to exist.'[25]

In this agitation the Hitler Youth entered a short-lived alliance with other right-wing youth movements, but Hugenberg the owner of a vast press and film empire and since 1928 the chairman of the right-wing German National Peoples' Party (DNVP), was said to have expressed his concern over the style of Hitler Youth agitation, particularly its proletarian tone, as evinced in this HJ appeal: 'Young Workers. Cast off the shackles of international world capitalism. Rise up against the dictate of slavery from Dawes to Young. Must we perish as the paid slaves of a capitalist world clique? Working Germany. Young manual and intellectual workers of Germany awake, shake off your chains.'[26]

The geographic location of the Hitler Youth headquarters up to 1931 in Plauen also ensured the continuance of social revolutionary attitudes. The contrast between Munich and Plauen is as significant as it is important. In Munich the experience of revolution and a Soviet republic had ensured the dominance of a frame of mind that considered terms such as socialism and revolution to be almost a provocation to violence. The financial backing for the NSDAP there was not so much the voluntary pennies given by the workers of Krauss-Maffei or Rodenstock but the contributions of wealthy Munich families such as the Bruckmanns and the Hanfstängls whose aim was hardly a national 'socialist' revolution but the consolidation of the social status quo of the Munich burghers which had been so severely shaken by revolution, inflation, and then depression.[27] The political climate in Munich, whether represented by the NSDAP, by the Wittelsbach monarchists, or even by the Bavarian separatists, was conservative and not revolutionary. If revolution was at all the aim there, it was the revolution of the *Spiessbürger*, a yearning to return to the alleged good old days of pre-1914 vintage, though preferably under a house of Wittelsbach rather than one of Hohenzollern.[28]

Plauen, by contrast, was part of what at the time was described as 'red

Saxony', in which Communist revolutionary activity had been one of the main features of political life between 1919 and 1924, an area which had produced its own kind of Communist Robin Hood in the person of Max Hölz, whose fame became legendary and whose exploits elicited grudging admiration even from those who opposed him.[29] In a region such as this Hitler Youth existence was not the comfortable pseudo-revolutionary one in the midst of the Munich bourgeoisie, but one cheek-by-jowl with the working class from which the majority of the Plauen members originated in the first place. The revolutionary ethos, though vague and ill-defined, had a more natural home there than in Munich, where at the NSDAP headquarters the *revolutionären Machenschschaften*, the revolutionary goings-on elsewhere, caused more than one eyebrow to be raised. The Plauen situation is equally applicable to other cities and areas with highly-developed industries like Berlin, Hamburg, and Bremen, the Ruhr, and the Rhineland.

Whether this makes the Hitler Youth or any large part of it 'socialist' is doubtful, though it is claimed that relative to the meaning and the interpretation of 'socialism' within the rest of the organizations of the NSDAP, its 'socialism' was certainly more pronounced than, say, among the storm troopers.[30] This did not change immediately after the departure of Gruber and the ascent of Schirach who, aware of contrast in backgrounds between himself and some of his immediate subordinates, tried at first to adopt social revolutionary aims and slogans which were more radical than those of his predecessor. But his conviction that in order to succeed he would have to draw the nationalist youth leagues into the Hitler Youth fold soon caused him to abandon this masquerade. Instead, whenever the question of the definition of socialism had to be faced, it was answered with reference to Oswald Spengler's *Preussentum und Sozialismus* in which Spengler argues:

'The essence of socialism is not the domination of life by the contrasts of rich and poor, but by effort and ability. This is *our* liberty, the liberty from the economic despotism of the individual.

'What I hope is that no one remains below who by his abilities has been born to give orders, and that nobody issues orders who has not a natural gift to do so. Socialism signifies being able to achieve something, not merely wanting something. Not the degree of the intentions is decisive, but the quality of the achievements. I appeal to the youth. I appeal to all who have marrow in their bones and blood in their veins. Educate yourselves. Become men. We do not need ideologues any more, no idle talk about *Bildung* and world citizenship and the spiritual mission of the Germans. What we need is hardness, we need a brave scepticism, we need a class of Socialist rulers. And again: Socialism means power, power, and forever again power. Plans and introspection are nothing without power. The path to power is mapped out before us: the most valuable part of the German workers in conjunction with the best bearers of the traditions of the old Prussian state both decided on the foundation of a strictly Socialist state, and to a *democratization* in the *Prussian* sense, both welded together by the consciousness of the unity of a sense of duty, through the awareness of a great task, through the will to obey in order to rule, to die in order to conquer, through strength to make immense sacrifices in order to accomplish that for which we are born, *for what we are*, what without us would not exist.

'*We* are Socialists. *We do not want to have been it in vain.*'[31]

Whenever pushed into a tight corner by its opponents about its theoretical socialism the Hitler Youth took refuge in the slogan of *Sozialismus der Tat*, the socialism of action, which was often enough summarized in the Prussian motto of *suum cuique*, to each his own, rather than the utopian 'everything to everybody'. This socialism of action was exemplified by Hitler Youth pressure for legislation beneficial to youth as well by its own actions, such as its organization during the disastrous winter of 1930–31 of free meals for starving children in various parts of Germany and in some cases even of free holidays in the Bavarian Alps. The scheme, however, was suppressed by the government since it was feared that it would help to swell the ranks of the Hitler Youth.

Schirach often argued that the Hitler Youth represented the microcosm of a successful national community:

'All work serves the one great ideal, before which differences of occupation, of background and of possessions disappear. One stands next to one another in this youth, all with equal rights and equal duties. There is no special Hitler Youth for the poor or the rich, no Hitler Youth for the grammar-school pupil or girl, or for the young worker. There is also no special Catholic or Protestant Hitler Youth. Everyone who is of German blood belongs to our group. Below the flag of youth, everyone is the same. . . .'[32] The son of the millionaire does not dress differently from the son of the unemployed worker. Both wear the garb of the community of comrades: the brown shirt of the Hitler Youth. The uniform of the Hitler Youth is the expression of an attitude that does not ask after class or occupation, but only after duty and achievement. . . .'[33] The symbol of the classless community of our youth is the flag of the Hitler Youth. In it has been fashioned the socialist will of the new generation.'[34]

If Schirach's professions of socialism by background and aspirations must be taken with more than a pinch of salt, the credentials of his successor Arthur Axmann, of working-class origin and for a time one of the spokesmen of the social revolutionary wing of the Hitler Youth, who between 1933 and 1940 was head of the Social Affairs Office of the *Reichsjugendführung*, were more impressive, at least before 1933 and during the early years of Hitler's rule. But when in the course of the war, after he had become *Reichsjugendführer*, Schirach developed a luxurious style of life, he lost the respect of many who had admired him.[35] Nevertheless Schirach's professions were believed and followed by many. One BDM leader writes:

'Our camp community was a reduced model of that which I imagined our national community to be. It was a completely successful model. Never before or since have I had the experience of such a good community, even in cases in which its composition was more homogeneous. Among us were peasant girls, students, workers, shop assistants, hairdressers, pupils, clerks, and so forth. The camp was led by an East Prussian farmer's daughter who had never crossed the frontiers of her own home district. Although she could never pronounce a foreign word properly, no one would have thought of ridiculing her for that. She managed us in such a way that after we had recognized one another's strengths and weaknesses, she led us to accept one another as we each were, with everyone endeavouring to be helpful and reliable.

'The fact that I had experienced this model of a national community intensely created in me an optimism to which I held on stubbornly until 1945. Supported by this experience I believed in the face of all evidence pointing to the contrary that this model could be extended infinitely. If not in the next, then in future generations.'[36]

Certainly in its pragmatic down-to-earth approach the 'socialism' of the Hitler Youth differed rather radically from the airy romanticism of the other nationalist youth movements. Before 1933 it advocated the enactment of a *Reich* Youth Law which would provide effective social and economic protection and secure equality in economic and social matters, including the prohibition of child labour, medical supervision for young workers under the age of twenty, a forty-hour week, as well as three weeks' paid holiday. The abuse of apprentice labour was pilloried, and the party demanded that youth should not be employed in dangerous jobs.[37] These and many other points were actually enacted in the *Jugendschutzgesetz*, the Youth Protection Law, of 30 April 1939.[38]

However, pragmatism cannot hide the absence of a clearly defined 'socialist ideology'. Whether this is an asset or a liability is an open question. The Hitler Youth borrowed ideas from different sources without shaping them to fit into a coherent structure of thought. It failed to produce a synthesis and instead left the 'socialist' components floating in an ideological vacuum. Hence the question of how and what to provide for 'ideological training' was and always remained a problem. It was as unsystematic as was its 'socialism', exhausting itself by preaching a nationalist and racist gospel. From 1931 onwards special educational letters, *Schulungsbriefe*, were issued monthly to Hitler Youth leaders with detailed instructions on how to run meetings of individual Hitler Youth units and advise on the content of these meetings (which every *Jungzug* or *Schar* held once a week). Hitler Youth calendars made specific reference to days of national importance each week, which together with whatever arose from current affairs were to be central topics around which instruction and discussion should revolve.[39] The content of a *Heimabend*, the 'evenings at home' as these meetings were called, actually mattered very little before 1933. This was because the active political deployment of the Hitler Youth in the political campaigns of the last few years of the Weimar Republic left very little time for other than purely practical matters. But soon after Hitler's establishment in power the *Heimabend* could be rather a bore. As one BDM veteran wrote:

'The *Heimabende*, for which we met in a dark and dirty cellar, were marked by a fatal lack of content. The time was spent on collecting fees, on checking uncountable lists and learning off by heart the words of songs whose poverty of content could not be missed even with the best of effort. Discussion of political texts, as for instance from *Mein Kampf*, quickly ended in general silence.'[40]

This experience was fairly general and the practice soon developed of unit leaders at *Heimabend* making due reference to whatever occasion was to be remembered and then either reading aloud war or adventure stories or taking the boys or girls out for some square-bashing, followed by a disciplined march through the district where the repertoire of army and Hitler Youth songs was shouted out. The meeting was concluded either with a field game in the streets or in a park, or simply by raiding a neighbouring Hitler Youth unit with which one had a 'feud'.[41] In place of 'ideology' emerged physical activity which unintentionally had to make good the lack of intellectual content manifest in the National Socialist movement. In cases where ideological instruction was rendered it often bordered on the ridiculous. In Berlin, for instance, junior Hitler Youth were taken on a conducted tour of the 'Free Mason Museum':

'In a glass showcase we saw a little bottle containing a brownish liquid and next to it an object which reminded me of a knitting needle. With that needle, the Museum guide explained to us, Goethe, a well-known Free Mason, had murdered poor Schiller. Naturally the international clique of the Free Masons had taken care that to this day the crime was not known to the general public. Also the party leadership did not desire any public discussion on this topic; only a highly select group of reliable people was to be given insight into this sad and shameful secret. At our next meeting someone brought a book entitled "The Chained Goethe". On its dustcover was one of the later Goethe portraits ... to which a clumsy montage had added arms and hands securely bound together by chains. From this book readings were taken and so far as I remember the text contained the confirmation of the mad thesis about the murder of Schiller by Goethe. To the same meeting I had brought with me the correspondence between Schiller and Goethe with which I was fairly familiar. But my protests against the suspicion of Goethe were not listened to.'[42]

One aspect of Hitler Youth 'ideology', more thoroughgoing than its 'socialism' or the propagation of conspiracy theories, was its totalitarian claim. Hitler had expressed that much in *Mein Kampf*, and that which had been his aim in 1924 he considered already achieved in 1938:

'This youth does not learn anything else other than to think German, to act German and when those boys at the age of ten come into our organization and there for the first time begin to breathe fresh air, four years later they move from the *Jungvolk* to the *HJ*, and there we keep them for another four years and then we do not return them into the hands of our old originators of classes and estates but take them immediately into the party, into the Labour front, into the SA or the SS, into the NSKK and so forth. And if they have been there for two years or a year and a half and they still have not become thorough National Socialists, then we put them in the labour service and for six or seven months they work at square-bashing, all with one symbol, the German spade. And any class-consciousness and pride in one's social position still remaining after six or seven months will be taken over for further treatment by the *Wehrmacht* for two years, and when they come back after two, three, or four years then we take them immediately back into the SA, SS, and so on to prevent relapse and they will never be free for the rest of their lives. And if somebody comes to me and says, well but some will always remain (then I reply): National Socialism does not stand at the end of its days but only at the beginning.'[43]

The reality of this totalitarian claim was forever present, both in the Hitler Youth and in the entire educational system of the Third *Reich*. The actual attainment of the claim is a different matter, but there can be no doubt that it would have been achieved had Hitler's Germany lasted longer than it did. The *Reichsjugendführung* certainly made serious and persistent attempts in this direction, especially its department of ideological training which was 'the centre of the effort to mould the minds of German youth. Most of the youth publications are sent out from here in a continuous stream of literature, educational pamphlets, and the like. The radio department has been of increasing importance. From this office is directed the widespread network of youth broadcasts; most important of these is the weekly home evening broadcast at 8.00 p.m. each Wednesday, when for a whole hour the entire German youth assemble about the radio to hear a specially prepared educational programme. Subsidiary broadcasts are made and directed by the Hitler Youth during the week. The department for press and propaganda takes care not only of Hitler Youth publications but also keeps the daily and weekly newspapers informed of Hitler Youth activities. This work is, so far as possible, left to the initiative of the youth themselves.'[44]

This, of course, is an exaggeration, but nevertheless illustrates the claims of the Hitler Youth. For example the regular broadcasting time was soon cancelled with the outbreak of war, since it coincided with peak listening time. But if the ideological training was not all-pervasive, the consciousness of continuous activity was, with a deliberate attempt to eliminate as far as possible the notion of the existence of a private life. Young people, deliberately as well as by force of circumstance, were conditioned to be continuously on duty. Whatever they were doing was in relation to or directly on behalf of the National Socialist state. Childhood ceased at the age of ten when the young German entered the *Jungvolk* or the *Jungmädels*. From that moment the 'marshal's baton of youth is carried by every *Pimpf* in his knapsack. But it is not the leadership of youth alone that is open to him: the gates of the state too are wide open. He who from earliest youth onwards fulfils his duty to Adolf Hitler's Germany, who is diligent, faithful, and brave, need have no worries about the future.'[45]

'The Hitler Youth was a youth organization. Its members could be uniformed and regimented, but they did not cease for this reason to be youths and to behave like youths. The excess of the desire for activity and movement found a wide field of expression in the activities of the Hitler Youth which always ran at a top pitch. It was part of the method of National Socialist Youth leadership that everything took the form of competitions. One did not only compete in sports and in one's job for the best achievement. Each unit wanted the best meeting hall, the most interesting hiking book, the highest collection for the winter aid fund. . . .'[46] Though individual effort was rewarded, great care was taken that it was never obtained at the expense of the unit; in the main the competition was between groups and not between individuals, all the emphasis centring on obedience, duty to the group, and helping within the group.[47] *Fähnlein* competed against *Fähnlein* within the *Stamm*, *Jungzug* against *Jungzug* within the *Fähnlein*, and *Jungenschaft* against *Jungenschaft*.

'This continuous struggle for attainment even in peacetime brought elements of disquiet and forced activity into the life of the groups. It did not simply absorb the youthful urge for activity but kindled it further at times when it would have made more sense and served a better purpose to create for the individual in the group and for the group as a whole opportunities for a process of inner maturing and development. . . .'[48] The leadership of a youth drilled for activity and effort slowly developed its own manager style. It was chased from one activity into the other and consequently chased its followers too in the same way. The young men and women of the *Reichsjugendführung* who triggered off this activity were subjected to the same restless dynamism. The wheel of unending activity continuously gained new force from its own movement and pulled every one with it who was within its reach.'[49]

The enthusiasm innate in most young people to put their life to a meaningful arid useful purpose was fully exploited and never more successfully so than in the early years of the Hitler Youth and in the later war years, when for essentially unpolitical reasons, and certainly not for those of National Socialist imperialism, it was willing to sacrifice more than just the largest part of its free time. Inevitably that policy and the enthusiasm with which it was received and carried out posed over the long term a serious threat to traditional social structures, such as the family, for example. The long term, though, was cut short in 1945 and consequently what might have become rather radicalized forms and expressions of the generation conflict never matured.

The one constant 'ideological element' of the Hitler Youth and Hitler Youth training was the blind belief in Adolf Hitler, which in Schirach's pronouncements often bordered on blasphemy, when Hitler was presented as the God of the Germans: 'We do not need intellectual leaders who create new ideas because the superimposing leader of all the desires of youth is Adolf Hitler'[50]; 'Your name, my *Führer*, is the happiness of youth, your name, my *Führer*, is for us everlasting life'[51]; 'This plebiscite [held on the occasion of the *Anschluss* of Austria in 1938] is for us not an election, for us it is a German prayer of thanksgiving and this prayer says: Yes, *mein Führer*',[52] 'He who serves Adolf Hitler, the *Führer*, serves Germany, and whoever serves Germany, serves God';[53] 'When we lead the youth to Germany, we lead it to God.'[54] – a somewhat macabre and unintended prophecy. 'Don't cry mother, I know I must die for Hitler' were the last words of the Hitler Youth Werner Gerhardt, when he was killed by political opponents in 1932.[55] Schirach accepted the responsibility for introducing and furthering this pseudo-religious adoration of Hitler at the Nuremberg Trials: 'I have educated this generation in the belief of and in faithfulness to Hitler. The youth movement which I built up carried his name.'[56]

Hitler's own attitude to his youthful followers changed considerably in the course of time. He had realized the importance of winning the youth over to his side from the very beginning. However, before 1933 other priorities by necessity led him to pay less attention to the Hitler Youth than after 1933. Much the same appears to apply to most of the leading functionaries of the Third *Reich* but Schirach himself in 1932 pointed to the existence of a 'clique alien to youth who do not understand our struggle and do not want to understand', within the NSDAP.[57] After 1936 the Hitler Youth became one of the organizations in which every other NSDAP formation or branch of the armed services showed a lively interest.

The adulation of Hitler combined with a fervently held belief in the creation of the *Volksgemeinschaft* devoid of social divisions but with emphasis on effort and attainment made up the basic creed of the Hitler Youth. The achievement of totalitarian claims had to be pursued and enforced, and this raises the fundamental question as to what extent National Socialist Germany was actually a fully totalitarian state, capable of enforcing its will and imposing its ideas upon every single member of the national community.

Hitler had promised to complete Bismarck's work, and indeed for a very short time he did. But for Hitler to successfully bring about a completely totalitarian state he would have had to utterly destroy the established traditional German social structure, to sever the traditional social ties of the German people, as the Bolsheviks had done in Russia after 1917. Instead, he posed as their stout defender (which brought him support from even the ultra-conservative camp) knowing that he needed the backing of the traditional powers to pursue his policy successfully, but at the same time planting the germinal cells for the fully totalitarian state of the future. For the time being, the old institutions co-existed with those of the party, but never without uneasiness which increased rapidly during the later years of the war. This uneasiness could certainly be observed in the relationship between Hitler Youth and parental home, for the Hitler Youth stood for a fundamentally different model of society from that of many of the parents of its members, whose values were still mainly those of an age gone by – that of Wilhelmine Germany in fact. Fortunately the reality of Hitler Youth life limped a considerable distance behind its 'ideals'. The shortage of well-trained youth leaders was never really overcome, nor the shortage of other educational facilities or means of ideological indoctrination and conformity.

Although during the war years Germany was becoming more and more 'totalitarian' in character, by embracing every single member of the state and forcing every citizen into the political process, the National Socialist government still allowed the existence of a wide sphere of 'political privacy'.[58] In other words, if one detested the methods of Hitler and his party but was not prepared actively to oppose him, it was still possible to opt out of politics altogether. For writers or journalists, for example, it was still possible to seek refuge in that quiescent state of mind which since the war has become known in Germany as 'inner emigration'.[59] They simply turned to fields other than politics and wrote under pseudonyms which were known, of course, to Goebbels' ministry but not to the general German public.

Inside Germany the totalitarianism of the National Socialist state never reached the point at which it managed to penetrate the innermost recesses of every individual's life, making every single action, private or public, subject to judgment according to the criteria of National Socialist ideology.[60] Quite apart from that, during the full twelve years of Hitler's rule, ideological coherence, which would have made it possible to establish clear and unequivocal ideological criteria of judgment, was never attained.

Any systematic study of the official publications for use of the Hitler Youth reveals how little space was given to actual direct political and ideological indoctrination. Most prominent in every one of them are reproductions of Hitler's utterances in stylized Gothic lettering, and for the rest one reads about Hitler Youth activities in various parts of the country.

Looking at the institutional position of the Hitler Youth within the NSDAP apparatus the impression gained is that it was compressed tightly into the party structure, which left little room for spontaneity and autonomous development. This would be true to say of the *Reichsjugendführung's* position vis-à-vis the NSDAP, but at a lower level where youth was in fact led by youth the picture was a different one. The average age of a *Bannführer* was twenty-four, an age drastically reduced after the outbreak of war. A *Gefolgschaftsführer* was rarely older than seventeen, a *Fähnleinsführer* in the *Jungvolk* between fourteen and fifteen. By 1945 a *Jungzugführer*, responsible for a unit ranging in numbers of between 30 and 50 boys, could even be eleven years old.[61] Consequently, it is true to say that never before or since in German history did youth occupy such positions of power – relative to their age, never did every action of theirs seem of almost national importance, as in Hitler's Germany. One inevitable by-product of this was an air of nonchalant arrogance with which many Hitler Youths tended to look down on the older generation – the generational problem was reversed. The continuous pressure for action, whether for propaganda marches, sports competititions, or Winter Aid collections, left very little room or time for thought, let alone for systematic ideological indoctrination. High-pressure activity was the substitute for ideology. This applies to an even greater degree to the war years, when from its outbreak HJ, *Jungvolk*, BDM, and *Jungmädels* became more and more involved at the home front, until finally many of them stood in the frontline themselves, already more familiar with all forms of tortuous death than with 'the facts of life'.

The image of millions of little Hitler Youths diligently and enthusiastically studying or learning by heart Hitler's *Mein Kampf* is one derived from fiction and not from reality. What was found to be too indigestible at SS-*Junkerschulen* was bound to be even more so among younger age groups. Such so-called ideological tenets as nationalism and the belief in the moral and physical superiority of one's own country and a latent and overt racialism among youngsters were not specifically National Socialist but could have been found in any moderate right-wing party before 1933.

What has often been called National Socialist ideological indoctrination of the youth seems to be a confusion of ideology with the 'party historical mythology' much cherished in so-called ideological indoctrination. It concentrated upon the glamorizing of every stage of Hitler's life, the *Blutzeugen der Bewegung*, the blood witnesses of the movement like the sixteen dead in the Munich putsch of 1923, and, of course, the martyrs Horst Wessel, who in 1930 had been murdered by a *Rotfront* department, and Herbert Norkus.[62] Given this limited range, the official Hitler Youth publications were rather dull, and by the rank and file were taken for what they were; clumsy propaganda.[63] The *Reichsjugendführung* had ventured into the film business as early as 1932 when the *Reichsjugendtag* at Potsdam was filmed,[64] but its subsequent endeavours in this field remained, with possibly one exception, as dull and as uninspired as its publications.[65] The only two Hitler Youth films with claims to distinction were not made by the Hitler Youth but by existing commercial or state film enterprises respectively. One was *Hitlerjunge Quex*, a film based on the fate of Herbert Norkus shown in November 1933; the other, first shown in May 1944, was *Junge Adler (Young Eagles)* concerning the rehabilitation of the delinquent son of a rich aircraft manufacturer through his work as a Hitler Youth labourer in his father's factory. However, the vast majority of films produced under the auspices of the *Reichsjugendführung* were renowned for their tedium, and Hitler Youth members had to be commanded to attend performances.[66]

Of course another indirect ideological influence was exerted through the 'co-ordinated' mass media such as the press, films, and theatres, especially the latter two, which after all mixed entertainment with indoctrination.

The absence of effective means of ideological indoctrination appears to have been a shortcoming of which the *Reichsjugendführung* was aware, for in 1943 it introduced a 'Hitler Youth Catechism'.[67] This publication was received with indifference. A check on supplies of the book in Hitler Youth headquarters in Berlin, Munich, Hamburg, Dresden, Essen, Düsseldorf, Breslau, and Königsberg showed that the stocks delivered had not even been collected.[68] Nor was it a compliment to its quality when a little later it turned up in bulk in the regular 'old paper' collections, that were conducted by the Hitler Youth.[69] And besides, by that time Hitler Youths frequently expressed their opinion that they were kept far too busy anyway to have any time for concentrated reading.[70]

Perhaps the major traditional institution which the NSDAP could not weaken was the Roman Catholic Church. The Concordat of 1933 seemed to have settled the relationship between the National Socialist government and the Church. But as already indicated the truce was short-lived, and virtually open warfare between church and the NSDAP broke out again soon afterwards. Officially Hitler chose to ignore the churches as long as they did not directly interfere with his actions. If they stepped on forbidden territory, the nature of his response depended upon circumstances. When, for example, during the first few years of the war the implementation of the euthanasia programme became public knowledge and Catholic and Protestant clergy spoke out openly against it, he agreed to have it stopped.[71] At a time of national crisis he could not afford to alienate the churches completely. But before the war and during a large part of it the *Gauleiters* of the NSDAP lived an almost autonomous existence. Hence the relationship between the NSDAP as well as the Hitler Youth and the churches depended very often on the attitude of the local *Gauleiter*. But even his power of action within his *Gau* had its limits. When in 1939 *Gauleiter* Wagner of Upper Bavaria ordered the removal of all crucifixes from school rooms, the public outcry of a traditionally Roman Catholic province was such that for reasons of expediency he had to be replaced by *Gauleiter* Giesler.[72]

In the years between 1933 and 1937 individual party leaders could assume a greater degree of militancy against the churches than at a later date. The Bishop of Munster, Count Galen, for instance, had a considerable record of denunciations against the Weimar Republic and shortly after Hitler had come to power he asked his congregation to co-operate with the new regime in order to restore Germany to her 'rightful position' among the nations. But he made a clear distinction between Hitler and the chief advocate of 'neo-heathendom', Alfred Rosenberg. When in 1935 the news came that Rosenberg was to address a public rally in Munster he immediately addressed a letter of protest to the *Gauleiter* of Westphalia stating categorically that 'the overwhelming Christian population of Westphalia would regard the appearance of Rosenberg only as an outright provocation, designed to pour contempt on their holiest and most cherished religious convictions'.[73]

Nevertheless Rosenberg did come on 7 July, and the local party administration turned the occasion into an ostentatious rally held in Munster's main square which also happened to contain the Bishop's residence. Count Galen was denounced as epitomizing the forces of reaction, and Frick, Minister of the Interior, whom Rosenberg, against the former's original inclinations, had persuaded to attend, made a speech on the separation of church and state. Rosenberg, in his speech, attacked the Bishop, asking him whether the NSDAP had not done more than any other political force to overcome the Bolshevik menace. He asserted that religious toleration was one of the basic constituents of government policy, illustrating this 'toleration' by the example of the bishop himself who had written letters defamatory of Rosenberg and could do so without the risk of imprisonment.[74]

The rally ended with Hitler Youth formations marching up in front of the bishop's residence and chanting personally insulting as well as anti-clerical slogans. Formations of Hitler Youths were used in similar demonstrations against the Bishop of Trier and the Archbishop of Paderborn; but in all three cases the Hitler Youths had been specially 'imported' from other German regions. Hitler Youth units were used for similar purposes in other parts of Germany also,[75] but whether these young boys were genuinely motivated by the new 'ideology' is doubtful. It seems more likely that the parades and marches gave vent to their excess energies, and that the idea of a free journey to a different part of Germany, a plentiful supply of food, and a few days off from either school or work appealed to them on a very basic level.

Occasionally attempts were made, especially among Hitler Youth leaders, to persuade them to leave the church. One German historian records his own experience as a Hitler Youth:

'Our headmaster was a National Socialist, an "old fighter", who soon after Hitler's seizure of power was given his chance. He was no one's favourite, nor was he hated. He was considered as somewhat thick-headed but well-meaning. He was one of the many who in those days made small careers for themselves. One day – I was a sixth-former – he stopped me and asked: "You are a Hitler Youth leader, how is it that you are still attending Catholic religious instruction?" I personally did not like attending religious instruction because I found it boring. But I was angry at being approached in this way and therefore replied: "Sir, it so happens that I am a Catholic and intend to remain one." He said: "You are right. One should always remain faithful to one's convictions." He was typical of the National Socialists of a bourgeois brand who wanted to dispel any suspicion of personal opportunism and who in the continued existence of the churches found their moral alibi.'[76]

Schirach clearly disassociated himself from the extreme anti-Christian wing within the NSDAP when he said: 'It is my purpose neither to re-erect in the forests of Germany heathen altars and introduce youth to any kind of Wotan cult, nor in any other way to hand over young Germany to the magical arts of any herb-apostles.' 'I shall not suffer in this youth movement anyone who does not believe in God,' he exclaimed on another occasion.[77]

It has frequently been argued that the imagination of the young was caught by teutonic ceremonies and rituals which were allegedly widely practised. Moreover, it is often said that ideological indoctrination was particularly effective and carried out by highly skilled instructors familiar with the entire range of techniques of ideological persuasion. This range included the pulsating rhythm of the marching columns and the united singing of Nazi songs endlessly repeated. Each boy and girl was supposedly introduced into the collective experience which dissolved their individuality and united them with their comrades.[78] It is impossible to substantiate an account of this kind. As far as the last point is concerned any organized camp experience produces to a greater or a lesser extent that result. It would hardly be skilful to keep up indoctrination by endless repetition of Nazi songs, and it is surprising to see just how few of the songs sung were actually of Hitler Youth origin. The main body was derived from those of the pre-1914 German Youth Movement, which in turn had adapted many of the songs and ballads of traditional German folklore. Thus when, at his interrogation at the Nuremberg trials, Schirach was accused of having anti-clerical songs composed and written specially for the Hitler Youth such as *Wir sind des Geyers schwarzer Haufen* ('We are the Geyer's black band' — black being the colour of the peasant rebels' flag), Schirach could validly point out that the song in question had originated in Germany four hundred years before, during the peasants' rebellion which was aimed against the aristocracy and the rich monasteries.[79]

To teach the Hitler Youth to despise their Christian heritage and to denigrate clergymen as traitors to their own country would hardly have been the operation of a 'skilled instructor' who must have been aware of the important role family life still played in Germany and of the important influence exercised by the church.

The National Socialist regime had to tread carefully in its relations with the church before the war. The extravagances of individual NSDAP leaders pursuing their own anti-clerical campaigns could prove rather embarrassing, and the fabricated show trials of priests because of sexual or currency offences were stopped.[80] As yet the time had not come when Hitler could afford a direct confrontation with the church. And even less so once the war had begun. Though in his 'Table Talk' he raged against the church, the prophecies he made refer to what he would do with it once the war was over.[81] While the war lasted the most he required was its tacit acquiescence in his rule, and even that at times, as over the question of euthanasia, could not be obtained.

The war also made a considerable difference to the Catholic as well as some Protestant youth groups still in existence. In one Munich parish such a group dissolved itself in order to play an active part in the Hitler Youth.[82] Youngsters now realized that the struggle of religion against National Socialist extremism had been superseded by the 'cause of the Fatherland against its enemies'. It was quite a common feature in Munich churches to see complete Hitler Youth formations in uniform among the congregation at mass and a Hitler Youth serving at the altar.

Had the ideological permeation of Germany's youth and its anti-Christian indoctrination between 1933 and 1945 been as thorough and as perfect as has frequently been suggested, one wonders why the Nazi creed was so quickly shed by the majority the moment Hitler's state had been defeated. However, it is clear that whatever can be described as National Socialist 'ideology' could, on the surface at least, give the impression of coherence, because many of the elements used, especially nationalism and racialism, had been present for decades and had percolated into the political consciousness of young Germans by way of the most popular avenue – literature.

VII Literature

Literature, one of the most formative influences upon the young mind, was subjected to extensive control in Nazi Germany. But even this control could function only up to a point, because the National Socialist regime – except in cases where an individual was identified as an active enemy – rarely ventured into the intimate sphere of the private family. Hence, while books could be withdrawn from publishers' stocks, schools, universities, and public lending libraries, they could not be withdrawn from a personal library. It is likely that far more works of authors proscribed by the NSDAP were destroyed as a result of Allied bombing during the war than because of direct drastic actions by the NSDAP and any one of its formations. There must have been many boys who read officially-condemned books like Erich Maria Remarque's *All Quiet on the Western Front,* followed by 'accepted' books like Hans Zöberlein's *Glaube an Deutschland* and Ernst Jünger's *Storms of Steel* – not necessarily in that order – or Kurt Tucholky's political satire, and Ernst von Salomon's *The Outlaws.* Thomas Mann's works might well have been publicly burnt in Berlin in 1933, but in many a German home his *Buddenbrooks* continued to occupy a respected place on the bookshelf.

Bearing these and other limitations on the otherwise wide powers of control and censorship of Germany's literary output in mind, National Socialist policy towards youth literature has to be considered. Institutions for censorship of youth literature were no novelty in Germany – they had their established place throughout the nineteenth century. In 1890 they were united as one body under the name 'The United German Censorship Committees for Youth Literature', which in 1933 was immediately subordinated to Rust's Ministry of Science and Education.[1] Also the various party offices endeavoured to exercise their influence upon what Germany's youth should and should not read. Just before the outbreak of the war in 1939, the NSDAP had its own department for it,[2] so had the National Socialist Teachers' League, the *Hauptamt* for Educators,[3] the Hitler Youth, which in the *Reichsjugendführung* had its own department for literature,[4] Goebbels' Ministry for Popular Enlightenment and Propaganda, the Office of Public Lending Libraries,[5] and the Labour Service.[6]

The most effective control, however, was exercised by the NS Teachers' League, which after Hitler's coming to power drastically reorganized the United German Censorship Committees to ensure ideological conformity. In a flood of circulars, guidelines were issued as to who and what should *not* be read. Rust's ministry subsequently supplemented this effort by directives issued from time to time which in effect legislated on the subject of youth literature throughout the duration of Hitler's Germany. As time went by the United German Censorship Committees disappeared completely, being absorbed into the *Reichsstelle für Jugendschrifttum* of the National Socialist Teachers League.[7] This office in turn was subdivided into 41 regional offices of the NSDAP administration. Its aims were clearly set out:

'National Socialist cultural work requires a complete change in the aims of library work in general, and steps must be taken to ensure these aims become practice. . . . In place of the absence of direction, selection based on the *völkisch* concept and directed towards the state will be introduced. The popular lending library treasures the traditional and undying legacy of the German past, and with the aid of the book keeps it alive and effective. Beyond that it cares for the *Volkstum* in its politically active form in the major libraries and thus helps to further the militancy of the German spirit.'[8] Jointly with the *Reichsjugendführung* it issued annually the volume *The Youth Book* which listed those books suggested as suitable for young Germans.[9] This publication was supplemented by a slimmer one which under the heading *We Reject* listed books considered unsuitable, giving a short reason for doing so.[10]

The position of Schirach's *Reichsjugendführung* in the network of censorship was secured as early as 1933 by taking over one of the most important collections of youth books in Berlin, renamed *Reichsjugendbücherei*, which contained samples of five centuries of German youth literature.[11] Schirach was also quick to establish direct contact with renowned German publishers, a connection through which he and his advisers could successfully influence the programme of important publishing houses. In 1933 the *Reichsjugendbücherei* stated as one of its immediate aims the intention of establishing a publishing house 'in which valuable, almost forgotten texts will be reprinted. . . . Besides this the *Reichsjugendbücherei* will organize travelling exhibitions every Christmastime, whose function is to exert an instructive, exciting influence and to advertise books; it also issues lists of recommendable youth books.[13]

'In that way the *Reichsjugendbücherei* will endeavour gradually to attain the position from which to wield a decisive influence on all youth libraries. The aim is to find among the people a greater understanding of the significance of youth literature in relation to youth education, and it is hoped that this institute through a further extension of its activities will attain world-wide significance.'[14]

For both the *Jungvolk* and the HJ fortnightly folders were issued each dealing with a specific subject such as the 'Versailles Treaty' or the 'Jewish World Conspiracy', naming a list of books which by way of local libraries would be easily obtainable for further 'enlightenment'.[15] How much and to what extent these folders were actually used in weekly Hitler Youth group meetings, and how much they represented yet another set of papers or books issued by the NSDAP publishing house, *Eher Verlag* in Munich, or the *Reichsjugendführung* with which Hitler Youth homes were inundated, but which lay about unread and in disorder unless a party inspection was imminent, is a question unlikely ever to be satisfactorily answered. By 1938 the Hitler Youth also founded a book club to 'enable all youths to obtain a good youth book at a low cost'.[16] The Press and Propaganda Office of the *Reichsjugendführung* was responsible for Hitler Youth periodicals which, as is symptomatic of most explicitly National Socialist journalistic products, never managed to capture the imagination of the young. Hitler Youths had virtually to be compelled to buy them and much preferred weeklies or bi-weeklies such as were published by the OKW, like *Die Wehrmacht* or *Der Adler* which in excellently illustrated and action-packed features about Germany's arms and soldiers dealt with a subject-matter particularly interesting to boys. The endlessly repetitive claptrap of the Hitler Youth press could not compete with that type of product.

A *Lektorat* consisting of over a hundred freelance Hitler Youths worked from 1935 under the *Reichsjugendführung* and within the *Reichsjugendbücherei* reading books or manuscripts submitted to them throughout the year.[17] After 1936 when the Hitler Youth had become Germany's compulsory state youth organization publishers specializing in the field of youth literature found it advisable to send the manuscripts of their authors first to the *Lektorat* of the Hitler Youth to gain their approval.[18] The dominant criteria which determined its decisions were summarized by the head of the *Lektorat*, who in an attack on publishers wrote in 1936:

'In order to recognize and to understand the reason which led clearly and without compromise to either approval or rejection one has to understand first the task set for the Hitler Youth. It is further necessary to liberate oneself from the remnants of a liberal ideology which by its emphasis on the principle of art for art's sake in the arts and the sciences, saw a literary work as something in its own right and which derived its scale of values from some indeterminable laws of art. The precondition for any understanding is to know one of the basic principles of National Socialist ideology – that that is good which serves the people, and this is harmful which does harm to the people.

'The practical work in which we are involved for the sake of our youth and for the sake of our people has given us shocking insights into concepts and views still operative in the circles of those who produce books three years after the National Socialist revolution. In the course of this year several thousand books have gone through our *Lektorat* and several hundred manuscripts have been examined and evaluated.'[19]

The influence such a sharp attack could wield is illustrated by a contribution to the professional journal of German publishers by Dr Herbert Beck, the head of the renowned academic publishing house C. H. Beck Verlag in Munich. In his response he wrote: 'When the Head of the Cultural Office of the *Reichsjugendführung*, Fritz Helke, who is also the author of significant youth books, adopts in so sharp a fashion an attitude of rejection to the autumn list . . . then this requires some fundamental attention . . . . Helke's radical condemnation, which declares a whole profession rotten and incapable, is naturally understandable when one considers that it originates in the passionate devotion to his task and his combative zeal. . . .'[20]

The *Reichsjugendführung* occupied itself with everything from fairy tales to adventure books. In the former category distinct limits were defined in consultation with the *NS* Teachers' League. The principle of free selection was rejected outright: 'It would be a complete mistake to offer to our children the fairy tales of primitive exotic peoples. . . .'[21] instead, 'We must by considerable care of our youth literature ensure that the generations growing up will have a close relationship with our fairy tales, sagas, and the faith in the ancient gods of our people. From that depends whether we shall succeed in establishing a real German ideology as the unshakeable foundation of our new *Reich* and the racial self-determination of every German.'[22]

In a multi-volume work for children in primary schools under the title *Volk und Führer* issued in 1939, the first volume consists of a selection of fairy tales, determined solely by ideological considerations.[23] The fairy tale was to act as a preparation for the struggle for existence, and that this was not recognized everywhere was a fact which caused its editor to comment in 1940: 'To conceive of the fairy tale as an expression of ideology and to use it as a means of education for this ideology is something still unknown to the mass of German teachers. . . .'[24] The selection 'must not be orientated along considerations of the past because what would then emerge would be a collection of the most well-known tales. Rather the selection must be based on those tales in which combative contrasts emerge most clearly. In order to drive this lesson home in the book and engrave it indelibly upon the child through repeated reading they must also be grouped and headed by specific slogans: The boy must be strong; A German child must be faithful and true; The fearless knows no danger; No risk is too great for the saviour from danger; Faithfulness is stronger than death. . . . The fairy-tale figure is certainly not a hero. But National Socialism endeavours to lead to the hero and heroism. Therefore fairy tales must be considered as an avenue which leads towards it or forms the transitional stage to the saga. Thus the heading of one section should read "Only heroes master the world. . . ." In that way we achieve what we have to say while at the same time preserving the actual text and the classic Grimm's fairy tale. Maybe the aura and the tenderness, which characterize fairy tales more than any other literature, will be affected. Maybe this aid will become superfluous once all teachers have understood the purpose of the fairy tale. But as long as this is not the case I accept this as a minor impediment to the poetical impact of the tale, in favour of a clear outline of a combative attitude and thus a greater educational impact.'[25]

To the possible objection that ideological training was likely to exceed the intellectual capacity of a seven-year-old, the writer cited quoted an example of his four-year-old daughter who asked him whether he knew who was bravest. He did not, but asked whether she knew. Whereupon she replied:

'"You and Adolf Hitler." This answer characterizes the inner life of the coming generation even in its most tender age. It is no longer limited to the family and close environment. Of course, the father still occupies the foreground, but behind him and the family, to this young eye, the community of the *Volk* becomes visible, and the mighty figure of the *Führer* stands out. And with this early glimpse of *Führer* and *Volk* comes equally early the will for the social virtues, which determine the value of the human being for the national community.'[26]

Irrespective of whether this corresponded to their true origins, fairy tales had to originate in an Aryan background; indeed Professors of Literature went so far as to declare that the fairy tale originates only among the Aryan races because only they had the kind of traditions which would ensure that tales of old would be handed on from generation to generation: 'The figures of the world of fairy tales are no products of accidents but witnesses of an ancient, northern-racially conditioned *Weltanschaung*.'[27]

Consequently the 'ideologically' acceptable interpretation of Cinderella argues that this tale symbolizes the conflict between a racially pure maiden and an alien step-mother. Cinderella is rescued by a prince whose unspoilt instinct helps him to find the genuine Cinderella. The voice of the blood within him guides him along the right way.[28] An analysis of 'the brave little tailor' finds that at first sight he appears as a man who on the surface has all the characteristics of the Jew. His excessive self-advertisment 'Seven at one stroke', the way in which he outwits the giant, the way in which he arranges his reception at the royal court and there gradually displaces all other favourites, all this could be considered as typically Jewish. 'But for the sake of justice it must be said he does not only profit, he also takes a risk in doing so. The aim which the Jew pursues is, in its final analysis, simply diabolical: all the empires of the world and their glory! On their way to the achievement of that aim he walks over corpses, and wades through a sea of blood. These are facts, which among reasonable people are beyond discussion.'[29] Fairy tales should illustrate the eternal victory of the powers of light over those of darkness, a lesson which mothers at Christmas-time especially should take care to teach their children. And there is a suggestion that the crib, though the centre of a true Christian Christmas, has no relationship with a true German Christmas, and should be replaced by a wintry scene, dominated by tall pine trees and snow radiating an atmosphere of serenity but not 'diluted' by any Christian conceptions.[30]

If fairy tales were only a transitional stage, the saga was 'national educational material of the first degree, because it is the repository of the heroism of the past, and woe betide the unheroic nation which inevitably declines to the level of slavery'.[31] At the first *Reich* Youth Rally at Potsdam in 1932 Hitler in his speech before the assembled Hitler Youths had pointed to the great examples of heroic behaviour that could be found in the German sagas: 'The National Socialist movement wants to educate the German boy, make him proud and courageous and teach him in time not to bend down the little head when others want to inflict an injustice on him. A German boy remains faithful to his people particularly when it is in its greatest danger. What you, my dear German boy, admire in our heroic sagas and epic poems, is something you strive yourself to become, in order that your people will once more be sung about in heroic epics.'[32]

Sagas, too, provided the illustration of the *Führerprinzip*, the supremacy of the *Führer*, whose greatness lies beyond the measure of any rational criteria. The popular prince or duke, the *Volksherzog*, provides the analogy for Adolf Hitler: 'Can all that which we owe to our great *Volksherzog* . . . our fellowship, can that faithful fellowship be purer and more excitingly embodied than in the old epic poem, where we find the most marvellous examples of the close association between the leader and his men, can there be a more marvellous example for the education of our youth than sacrifice of the men for the King and that of the King for his men?'[33]

Alfred Rosenberg too points to the importance of Nordic sagas in the educational process of a National Socialist Germany: 'In place of the procurer and stock trader stories of the Old Testament will emerge the Nordic Sagas and fairy tales, at first simply told, and later understood as symbols. It is not the dream of hatred and a murdering Messianism, but the dream of honour and freedom which must be awakened through Nordic, Germanic sagas. From Odin onwards over the old tales to Eckehart and Walter von der

Vogelweide.'[34]

One of the most influential figures whose new rendering of the German sagas was read around many a Hitler Youth camp fire before and during the war, and probably the most able of this 'northern renaissance', was Hans Friedrich Blunck, a member of the German youth movement before the war and infantry lieutenant in the First World War. For three years he was President of Goebbels' 'German Writers' Chamber' and generally highly honoured by the party.[35] His particular rendering of the German sagas, which places considerable emphasis on the leadership principle, has remained to this day one of the best-selling German youth books.[36]

Whatever the plot of each saga, the basic idea is common to all, that of a group of heroes inseparably tied to one another by an oath of faithfulness who, surrounded by physically and numerically superior foes, stand their ground. The man who represents the centre of the small band is the *Führer* who is the strongest and boldest in the fight, yet at the same time not a rash man but one who thinks clearly about what he does. Either the band of heroes is reduced to the last man, who is the leader himself defending the corpses of his followers – the grand finale of the *Nibelungenlied,* or through its unparalleled heroism brings about some favourable change in its fortune.[37]

The sagas also offer a useful bridge to the National Socialist myth of the 'First Germanic *Reich*', allegedly forged by the Ostrogoths under Theoderic the Great. Those who built and defended that untenable construction have usually lost sight of another book equally as popular when it was first published in the late nineteenth century, and popular among German youth throughout the past seven decades, Felix Dahn's *Kampf um Rom.* Here too that first Germanic *Reich* exists but finally perishes at the foot of Mount Vesuvius, when its last defenders, rallied around their King, are, like Hitler in Berlin, reduced to defending a few square yards of earth.[38]

The didactic conception of the heroic saga of National Socialist Germany is that of a direct appeal to the youth to see themselves against a racially homogeneous Germanic background, which provides ample evidence that they too can participate in the forging of the new *Reich*, to fight for its expansion, and if necessary to perish for it. The age groups to which this appeal was directed were the twelve to fifteen-year-olds who had reached what the NS Teachers' League chose to call the 'Viking Age': 'With the onset of puberty the youth steps into the Viking Age. Risk and adventure and heroic actions are being looked for. Yearning for countries and places far away and enjoyment of adventurous events and courageous actions are inborn elements of every healthy young German. The death-defying fighter who in the blind confidence in his own ability and physical strength overcomes unusual difficulties, and the hero who can manfully carry suffering without his substance being damaged, they are his ideals.'[39]

In this context a natural and particular eminence was enjoyed by the *Nibelungenlied* because, as was claimed, it preserved the best racial legacy, which must become the common background for German youth and the German people as a whole.[40] Rosenberg declared it as 'probably the mightiest precipitate of wilful occidental art creation; it illustrates the highest value of the Nordic race.'[41] He interprets the hero Siegfried as the epitome of Germanic generosity 'which presupposes in the enemy the same conception of honour and the same form of open combat; who in childlike straightforwardness can never accept that the contrary of his presuppositions happens to be the case. This generosity has brought the Germans in the course of their history many serious shocks, such as when they began to admire Rome, and in recent times when by the emancipation of the Jews, by the granting of equal rights, it allowed healthy blood to be poisoned.'[42]

Hagen, the assassin of Siegfried, was elevated to a position equal to that of his victim; what Germany really needed, so the literary advocates of the Nordic mission argued, was a combination of both Hagen and Siegfried. A man with the watchfulness and circumspection of a Hagen and the dynamism and magnetism of a Siegfried would be invincible.[43] Siegfried's personality is archetypal of the German fate, a radiant heroic figure at an early stage, an example of virtuous knightly manners and generosity, full of strength of body as well as of mind. During centuries of German weakness the image of Siegfried had receded or been perverted into one not far removed from being a fool. Only the Romantic movement resurrected him and since the middle of the nineteenth century he had appeared again in German school reading books, and in the new editions of German sagas he had entered once more the national consciousness of the youth of Germany. Siegfried's example is said to have inspired the youthful regiments of Langemarck.[44] He inspired heroes of the National Socialist movement like Albert Leo Schlageter and Horst Wessel; he is also the figure whose fate prompted a decisive slogan of the 1920s – that of the stab-in-the-back which, it was claimed, the army had suffered from defeatism and Bolshevism at home. Hindenburg in his testament summarized the parallel thus: 'Like Siegfried under the impact of the spear thrown by a grim Hagen, so our exhausted front collapsed; in vain it had tried to gain new strength from the well at home. . . .'[45]

The Nordic epic was also a veritable source of National Socialist 'ethics', especially the Edda, the main work of Germanic literature dating back to the ninth century and beyond and consisting of heroic epics and poems. Analogies were drawn between Grimm's fairy tales and the Edda, which was said to represent a true reflection of Germanic life.[46] The 'genuine' Germanic characteristics of the Germanic gods were said to be much closer to the character of the Germans than were those of the sagas of Greek or Roman antiquity.[47] One of the most widely circulated introductions to the Nordic epic demonstrates the range of politically suitable interpretations, whose aim is summarized by the author as follows:

National Socialism has subordinated German life again under the law of honour and has thereby established a clear and compelling order of values. It has rejuvenated that attitude according to which our forefathers out of the nature of their character have once lived and acted. What that attitude was once like, how it affected the entire conduct of one's life, is nowhere as apparent as in the old Nordic poem. It shows us a human character whose life was a continuous preparation to meet fate, a will for self-assertion and therefore struggle, and that life was mastered with the aid of the basic values of honour, faithfulness, and bravery. To lead back to these values, to create once again a sense of what is exemplary and valid, to bring to life for our youth again something of the brave and noble character of our ancestors and in that way help the Germanic legacy to dominate within us, that must be the ultimate purpose of any occupation with old Nordic poetry. In the final analysis it is not a matter of knowledge, but a matter of instilling an attitude of value. Only then poetry becomes a creative force of power of life.[48]

From the fairy tales and Germanic sagas it was only a logical step to deploy historical material to produce and shape the 'National Socialist Character' of youthful readers. Hitler himself had outlined in *Mein Kampf* how Germany's greatness and that of its historical leaders should be systematically used to awaken the national pride of youth and to illustrate Germany's mission: 'From the innumerable great names of German history the greatest are to be selected and projected to the youth in such an intense way that they become the supporting columns of an unshakeable national feeling. From this point of view the teaching material is to be systematically structured and the teaching is to be planned and carried out so that a young person when leaving school is not half a pacifist, democrat and what not, but a thorough German.'[49]

Rosenberg equally underlined the importance of history, and the teaching of history, which would have to serve National Socialist ends, to strengthen those values 'which lie deep in the Germanic character and which have to be tended carefully to bring them to the surface again ... the weaknesses of our great men should not be covered up; but that which raises them above the ordinary, the eternal, mythical should be detected with a searching soul and shaped accordingly. Then a row of spirits will emerge from Odin, Siegfried, Widukind, Frederick II the Hohenstaufen, Eckehart, von der Vogelweide, Luther, Frederick the Great, Bach, Goethe, Beethoven, Schopenhauer, Bismarck, inclusive of their Germanic enemies.

Far removed from this spiritual and racial line of the development stand for us the Institoris, Canisius; far removed too will one day lie Ricardo, Marx, Lasker, and Rathenau.

'The schools of the coming German Reich will have to serve this new evaluation, it is their noblest if not their only task for the coming decades, until these values are taken for granted by all Germans. These schools are still waiting for a great teacher of German history with a will for a German future. He will come when once myth has become reality.'[50]

The demands, then, that historical material in youth literature would have to meet National Socialist requirements were quickly articulated by the NS Teachers' League in 1933. The content of historic literature for youths was not to consist merely of a chronological list of historical events, but should correspond with the requirements of the time, arising out of the racial tasks for the future. Whatever historical insight is necessary for the new *Reich* of the Germans and for the education of those who will one day run it should determine the content of historical youth literature. In this way the historical consciousness of the Germans would be remoulded, creating an awareness of 'the blood stream' which connects Germans with the epochs of the past. In the light of this new consciousness a fundamental reinterpretation of German history would be inevitable.

Not Rust's Ministry of Science and Education but Frick's Ministry of the Interior early in 1933 established guidelines for the teaching of history which was to be conducted with special emphasis on early Germanic history, the significance of the race as the roots of the *Volk*, the racial thought, and the heroic idea, as well as the figure of the *Führer* as a source of strength 'in the racial struggle for existence amidst a hostile world.'[51] The result of this approach was apparent above all in biographies and in widely popular books such as the *Deutsches Wesen und Schicksal* where one could find chapter headings like 'A thousand Years of the German Middle Period', 'The Second *Reich* of the Germans' and 'The *Reich* since 1933 – Hitler builds Greater Germany', the three of which span the period from the 'First' to the 'Second' and from there to the 'Third' *Reich*.[52]

The notion that history could also be read by youths, or anyone else for that matter, as a form of relaxation was rejected, as was also the notion that popular history should be dry and dull instruction. It served ideological orientation, nothing else.[53] Examples of 'leaders' in all spheres of life were cited, and ideally suited for this purpose was Frederick the Great whose stock had risen considerably since 1871 and who had been the subject of countless youth books before 1933. In his personality, it was alleged, Prussia reveals itself in its purest form, and it is by no means an accident that the National Socialist movement was a fusion of Prussian order and Prussian will to sacrifice, and the concept of the German race.[54] The fact that this

National Socialist leadership cult contained inherent dangers, that some of the writers made their 'heroes' really incredible, did not pass by unnoticed: 'But also one should be wary of dressing up the figures of our past in a National Socialist sense, and turning their conversations into a recitation of half the party programme. Show them to our youth as whole German men. This is sufficient. The subject of National Socialism is best left to the present and its problems.'[55] Another criticism of 'period' youth literature was directed at the stereotyped view of history and the preference for always using the same heroes, such as the Viking stories, the peasant risings of the sixteenth century which lent themselves very well to anti-clerical agitation, and the Seven Years' War with its outstanding figure, Frederick the Great.[56] Attention was directed to equally important but hitherto neglected areas such as the Crusades, Bohemian history because of its impact on and its importance for the *Reich*, and those epochs which demonstrated the essential territorial unity of an area from which parts had since been lost for the *Reich* such as Switzerland and Holland, where young Germans could be shown the extent of territory in Central Europe once occupied by the German people. More attention, too, was to be paid to the racial minorities and their leaders and to the cultural achievements in the German east, which were not to be limited solely to a history of the Teutonic Order; also to the Greater German achievements in Austria and the struggles of the nineteenth century which were in need of reinterpretation, since the nineteenth century's little German approach, like the 'Hurra patriotism' of the Wilhelmine period, no longer sufficed.[57]

There was certainly no shortage of writers who were willing to lend their services to the writing of youth literature of this kind, though the classics of this period had in many cases been written before 1933 and some of its authors left the party or in fact never joined it. Will Vesper, next to Kolbenheyer one of the very few genuinely good writers whom the NSDAP managed to attract to its ranks, had been specializing in his novels on subjects taken from Germany's early history.[58] His work is marked by a pronounced nationalism and anti-Semitism; one of his most popular editions was a new translation of Tacitus's *Germania* which he had published as early as 1906 but which after 1933 became the sole 'official' translation.[59] Vesper's translation was introduced with an interpretation of Tacitus as a historian and chronicler who, aware of the growing degeneration of Roman society, saw in the Germans the exact opposite. In the Germans the strength of regeneration was considerable because they were aware of the three-fold sources of their society: first, the age-old roots in the soil and the strict preservation of the race; secondly, the political structure of their tribes, and the operation of the leadership principle; and thirdly, their unique purity and the health of their marriage customs and their ethics.[60]

Edwin Guido Kolbenheyer, whose *Paracelsus-Triology*, a biography of the German doctor and philosopher of the early Renaissance, was one of the most widely read books in Germany by old and young alike, and which also inspired a film of the same name, interprets the state as a metaphysical and biological necessity and its members as the exponents of the race. History, and this his *Paracelsus* makes quite clear, can only be understood in terms of biological necessities.[61]

However, the man who provided Hitler and his party with a ready-made slogan never joined the party, refusing outright to do so on the grounds that for a writer to be a member of a political party would deprive him of the distance which allowed him detached judgment and put him in a position in which he could counsel no longer. Hans Grimm's *Volk ohne Raum*, (*People Without Space*), is perhaps the only explicitly German political novel of literary standing produced by German national and philo-national socialist literature. Among other things it is an indictment of Germany's post-Bismarckian industrialization, and bears strong features of alienation from it. The cure for the evils of industrialization Grimm puts forward in his novel is more space, space for overseas colonization, because only that will restore the balance between the inevitable progress of industrialization and the forces of social unrest. The novel, well over 1300 pages long and written in a very idiosyncratic style, has proved very successful especially among the young generation. Republished in 1956, nearly one million copies have been printed so far.[62]

The historical context of the German classics too was in need of re-interpretation because they stemmed from 'the world of humanist-liberal ideas. We know the aim of the culture of this period: to produce the greatest possible individualism, an aim which our racial feeling and desire fundamentally oppose.'[63] Whatever reinterpretations were suggested, National Socialism failed here in the face of the traditions of German schoolmasters who interpreted Goethe, Schiller, Kleist, and Hölderlin for their pupils in much the same way as these writers had been interpreted in the past. In any event, as with the classics of most other countries, their real value is generally discovered after the school desk has been left – the classroom rarely contains an atmosphere conducive to their understanding.

But outside the classroom was a subject much more compelling for a generation born after the First World War – the War itself. Especially so, since its literary yield was of an infinitely higher standing than anything produced, for instance, after the Second World War. Within the framework of 'ideological' training, the National Socialists paid particular attention to the war-generated literature 'because the idea of National Socialism with all its demands was born in the war'[64] – hardly correct, but nevertheless at the time believed by many, to whom the mention of the name Friedrich

Naumann, the German liberal who even before Hitler was born had argued the case for a national socialism, would have merely caused shrugged shoulders. The war, from the National Socialist point of view, was an overwhelming assertion by the German people of their right to live, an activation of all racial resources. Consequently 'the war literature is the most important aid to awaken those educational effects which the World War produced. And because the experience of the World War was infinite and manifold, the great number of war books is both necessary and good, as even their entire range can only indicate in a very fragmentary fashion the whole of the war experience.'[65]

The war literature and the glorification of the subject were of course not exclusively a product of the 1930s. The great classics had by then already been produced, accompanied by a spate of lesser works. What is symptomatic about the war literature after 1933 in Germany is the exclusive concentration upon the glorification of war and the suppression of any countervailing force. War literature in all forms from battle descriptions to adventure stories was aimed at German youth. 'We want to see that man described who understands how to be victorious.'[66] That the hero of the First World War had to be the epitome of racial virtues is self-evident.

'The word Hero needs to be understood in its widest sense and always in a reciprocal relationship to "followers" or those who resist him. Whether it is Herman the Cheruscan or a daring Viking, whether Hauptmann Erckert in the Kalahari [Hans Grimm: *Volk ohne Raum*] or the war volunteer Siewert in *Gruppe Bosemueller* [Werner Beumelberg] . . . we are always dealing with a personality, with the risk of will, life and limbs for a great cause, with a great example, the test in need, a picture and example of racial virtues, irrespective of the examples to the contrary, which are as necessary as is shadow to the light.'[67]

What was considered to attract youthful male readers was a combination of the technical and the adventurous, as one can find in the various accounts of the exploits of Baron Manfred Freiherr von Richthofen, and those of the U-boats and the cruiser *Emden*. The offensive element was believed to make a book a sure success among a young readership: 'Forward and through!' This was considered to be the best means of introducing youth to war literature.[68] Only from the age of sixteen onwards were classics like Ernst Jünger's *Storms of Steel* recommended.[69]

The kind of war book advocated and produced also lent itself ideally to the illustration of the leadership principle in operation; but the results did not reach the expectations of that body most directly affected by this kind of propaganda. As a *Wehrmacht* general pointed out to publishers in 1939:

'War memoirs are going into the hundreds, but only a few of them fulfil the purpose for which they are needed. Many far from reach the level of a

Beumelburg, Jünger, Zöberlein, and Schauwecker who honestly and truly describe the war as our frontline soldiers experienced it. Very often there are exaggerated adventurous stories, which clearly carry the stamp of the lack of personal experience and which are surrounded by an aura of Hurra patriotism and mothballs. In others the naturalist element comes out so strongly that it tends to push aside the heroic one, strongly reminiscent of Remarque. Yes, now and again even an explicit defeatist surfaces who in order to make his book more acceptable just attaches the fashionable call for the fraternity of all frontline fighters. To describe the experience of war and its innermost drive is truly a very difficult task. Part of it is that one must not only have seen these things but felt them as well, out of that spiritual attitude which in the suffering of one's own people comes the greatest motivation for courage and sacrifice.

'I must add here a reference to one of the errors, which is frequently made, but which is really a leftover of the symptoms of decay of the last years of the World War: to ascribe to every frontline soldier rough and bad behaviour as one of his most important characteristics. First-rate armies under great leaders who fought for an ideal have always believed that the honour of the troops does not simply consist of fulfilling their soldierly duties, but that this requires also the unobjectionable behaviour of every single man. Especially since the Prusso-German army has been based on the principle of national service, this conception of human decency has been at home there.'[70]

No doubt the critic, however right he may have been in the early part of his criticism, was as much a victim and purveyor of illusions as those he accused.

A completely new category of youth book saw the light of day after 30 January 1933: that which glorified the heroes of the party.[71] The Ministry of Science and Education issued regular lists of books which should be included in school libraries. Their subject was the history of the National Socialist movement and the life of those who died for its cause. Since the *Horst Wessel Lied* had become Germany's second national anthem anyway, the storm trooper Horst Wessel was an obvious subject; so was Albert Leo Schlageter who practised active resistance against the French after their Ruhr occupation, and so, of course, was Herbert Norkus. But with the exception of Aloys Schenzinger's *Hitlerjunge Quex* none of the literary treatments managed to establish any widespread popularity. In Hitler Youth libraries a decade after their publication one could often come across them but as well as being dusty they were obviously unread, while First World War books and those on the Second World War had been very heavily thumbed.[72]

After the renunciation of the military clauses of the Versailles peace treaty and the reintroduction of conscription, the German Army High Command supported a publicity campaign aimed at making the new *Wehrmacht* more familiar to everyone. The periodicals and books published with that aim were in the main highly successful as they imparted a good deal of technical information to an interested readership. After the outbreak of war besides providing information as done by the *Wehrmacht*, the *Reichsjugendführung* considered it imperative to infuse Germany's youth with enthusiasm for the 'German struggle for liberty'. Education in preparation for military service now became one of the major aims, directed at the older boys:

'Education to bring forth the will to bear arms is now all important. It is important to educate young people consciously and with conviction so as to produce a fighting spirit and fighting attitude. Therefore the first yardstick with which our school libraries should be measured is to what degree they can produce this fighting spirit. Mental readiness for the military call among youths requires a certain knowledge of military matters. Put informative military books into the school libraries! The boy wants to know about the structure and the equipment of the *Wehrmacht*. . . .

'Furthermore every youth should be informed about every branch of the armed forces: army, navy, and air force. He should be familiar with their weapons, their specific tasks and methods of fighting. Finally the pupil must also read books which familiarize him with armies of other countries, but all books must be full of lively tension . . . otherwise they could create the very opposite of military enthusiasm.'

From 1940 until late 1943 books on the achievements of the *Stukas*, the *Panzers* and the U-boats flooded the German book market, a flood halted only by shortage of paper. In schools boys and girls from ten upwards were to be familiarized with the deeds of those soldiers who had been awarded the Knight's Cross for bravery, and one of the last volumes published before the end of the war portrayed Hitler Youths in action – at a time when the invocation of the Langemarck myth was demanding again its bloody sacrifice.

The utilization of various forms and expression of imaginative and historical literature for the purposes of political indoctrination does not imply that literature for direct political National Socialist education did not exist. On the contrary, special importance was given to that subject.[76]

'What function does political youth literature fulfil within the general field of literature? It should serve the political education of the youth. Hitler's demand is that the youth should be trained to be the future bearers of the National Socialist state. Regarding political education, it does not matter whether one creates a formal feeling for the state, but one must instil a lively enthusiasm for it, a feeling of surrender and sacrifice for the state, the embodiment of a racially determined order of life. Political youth literature should not consist of theory and practice, it should not teach; no, it should elevate the child, the young man, it should arouse enthusiasm, raise the forces of his will, to activate it and assist in mentally preparing the young generation for service to the state and to the nation. Within the national educational work of National Socialism political youth literature is an important factor, and therefore we cannot be indifferent to the spirit exuded by a particular piece of political youth literature.'

In other words, the gradual and rational education with the aim of producing a responsible citizen of the state was not the purpose of National Socialist political education, but rather the development of the racially conscious *Volksgenosse* (national or racial comrade). Politically motivated literature was to appeal to the emotions, elicit reactions of blind obedience and total surrender and cement a 'fanatical faith in the *Volk* and *Reich* and in the *Führer*, whose legacy they will one day have to preserve'.[78] Hitler himself had underlined that no boy or girl should ever leave school without being aware of the importance of racial purity. The chief aim of the political education of Germany's youth should be indelibly to 'burn' in their hearts and minds a sense and feeling of race.[79]

Books and brochures on racial instruction made up a good part of every school and Hitler Youth library, which when discussed in Hitler Youth meetings made for many a dull evening. But in many they produced the desired effect, especially when read in conjunction with the viewing of the film *The Eternal Jew*, and ultimately provided the basis for young men regarding the Jews as vermin and treating them accordingly. Party history too belonged to the field of education in which the two primary books were Goebbels' *Vom Kaiserhof zur Reichskanzlei* and the party's press chief Otto Dietrich's *Mit Hitler and die Macht*. The person of Hitler became a subject of 'literary' treatment for youth books but of a quality which caused acid comment from, at first glance, as unlikely a source as Himmler's SS-paper *Das Schwarze Korps* which ran a whole series on Kitsch and commercialism in the Hitler cult.[80] Actually only very few of the volumes on Hitler were officially recommended for inclusion into school and Hitler Youth libraries. Moreover, regularly reissued volumes for the branches of the Hitler Youth, *Pimpf im Dienst, HJ im Dienst,* and *Mädel im Dienst,* limited their political information to a minimum. Of one issue of *Pimpf im Dienst* of 349 pages, only 14 have an explicitly political content. The remainder concerns itself with various forms of physical exercises, sports, games, para-military field exercises, air rifle shooting, camping, hiking, and first-aid.[81] The political content of *HJ im Dienst* and *Mädel im Dienst* was more pronounced, and in the latter 'racial advice' was given.

Baldur von Schirach made sure that his own works received wide circulation though they contained little which was of practical use to a Hitler Youth, except the poems which had to be recited on special national or party holidays.[82] Biographies of other men important in the party's history were in circulation, with Göring being most prominently represented. However the sections of his biographies most widely read were those describing his part in the Richthofen Circus (the famous air force formation of the First World War), which he was the last to command.[83]

Also in the 'literary field' belong the speech choruses which accompanied Hitler Youth events and public appearances of other party formations. These were never entirely successful and could be a source of definite embarrassment when staged badly, as Leni Riefenstahl unintentionally documented in the case of the Labour Service in her film *Triumph of the Will*.

Throughout the pre-war period, the Third *Reich* time and again laid claim to Germany's lost colonies. But colonies, as was later to be demonstrated, need not necessarily be overseas. In order to meet a widespread sentiment for colonial expansionism as well as to train young German eyes outwards for the future quest for *Lebensraum*, attention was drawn to both the former colonies and 'borderland Germans' and racial Germans. The specifically racial task of the youth book when describing the life of Germans living outside the frontiers of the fatherland was mentioned in 1941:

'The youth book has a particularly important racial function: to convey to our youth the knowledge of Germans living outside the frontiers, to elicit the necessary warmth of heart for the fate of our fellow Germans in foreign lands, and out of that to create a readiness to act on their behalf. From this sense of participation and the readiness of the people in the *Reich* to act on their behalf will depend the degree to which those German groups outside our frontiers will support the *Reich*, or alternatively to what degree they will allow themselves to be absorbed by a foreign race.'[84]

The fate of the racial Germans found expression in some widely-read books on Volga German refugees during the turmoil of the Russian revolution, and also in books on the former colonies, or the struggle in them during the First World War as portrayed, for example, in General von Lettow-Vorbeck's memoirs.[85] On the other hand, James Fennimore Cooper's *Leatherstocking* tales caused annoyance in some quarters of the National Socialist Teachers' League because they involved the minds of their young readers in the power struggles between the British and the French, a struggle which was not of interest to Germany. The agitation never went so far as to call for a ban of the book, but literary endeavours to produce a German Leatherstocking based in Togoland, the German Cameroons, or South-West Africa were given support.[86]

The fate of the Sudeten Germans had been a favourite topic before 1933 and remained one until 1938, as did that of the German minorities in Poland.[87] The troubles of the Southern Tyroleans however remained unmentioned, even though, in fact, they experienced a higher degree of suppression than was ever inflicted on the Germans of Czechoslovakia. But Hitler's Italian policy, culminating in the Axis alliance, carried its repercussions even into the distant corner of youth literature. Except for novels on the mountain warfare in the Dolomites in the First World War, the fate of the ethnic German South Tyroleans received no 'literary' treatment.[88]

In order to bridge social gaps at an early age the 'community of race' was supplemented by the 'community of work'. Heroic qualities need not exclusively be found in the soldier, they could be found also in the worker and his everyday life because at this level the continuous struggle between man and matter took place. The worker was to be as much a subject of youth literature as the soldier, while the portrayal of the life of the leisured class was considered taboo – at least in books directed at a male readership.[89] Especially for those approaching school-leaving age, books of this content were thought essential. They would assist the young individual in the process of integration into the 'racial community' as well as into the working community and render a higher sense of purpose to his work than merely that of earning a living. Emphasis on the racial-social aspect would reveal the average German in his day-to-day environment, fulfilling his duty as member and servant of his national community. Apprehension was expressed lest over-emphasis on nation and race would produce among the youth an ignorance of and an indifference to social problems. It was all well and good to paint on the large canvas of nation and race, but it was equally important to explore in youth literature those areas which affected the individual youth more immediately and more directly. That this would be a difficult task for any writer was recognized. Modern industrial and social complexity tended to touch a host of problems which would be difficult to describe with that element of suspense and struggle which appealed to the youthful reader. However, the struggle need not be one of man against man, but of man against nature, and possible examples such as the miner at the coalface or the attitude of a ship's stoker in a gale-force-nine storm were suggested.[90]

A potentially realistic school of literature found advocacy in the observation that 'the real hard-core problems of the production front have not yet been discovered' and in the demand to 'get into the coal mines, into the foundries, into the construction offices.... There the true battles are fought. There, even in peace-time, whole armies of workers are engaged in continuous battle. That it is really a battle the civilian notices only when, in the front sector "coal", another one hundred and fifty men have been killed.'[91] By comparison the people of leisure reposing on their deckchairs were of no interest.[92] Adventures in North America may well be exciting but they had little relevance to the problems of the day. Adventure could equally be found along the railway tracks, water locks, foundries, and laboratories They produced problems and situations requiring as much coldbloodedness, presence of mind, decisiveness, and comradeship as did the Wild West. They produced the genuine every-day hero.[93]

It cannot be said that these demands brought forth any adequate response. The National Socialist 'Hero of Labour' did not perhaps remain fiction but he found no literary embodiment, either in youth or adult literature. Reading about adventurous exploits in far-away lands and about heroes of ages past was something National Socialist cultural policy was simply unable to stop.

Nor could it completely deal with a cause so dear to the heart of early National Socialism: the use of foreign words in the German language. Georg von Schönerer, the Austrian Pan-German one of the two men to whom Hitler paid his respects in the opening pages of *Mein Kampf*, had once started a systematic campaign to eliminate all words of foreign origin used in everyday German. 'Window' became the Germanic *Windauge* to replace the Latin-originated *Fenster*. The names of the months were Germanized out of recognition. In this respect Nazi policy did not go as far as that, but the slogan and the admonition was that to be German was also to speak German.

'The entire life and the entire struggle of our youth of today culminate in their affirmation to be German. This affirmation is for them the beginning and the end. Woe to those who do not understand them! Three times woe to those who oppose them!

'That this claim to totality also embraces the language is for our youth something natural. They conceive of and experience the language as the form of expression of the German soul born in its blood.

'To be German does not only mean to feel, to think, to act as a German, but also to speak like a German. The foreign word is not only an insult to the honour of our language. . . . Whoever uses foreign words thinks as a member of a class and does not act in the spirit of comradeship, whoever chooses the German word instead eliminates his own ego and feels with his fellow comrades. Only in this way the speaker as well as the listener becomes aware of the common legacy of our ancestors. The foreign word separates, the mother language unites. . . .

'These are the basic images and feelings alive in a young German when he takes hold of a book, especially a youth book.

'Language is not, but continuously becomes. This process of growth is both original as well as close to the contemporary scene; therefore to create in German is a great task. To assist Germany's youth in this and to lead it is the duty of the youth book. The author of youth books must be a master of the discipline of language, a fighter for the treasure of the German language, a man who arouses a sense of honour for the German language.'[94]

Writers who were attacked for using foreign-derived words frequently objected, and referred in defence to the language of Hitler's speeches which were hardly models of Germanic purity. But:

'We consider it an impertinence when an author of youth books excuses his use of foreign words with reference to the *Führer* who also uses them. The *Führer* knows why in his great political speeches he uses them, speeches addressed to the whole of the world in which foreign words are clearly defined meaning the same in every language. But many an author of youth books does not know why in a book addressed particularly to young boys he throws about foreign words. In spite of all the usefulness of the material and the spirit, books of that kind because of their inadequate language must meet rejection. This is not simply the opinion of schoolmasters, it is the opinion of the *Reichsjugendführung* and all responsible circles.'[95]

As in the literature of every country the pure adventure story occupied for young and old a special position – the kind of book the youth had read at ten but which lost none of its inherent excitement and suspense over the years, and which, decades later in moments of leisure, the adult reads with the same enthusiasm as in childhood. But National Socialist literary critics insisted that life, as reflected in the main characters, had to stand in the service of an idea, in the service of the community, and that the 'heroic' element must predominate.[96]

'The adventure book does not represent a category which lies outside the valuation of the principles of our ideology, it need not, because a fair shot of adventure runs through the blood of every German. . . .

'It is the kind of literature which forms a preliminary step towards the heroic or can already be heroic if a dangerous mode of life stands in the service of an idea, a task a community, a life lived for a useful purpose, not a life consisting of the unmotivated inspirations of the moment.'[97]

Rudolf Hess in 1940, little more than a year before his flight to Great Britain, at a Hitler Youth sponsored occasion publicly referred to the role of the adventure book and its importance because in every healthy boy and girl it awakened enthusiasm for heroic action:

'You read with the same passion what we read in our youth: Karl May and Leatherstocking, about adventures at the far away Gold Coast, fights with wild animals, the hunt of giant fishes. You read the books about daring seafarers and their stormy voyages around Cape Horn. You read the heroic sagas of your people, you want to know how Frederick the Great once fought, how Bismarck and Moltke have conquered, how a Weddigen, a Boelcke, a Immelmann, a Richthofen, a *Graf Spee*, an Admiral Scheer have achieved their great victories – you absorb all that into your hearts, it excites your enthusiasm, it lives in your fantasy.'[98]

While Hess described the realm of adventure, the National Socialist Teachers' League also stated what an adventure book should not contain and the kind which should not be carried by school libraries. The detective story, the whole range of crime thrillers including the technicalities of detection and identication, was declared undesirable.[99] The detective had none of the heroic qualities of a Luckner, Richthofen, or Prien. Only the latter category embodied virtues worth emulation by the young reader.[100] Where opinions were divided was concerning that group of adventure books which since the nineteenth century have entered the literature of every European language: the 'Red Indian' story. Will Vesper represented the opponents of 'the outdated Red Indian fiction in the youth books' since it was not reconcileable with the racial doctrines of National Socialism:

'We must finish all the soft literary dreaming about the coloured races, whether now in scientific works, poetical and entertainment literature, or in the long-obsolescent Red Indian fiction in our youth books. We are a white people. We represent the core and major people of the white race. The white race is in danger. It is our responsibility to recognize in time the necessities of the future and to open the eyes of our people to the threatening dangers. Be it warning enough for us that every Jew is the pace-maker of coloured intermixing and the destroyer of white watchfulness. We should meet the coloured danger with all the necessary sharpness there, where for the moment it is most immediate for our people, in the admiration of the coloured in a literature that is tired of Europe.'[101] Vesper did not succeed in his plea; Red Indian stories remained as popular as ever.

One of the most successful authors of this genre in Germany at the time was Erhard Witteck, who published his youth books under the pseudonym Fritz Steuben, the major one of which was the multi-volume fictitious biography of the Indian Chief Tecumseh. In opposition to Vesper he argued that the Red Indians illustrate amply that the lack of a racial consciousness and the failure to grasp the importance of establishing racial bonds among themselves caused their downfall.[102] The Red Indians were not the only adventure subject on which opinions were divided. *Robinson Crusoe* gave cause for discussion too. Some argued that the book could be put without reservation into the hands of every youth because Robinson Crusoe represented the Nordic blood of adventure, the typical Nordic Hero capable of surviving and mastering even the most adverse conditions.[103] Others however objected to Robinson Crusoe's friendship with the native, and maintained that it was necessary to revise the text in order to bring into relief his racial superiority. Equally, they demanded the elimination of the passage in which the Spaniards remaining on the island marry native women, and recommended that Friday be left on his island, a course which 'for him as well as for the white race is the best'. Regret was also expressed that Robinson Crusoe had not been turned into a German boy – which may be of importance to a reader ten years of age.[104] *Uncle Tom's Cabin* was withdrawn from all school and Hitler Youth libraries because its content ran counter to the ideas of 'National Socialist racial political education'. Nor was Tom the right kind of hero. He is a humble sufferer and as such hardly an example for Germany's youth which was being educated in unconditional readiness for action and the struggle for *Volk* and Fatherland. Moreover, Tom could be interpreted as a piece of literary counter-propaganda to the colonial idea.[105]

By far the most widely read and admired German author of adventure novels from the turn of the century to the present day is Karl May.[106] The son of a poverty-ridden family in central Germany he managed to advance his education sufficiently to gain admission to a teachers' training college. There he was involved in a number of criminal activities which led to his being sentenced several times to short terms of imprisonment. He was successful in breaking away from his criminal past, but with a teaching career now closed to him he turned to writing adventure stories for popular weeklies. From there it was only a short step to writing adventure books, mainly in the first person and in such convincing detail that at first reading one would believe Karl May had been in all the parts of the world in which his adventures take place. Yet everything was fictitious; he did not visit North America or any other part of the world until his books had made him a rich man. His works, totalling 70 volumes each averaging between 500 and 600 pages, have remained best-sellers and his German readership comprises virtually all age groups from eight to eighty.[107]

Hess referred to him in the speech quoted above, and Hitler had been an equally ardent reader of Karl May; so had many of his opponents. In the early years of the Dachau concentration camp possession of a Karl May volume from the camp library was worth a day's food ration. In view of the support from people in such high places few dared to attack the ethical content of Karl May's work, in which the hero never commits violence for violence sake, in which he never actually kills, where retribution usually occurs in some form of divine intervention or a godly justice. The evildoer in some wild chase on horseback fails in jumping a crevasse and disappears in the depths. The hero is always straightforward and without complications, but always superior even to his own friends. He really is too perfect and virtuous to be alive. *Das Schwarze Korps* once attempted to demolish the Karl May cult, but without success.[108] As late as 1944 the *Reichsjugendführung* still issued Karl May volumes as prizes for Hitler Youth competitions and the Army High Command ordered 3000 volumes for troops engaged in anti-partisan warfare.[109]

Precisely what results National Socialist policy in the field of youth literature has yielded is very difficult to assess. At no time during the Third *Reich* could the regime completely eliminate existing countervailing influences.[110] The party produced no writer capable of putting National Socialist ideology over in the form of a youth book. All it did was to rely on writers already established, like Karl Aloys Schenzinger who wrote what was to be a party classic, *Hitlerjunge Quex*, something which, in his case, was deeply regretted within a matter of years before the outbreak of war. The NSDAP could rely on the nationalist literature of the Weimar Republic, but effectively its action was one of negation – it failed to create, so it let alone what was considered suitable, and banished what was considered unsuitable. The NSDAP's function was one of control, not one of creation. The stuff created by party poets, like the *Reichsjugendführer* himself, could be disposed of only under duress. What was novel was the broad front of racially motivated anti-Semitism which was established and in no sector more strongly than in that of the youth book. In itself, of course, anti-Semitism was nothing new; National Socialism merely touched a chord *already* existing from early childhood, when the story of Judas and the thirty pieces of silver, and the crucifixion of the Lord by the Jews, had been heard.

The party's control function and its intervention in the sector of youth book production was unprecedented, and would inevitably have resulted in serious psychological damage among German youth had the Third *Reich* lasted even a generation, rather than the promised thousand years. As it happened the damage was serious enough but not in depth, as post-war Germany has shown. It is relatively easy to indicate a measure of consistency in National Socialist literary policy by quoting relevant extracts of policy statements, but even here inconsistencies can be demonstrated. Be that as it may, however, a much more difficult problem is posed by the question of how much of what the party demanded should be read, was actually read, and what else was read besides, and this question defies empirical measurement. Personal experience would indicate that *Mein Kampf* was unreadable while *Hitlerjunge Quex* was very readable, that anti-Semitism was present but its roots lay in the religious rather than in the political sphere. It would indicate also that German youths at that time eagerly read a wide variety of war books, but that especially those dealing with the Second World War enjoyed little popularity because they shared a feature common with most newsreels at the time: much-of-a-muchness. German youth was not cut off from the pre-1933 literary world; Thomas Mann, Döblin, Zuckmayer and Remarque stood on the same shelf as did Salomon, Fallada, and Grimm. However, personal experiences such as these, even when supplemented by identical experiences of contemporaries, do not allow any generalizations.

Outside appearances are misleading, as are the massive columns of a Nuremberg party rally. The swastika flags, the pennants, the roll of the drums, and the brownshirts suggest as much a uniformity as does the catalogue of a Hitler Youth library – a picture that is very deceptive. One can point to the vast number of youth journals issued for school children and Hitler Youth, mostly handed out free, but one cannot make any deductions about the response of the readership. Whether most readers did more than look at the illustrations – and to manipulate expertly with pictures as in the propaganda journal *Signal* was something the Hitler Youth and National Socialist Teachers' League never thought of – is another matter and impossible to assess. Even an analysis of school reading books would show nothing of the response, but without wishing to generalize too much, the specimens supplied to this author at the primary school level had the stories about the *Führer* so thickly laid on that one tended to look for something more interesting, even at the age of eight.

The war produced its own pressures and necessities and developed a trained eye for propaganda of all kind. The spirit of invincibility of 1914 was not there in 1939; it had already been contradicted once. A spirit of euphoria at Germany's string of victories, yes, but at the same time an awareness of the German proverb – 'He who laughs last also laughs best.' Scepticism is a bad bedfellow of ideological propaganda and in such an environment control of reading matter was officially admitted not to be entirely successful:

'Young people? – no one, in order to understand them, should refer back to the experience of one's own youth – however short the interval. Those boys standing continuously amidst a dangerous life confronted by serious tasks – they cannot be compared with the irresponsible youth of the Weimar period. Equally it would be a mistake to use as a yardstick the happy and richly endowed Hitler Youth of 1939. It would result in very little if one were to force upon a 14-year-old railway helper material for political education. If he finds the way to the library at all then one must be glad if he remembers good old acquaintances from his childhood like *Bill and the Red Snake*.[111]

'After clearing-up operations following an air-raid, a Hitler Youth came to the local library 'hollow-eyed' and expressed the wish to read something light and funny like a boys' adventure story. The librarian advised him to have a good sleep first. Her colleague however disagreed, for a little light reading would have been a form of relaxation for this 17-year-old HJ section leader. And how typical was this youth of the rest of his contemporaries?'[112]

During the war youth turned away from most forms of direct

propaganda, with the exception of historical biographies and fairy tales. As one German literary historian put it, 'never in recent times did German boys and girls read fairy tales as intensively as during the last years of the Second World War'.[113] As war increasingly became grim reality, the less were war books in demand; consequently while National Socialist ideas of the reading interests of the German youth were directed towards ideological criteria, with the continuation of war these corresponded less and less to reality. Propaganda defeated its own ends.

If it is difficult to assess the actual response of the youth readership, it is equally difficult to assess how far the National Socialists managed to overcome countervailing forces such as the parental home.[114] One can document that attempts to that effect were made in youth literature, but certainly the family unit in 1945 was still more intact than it is today. In schools of course National Socialism could exert its influence far more, firstly through the direct control of the teachers and library, and secondly by making use of the eternal teacher-pupil dichotomy.

To control and contain the countervailing influence of the church was as difficult as it proved to be with the family. Both Roman Catholic and Protestant churches throughout the duration of the Third *Reich* issued in very informal ways their own lists of recommended youth books, and some dioceses maintained their own libraries whose independence was, because of the Concordat, successfully defended.

Therefore, given the relatively short duration of Hitler's Germany, the psychological gains made by the control of youth literature can only have been very limited and in most cases only temporary. However, what must be borne in mind is that National Socialism could build upon and utilize a popular nationalistic literary tradition in youth literature, which since 1871 had been at work instilling in Germany's youth a spirit of superiority and militant aggressiveness.

VIII Education

Hitler's own ideas on the subject of the education of Germany's youth are exhaustively summarized in his *Mein Kampf* and they remained unchanged throughout his career.[1] Irrespective of the place of utterance or his audience in later years, the same ideas and commonplaces crop up, time and again.[2] According to him the state's primary educational task for the welfare of the German race was to instil a racial consciousness into every boy and girl. This and this alone would ensure that the child would become a valuable member of the national community.

What were the tenets of this racially-oriented educational philosophy? High intellectual qualities were said to be non-existent outside the Aryan race. The quality of the race would determine its intellectual capacity. Physical degenerates rarely produce a genius, and examples of them in history are exceptions that prove the rule. In general a healthy and strong intellect will normally be found only in a healthy body – itself the product of rigorous physical training:

'By recognizing this, the *Völkish* state has to adjust its educational work not merely to the indoctrination of knowledge but in the first place to the production of bodies physically sound to the very core. The development of intellectual ability is secondary to this. But here again, priority must be given to the development of the strength of will and decision, combined with a training in readiness to assume responsibility. Finally comes the purely scientific education.'[3]

The basic assumption of a racially-organized state must always be that a physically healthy human being of good character is more valuable to the national community than a weakling however high his intelligence may be. A nation of learned but physically degenerate and cowardly pacifists could neither conquer heaven nor secure their existence in this world. In the struggle for existence it is seldom the personality who knows least who loses, but he who is unable to draw conclusions from his knowledge and act accordingly.

Physical education therefore, being of national importance, was no longer a matter for the individual, or even for parents, but directly a matter of state-concern for the protection of the race. In the same way as the state was already interfering with the right of the individual by instituting compulsory education for the welfare of the whole, so the racial state was to exercise its authority to correct the ignorance of the individual in questions of the maintenance of the race. The educational work of the state was to direct its endeavours purposefully so that young bodies were given the necessary training and toughening from earliest childhood onwards. The formation of a generation of bookworms was to be avoided at all cost.[4]

The school curriculum had to make more time available for physical exercise on the grounds that there was no point in loading young minds with an excess weight of knowledge of which only a fraction would be retained anyway. Instead of the customary weekly two hours of physical training, the minimum now recommended was one hour every morning and one every evening. Hitler then turned to what he considered to be one of the best forms of sport: boxing. He dismissed the disapproval of that sport as being rough and vulgar in comparison with fencing. Why should the latter be noble and commendable for a young man and the former vulgar? There is hardly any other sport, so Hitler declared, which advances the aggressive spirit more, and which demands lightning power of decision in a greater degree than boxing. It is not more vulgar for young men to settle their differences with fists than with two pieces of metal. A healthy boy should be able to give and take blows, something which 'intellectual fighters' might regard as wild. But it is not the racial state's task to train a colony of peace-loving aesthetes and physical degenerates. Its ideal is not the honourable *petit bourgeois* or the virtuous old maid but rather the forceful embodiment of male strength and the development of women who were capable of bearing such sons.[5]

The failure of the educated German upper class after the Great War, Hitler claimed, was due to the lack of hard physical training – had it, for instance, learnt to box, a revolution made 'by pimps, deserters and similar trash would not have been possible'.[6] Purely intellectual training led to defencelessness once weapons other than those of the intellect entered the political arena. On principle German higher education had not set out to produce men but civil servants, technicians, and professors.[7] The only institution which tried to make good these shortcomings was, according to Hitler, the German army. The ethos of that army and its indoctrination of recruits with belief in its invincibility and superiority were responsible for the aggressive spirit displayed in the attacks of 1914. The courage displayed in the first few months of the World War was the result of untiring training in the army which managed to draw out the maximum of effort even from the weakest bodies and instilled the kind of self-confidence which was not lost during the later battles:[8]

'Particularly our German people, today collapsed and defenceless against the kicks of the whole world, needs that suggestive power inherent in self-confidence. But this self-confidence must be instilled from childhood into every German. His entire education and training must be designed to convince him of his absolute superiority over others.'[9]

Next to physical fitness comes fitness of character with its emphasis upon faithfulness and readiness to sacrifice, and this is followed by the training of willpower and the readiness to take on responsibilities.[10] Only then, in the order of Hitler's priorities, comes scientific education, for which he advocates changes.[11] The subject of history is in need of serious pruning. Its teaching abounds with an excess of dates, reigns, and battles while it lacks that thread of political continuity which alone makes the significance of the events intelligible to the student: history, in fact, must be geared to show the great themes and the pattern of development rather than a lot of unnecessary detail. This will ensure that history is of benefit to the individual as well as to the whole community.[12] Hitler's positivist streak clearly dominates in his assertion that history is the teacher for the future and the guarantor of the continued existence of the race. This is the end to which history is the sole means. The individual needs only as much history as is necessary to provide that degree of historical insight which will foster a firm ideological attitude in questions of race. National history seems of less importance than the history of racial development.[13] 'It is the task of the racial state to ensure that at long last world history will be written and that within its context the racial question will be elevated to the dominant position.'[14]

General education as a whole was in need of pruning and concentration; after that specialization could take place. One of the main functions of general education should be to raise nationalist enthusiasm in youth – a precondition for a prosperous industry, trade, and commerce. Prosperity would arise from readiness for sacrifice by the individual on behalf of the nation rather than from materialistic egotism. The kind of purely vocational training that youths were presently receiving in schools and universities was very unlikely to raise national enthusiasm.[15]

In Hitler's view the humanities, as well as the sciences, were auxiliaries in the process of cultivation of racial and national pride. History and cultural history must therefore be taught from that point of view. For whatever reasons a man may be great, he must not be considered as a great individual but as a great fellow-member of the race. The great names in German history must be portrayed in such a manner as to make them pillars of an unshakeable racial and national community for Germany's youth and the lesson driven home to young minds must be that 'He who loves his race,

Above Hitler Youth cavalry in Pomerania. HJ riding detachments enjoyed considerable popularity in Germany's rural regions
Below Para-military training. Hitler Youth members engaged in a river-crossing exercise

Marine-HJ: a crew of the naval Hitler Youth rowing on Lake Constance

Above Motor-HJ: Hitler Youth
motor-cyclist during a national
motor-cycling cross-country
competition
Above right Rock-climbing – a
favourite 'courage test' in the Hitler
Youth

R

Right Another HJ sport – dummy
hand-grenade throwing

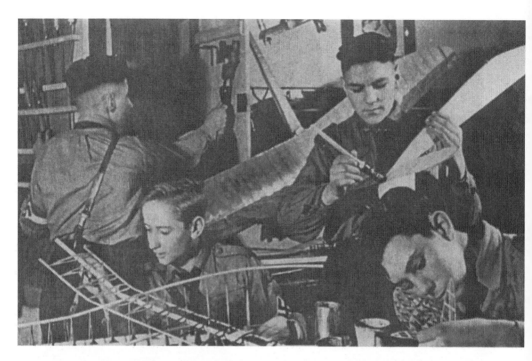

Flieger-HJ: from the model glider to the first solo flight

demonstrates this only by the sacrifices he is prepared to make for it.'[16] The close connection between nationalism and a sense of social justice must be implanted into the young heart. Then a nation of citizens will emerge closely bound to one another and forged together by common love and common pride, invincible forever.[17]

'The fear of chauvinism in our time is the symptom of the impotence of society. Since it lacks exuberant strength, and since such strength appears to be unpleasant, it can no longer achieve great deeds. The greatest changes on this earth would have been unthinkable had their driving force been the bourgeois virtues of peace and order instead of fanatic, even hysterical passions.

'Surely the world is moving towards great changes. The only question is whether they will be of benefit to Aryan mankind or to the eternal Jew.

'The racial state will have to ensure a suitable education of its youth so that a generation will emerge capable of facing the final and decisive decisions on this globe. The nation which first sets out on this path will conquer. . . .'[18]

'The crowning achievement of the entire educational work of the racial state must be to burn a sense of race and feeling for race instinctively as well as by the force of reason into the youth entrusted to its care. No boy or girl should leave school without realizing the necessity and the nature of the purity of blood.'[19]

This provided the 'ideological' basis upon which, in the words of Baldur von Schirach, 'the revolution of education' was to be carried out from 1933 onwards.[20] 'National Socialism is a *Weltanschauung* whose claims are total and not simply a matter of opinion. The means by which to enforce this claim is through education. German youth shall not as under Liberalism in a so-called objective way be given the choice whether it wants to grow up materialistically or idealistically, racial or international, religious or godless, but it will be consciously formed according to those principles which have been recognized and proved as right: the principles of the National Socialist ideology.'[21]

This pronouncement by the leading National Socialist pedagogue Ernst Kriegk reflects of course Hitler's own postulates, and upon the question 'Reason – what belongs to it?' the founder of the National Socialist Teachers' League, Hans Schemm, provided his own answer: 'Logic, calculation, speculation, banks, bourses, interest rates, dividends, capitalism, career, usury, Marxism, Bolshevism, crooks, and swindlers.'[22] Hence the corollary of this definition was to replace the primacy of reason with that of physical prowess which would train and develop man's innate aggressive spirit.

Shortly after coming to power the Minister of the Interior Dr Wilhelm

Frick issued the guidelines for the future National Socialist education programme: 'The period in which the task of the school was considered to be to develop the individual is past. The new school proceeds on principle from the idea of the community, which is the age-old legacy of our Germanic ancestors.'[23] But teachers, who might well pay lip-service to these principles, if proved too settled in their ways and methods to pay much serious attention to them, would then have to be displaced by an entirely new body of teachers. As this was of course impracticable for the time being, it was, in Schirach's view, up to the Hitler Youth to supplement the educational functions of the school both in the realm of 'ideological training' and of physical training.[24] The final aim was that out of the Hitler Youth would eventually come 'the youth leader and educator of the future' who would be the 'priest of the national socialist faith and an officer of National Socialism'.[25] The priest and the officer of National Socialism were meant to produce ultimately 'the eternally enthusiastic fighter' and 'the political soldier.'[26] The 'fighting instinct' was alleged to have been racially derived and those who could not fight were not fit to live, because life was nothing but an eternal struggle for existence. In the past, Germans, because of their lack of militant national pride and their divisions, had always been cheated of their rightful victory, a victory which a generation of youths, educated according to National Socialist principles, would soon secure and benefit from. As the benefits of victory would always be threatened by that race which was forever prepared to fight, Germans would have to become politically orientated soldiers, soldiers capable of fighting with ideological as well as with more conventional weapons.[27] But the way this was done revealed the sham and vulnerability of National Socialism as an ideology. It could not be exposed to rational discussion, and when confronted by debate its character as a faith, which by its very nature could not be empirically verified, was insisted upon.[27]

The intrusion of the rough and tumble of day-to-day politics into the German educational fabric was of course nothing new; the political divisions of the Weimar Republic reached too deep not to have affected the educational system, particularly at the secondary school and university level. At first, with the establishment of the Republic, it had seemed as though the fall of the Hohenzollern Empire had cleared the way for reform, with the attempt to create new and less formal relationships between teacher and students and to clear the classrooms of their stuffiness.[28]

That impulse, however, was soon stifled by the interference of social, political, and religious interest groups. The arguments between 'republicans' and 'nationalists' had invaded the lecture halls of the universities from the very beginning, and as the party struggle on the public forum intensified, it inevitably invaded school classrooms too.[29] If, as in the case of

Bernhard Rust, a teacher allowed himself to be too actively involved in politics he could expect dismissal – with certainty if he was a National Socialist or a Communist.[30] Pupils, because of their age and lack of maturity, were likely to be much more active in the form and expression of their political engagement, in which case they risked being prevented from taking their matriculation examination. One of the first decrees issued by Rust when he became NS Minister for Science and Education nullified 'all disciplinary measures taken since 1 January 1925 against pupils for actions which had a solely national motivation. Pupils who have been dismissed for these reasons must be readmitted without previous examination into the forms in which they worked at the time of their dismissal.'[31] Those concerned and readmitted were celebrated as martyrs for the 'national cause' – and made the most of it.

The reluctance to display direct outward political commitment by many of the German teaching profession was carried well into the Third *Reich*. In 1933 no one could foresee with certainty how long Hitler would last as German Chancellor, and a substantial body of opinion, inside as well as outside Germany, forecast for him a stay no longer than any of the previous governments. However, this reservation changed rapidly after those events which quickly consolidated Hitler's position in 1933 – the *Reichstag* fire, the March elections, and the passing of the Enabling Act. Teachers and civil servants alike now rushed to become members of the NSDAP or of any one of its sub-organizations. But this, in most cases, was a step dictated by opportunism and the need for economic survival rather than by political conviction. It was by no means uncommon that a teacher of say, German history, would with a straight face discuss a particular piece of German literature or history as interpreted by the canons of National Socialism, but then by particular emphasis clearly indicate both his own position and the absurdity of the underlying NS assumptions. Over the years a peculiar kind of double-talk developed in which everyone knew what was meant, yet which at the same time always followed the accepted jargon and ideas and so could never be pinned down as seditious. Nevertheless, outwitting National Socialism can hardly be considered an act of 'resistance'. Little enough was risked in this way and none of the horrors committed in the name of the German people was prevented.

But in many German urban centres even before the teaching profession succumbed to the 'dictate of reason', the Hitler Youth had carried out their own form of 'seizure of power'. In many schools, against the opposition, frequently physical, of headmasters and caretakers, the black, red, and gold banner of the Republic was torn down from the flagpoles and in its place was flown the banner of Hitler's party. Pictures of prominent Weimar politicians which adorned the walls of classrooms, like that of the late President

Ebert, were subjected to ceremonial burnings in the school playgrounds.[32]

After the co-ordination of the German provinces later in 1933, Rust, aided by the militant NS Teachers League, carried out a systematic purge of the entire teaching profession. Teachers at secondary school or university level who belonged to one of the democratic parties Left-of-Centre were removed, mainly into a premature retirement, a measure which also affected all Jewish teachers, irrespective of previous party affiliations. They were replaced by men and women who were often better National Socialists than teachers.[33]

The dichotomy between pupils and teachers is probably as old as the relationship between them, and during the Weimar Republic the attitude of 'we' against 'them' was inevitably aggravated by sharp ideological cleavages. But when in 1933 'the moment of youth' had come many Hitler Youths thought the time ripe to pay back the 'liberal bourgeois hypocrites'. One *Jungzugführer* took his unit, broke into his school, and in well-established 'beer-hall-battle' manner disrupted and finally dispersed the meeting of a teachers' association.[34] In another case, in Munich, uniformed Hitler Youths smashed the windows of the flat of a Latin mistress notorious for giving low marks, and after they had completed their destructive work they assembled before the house singing sentimental folksongs. Police when they arrived at the scene were bewildered and as they could not arrest a Hitler Youth in uniform merely took down their names.[35]

Between 1933 and 1934 reports of incidents ranging from disobedience to the use of physical force by Hitler Youths against teachers reached such dimensions that it became a matter of grave concern for the NSDAP. During the middle of November 1933 a National Socialist Committee for Education was convened and met to discuss the threat to school discipline posed by the Hitler Youth and to consider ways of meeting it. The conclusion reached by the committee was that this was primarily the result of a 'leadership crisis' within the Hitler Youth – a crisis which genuinely existed – and that one way towards at least a partial remedy would be to press as many young teachers as possible into service with the Hitler Youth.[36] Obviously a head-on confrontation with the Hitler Youth was to be avoided, but nevertheless the return to 'law and order' – as Hitler's appointment was interpreted by many – had to be ensured. In this the teachers had the full backing of Rust's ministry. Rust himself declared that 'the authority of the school in the racial state must not be violated' and later, 'It is the task of headmasters to ensure that pupils obey their teachers unconditionally and that law and order reign supreme throughout the school.'[37]

Some ideas of the function of the schools were expressed in the formula, 'The supreme task of the schools is the education of youth for the service of *Volk* and state in the National Socialist spirit. Any controlling function is to be exercised solely by the immediately superior administrative organ.'[38] This last sentence was added by the NSDAP itself, lest Hitler Youths interpreted their role as being one of controlling the teachers. From the point of view of National Socialist teachers, then, the Hitler Youth's function was supplementary to that of the school, not superior. And in order to reassure schools as well as parents, the Hitler Youth was explicitly admonished that it 'had to respect the authority of the school unconditionally, and its leaders are to remind their members to fulfil the school requirements for work and discipline. Schools, as well as Hitler Youth, in their demands upon the youth have to respect the participation of parents as well as the maintenance of a healthy family life. In the new state the family in particular represents the germinal seed and the basis of the *Volkstum*; its existence is to further and to be protected.'[39]

Schirach, however, was not prepared to accept the primacy of the school unconditionally. He rejected successfully any claim by teachers to influence and guide Hitler Youth service: 'To teach and to lead are two fundamentally different things. The teacher as such should not be a Hitler Youth leader. The *Reichsjugendführung* does not accept a prior suitability of a teacher for Hitler Youth office, any more than of any other fellow German.'[40] This of course reflects not so much a contradiction of Schirach's previously mentioned ideal of the 'leader and educator' but rather his own adjustment to the existing realities.

The Hitler Youth endeavoured to secure and institutionalize its own position within the schools by having at least one teacher on the staff, preferably a former member, who would represent its interests and act as a kind of liaison officer between school and Hitler Youth. As it proved impossible to do this for every school a *Vertrauensmann* (or liaison officer) for the relations between Hitler Youth and schools was set up at local party district level.[41]

It is as difficult to document the attitude of teachers towards the Hitler Youth as it is to generalize about it. Certainly a large part of the profession, including party members, viewed the pedagogic and educational attempts of the Hitler Youth with reservation and scepticism. But areas of direct friction were relatively few. Hitler Youth activity was too well planned and regimented to cause overlap and conflict with the school.[42] Also ideological differences were, a few isolated exceptions apart, virtually non-existent. Teachers could reasonably well maintain their own position where, as for instance in rural Bavaria, they enjoyed the full support of parents as well as pupils. However, through the centralization of the entire German educational system, Germany's schools too became important executive organs of the National Socialist state, whether by compelling all children from the age of ten upwards to be members of the Hitler Youth, or through suppressing potential opposition among pupils by the threat of not allowing them to take their matriculation examination.[43]

In its relationship with the parental home, the Hitler Youth between 1933 and 1936 made genuine attempts to win over the loyalty of the parents. Schirach in public speeches pleaded for their support. Hitler Youth units staged parents' meetings. But once the Hitler Youth had become the state youth such endeavours were no longer thought to be necessary; parents had to accept the Hitler Youth as they accepted the labour service and military service.

The war offered further possibilities for Hitler Youth inroads into school and family life, and one such possibility offered itself in the *Kinderlandverschickungs* homes. Originally the KLV project had been designed by the NSDAP to facilitate holidays for children from urban centres whose health was endangered. At the beginning of the war the scheme was extended to house children from border districts potentially threatened by war action. With the onset of the Allied bomber offensive in 1943 entire schools were moved from the cities to KLV camps in which the Hitler Youth leadership of the respective *Gau* closely collaborated with the local school administrative offices. Formal education and Hitler Youth service were thus merged and ultimately the aim was that the teacher and camp leader should also be the camp's Hitler Youth leader – the educator should also be the leader. This aim was achieved only in a very few camps before the end of the war.[44]

In the meantime a more pragmatic course was steered by the Hitler Youth in its relations with school and home which in practice led also to the absorption of the generation conflict. At first sight this seems a contradictory result considering the original claims of the party and the Hitler Youth, especially before 1933 when the National Socialist movement, unlike any other political movement in Germany at the time, was accepted as being the 'Movement of Youth'. Certainly the Youth Movement before 1914 and to some extent also after 1918 was in part a protest movement against the older generation. The National Socialist movement too put forward its claims to represent the ambitions of the young against the forces of the status quo supported by the old. Its mode of agitation, its propaganda slogans which equated the 'Weimar System' with the 'system of the old', was essentially directed at the younger generation and therefore allowed also its older generation membership to identify itself with the cause of youth. Since it was this age-group, on the threshold of middle age or already well advanced into it, which actually took over the reigns of government the generation conflict as such had to be ended. After 1933 Hitler Youth leadership emphasized in its publications the organic unity of the *Volk* and opposed the 'youthful spirit of opposition for opposition sake'. When in

1936 the Hitler Youth was institutionalized as the only German youth organization Schirach declared: 'The contrast between the generations has now been overcome. And that is well. Because youth movements have only a right of existence as organizations of immature forces of opposition directed against the [incapable] leadership of their racial community.'[45]

The generation conflict was thus absorbed and defused at the highest institutional level by the reinterpretation of the conflict of 'youth' against the 'forces of reaction' – a reinterpretation that was activated only in instances of direct internal opposition in Germany to National Socialist policies, as that offered on occasions by the Roman Catholic Church. Of importance in this absorption of the generation conflict is the vast extension of the range of activity and responsibility for the individual Hitler Youth. There has never been a period in German history in which youth wielded such wide administrative and executive powers, a development that was further forced by the impact of war. 'Youth would not have been youth had it not tasted with pleasure and high spirits its new power.'[46] Such active involvement furthered the self-consciousness and arrogance of youth.

Symptomatic of this spirit was the conflict that arose between Schirach and Rommel. As most forms of para-military training received high priority over more conventional sports the question arose as to who should provide and supervise this training, and this brought the German army into the picture since it alone possessed the necessary resources. The SS-*Verfügungstruppen* at the time could hardly be considered for the job, as they themselves were in the process of rigorous training partially carried out by army officers delegated for the task. The army, of course, saw in the Hitler Youth, as well as in the younger age groups of the storm troopers, an ideal reservoir of manpower well suited to plans envisaging the rapid expansion of Germany's military forces. Co-operation between army officers and Hitler Youth units already existed at various levels, but the attempt to institutionalize this relationship was not made before 1937 when the then Lieutenant-Colonel Erwin Rommel, at the time an instructor at the War Academy in Potsdam, was assigned to the Hitler Youth to supervise their general standards of training and discipline. A wearer of Germany's highest decoration of the First World War, the *Pour le Mérite*, he was immediately hero-worshipped by the boys. By comparison with this battle-hardened soldier, Schirach, in his arrogant attempts to assert himself, was bound to appear bombastic and effete. Rommel had nothing against the para-military training of the Hitler Youth, but the acquisition of a sound educational grounding coupled with good character-building appeared more important to him. He despised the kind of upper echelon Hitler Youth leader who advertised his new-found prominence with a chauffeur-driven car. As the son of a schoolmaster he could very well appreciate the early difficulties between Hitler Youth and the educational authorities, and on a number of occasions sided with the latter against the former. When Rommel tried to act as mediator between Rust's ministry and Schirach, the Hitler Youth leader, immediately suspecting a plot against him by a combination of schoolmasters and army, took personal offence. Rommel told him point blank that if he, Schirach, was determined to be the leader of a para-military force he should first become a soldier himself. It was the end of Rommel's assignment with the Hitler Youth and thus for the time being the end of any formal relationship between army and Hitler Youth.[47]

While the Weimar Republic had made serious and successful attempts to improve the quality of primary-school teachers, after 1933 it became regular practice to take into consideration work done for the NSDAP in deciding teaching appointments. This could mean the waiving of many professional examinations which had previously been compulsory.[48] To start producing a 'National Socialist teacher', institutionalized short cuts such as the 'Institutes for Teacher Training' ran short, condensed courses and its students wore Hitler Youth uniform throughout and were organized along Hitler Youth lines.[49] The outbreak of war resulted in an even more acute shortage of teachers and this provided the opportunity for the Hitler Youth to participate directly in remodelling teacher training courses in order to produce the 'political teacher'.[50] Hitler Youth leaders and headmasters alike were directed to observe their subordinates and pupils respectively for two qualities: 'leadership quality' and 'teaching ability'. Those endowed with the first quality would be asked to go through special examinations which, if passed, would get them a scholarship at one of the 'élite' schools; those who displayed an ability to teach would be encouraged to take up the teaching profession.[51] Selection for teacher training was made jointly by officials of the Ministry of Education and representatives of the Hitler Youth.[52] The heads of the training institutes were to be, in principle, Hitler Youth leaders with the ultimate objective of creating a teaching body 'united and strengthened by membership in one organization, an instrument close to the political leadership which would disseminate one political shape through every facet of education'.[53]

While these ideals were awaiting fulfilment, schools still had to be run with the existing personnel and the curriculum still contained a good deal with which the 'reformers' would gladly have dispensed. Before the war the schools directly affected by Hitler's rule were the religious denominational schools which were abolished in 1936 – a clear breach of the Concordat.[54] Whether this step had detrimental effects upon the pupils is a matter of opinion. From this time Catholics and Protestants were educated in the same school, dividing up into their respective denominations once a week to receive religious instruction by a clergyman. During the same year church holidays during weekdays were no longer celebrated as public holidays and special prayers on such occasions were banned at school. Two years later all teachers were ordered to resign from any denominational professional organization of which they might be members.

German teachers were encouraged to ignore the classics in favour of the study of the German heritage and the German national community. Rust's ministry went as far as issuing examples of essay topics for use in German language classes. To what extent these were used is impossible to assess. A very narrow survey among Germans born between 1925 and 1935 may perhaps indicate the general trend. Only ten per cent remember being subjected to up to five 'NSDAP Essays' during their school career and those who wrote them were all in the 1925–32 age group, while of those questioned born between 1933 and 1935, not one ever wrote an explicitly party political essay,[55] such as 'Adolf Hitler, the Saviour of the Fatherland', 'What enables Adolf Hitler to be the German *Führer* and Reichschancellor', 'The Renewal of the German Racial Soul', 'Analyse structure and plan of Adolf Hitler's Speech of 17 May 1933'.[56] In the entrance examination to the *Nationalpolitische Erziehungsanstalten* German composition was tested until 1943 by essentially non-political essays.[57] In the requirements for admission to the *Adolf Hitler Schulen* the essay was of secondary importance anyway. The literature chosen was intended to illustrate the bonds unifying the community in its present struggle. But literature for this purpose was extremely hard to come by and only two alternatives remained: recourse to war books written by National Socialists or approved by them, or a return to the classics, excluding those written by Germans of the Jewish faith. The classics prevailed.

National Socialist education carried to the extreme a tendency inherent in German historiography since the nineteenth century – the concentration upon the 'world historical individual'. History, it was alleged, could almost be completely taught in terms of political and military biographies. Recent history, which was introduced from the first form of the primary school, was exclusively the history of the NSDAP, with a strong mixture of National Socialist hero-worship and mythology. Guidelines for the teaching of history in the upper forms of grammar schools laid down that the period between 1918 and 1932 was to be treated as the attempt by Germany to realize on its territory the Western European ideas of 1789. Political Catholicism was to be portrayed as an ally of the Marxist and the Capitalist International. The expansion of Jewish world dominion in Germany was to be demonstrated and parliamentary democracy was to be interpreted as an inevitable step in the process ending in the seizure of power by the Bolshevik world conspiracy. Finally, January 1933 brought about Germany's liberation at the hands of Adolf Hitler. Geography was to be taught in terms of geopolitics, of living space, of demographic movements, racial expansion, and acquisition of colonial territory.[58]

In the natural sciences biology was the subject worst affected by racial teachings. Unverified and absurd theories found their way into the textbooks with the purpose of producing 'racial consciousness' and 'racial feeling' in Germany's youth.[59] Even arithmetic problems were set so as to influence children in this direction. The question 'How many children must a family produce in order to secure the quantitative continuance of the German *Volk*?' was by no means unusual. Children were also confronted with more grisly problems such as, 'A mentally-handicapped person costs the public 4 *Reichsmark* per day, a cripple 5.50 *Reichsmark* and a convicted criminal 3.50 *Reichsmark*. Cautious estimates state that within the boundaries of the German Reich 300,000 persons are being cared for in public mental institutions. How many marriage loans at 1,000 *Reichsmark* per couple could annually be financed from the funds allocated to institutions?'[60]

However, because the 'political teacher' could not be produced in sufficient quantities in time, education was mainly left in the hands of those who had carried out the task for decades. Many of the teachers, if not most, were nationalistic; only a small minority were rabid National Socialists. For the most part, lip-service was paid to National Socialist ideals during lessons, followed by a quick transition, as in the case of German literature, to the German classics or to the staple fare on which the teachers themselves had been fed in pre-1914 or pre-1933 days.[61]

An important by-product of this discrepancy between the National Socialist theory and the actual practice in the teaching profession was a sense of insecurity among teachers – the fear of being denounced. Though actual cases of this happening were very rare, a teacher in German literature who for lack of National Socialist material put the emphasis of his teaching upon the literary masters of the past was risking a potential challenge by a member of the form he instructed. And this sense of insecurity was further aggravated by the awareness, as in biology, that what one was teaching was complete nonsense. Insecurity bred uncertainty and uncertainty led to a lowering of educational standards. When, as well as this, 'Total War' mobilized most of the German youth in one form or another, when entire school days were devoted to the collection of scrap metal, when entire grammar-school forms manned anti-aircraft batteries and teachers taught them in between raids, education as such slowly ground to a halt.[62]

In 1943 a member of the *Reichsjugendführung* compiled a report assessing the general situation of education in Germany. The author of the report was extremely outspoken, and that in itself was an exception at a time when every subordinate was only too eager to draw the most favourable picture for his superiors. The report stated that after the war, the consequences of the war apart, of every hundred grammar-school teachers required only 35 would be available. While during the inter-war years thirty per cent of all university candidates intended to study philology, in a faculty which comprised a range of subjects essential for the majority of grammar-school teachers, the percentage had sunk to ten per cent in 1939 and to five per cent in 1941. The decline in the prestige of the intellectual professions and the growing attractions of competing careers in industry and in the army was mainly responsible for this reduction but it was a decline that had already been noticed at ministerial level as early as 1940. The anti-intellectualism of National Socialist policy was showing the first signs of paying somewhat unexpected dividends, and that, combined with the decline of standards of instruction through lack of time and the physical exhaustion of pupils through exertions during and after air-raids, forecast a very gloomy picture for German education if this deterioration was allowed to continue.[63]

What applied to primary and secondary schools applied equally to university education. Universities, probably more than any other educational institution in Germany, were strongholds of National Socialism, even before 1933.[64] The National Socialist German Students League, though small in numbers, was tightly organized and had managed to put itself at the head of Germany's Student Association as early at 1931.[65] Schirach aimed at creating also a new type of student, a new type of university teacher, and a new concept of the 'body of knowledge', in other words an overall reform of the German university structure and the content of its teaching.[66]

University teachers were rather under-represented in the ranks of the NSDAP before 1933.[67] This does not mean that they were supporters of the Weimar Republic. On the contrary: they tried to be as unpolitical as possible, maintaining their distance from the German Republic as much as from its most radical right-wing opponents. Yet after Hitler's appointment the call by the students for university reform was reciprocated in many quarters of the German university teaching world. Radical student reformers may well have complained that 'the main difficulty in universities is that we have no National Socialist lecturers', but many of them expressed doubt, scepticism, even sarcasm about the traditional concept of the German university.[68] German academic journals and brochures of the early 1930s abound with the demand to abandon old ties and traditions and to establish new ones, to define anew the body of knowledge.[69] National Socialist students were by no means the only ones in Germany to call for a reform of the pluralist anarchy of the universities, to establish the university as one organic community with only one sense. Vague and nebulous as these demands may have been they were widely popular. However, the responses of the rectors of German universities were hardly more concrete than the demands. In reply they argued that any reform presupposed the maintenance of the existing substance but a new definition of the body of knowledge could be based on 'Germanic-German basic values' – as Heidegger put it, on the 'activist-heroic intellectualism in the sense of existential self-assertion' – but these were as vague and confusing as any of the demands put forward by the National Socialist students.[70] In practice though, National Socialism offered rectors an ideal line of defence, that of the *Führerprinzip*. As 'leaders' of the intellectual community of their university, they could reassert the power of the status quo and defend the brown academic gown against the troublesome Nazi radicals of the brown shirt.[71]

Co-ordination of universities began in May 1933 but affected the content of the teaching very little. From the point of view of the attempt to overcome the social and political divisions in Germany and to unify a spiritually divided nation, it was not a bad thing to abolish exclusive student corporations and prohibit the barbaric habit of duelling. The drive for radical reform of the German university, whose prominent spokesman was Alfred Rosenberg, encountered strong opposition inside the National Socialist party. None other than Goebbels himself issued instructions to his subordinates, saying, 'It will not do that the entire German history and its heroes are examined with the aid of National Socialist yardsticks to see whether they have thought and acted as good National Socialists. With the exception of the period 1918 to 1933, which can only be looked at under criminal auspices, it is insufferable to measure everything with the yardstick of a new time, to act as though German history had only begun with National Socialism. By that yardstick no German intellectual hero will stand up to measurement, neither Mozart, nor Beethoven, nor Goethe, nor Schiller, nor Frederick the Great. Tó describe Goethe as a freemason and as the poisoner of Schiller, to describe Mozart as the victim of poisoning, and them all as freemasons, is as stupid as it is revolting. The consequence of this would be an impoverishment and a superficiality without example in our cultural life. Christianity has brought forth artistic creations before which we bow in respect to this day; Charles the Great has been no less than the creator of the idea of the German *Reich*. This "Total Sale of German history" does not lie in the interest of National Socialist popular enlightenment.'[72]

What German universities could have opposed and did not was the suspension, dismissal, and premature retirement of those members of their teaching staffs who had been politically engaged on the Left, or were 'non-Aryans', or both. Within the first twelve months of National Socialist rule

14.34% of the entire university teaching staff and 11% of university professors were dismissed. These figures obtain their true significance only if one looks at the impact of the dismissals or suspensions on the individual universities. Düsseldorf lost 50%, Berlin and Frankfurt/Main 32% each, Heidelberg over 24%, Breslau 22%, Göttingen, Freiburg, Hamburg, and Cologne lost between 18 and 19% of their teaching body. Famous holders of the Nobel prize were banned.[73]

Side by side with the reduction of the teaching staff was the reduction of the student body. Particularly affected were Jewish, foreign, and female students. National Socialist students demanded that publications of lecturers who did not possess the confidence of the student body should be removed from the university libraries, that Jewish professors should henceforth be allowed to publish in Hebrew only, and at the university of Kiel they demanded under the threat of force the dismissal of no less than twenty-eight professors. New appointments should be made only with the approval of the students. This wave of student militancy reached its height in May 1933 with the public burning of the works of undesirable authors, including Thomas Mann and Erich Maria Remarque.[74]

Rust recognized the need to curb student activism and indirectly introduced new disciplinary measures by creating new student organizations. Furthermore, it became a precondition for students to serve in the Labour Service before they could conclude their studies. On 16 June 1933, in a speech before students in Berlin, Rust emphasized: 'One thing I must say here and now: the truly great and practical school is not to be found across there [meaning the university], nor in the grammar schools, it is to be found in the camps of the Labour Service, because there teaching and talk ends and action begins. . . . Whoever fails in the Labour Service camp has lost the right to lead Germany as an academic.'[75]

The National Socialist German Students League now replaced student corporations and membership became compulsory. The new type of student was to be very much the same as 'the new type of German youth' which the Hitler Youth set out to produce. As in schools so at universities complaints increased from staff and students alike regarding the excessive extra-mural activities forced on the students, which diverted them from their scholarly pursuits and led to a general lowering of standards. The practice of National Socialism soon had its sobering effects upon the National Socialist enthusiasm of the students. The SS-*Sicherheitsdienst* in its confidential report for 1938 observes in regard to Germany's students: 'Generally among young students the tendency is noticeable to keep away from any kind of political activity and . . . to conclude their studies as quickly as possible.'[76] The new type of student then proved as unattainable as the new type of university teacher. National Socialism, for the time being, had to accept the teachers and the students they had. It was a natural consequence of its intellectual inferiority that it could never produce anything of intellectual excellence.

As far as a new formulation of 'the body of knowledge' was concerned, this too did not find any later clarification and definition and remained a nebulous fragment in the field of higher education, which could at no time ever fill the void of meaningless political hyperbole.

IX Elites

As in all authoritarian and totalitarian states – but occasionally also in democratic societies – a political, military, economic, and administrative élite was required for the continuance and expansion of the National Socialist régime, an élite which by the very nature of the National Socialist *Weltanschauung* had to be trained from childhood. The training of the élite was to be carried out by a three-tier system: first, the *Nationalpolitische Erziehungsanstalt* (NPEA, more popularly known as the NAPOLA)[1] and the *Adolf Hitler Schools,*[2] secondly the *Ordensburgen,*[3] and thirdly the *Hohe Schule*[4] of the party. Those entering the *Ordensburg,* or later the *Hohe Schule,* were outside the age group in which they would have been members of the Hitler Youth. However, the impression of a well thought out and detailed system of educational institutions for the training of the National Socialist élite is deceptive. As far as the National Socialist *state,* as distinct from individual leaders, is concerned one cannot say that such planning as existed included provisions for the training of a sociologically definable future élite. There never existed a functional definition of an élite. Indeed behind the facade of this three-tier system lay in reality the chaos of a pluralist anarchy, resulting in educational establishments originated or supported by the party on the one hand and by the *Wehrmacht* and the SS on the other, or even by conflicting individuals within the party hierarchy such as Ley and Rosenberg.[5] Between the schools such as the AHS or the NPEA little or no co-ordination existed and the competition between them was at times as fierce as the in-fighting at the higher levels of the National Socialist leadership.[6]

The aims of NPEAs lay in their origins.[7] They were designed by their protagonists to produce an élite which could fill posts in all spheres of German life, including the academic sphere. In contrast to the other institutions which were without precedent in Germany, the antecedents of the NPEA reached back via the Weimar Republic to the cadet institutes for the training of future officers of Imperial Germany and also to those of Prussia where they had been founded by King Frederick William I, the father of Frederick the Great, who emulated the example first set by Louis XIV in France. In the wake of the Versailles Peace Treaty, these *Kadettenanstalten* were officially dissolved on Allied orders in 1920.[8] Nevertheless, some of them continued to function – though not for the explicit purpose of training future officers – during the Weimar Republic as 'State Institutes of Education', or as private 'public schools' in which a special emphasis was placed on 'soldierly traditions'.[9] Hitler's forty-fourth birthday provided the occasion for the foundation of the first three NPEAs; five more followed in 1934 and seven in 1935, of which the majority had previously been cadet institutes.[10] The original base of power of the NPEA was very much in Prussia. Nine more followed in 1941 and between 1942 and 1944 a total of eighteen were founded, of which two were for female pupils.[11] NPEAs were also founded outside Germany where they were termed *Reichsschulen*, two of them in Holland, at Valkenberg near Maastricht and at Heijthuijsen, and one in Belgium at Quatrecht near Ghent.[12]

The end product of the NPEA was to be the political soldier, the individual who could be used on all 'fronts', that is to say in all sectors of German public activity.[13] Unlike any of the other educational institutions, the NPEA was not directly subordinate to the National Socialist party. Its immediate superior authority was the Ministry of Science and Education and its curriculum was that of a German grammar school.[14] Different NPEAs catered for different needs, some for instance specializing primarily in the humanities and others in the natural sciences and foreign languages.[15] Until the outbreak of the Second World War no party officer could exercise any direct or supervisory function in these schools, and the Hitler Youth gained influence only in so far as from 1936 onwards all NPEA pupils had to be members of the *Jungvolk* or the HJ.[16] The organizational structure within each school was modelled on that of the army; in place of school forms there were 'platoons', and some schools would carry on the tradition of an historically-famous German regiment.[17] But while in the old cadet institutes of imperial Germany the teachers had been mostly army officers, this function in the NPEA was fulfilled by civilians who shared living accommodation with their pupils.[18] A distinct attempt to emulate the British public school system can be discerned,[19] but unlike the public schools the NPEAs lacked the explicit class bias. The endeavour was to cream off the best of Germany's youth irrespective of social origins; its pupils came from all social levels of German society, and in cases where the parents of a pupil could not afford the payment of the school fees this was usually waived.[20]

The actual founder of the NPEA, Joachim Haupt, came from the German Youth Movement and endeavoured to carry its traditions into the schools.[21] He had been a *Freikorps* member and was associated with the social revolutionary wing of the NSDAP. August Heissmeyer, the second inspector of the NPEA (they were all officials of the Ministry of Science and Education) also came from the Youth Movement and not from the Hitler Youth and had known Haupt closely since the early 1920s.[22] The policy of recruiting teachers during the years before the war shows that applicants with a youth movement background appeared to have a clear advantage over those whose youth activities had been confined solely to the party-political sphere.[23]

Throughout the history of the NPEAs all their full-time staff from headmaster downwards were employees and civil servants of the German state, and headmasters were allowed considerable liberty in the selection of their staff. Criteria of selection were academic rather than political.[24] Although Hitler's pronounced preference for physical toughness rather than intellectual refinement could never be completely ignored, the aim was nevertheless to fuse the traditions of cadet corps of days gone by with those of the British public school, or rather what British public-school traditions were taken to be.[25] National Socialist educationalists understood the basis of the British public school system to be a hierarchical, clearly defined, and tightly organized community. And they compared their own version of élitist education with that of the British:

'The boy is removed from the spoiling influence of the parental home at an early age, and at first has difficulty in establishing his own position among his fellows. But as a rule the need to survive wakens the necessary forces in him, which toughen him and provide him with security and a firmness of will.

'By means of the strictly authoritarian prefect and fagging system he becomes accustomed to obeying as well as to giving orders, and by stages he acquires new rights within a system of an authoritarian self-administration. . . . Public schools are therefore explicit instruments for shaping the individual pupil into a uniform national type, with an equally uniform system of values.

'Our most recent educational endeavours in the National Political Educational Institutes . . . appear to run along the same principles. Like the public schools in England they are meant to train an élite, a reservoir for leadership. The principle of a common education within an institution is also pursued in particular by the compulsory participation of all in sports, and in general by physical and intellectual training within a relatively small community. Team competition is more highly valued than individual achievement. The emphasis on a healthy way of life will eradicate damages created earlier on by overfeeding pupils with dry knowledge. That does not mean that they [the NPEAs] do not convey regular and

thorough instruction. Through the strengthening of historical consciousness, German consciousness ... an awareness of the national community, perspectives are being created which ultimately culminate in an
organic view of the whole. As in public schools, the authoritarian principle
is indispensable ... [and] the tutorial system also has its German
equivalent.'[26]

On the one hand emphasis was placed upon duty, courage, simplicity,
and commitment to the collective; on the other the intention was to nurture
the attributes of the 'colonial ruler' – the air of superiority and aloofness,
impeccable manners and style.[27] At the same time absolute dedication to the
National Socialist 'ideology' was demanded, although because of its
vagueness this proved the most difficult, if not an impossible, task. Dedication to duty, racial superiority, and ideological conviction would eventually bring forth a new class of leaders, drawn not from one but from all
social classes within Germany.

The NPEAs tried to combine the triple functions exercised by the parental home, school, and the Hitler Youth, and a high level of academic performance was expected from all its pupils.

The individual NPEAs were regularly inspected by the Ministry of Science and Education, which also carried out any promotions within the
teaching body. Although formally Hitler in his capacity as leader of the
NSDAP appointed all NPEA teaching staff, in practice teaching appointments were made by the Ministry, and teachers had to possess all the qualifications normally necessary for German grammar-school staff. In spite of
regulations setting out the criteria for teacher selection, among which
National Socialist conviction and party membership occupied first place, in
the actual practice of selection this criterion ranged sixth while natural
pedagogic talent and academic ability occupied first and second places
respectively.[28]

Joachim Haupt, who had been a tutor at the Plön State Institute of Education during the Weimar Republic, stressed the significance of the choice
of the name NPEA – a choice originally made by the NS pedagogue Ernst
Kriegk.[29] The identification of school, teachers, and pupils with the 'state'
rather than with the National Socialist Party was to him most important, a
choice which also illustrates the fact that at this early stage the distinction
between party and state could still be made and was allowed to be made.
The slogan 'the state is the party and the party is the state' found its expression only at a later stage, as did its practical consequences. Schirach,
who disliked Haupt's popularity immensely, especially with the youth associations which still existed outside the Hitler Youth, viewed him as a
serious potential rival and in the aftermath of the June purge of 1934 the
necessary pretext was found for his removal.[30] Fortunately for Haupt he

did not share the fate of Röhm and others. For a few months his deputy Sunkel carried out his functions.[31]

From its very beginnings the NPEAs represented an area over which the diverse party bodies tried to obtain control and exert their influence. By late autumn of 1933 the SA formulated plans according to which each tutor or teacher besides being a civil servant should also have a rank corresponding with his position in the SA.[32] Haupt successfully stalled, but after June 1934 this idea was dropped, to be taken up again by Haupt's successor, August Heissmeyer, with the slight change that instead of SA commissions teachers were to hold general or honorary commissions in the SS.[33] Heissmeyer thought that in this way the demand for party influence would be appeased. Heissmeyer, who was brought in by Rust personally, occupied a very peculiar dual position. Up to 1944 he divided his function first as Head of the *SS-Hauptamt* and then as head of the *Dienststelle Heissmeyer* with that of a civil servant for Rust. Only after that date were the two positions amalgamated into one office under SS control.[34]

Schirach from the beginning endeavoured to bring the NPEAs under his wing, but failed.[35] Not only did he face Heissmeyer's own spirited opposition and that of Bernhard Rust, but also that of Himmler and other party dignitaries who argued that Schirach lacked both the experience and the maturity to be entrusted with the training of those who would be the coming élite.[36] Moreover, up to 1936 Schirach was still too preoccupied with establishing the Hitler Youth's position to be able to pursue the matter more than sporadically. Himmler, who during the Second World War was to achieve more influence over the NPEAs than anyone else, let time work for him.

Superficially the same standards of admission and the same process of selection had existed for all NPEA schools since 1933. In practice, however, individual headmasters could exercise their own discretion. But pressure for admission caused Rust in a ministerial directive of October 1937 to formalize the process of selection. In it he stated:

> It is of the utmost importance that the *Nationalpolitische Erziehungsanstalten* receive those German boys who by their attitude and ability meet the special requirements of these institutes. I therefore order:
> 1) Every elementary school pupil of the third or fourth form who seems suitable for a NPEA should be mentioned to the local school administration by 1 November each year. Its head will then forward the proposals to the nearest NPEA by way of the official channels. A list of these is enclosed.
> 2) Heads of NPEAs or individuals delegated by them, together with representatives of the local school administration, will be enabled to attend and monitor the lessons of primary school forms which the proposed candidates attend, as well as attend the examinations which would lead to admission to grammar

school.[37]

The directive was later enlarged upon:

As places of national political community education, the *Nationalpolitische Erziehunsanstalten* have the task, by means of a particularly varied and specially hard training, of providing the German people with men measuring up to the demands facing a *coming generation of leaders.*

To fulfil this task they require a continuous intake of pupils which is *completely healthy, racially unobjectionable, of clean character and of above average intellect.*

Applicants who do not meet these high requirements will have no chance of being accepted. In order to avoid misunderstandings it must be emphasized that unfavourable economic or domestic circumstances of the parents do not represent a reason for acceptance into the *Nationalpolitische Erziehungsangstalt. The qualities of the candidate alone will be the decisive reasons for acceptance, and his remaining in the institution will depend on his success and conduct.*

For this reason – after a successful entrance examination – acceptance is probationary for the first six months. But even after the probationary period the *Jungmann's* ability in all areas is subject to continuous assessment. Should he, in the course of time, prove incapable of meeting the continuing increasing physical, character, and intellectual demands, he can, after due notification to his parents, be released by the next half year without this meaning that he has been removed from a secondary school. . . . Ignoble conduct in serious cases will result in the immediate dismissal of the *Jungmann*. . . . Besides thorough educational and scientific training and character shaping, all institutes, in the interests of a varied training, place considerable value also on varied forms of physical education. This comprises gymnastics, games, field games, boxing, fencing, riding, skiing, rowing, sailing, gliding, and motor sport (motor cycle and motor car). The knowledge and faculties gained will find their practical application in spring and autumn exercises, stays in country homes, holiday hikes, and travel abroad.

By his membership of the *Nationalpolitische Erziehungsanstalt* each *Jungmann* belongs to the Hitler Youth.

In view of the often very considerable distances between home and institute the school year is broken up by three longer vacations, at Christmas, Easter, and in the summer.

The stay at the school is considered successfully completed with the handing over of the matriculation report, which provides the right to attend university or other institutes of higher education. No rights for an officer or leadership career in the party can be derived from matriculation from a *Nationalpolitische Erziehungsanstalt.*

Acceptances are made in principle only after a successful examination, the duration of which is eight days. It does not simply test what has been learnt by memory, but endeavours to test also the physical capacity and the character of the candidate. The head of each institute *alone* decides the acceptance into the *Nationalpolitische Erziehungsanstalt.*[38]

As Rust's ministry pointed out in this directive every candidate had to be racially unobjectionable, which in practice meant that the family tree must not show any traces of Jewish ancestry; nor were the physically handicapped accepted, or those whose sight or hearing was in any way impeded. While poverty was no reason for acceptance, nor was wealth and social status.[39] Provisions were made for 'late developers', but at the point of joining the NPEA their performance had to be equal to that of the form or 'platoon' entered, 'because in view of the strenuous syllabus there will be no possibility of making up for lost time'.[40] The NPEAs could allow themselves a great measure of selectivity in their choice of candidates, and the composition of the teaching staff ensured that only those whose appearance as well as scholarship measured up to their high standards were admitted.

Pre-selections were carried out between October and December each year, conducted by the doctor of the nearest NPEA and several teachers. On average each NPEA received 400 applications annually, of which only one-fifth were admitted to the entrance examination. The final pass rate was approximately one-third of those taking the examination.[41]

Although parents could apply for admission of their son, he would only be considered if his teachers supported the application. The more standard procedure removed the parental influence regarding application and selection completely.[42] The proposal could be put forward by the headmaster of a primary school, and although the parents were notified before the pre-selection process there was nothing they could do either to further or much less to hinder it. A widow whose eldest son served with the German armed forces in Russia and who objected to her one remaining son being considered even for pre-selection received the reply: 'My dear lady, you had better adjust your ideas. Your son is not your personal property, solely at your disposal. He is on loan to you but he is the property of the German *Volk*. To object to his name being put forward for an élite school is tantamount to insulting the *Führer* and the *Reich*.'[43]

Entrance examinations took place at the NPEAs and, though they varied slightly from school to school, generally they were spread over a week, the mornings being taken up with an examination of general subjects comprising German composition and spelling, arithmetic, history, geography, biology, and general knowledge. The afternoons were devoted to physical exercise tests including swimming (or a 'courage test' for those who could not yet swim and who were thrown into the deep end of the swimming pool, with a troop of life-savers standing by), athletics, obstacle races, and field exercises which included map reading. Part of the field exercise test was also carried out at night, usually taking the form of a para-military exercise, the capture of a defended forest bridge, or being dropped from the sidecar of a motor-cycle miles from anywhere and being ordered to make one's way back in the dead of night in totally unfamiliar territory.[44]

The selection procedure was meant to ensure the inclusion of talent from every social stratum. Class lists and statistics are too fragmentary to provide an entirely reliable picture of how far the NPEAs succeeded in eliminating class bias. The *Nationalpolitische Erziehunganstalt Oranienstein* for the year 1938 produces the following breakdown of its intake. Of a total of eighty-two boys that year – in itself an exceptionally high intake explained by the expansion of numbers of NPEAs, which, being not yet completed for occupation, were forced to 'double up' on the understanding that the surplus would later move on to the new schools – nine boys were the sons of manual workers, three were sons of peasants, six of artisans, seven of commercial employees (non-executive), twenty of civil servants, eight of army officers and SA leaders, twenty of self-employed, and four of doctors. For 1941 a complete breakdown of the social origins of all NPEA pupils exists, showing that 1.5% of the pupils were sons of NSDAP leaders, 26% of civil servants, 5.6% of regular soldiers, 22% of employees, 13.1% of workers, 7.2% of peasants, 16.3% of commercial employees, 6.6% of the professions, and 1.7% without jobs.[45] These figures of course point to a middle-class dominance, yet nevertheless the representation of sons and daughters of working-class origin is significantly higher than at any other level of higher education in Germany then and now.

There is some evidence to show that at a pre-selection level preferential treatment was occasionally given to the sons of 'old fighters', that is to say to sons of those who had been storm troopers before 1923, and also during the war to those whose fathers had been killed in action or had suffered heavy physical injuries in the frontline.[46] However, the Oranienstein sample seems to suggest that in practice neither category benefited very much. In the 1943 intake at Bensberg near Cologne there was not a single pupil whose father was a party member, but, as one would expect at the time, the majority served on the front.[47] A scale of school fees had been established by 1937, but in the final analysis these were determined by the income of the parents and ranged from 20 *Reichsmark* to 150 *Reichsmark* per month (according to the official rate of conversion of those days, from £1 to £7.50).[48] During the first six years of their existence free places or scholarships at NPEAs were extremely rare; after the outbreak of war, however, they increased rapidly and taking once again the 1943 Bensberg example only three pupils in their first year paid any fees at all.[49] The position was rather similar with regard to textbooks, exercise books, and similar items. At first parents were required to pay for them but later they were issued free.[50]

The curriculum within the various NPEAs varied considerably. Thus Bensberg placed its main emphasis on modern foreign languages, Schulpforta in Thuringia on classical languages, Oranienstein on mathematics and the natural sciences.[51] But in the upper forms the curriculum consisted of four weekly periods of German, four of Latin, five of English, three of mathematics, two periods of art, one hour of religious instruction, one of music, and five periods of sport.[52] In contrast to the curriculum of traditional German grammar schools which taught academic subjects in the morning and left the afternoon free for homework or sports, NPEAs began their school day at eight o'clock in the morning with two hours of lessons followed by three hours of sports, which could mean any form of sport or cross-country exercise. Afternoons would follow a similar pattern, beginning with academic subjects and then moving on to art, music, or athletics. The impression intended to be conveyed to the pupils was that education consisted of more than a mere process of book learning – rather it was the interaction of intellectual, physical, artistic, and political faculties. What favoured the success of this education was also a very favourable teacher/pupil ratio ranging from 8.5 to 14.4 pupils per tutor.[53]

Relationships inside the school took their model from the military establishment, and political activities were carried out within the ranks of the *Jungvolk* and the HJ. From the very first year pupils were compelled to involve themselves in the activities of the surrounding community.[54] While younger ones would work with farmers, harvesting or picking potatoes or fruit for example (the latter was usually preferred), the older ones were sent to nearby factories, to steel foundries, or into the coal-mines. The report on each *Jungmann*'s performance in these capacities was as important in his final assessment as a pupil as were his academic or other achievements.

These reports make interesting reading. Thus one pupil writes that although the miners with whom he lived and worked suffered no shortages, considering the kind of work they performed they ought to be paid better and, even more important, they deserved a greater social prestige than they in fact enjoyed. Another one blames the existence of social and sexual misdeameanours among young miners on the absence of firmly established religious foundations. The general impression conveyed in these reports is that while every sector of National Socialist Germany had benefited by the Third Reich the miners had been left out in the cold.[55]

One vital element in furthering 'the spirit of the national community' was frequent celebration by all the companies of the NPEA, either of national holidays or, during the war, of ceremonies of mourning for former pupils who had been killed in action.[56] The style of these celebrations was very often a curious mixture of post-First World War Youth Movement ritual and Nuremberg rally choreography in miniature. The mysterious magnetism radiated by the mass of the pupils, in the same uniform, singing the same song, or exclaiming the same speech choruses in a flag-draped yard in front of roaring log fires – all exercised upon the individual pupil the same fascination as had done the camp fires of old and gave him a sense of 'belonging': *Du bist nichts, Dein Volk is alles!* ('You are nothing, your people is everything.')

Before the war one of the main features of NPEA schooling and a cause of much excitement among those affected was an exchange visit abroad. Connections were fairly widespread. Some pupils were sent to Windhoek, the capital of Germany's former colony in South West Africa, others even to the United States of America,[57] but the most frequently visited 'Western' contact was Great Britain where visits were usually arranged on an exchange basis, as, for example, with St Paul's, London[58], or with Rugby.[59] The German reports about Great Britain make interesting reading. They stress the importance which tradition plays in the British way of life on the one hand and 'a lack of toughness' in games on the other.[60] The feature of general astonishment for the German visitors was the extent to which *die Engländer* were 'ill-informed' on the subject of Hitler's Germany and the degree to which they gave credence to 'anti-German propaganda'.[61] Pupils from Harrow also visited Oranienstein in 1936; an Anglo–German football match ended in a draw, while the British won the fencing competition.[62] Among other schools included in NPEA-sponsored Anglo–German visits was Dauntsey's School in West Lavington.[63] But the reports German visitors submitted were all fairly uniform in content. They unfailingly mention the friendly reception, the degree of historical consciousness of the average Briton, and the general helpfulness. But on the debit side, on a purely political level, they note strong hostility to the Third *Reich*, while the attitude of the British press is described as being 'anti-German', with the notable exception of *The Times*.[64]

Exchange visits continued up to and including 1938. They were also arranged at the teacher level.[65] One British teacher described his experiences thus:

'I spent the whole of last year in one of the NPEAs and visited a large number of other boarding schools in Germany; and I propose now to briefly describe the kind of life the boy lives there. Firstly the boys must be racially sound. Secondly they must be physically fit – the standard of physical fitness is extraordinarily high. And thirdly they must look reasonably honest (though their honesty is sometimes taken for granted if they have fair hair and blue eyes). In England we constantly hear the sportsman held up as a model type and an example to follow. In Germany it is the soldier: boys are taught to develop a soldierly attitude towards life.

'Games take a very large part of the day's programme. There is no specializing. They are not out to produce record breakers, but boys who have reached a reasonable degree of efficiency in a large number of games. The Germans demand roughly two things of a game: firstly it must develop the muscles efficiently; and secondly, it must be a form of *Kampf* sport –

that is to say, it must give ample scope for the fighting spirit. . . .'[66]

But there is also evidence to show that British teachers judged the NPEAs higher than their own public schools.[67] After the final year, in which each NPEA pupil would sit his matriculation examination, two types of national service followed, first nine months in the Labour Service, the *Reichsarbeitsdienst*, second, and immediately following, service in the armed forces. Although Rust had stated that completing the NPEA gave no automatic entry to careers in the top echelons of army, party, or civil service,[68] practice showed that NPEA pupils were rapidly snapped up by all. After national service the choice of the career had to be made and a large proportion of those who chose to make their future in professions other than the army went on to university and throughout their studies could rely on the helping hand of the party. Actually the course of events did not allow this development on any large scale and the first batches of graduates were immediately swallowed up by the army, where they soon left the impression of being 'excellent officer material'.[69]

Himmler's *Waffen*-SS was not slow in making successful attempts to turn NPEAs into recruitment bases for its officers, and with Himmler's growing influence new tendencies came to the fore which prior to 1940 had not existed.[70] Pupils in upper forms began to receive specifically anti-religious indoctrination by SS-officers from the SS-*Hauptampt*, and these lessons regularly ended with veiled and sometimes more explicit invitations to the pupils to leave their respective religious denominations.[71] Members of the 'Germanic' *Waffen*-SS mainly Flemings and Dutchmen, were seconded as tutors. Racial criteria in the pre-selection stage became more specific, including skull measurements, while the doctors examining applicants for admission were no longer those from the NPEA but from the SS.[72]

The war put an end to the exchange visits, but older pupils were sent into Germany's eastern territories and often from there for a short spell into the German-occupied Eastern European territories. On his return each pupil, as in the case of the pre-war visits abroad, had to submit a detailed report. One dating from August 1941 in Poland referred to the activities of a NPEA harvest team in the German-annexed *Warthegau*. Its author complained about the excessive reliance the German 'settlers' had to place upon the availability of Polish labour which caused the Poles to drive the wage rates up.[73] One 'settlement supervisor' received a favourable mention 'for teaching the Poles the only effective lesson with horsewhip and stick'.[74] The introduction of greater mechanization into farming methods which would reduce the dependence upon Polish labour was recommended.[75] The local police received severe reprimands for the neglect of duties, as did SS-building staffs who hired Polish labour to build roads and bridges and then left the Poles to themselves to get on with the job.[76] According to the author of this report, the SS paid wages that were far too high and the Poles for their part seemed to make the most of it by working correspondingly slowly to make the job last as long as possible.[77] A visit to the Jewish ghetto at Lodz was also in the programme. The pupils 'were amused by the sight of the ghetto'.[78]

One NPEA platoon leader who spent some time with his unit in Holland submitted an interesting report which throws some light on the divisions within the camp of the Dutch Hitler sympathizers. While they found the co-operation between Germans and female members of the Dutch Labour Service good, co-operation with the male Labour Service was much less so 'because it is led by anti-German Dutch officers whose removal even to this day causes some difficulty'. The Dutch youth movement of Mussert's NSB (the Dutch National Socialist Movement) left a completely negative impression because of their 'moral laxity'. The NSB also lacked unity. Some of its leaders were found to be in favour of a Greater Germanic Empire, others were primarily interested in Dutch independence. Members of the Dutch SS told NPEA pupils that as long as the Dutch youth was with Mussert, it was in the wrong hands completely. The best thing that could happen was for Mussert to 'disappear altogether'. By comparison, the Dutch SS 'is ideologically unobjectionable and consciously orientated along the Greater Germanic concept'. The German army, however, to the visitors at least, seemed to enjoy a good rapport with the civilian population; its public bandstand concerts were very well attended, though the sight of a German NCO with a Dutch girl walking down the street, arms crossed at the back with the girl's hand resting on the German's pistol holster, seems to have aroused some misgivings.[79]

By that time Himmler's influence had become considerable in the running of the NPEAs. In its early days uniforms worn by NPEA pupils were evidence of the attachment of the schools to military traditions. Late in the war some NPEAs were issued with uniforms similar in style to that of the *Waffen*-SS, the field-grey a minute shade darker than that of the army, the eagle on the left sleeve of the jacket.[80] To be caught by the Allies wearing this uniform meant some weeks or months as a prisoner-of-war – even for eleven- and twelve-year-olds.

The German military successes up to the autumn of 1942, which appeared to make the creation of a Greater Germanic Empire feasible, had their effect also on the educational concepts held by the leaders of the Third *Reich* and especially on those concerned with the training of the future élite. On 10 December 1940 Hitler delivered a great speech before a mass gathering of armaments workers in Berlin, in which he referred to the élite schools:

'You all know we have the National Political Education Institutes and the Adolf Hitler Schools. Into these schools we take the gifted children of the masses, sons of workers, of peasants, whose parents would normally never be in a position to pay for the higher education of their children. . . . Thus we have created great opportunities to rebuild the state from below. This is our aim. It is a marvellous thing to be able to fight for an ideal like this. It is marvellous that we can say that our aim lies almost within the realm of fantasy, that we imagine a state in which in the future every position will be occupied by the ablest sons of our people, irrespective of their origin, a state in which birth means nothing and achievement and ability everything. . . . But this image is confronted by a different one, that of another world. There the ultimate aim remains the accumulation of wealth, of capital, the struggle for family property, the struggle caused by the egotism of the individual. Everything else is simply a means to an end. These two worlds are the ones that confront each other today.

'We know quite well that if we lose this struggle this would not merely be the end of our socialist work of construction, but the end of the German people as a whole. The other world, however, says: "If we lose, then the entire capitalist structure will collapse. We have gold and put it into our vaults. It would lose its entire value. Because if the idea spreads among the people that work is the decisive factor, what then? Then we will have bought our gold for nothing." They can all see quite clearly how our nation is being restructured: on their side we can see a state governed by a thin crust, the upper class, who send their sons automatically to specific educational institutions like Eton College. On our side we see the Adolf Hitler Schools and the National Political Education Institutes. Two worlds. In the one case the children of the people, in the other only the sons of a financial aristocracy. I admit one of the two worlds will have to break, either one or the other. . . .'[81]

This speech of Adolf Hitler's, the only one in which he discussed at some length and before a mass audience the purpose of his élite schools, was the signal for the mushroom growth of new NPEAs, which between 1941 and 1944 took place predominantly in Germany's frontier provinces. Military success encouraged visions of a 'master race' capable of administering its newly won *Lebensraum* on what was taken to be the British model of governing India. Furthermore, in place of the idea expounded in Hitler's *Mein Kampf* and in his subsequent volume *Hitler's Second Book* of securing living space for the German people and concentrating all Germans so far scattered all over Eastern and Southern Europe, from the Baltic countries to the Volga, from the Balkans to the Southern Tyrol, in the heart of Europe, there now emerged the idea of an empire, resting upon the shoulders of the 'Germanic race'.[82]

Himmler was undoubtedly the most radical progenitor of this idea.

Already before the war he had opened his SS-*Verfügungstruppe*, the precursor of the *Waffen*-SS, to limited numbers of Northern and Northwestern Europeans who were not Germans. His ambition to expand the *Waffen*-SS, curbed, however, by the strict limitations on the recruitment of German nationals exercised by the *Wehrmacht*, led him as early as 1940 to circumvent *Wehrmacht* restrictions and to recruit Western and Northern Europeans into the *Waffen*-SS. Germany's invasion of Russia provided also the slogan of the 'Crusade against Bolshevism', but in the ensuing battles in the East Himmler's first-line *Waffen*-SS divisions were so seriously decimated that quick replenishment was found only through the recruitment of Eastern as well as East-Western Europeans. The notion of the 'Slav subhuman' had by necessity to be abandoned. Himmler would have pursued the 'Europeanization', such as it was, of his SS-state even more thoroughly had Hitler not curbed his zeal on occasions.[83]

During dinner on 5 April 1942 at Hitler's headquarters in Rastenburg, Himmler declared that, in his view, the best way of solving the French problem would be to carry off every year a certain number of racially-healthy children chosen among France's Germanic population. It would be necessary to try to settle these children while still very young in German boarding schools, to train them in a way that would alienate them from their French nationality, which was due to chance, to make them aware of their Germanic blood and thus inculcate in them the notion of their membership of the great group of Germanic peoples. Himmler, besides being fundamentally inclined to a larger than purely national conception of the future of the 'German race', had been further encouraged by reports, which were in fact accurate, that the recruitment of French nationals by the *Waffen*-SS was considerably more successful than that carried out under the auspices of the *Wehrmacht*.[84]

Hitler, however, remained sceptical. He did not foresee much success for this policy. 'The mass of the French people,' he declared, 'has petty bourgeois spiritual inclinations, so much so that it would be a triumph to succeed in removing the elements of Germanic origins from the grasp of the country's ruling class.'[85]

Himmler took the point and then suggested the creation in Holland of two *Nationalpolitische Erziehungsanstalten* for boys and one for girls, to be called *Reichsschulen* – a title approved by the *Führer*.[86] A third of the pupils would be Dutch and two-thirds German. After a certain period – the precise length would need some thought – the Dutch pupils would have to visit a German NPEA. Himmler further explained that, to guarantee that instruction would be given in accordance with the purposes of the Germanic *Reich*, he refused to make any demands for a financial contribution from Holland and had asked Schwarz (the NSDAP's *Reichs* Treasurer) to set aside a specific sum exclusively for the financing of these schools. A project was also being considered for the creation of similar schools in Norway. They, too, would have to be financed by the *Reichs* Treasurer. 'If we want to prevent Germanic blood from being absorbed by the ruling class of the country we dominate and which subsequently might turn against us, we shall have to gradually subject all the precious Germanic elements to the influence of this instruction.'[87] Hitler approved of this point of view. 'Under no circumstances should one make the mistake of training apparently racially valuable members of other nations in the German *Wehrmacht* before having ensured their ideological orientation upon the German *Reich*.'[88] This remark by Hitler amounted to a major concession to Himmler, who from it successfully claimed the supremacy of the SS in dealing with such diverse matters as educational policies in German-occupied Western Europe and the recruitment of foreigners into the *Waffen*-SS. From that date onwards the process of transfer of all originally *Wehrmacht*-recruited foreign units such as the *Legion Wallonie* or *Legion Volontaire Française* into the SS gained strong impetus.[89] Only Himmler's legions could be trusted with ideological indoctrination, not the *Wehrmacht* which by that time had in Hitler's view proved itself to be *weltanschaulich* unreliable.

With Himmler's growing ascendancy in influence over the NPEAs, procedures of racial selection and training used in German NPEAs were applied in all other German-occupied territories.[90] However, besides the Dutch and Belgian *Reichsschulen*, only the NPEA at Rufach in Alsace had a substantial proportion of non-Germans; the majority were racial Germans from the South Tyrol, Bessarabia, and Bukovina.[91] One basic principle insisted upon was that whoever gained access to a NPEA or a *Reichsschule*, whether German or non-German, whether Western or Eastern European, was ultimately to have equal opportunities for advancement.[92] Whether in practice this principle of equal opportunity irrespective of nationality would ever have become more than an object for lip-service one cannot say. As it happened, it was never put to the test.

It is doubtful whether without Himmler's direct influence so many NPEAs would have been set up from 1941 onwards. But since they represented an integral part of Germany's national system of education Himmler in order to establish the permanence of his influence moved slowly, though steadily and subtly.[93] At first he had simply appeared as one of the many guests at their foundation, but, with the increasing number of stipends and scholarships, financing them became rather a burden for the Ministry of Science and Education.[94] Here was an opening which Himmler was very quick to exploit. He declared the readiness of the SS to finance the cost of the uniforms and school equipment.[95] The *Wehrmacht* had similar ideas, but Himmler not only spotted the opportunity first but because of his power was able to make a quick gesture, whereas the *Wehrmacht* would have found it necessary to go through the entire complexity of the channels of command.[96] In addition, already in 1936, with the appointment of August Heissmeyer, the first SS-*Gruppenführer* of the SS had made his appearance in the NPEA system. This provided Himmler with a tactical advantage over the army, a lever with which he hoped to gain more direct and explicit influence upon the NPEAs. When the army suggested that its officers and NCOs be appointed as NPEA instructors, Heissmeyer, on his own as well as on Himmler's wishes, turned down the suggestion.[97] Only with the beginning of the war did *Wehrmacht* and *Waffen*-SS officers appear to supervise para-military training.[98]

Heissmeyer, although an SS officer and a convinced National Socialist, had his own ideas about how the NPEAs should be run, ideas that were not very different from those held by his predecessors. He felt that the quality of the schools, their curricular versatility, and the excellence of the teaching staff would not gain by their being turned into outright party schools.[99] The relatively large amount of independence which he allowed the heads of the schools and the teachers could only be maintained, he believed, as long as they remained under Rust's ministry and did not become an exclusive domain of the SS. Himmler at first looked at Heissmeyer's attitude as a personal challenge – after all as an SS officer he had sworn the SS oath and was bound by its statutes. But Heissmeyer was at the same time a civil servant and in this capacity quite independent of Himmler.[100] The man who inspired Himmler most with his ideas for a 'European SS', SS-*Gruppenführer* Gottlob Berger, also considered Heissmeyer as little less than a traitor for preserving the relative independence the NPEAs enjoyed.[101] Only in 1942 did the *Reichsschulen* outside Germany come under the direct exclusive control of the SS-*Hauptampt*,[102] the NPEAs in Germany remaining under the control of Heissmeyer, who was instructed to do his utmost to see that his graduates would volunteer for the *Waffen*-SS.[103] This did not eliminate the existing friction, if anything it complicated it, for Rust now came to believe that as an SS-officer Heissmeyer was intriguing on behalf of Himmler and Berger, while Himmler accused him of not furthering the interests of the SS in his sphere. One particular cause of annoyance for Himmler was that the independence of the heads of the NPEAs allowed them to turn down 'undesirable' lecturers, such as those provided by the SS for ideological or, more specifically, antireligious instruction.[104] As in the course of the war the internal balance of power tilted in favour of the SS its ultimate supremacy was assured and from 1942 onwards a great number of experienced NPEA teachers were drafted into the armed forces and replaced by SS-nominees.[105] Inevitably both Rust and Heissmeyer were losing ground[106] and this was confirmed when, in December 1944, Hitler issued a special *Führerbefehl* appointing Himmler personally as supervisor of all schools from which, in the future, officers for the *Wehrmacht* and the *Waffen*-SS were to be recruited.[107] Himmler had finally won, but at a time when all the *Reichsschulen* outside Germany had disappeared, and when some of the NPEAs, already exposed to the advancing forces of the Western Allies, had been dissolved pending 'the victorious end' of the war.

As the war increasingly involved the remainder of the German youth, inevitably it affected the élite schools as well. Under the growing impact of the Allied bombing of Germany, German children were evacuated into less exposed regions and grammar-school pupils into *Kinderlandverschickungs* (KLV) homes (essentially camps in the countryside where teaching was supposed to continue uninterrupted).[108] Those KLV camps close to a NPEA were immediately supervised politically by NPEA *Jungvolk* and HJ leaders, which in practice meant the introduction of a military discipline into the camps that was far more rigid than anything the ordinary Hitler Youth had been accustomed to.[109] KLV camps which enjoyed this doubtful benefit thus became, for political purposes at least, NPEA extensions.

The emphasis upon para-military training rose appreciably during the last years of the war, the weapons chosen depending upon the pupil's physical capacity to handle them.[110] At Bensberg, for instance, an attempt was made to train eleven- and twelve-year-olds to fire the short Italian carbine, Model 91, with the collapsible bayonet. However handy a weapon this carbine may have been, its recoil proved too strong for the children; moreover the available samples proved lethally defective.[111] But a youngster of that age could be trained to use a *Panzerfaust* or a 20-mm anti-aircraft gun. Members of the upper forms of that school actually manned several flak-batteries around Cologne, while the younger pupils were evacuated into the Eifel and rural districts of Westphalia.[112]

No official order or decree was ever issued dissolving the NPEAs in the face of the approaching Allies. Often the decision was left in the hands of the head of the school,[113] who was, however, frequently found to be reluctant to issue any order without the backing of a local *Gauleiter* or an officer of the SS. But as the Allies advanced, the future élite, in so far as it had not already been absorbed into the ranks of the *Wehrmacht* and SS, evaporated as quickly as it had been assembled.

The NPEAs for girls virtually vegetated on the periphery of élite education, since in view of the male orientation of National Socialist education policies the question of a woman's function in society – apart from the most obvious answer – created embarrassed bewilderment. Not until late in the war did the idea enter into the discussion that girls might be mobilized for tasks other than child-bearing.

The other important part of National Socialist élite training was represented by the *Adolf-Hitler-Schulen* (AHS), schools without precedent in the German educational system and established *outside* the existing national framework of education.[114] Plans for establishing schools separate from state institutions to produce exclusively an NSDAP élite go back to 1933, but more than three years of planning – which included the study of existing boarding schools including those run by the Jesuits – were to intervene before finally in December 1936 they were revealed to a greater circle inside the NSDAP.[115] The driving forces behind the AHS were the *Reichsorganisationsleiter* of the NSDAP and head of the Labour Front, Dr Robert Ley, and Schirach, who hoped by means of AHS to have an efficient rival instrument to Rust's NPEA.[116] In a decree signed by Hitler and published on 1 February 1937 the AHS were formally founded and control functions delegated solely to Ley and Schirach.[117] The latter established within the *Reichsjugendführung* a new post, that of the Inspector of the AHS, responsible directly to him,[118] while Ley had his office establish the organizational and administrative framework of the new schools.[119] Finance came directly from party funds. In contrast to the NPEA, the AHS was *in principle* a non-fee-paying school, but through the foundation of bodies like 'Adolf Hitler Gift' parents who could afford it were 'invited' to make contributions.[120]

The AHS was not only removed from the Ministry of Science and Education: it was equally removed from the Ministry of Justice. All judicial matters were exclusively the domain of party courts, and it was the NSDAP which assumed all responsibility for the individual pupil's welfare.[121] German male youths aged between twelve and eighteen years were eligible and were selected by the party officials of the respective *Gau* in which they were living. Rust's directives concerning selection for the NPEAs and equal opportunity for all were mirrored in the selection directives of the AHS.[122] In the pre-selection process local, regional, and *Gau* officials of the party and the Hitler Youth participated. Final selection of candidates was made early each year in what was described as a 'Youth Camp' but which amounted to a two-week examination in each *Gau*.[123] Admission to this examination was preceded by a thorough medical examination carried out by a Hitler Youth doctor, a stage at which a considerable proportion of the candidates always failed to measure up to the desired standards of physical fitness. In 1940 for instance, the *Gau* Baden nominated forty-eight candidates for the Youth Camp. In the medical examination alone fourteen candidates were rejected.[124] At the 'Youth Camp' the boys would be divided into groups of between five and eight boys usually with a *Bannführer* of the HJ whose task it was to observe each individual with regard to physical

Above American boy-scouts salute a Hitler Youth march-past in Munich in 1935
Below Leaders of the youth movements of the Axis powers at the 'European Youth Rally' held in Vienna, 1942

Above Danish, Norwegian, Flemish, Dutch and German youths under instruction by German Waffen-SS NCOs.   *Below* A Dutch NCO explains the terrain to two Hitler Youths at an HJ military training camp, 1943.   *Right* Dutch, Danish and Norwegian land-service leadership candidates

Above Leaders and instructors of a Hitler Youth *Wehrertüchtigungslager*: German and Latvian HJ officials and Waffen-SS NCOs
Below Devoid of uniform but playing drums and fifes – 'racial German' Hitler Youth in the Lodz area of Poland

toughness, emotional reactions, and intellectual capacity.[125] Much more than was already the case in the NPEAs, there was a stress on physical performance and general appearance rather than on intellectual capacity, one reason why, for instance, NPEA pupils tended to look condenscendingly upon their comrades of the 'proletarian élite'.[126] Sociologically, like the NPEA, the AHS reflected the predominance of the middle classes. Only 19.5% of those selected for the AHS in 1937 and 1938 entered the professions of their father as those of worker, artisan, or peasant, an obvious contradiction between National *Socialist* theory and practice, though one which at that stage was unavoidable.[127] Unfortunately, in the absence of further statistical data, it is impossible to say whether this social composition of the AHS pupils was maintained or whether any changes occurred.

Final selection was made by a commission frequently chaired by the respective *Gauleiter*, which compared the reports on each individual made by the group leaders together with all other material. The candidate was often invited to appear before the commission personally to answer questions.[128] After experience with the first two batches of AHS pupils it was recognized that 'leadership qualities' and fair hair were not quite sufficient prerequisites for a future party élite and more rigorous intellectual qualifications were required.[129] Of the 1941 intake of AHS pupils more than half had passed their entrance examinations into secondary schools. While the teaching staffs up to 1939 show rather doubtful origins and few qualifications other than that of a party career, from 1939 onwards for the teaching of traditional academic subjects only teachers with the qualification to teach at a German grammar school were employed. Of the total of 12 AHS the heads of six had before 1933 belonged to the various branches of the German Youth Movement, prominent among them the *Jung-Wandervögel*, and after 1933 had been HJ leaders.[130] When the war tore gaps into the ranks of AHS teachers, rather than use available teachers from among non-grammar-school types several AHS used university lecturers.[131]

Again, much more than was the case with the NPEA, up to 1942 the precondition for any successful career within the AHS was unconditional acceptance of the postulates of National Socialist ideology, which, because of its vagueness and heterogeneity, was reduced to the unconditional acceptance of National Socialist mythology.[132] There was hardly a subject taught in which the text-books, provided especially for AHS requirements in 1939, did not stress the superiority and the pre-eminence of the Germanic Aryan race. Thus, the history of Sparta was interpreted as the struggle for existence of a Nordic master race.[133] In persuasively-written and well-designed and illustrated text-books, whether of history or of mathematics, it was not so much that a subject was actually taught but that National Socialist mythology was propagated. An essay by a pupil on Richelieu portrays him as the subjugator and exterminator of the French aristocracy which was largely of Germanic origins. Germany apparently derived some advantage from the machinations of Richelieu and the Roman Catholic Church because the Huguenots emigrated back to the Fatherland, where its Nordic leader, Prussia, offered a welcome to them.[134] Literature was not presented as a subject in which critical examination of the text helps toward a deeper understanding, but a subject in which, by suitably compiled quotes and essays, party ideology could be illustrated. The theme which of course was identically treated in all NSDAP élite schools was the glorification of soldierly virtues, the fight for the country and the hero's death, a theme, however, which at least since 1871 had found entry into German school books and to which the National Socialists only added the racial component.[135] Modern poetry was represented by the rhymes and lyrics of storm trooper songs and poems.[136] Text-books issued between the summer of 1941 and that of 1944 are characterized by the predominance of subject-matter relating to Germany's quest for living space and the tasks that would emerge for Germany's youth.[137] Consequently, in spite of the greater emphasis on intellectual capacity, the very manner in which the subject was presented and had to be taught caused the stigma of ignorance and intellectual inferiority to remain with the AHS to its end. The natural sciences and mathematics were treated only very superficially;[138] equally so were foreign languages. Only Latin and English were compulsory; other languages, if taught at all, were optional. After all, the task was not to familiarize the pupils with the culture of other nations but to teach how to dominate and to administer them. A rudimentary knowledge of Polish and Russian was thought to be desirable but only to enable basic communication between ruler and subject.[139] As in the NPEAs, great importance was placed on sports and physical education, the main emphasis being on sports that would involve para-military training and combat sports like boxing, wrestling, and fencing.[140]

The creation of a pupil filled with propaganda slogans, capable of restating them as unalterable points of view which left no room for doubt and discussion – this is what Ley and Schirach considered tantamount to an educational revolution. The teaching methods were to be equally 'revolutionary'. Lecturing, as in a university, became the model, which frequently degenerated into the hectoring of propaganda which once delivered had to be discussed in small groups under the guidance of a teacher. Had any intellectual doubts arisen, the AHS pupil had already learnt at an early age that it would hardly be wise to voice them. Finally, each pupil was expected to sit down and produce his own summary of the lecture, which later on provided material for the teachers to criticize – for example, which point the pupils had omitted or stressed too strongly or misunderstood. It was not advisable to differ with the teacher.[141]

Numerical grades for effort and attainment, as were customary in other German schools, were completely abolished, as were the traditional school reports. However, this does not mean that examinations were abolished. On the contrary. But they were conducted unvigilated, relying on the sense of honour of the pupils not to cheat. In point of fact the AHS relied very much on the principle of pupils' 'self-government'. Instinctive judgment of the growth of the pupil's leadership potential was considered of greater importance than an exclusive assessment based on written examinations.[142] To provide some relationship between 'theory' and future 'practice' AHS pupils were sent to party administrative offices during their vacations in the *Warthegau* and in Alsace-Lorraine.[143] Here, as with the NPEA, pupils' experience for the future role of the colonial master was to be gathered. What that experience was like can be seen from a report of an AHS pupil who took considerable pride in having personally and publicly insulted the French population in Alsace-Lorraine.[144]

Ultimately the AHS, like the NPEA, was to fall under Himmler's domain, but too late to have any practical effect one way or another.[145] It has been argued that had Hitler won the war the AHS would have been an important contribution towards realizing and securing over the long term the National Socialist plans for ruling Europe, because the end result would have been a body of enthusiastic 'and doubtlessly intelligent' young administrators.[146] It is questionable whether, even if intelligent, the enthusiasm would not soon have worn off and accommodation with 'the facts of life' set in. One could object by referring to the Soviet Union which has apparently produced a party élite for all offices of state out of a training process which is extremely narrow and rigid.[147] But the comparison breaks down immediately once one looks at the national and cultural traditions of both countries, one for long periods sealed off from its Western neighbours, the other being throughout participator in as well as a shaper of Europe's culture and her political destinies. For Hitler and Himmler to succeed along Soviet lines they would have had to eliminate the awareness of centuries of tradition, in fact to reduce Germans to the level at which Lenin found the multitude of Russia's population in 1917, the level of illiteracy, and then start afresh. This could hardly be done and, in spite of some educational experimentation, the absence of coherent and systematically constructed ideological premises left little alternative but to rely on the established pattern of education.

No more successful in eliminating two thousand years of European cultural heritage were the *Ordensburgen*, the castles of order, which were founded in the same year as the NPEAs, in 1933.[148] They were ultimately to

cater for the eighteen-year-old AHS graduate, and because of their imposing architectural styles are the most visible remnant of the Hitler Youth to
this day, particularly the *Ordensburg* Vogelsang in the Eifel and Sonthofen
in the Allgäu in Bavaria.

Robert Ley had also been the originator of the *Ordensburgen*, the result
of a conversation between him and Hitler when both had visited the former
training school for German trade union functionaries in Bernau near
Berlin.[149] The term *Ordensburg* was not used then but that of 'training
castles', which were already in existence to produce functionaries for Ley's
Labour Front. At the outbreak of war the NSDAP operated a total of 136
such institutes for political indoctrination.[150]

But without having in mind any specific ultimate function, Ley, supported by Hitler's desire to build something representative of the 'new
spirit', began building first in Pomerania at Krössinsee the Falkenburg; a
year later, in 1935, this was followed by the commencement of the building
of Vogelsang in the Eifel, and at Sonthofen in Bavaria.[151] All three projects
were financed by the Labour Front, justified by Ley with the argument that
workers, artisans, and private enterprises owed a moral debt to the party.[152]
During the first phase of the building programme Ley declared that each
Ordensburg was to accommodate 1,000 men and 500 employees, but since
these figures tended to increase, havoc was played with the architectural
planning.[153]

Only by April 1936 did Ley finally arrive at formulating the actual purpose of the *Ordensburgen*.[154] They were to offer a three-year course for
young adults who were party members and were destined ultimately to
work within the party administration. Every year the course takers were to
change their location.[155] The first course began in Vogelsang in May 1936
but instead of lasting three years it lasted only ten months and provided Ley
with the cadre personnel for the three castles as well as the initial batch of
teachers for the AHS.[156] Pupils or students at the *Ordensburg* were
officially referred to as *Junker*. Only in conjunction with the conception
and the founding of the AHS did the whole project shed its image of an
improvization on an unknown theme.[157] At no time did the *Ordensburgen*
ever produce graduates who had run through the entire course of three (or
later four) stipulated years.[158] The outbreak of war put an end to them.
What was carried on during the war were courses of some three to four
months duration, frequently for disabled party members for whom a position in the party administration now had to be found.[159] Special courses
were also run for administrators of the eastern territories. During the war
Ley's grandiose buildings were used for pupils of Adolf Hitler Schools
founded but not built, or later for NPEA pupils who had been evacuated.[160]

The entire project from beginning to end was virtually a private venture by Ley, which was not unopposed by the party functionaries, many of whom resented the new élitism – for they themselves thought they already represented the party élite.[161] Furthermore, if there was to be an élite within the party, Himmler's claims and practical steps on behalf of his SS had by 1936 already been firmly established, and the corrupt Ley was hardly the man to oppose the pedantic and fanatic, but materially incorruptible, Himmler. Hitler too avoided, even at the public openings of the *Ordensburgen*, any reference that they were meant to train a party élite, nor did he ever use the term *Ordensburg* publicly.[162]

The quality of the candidates before the war also gave cause for comment. A report by many of the leading party functionaries to the NSDAP headquarters and also to the *Amt* Rosenberg (the party ideologue's personal office) remarked that 'the timetable of the *Burg* envisages at the most one lecture a day. Actually there is only one every second or third day. Many *Junkers* cannot digest a lecture delivered with spirit and intellectual content. They do their best to understand and to retain it but even then what has been learnt is isolated and a relationship to other preceding lectures does not exist. The frequently rather shallow prior education does not allow them to establish that relationship with what has been heard previously. . . . Working parties created well over a year ago were meant to cure this evil. In them the instructor was meant to discuss the day's lecture and to provide further explanation to allow those *Junkers* whose education was deficient to keep step with the others. But the success of these working parties was also a somewhat limited one; mostly they took place only every second day, and the knowledge of the tutors was not in every case at the level that would have ensured success.'[163] The *Junkers* were not in the course of time impressed either. At Vogelsang it was a well-known fact that before completing it, a large number of people tried to use all legally possible ways to get out of the course. And these were people who were party members already, that is to say they had completed their eighteenth birthday.[164] Within the established party apparatus little eagerness was shown by its younger members to become *Junkers*. For one thing, Ley's venture lacked any specific directives as to how the attendance at an *Ordensburg* would practically affect a career within the party administration.[165] The majority of young applicants were workers who had made their way through the Hitler Youth, had thus entered the party, and now hoped via the *Ordensburg* to arrive at something better.[166]

When Ley was asked in a newspaper interview what the training at an *Ordensburg* aimed at, he replied that it aimed at producing 'a whole man through and through' (*einen ganzen Kerl*).[167] But what these 'whole men' constituted, Ley left open. If toughness was to be included, the living conditions at an *Ordensburg* were hardly conducive to this. By comparison with the NPEA and the AHS life there was rather luxurious and the spartan example so frequently invoked was hardly practised, nor did the monastic seclusion of an order prevail. The *Junkers* were equipped with sufficient funds for visits to nearby cultural centres or even for journeys abroad. *Junkers* who were married were also catered for. Special quarters were provided at each Ordensburg so that their wives could enjoy lengthy visits.[168] From the first day of their arrival considerable pressure was exerted on the *Junkers* to sever their connections with the religious denomination of which they were still members, pressure that increased during the war. Apparently the first commander of Vogelsang was relieved of his office because he had one of his children baptized in a church.[169] The journal of the party leadership, *Der Hoheitsträger*, reports in 1943 that in the course for the war-disabled at Krössinsee half of the participants had left the church before the course began, 'the rest will follow'.[170]

Besides his AHS and the *Ordensburgen*, Ley also planned various educational schemes for the whole of German education, based as he put it 'on the indivisibility of responsibility of the party for *Weltanschauung and education*'.[171] According to the last version the party was to assume full responsibility for all *Volksschulen* (primary school from the first to the fourth form, secondary but not grammar school from the fifth form to and inclusive of the eighth form). At the same time as grammar-school selection was made, at the end of the fourth form, a boarding school for potential party functionaries was to be introduced. That he already had his AHS which fulfilled the same function seems to have escaped Ley. After the completion of their eighteenth birthday pupils were to move on to the *Gauburgen*, from where, after completion of studies and two years of practical party work, they were to move on to the *Ordensburgen*. Also a teachers' academy was to be established for the training of the party élite.[172] Ley's meddling in educational matters became ultimately such a nuisance that in January 1941 Martin Borman, as head of the party chancellery, forbade him to intervene in official educational policy.[173]

At this time the last tier of the National Socialist élite education was to be Alfred Rosenberg's *Hohe Schule*, the party academy.[174] Ley too had thought of a similar idea, as had Himmler. Rosenberg, suspicious of Ley's inconsistent efforts, calmly refused any co-operation with him. Himmler, equally as suspicious, decided to go his own way with his SS-*Junkerschulen* in Bad Tölz and in Braunschweig. So Rosenberg, left alone by both Ley and Himmler, could go his own way.[175] But not very far. Although Hitler had given his agreement to the establishment of the *Hohe Schule* and to plans for building, as well as to the course structure, the war intervened. In 1941 teaching activity was taken up for a short time in Frankfurt am Main in conjunction with the Institute for Research into the Jewish Question, but it soon petered out. How far this was due to the objective circumstances produced by the war or how far this failure reflects Rosenberg's own lack of drive and self-assertiveness is difficult to say.[176]

Academically the greatest success of the NSDAP élite training was the NPEA, but as an institution it had deep roots in German educational and military tradition. By comparison, the AHS and the *Ordensburgen* bear all the hallmarks of improvization and lack of thought, the latter even more so than the former. The *Hohe Schule* really remained stillborn. What one can observe in Hitler's attitude and among the majority of NSDAP leaders is a reluctance to break with the traditional model of German education once and for all. Certainly such plans as Ley and others produced proved more of an antidote to any attempt at a radical revolution than an aid to them. Consequently it was preferable to operate through the existing system than to replace it by chaos. The educational institutions of Hitler's party, the NPEA, AHS, or *Ordensburgen* never produced an élite that outlived their creators: this is equally true from the point of view of producing irrevocably convinced National Socialists as from the point of view of the administrator. This failure was inherent in the ideological ambivalence of National Socialism and the unco-ordinated schemes – themselves the product of personal rivalries – of its leadership.

x Dissent

Dissent from and among the Hitler Youth arose in essentially two forms. First, up to 1933, dissent, for whatever reasons, still only manifested itself as disagreements between individuals or between other youth groups and the Hitler Youth. After 1933, with the Hitler Youth's successful all-embracing totalitarian claims, culminating in the compulsory service of all German youths in the Hitler Youth, the identification of party and party organization with the state had been achieved. Consequently any dissent expressed in public was by definition dissent against the state of Adolf Hitler.

Dissent within the Hitler Youth before 1933 was a very frequent occurrence, its motivation ranging from personal rivalries and disagreements to ideological differences – quite often, as is usual in such cases, personal discontent was expressed under the guise of ideological dissatisfaction. At no time, however, did any disagreement seriously affect the development of the Hitler Youth. Those who broke away were in the minority and in no instance did any rival group to the Hitler Youth enjoy any degree of success. They vegetated on the periphery of political life and the life of the German youth organizations until, rather sooner than later, they faded into oblivion. At the time such dissent occurred the occasion was often taken more seriously than subsequent developments showed it to actually have been worth.

The radical social revolutionaries, as the left wing within the Hitler Youth tended to describe itself, continually demanded that the nationalist component of the NSDAP programme should not be emphasized at the expense of the socialist one. For some time they appeared to pose the most serious threat to the unity of the Hitler Youth, because at this level they reflected the debate going on within the party and SA between 1926 and 1931.[1] While the adults slithered from one compromise to another with the propagators of the orthodox party line until they either became absorbed by it or made the final break, the Hitler Youth from the very beginnings of the debate took a more radical view, even threatening rebellion, if necessary.[2]

Within the NSDAP the social revolutionary influence centred around the brothers Gregor and Otto Strasser, who had been instrumental in building up and expanding the NSDAP in northern Germany where industrialization and proletarianization made it imperative for the term 'socialist' in the party name to be more than just another convenient adjective.[3] The first practical issue which threatened to divide the party was the demand by the KPD and the SPD to expropriate the deposed German royal and princely families and to turn their estates and wealth over to the Republic.[4] The Strasser wing strongly supported this move; Hitler, on the other hand, was not prepared to co-operate with the left-wing parties of the Republic on a national level, nor for that matter to risk losing the present as well as the potential support of the middle class, to whom expropriation was just another milestone on the path to 'Red Revolution'. Hitler succeeded in maintaining the unity of the party and Gregor Strasser withdrew his demand for expropriation, though the defeat was strongly resented by him and his brother Otto and their supporters.[5]

Within the Hitler Youth this dispute left an immediate mark upon its Berlin contingent shortly after it had been set up in July 1926. A 'National Socialist German Workers Youth' movement (NSDAJ) was founded which stressed its social revolutionary aims, without actually being very clear as to what these were to be.[6] In any event the NSDAP paper, the *Völkischer Beobachter*, warned all members of the Berlin NSDAP and the Hitler Youth that the NSDAJ was not a recognized National Socialist youth movement and was sailing, so to speak, under false colours.[7] Until Goebbels' appointment as the *Gauleiter* of Berlin later in the year, the organization of the NSDAP there was rather chaotic; rupture and dissension were frequent and its youth movement reflected this.[8] When the BDAJ (*Bund Deutscher Arbeiter-Jugend*) was founded early in 1927 the Hitler Youth *Gauführer* Günter Orsoleck emerged at its head.[9] It gained no significant foothold but was a symptom of the continuing ideological dissension that affected the Hitler Youth.

Simmering below the surface for the next two years, it erupted again on the occasion of the 1929 party rally when the left wing of the NSDAP issued '14 Theses of the German Revolution'. Signed by the 'Social Revolutionary Left of the NSDAP', it demanded greater emphasis and radicalization of the party's socialist programme, and was in the main the product of Otto Strasser.[10] He had viewed with alarm the rapprochement between Hitler and Hugenberg's reactionary German National Peoples' Party (DNVP) in 1928.[11] Hitler, for his part, had become very suspicious of Otto Strasser's own supporters who included several prominent 'National-Bolsheviks'[12] whose publications were supported by Strasser's own publishing venture, the *Kampfverlag*.[13] Attempts by Hitler to win Strasser back to party orthodoxy failed, and finally on 4 July 1930, convinced that the NSDAP was following the wrong course, Strasser broke with Hitler publicly – announcing the news to the readership of his journal *Der Nationalsozialist* with the headline 'The Socialists are leaving the NSDAP'.[14] Among the signatories of Strasser's manifesto were members of the National Socialist left wing, among them three prominent Hitler Youth leaders: the *Gauführer* Richard Schapke, the former *Gauführer* of East Prussia Rolf Becker, and a member of Hitler Youth *Gauleitung* of Württemberg Karl Baumann.[15]

If Otto Strasser had hoped to cause a major secession or indeed exert any influence upon the NSDAP he was disappointed. His own brother proclaimed his loyalty to Hitler, and the men most prominently associated with the left wing of the NSDAP, like the *Gauleiter* of East Prussia Erich Koch, the future *Gauleiter* of Hamburg Karl Kaufmann, Bernhard Rust, the *Gauleiter* of Hanover and future Minister of Science and Education, the *Reichsjugendführer* Kurt Gruber and several others, all affirmed their loyalty to the *Führer*.[16]

Otto Strasser was not daunted. Four days after the publication of his manifesto he founded the precursor of his Black Front, the *Kampfgemeinschaft Revolutionarer Nationalsozialisten* (the Combat Society of Revolutionary National Socialists) which claimed to represent the social revolutionary and anti-capitalist forces of the NSDAP.[17] One prominent defection from the ranks of the Hitler Youth was Artur Grosse, the *Gau* education leader of the Hitler Youth in Berlin-Brandenburg-Ostmark. In language even more radical than that of Strasser he denounced Hitler in unequivocal terms as a traitor to the cause of a specifically German socialism. He accused him of having manipulated for selfish ends the German socialism of an idealistic youth, who had sacrificed everything for the cause, and of having diluted it to mere 'slogans of unscrupulous demagogues as a means to an end of wild petty bourgeois types and revolutionary mercenaries'.[18]

Schapke and Grosse founded a youth movement for Strasser's organization, the National Socialist Workers and Peasant Youth, the NSABJ, whose power base was in Westphalia and the Rhineland where it was led by a former Hitler Youth member Karl Kroll, who had been expelled as a result of petty intrigues.[19] As with most German youth movements of the time, the charts of their organizational structure look more impressive than the actual number of members. By September 1931 the *Gau* Westmark, which embraced the two provinces, was organized into five groups, Essen, Wesel, Dorsten, Düsseldorf, and Cologne – one of them led by another Hitler expelled youth.[20] By that time Strasser's organization had also renamed itself 'The Black Front' and its youth organization claimed to be inspired by the teachings of Moeller van den Bruck, the propagator of the application of Prussian Socialist ethics to the whole of Germany and author of the book *Das Dritte Reich*: 'The banner of its members is the black banner of Moeller, who is its great teacher and whose book *The Third Reich* is the basic book of the Black Front.'[21]

In its programme the NSABJ proclaimed its aim 'to secure the internal and external freedom and independence of the German people'. It promised to achieve the reality of German socialism and advocated the introduction of youth legislation which would protect the welfare of youth in all spheres of life, a programme somewhat analogous to that advocated by the Hitler Youth itself.[22]

To some extent — precisely how much cannot be measured in exact figures — the NSABJ profited by the partial absorption of the 'Group of Social Revolutionary Nationalists', a youth group founded two months before the NSABJ, by among others, the former Hitler Youth leaders Orsoleck and Becker.[23] This group never had more than a total of 200 members, though its membership claims greatly exceeded this figure.[24] Ultimately its founders associated themselves with philo-Communist groups such as the German socialist Combat Movement (the *Deutsche Sozialistische Kampfbewegung*), supporting an exclusively 'eastern' orientated German foreign policy, which advocated the welding together of a solid block consisting of Germany and Soviet Russia to confront the capitalist society of the West.[25]

Otto Strasser's secession was, in the end, of less impact upon the NSDAP and the Hitler Youth than was originally feared. The whole of Bavaria including its capital city Munich appeared to have suffered no defections at all.[26] In Berlin, according to a police report of September 1930, 'only a few individual members have left the Hitler Youth and joined the National Socialist Workers and Peasants' Youth'.[27] Reports from Württemberg indicate attempts by Strasser's youth group to gain a foothold in the Hitler Youth, but they met with no success with the exception of Karl Baumann, as already mentioned.[28] He too publicly attacked the 'numerous and capitalistic oriented personalities of the party', the despicable alliance with Hugenberg, and 'the openly anti-socialist and unrevolutionary character of the NSDAP'.[29]

In Berlin one Karl Heinz David was appointed as *Gauführer* of the NSABJ for Berlin-Brandenburg, but in a further Berlin police report of June 1931 the previous observation finds further confirmation: 'the NSABJ has made no progress ... the development in Berlin has not moved from its initial position'.[30] Goebbels kept a tight rein on his *Gau* and the NSDAP's success at the polls did nothing to encourage leaving what appeared to be a winning team.

In the north, in Schleswig-Holstein, the former leader of the sports section of the Hitler Youth, Werner Hansen, started a branch of the NSABJ without ever attracting more than twelve members. In Bremen, however, for a short time panic seems to have been caused in the NSDAP by the defection in September 1931 of Walter Burchhard, Hitler Youth *Gruppenführer* North, and Rolf Jänisch, the Hitler Youth district leader of Bremen. They were joined by the whole Hitler Youth leadership of the Bremen district.[31] Burchard, a man with Communist leanings and also in close touch with Strasser's Black Front, played a double game for three months, remaining formally a member of the Hitler Youth until he was expelled in December 1931.[32] What they lacked in numbers, the defectors often tried to make up by the radicalism and eloquence of their denunciations of the NSDAP, and the Hitler Youth dissenters of the *Gau* Mecklenburg-Lübeck under their leader, the former Hitler Youth *Graufführer* Lothar Hielscher, issued a proclamation in which they stated:

'We youths have followed the development of the Hitler Youth during the last few months with concern and gloomy foreboding. . . . As long as the NSDAP and its leaders honestly sought to fight according to the twenty-five points of the party programme . . . this situation was still bearable. In recent times, however, the NSDAP has on "tactical grounds" adopted courses which are in strict contrast to the National Socialist ideology, and no longer gives us youths the expectation that our revolutionary demands will ever be fulfilled.

'We declare that we will not participate in this continued betrayal of the twenty-five points of the National Socialist revolution by the NSDAP, and from this very day we leave the Hitler Youth. . . .'[33]

They went on to declare that they would go on fighting for the National Socialist revolution according to the twenty-five points.[34] But however great their vociferousness, however persuasive and convincing their eloquence, they could not make up their lack of numbers. The 'Black Front' and the 'National Socialist Workers' and Peasants' Youth' were, and remained, organizations which the NSDAP could afford to laugh about. Their failure to sustain the initial impact which their defection from the ranks of party and Hitler Youth had at first left on the party leadership and on Gruber quickly put the apparent danger into perspective. The defections from the Hitler Youth to the NSABJ were generally restricted to the highly urbanized and industrialized regions of Germany. Its attraction must have been very short-lived for by the time Schirach became *Reichsjugendführer* the strength of the NSABJ for the whole of Germany was estimated at not more than fifty youths.[35] This does not mean that the grievance expressed by them was that of a tiny minority but simply that those who believed themselves able to find an effective remedy outside the ranks of the Hitler Youth and its formations were in the minority. Attempts within the Hitler

Youth to organize 'pressure' groups which would ensure that the socialist aim would ultimately be accomplished continued; the *Roland-Kreis* concentrating mainly in southern Germany and pressing for reform from within, is one example, but this, as well as other similar attempts to organize social revolutionary groups within the Hitler Youth, failed to elicit any response.[36] They failed not because of the strict opposition of the *Reichsjugendführung* to anything that might introduce factionalism, but because to the mass of the Hitler Youths the opposition leaders were unattractive when compared with the *Führer*, whose position and personality had already at that stage been endowed with a 'divine' aura which was not to be fully dispelled until 1945. This unquestioned respect for authority ensured the continuance of the assumption that come what may Hitler knew what he was doing, while the dissenters were seen as mere men who had once been Hitler Youths like the rest of them, led by Otto Strasser who, when all was said and done, prior to joining the NSDAP had served the Social Democrats in the *Reichstag*. However, as a precaution, Gruber and his successor Schirach continued up to the end of 1933 to issue periodic warnings against the 'Black Front'.[37]

Walter Stennes' revolt of April 1931 was potentially dangerous. He was the leader of the SA for the whole of Eastern Germany and enjoyed substantial support from his immediate subordinates and particularly from the Berlin SA. Arguments over competencies within the SA in Stennes' region and opposition to Hitler's order for the SA to desist from street fights triggered off the revolt. Stennes thought he could successfully emulate Otto Strasser and when Hitler stripped him of all his offices he accused Hitler, saying 'that the NSDAP has left the revolutionary course of National Socialism for Germany's liberty, that instead it has followed the reactionary line of one of the coalition parties and thus, consciously or unconsciously, has abandoned the pure aim for which we fight'.[38]

The Hitler Youth remained generally untouched by this incident, but in view of the prominence of Berlin's storm troopers in the 'Stennes revolt', the Hitler Youth *Gauführer* for Berlin-Brandenburg-Ostmark, Robert Gadewoltz, thought it wise, after the event, to issue a declaration which in fact disassociated the Hitler Youth from the storm troopers. It stated that the quarrels between the NSDAP and SA in Berlin were not a matter of interest for the Hitler Youth of Berlin, whose guiding principle at all times would be unswerving loyalty to Adolf Hitler.[39]

Other social revolutionary youth groups associated in one form or another with the 'Black Front' continued to rear their heads from time to time, but unsuccessfully. In one case what appears to have been a devious intrigue by Schirach supporters with the ultimate aim of having Kurt Gruber expelled from the party was instigated early in 1933, when a Hitler

Youth confidential situation report claimed that he was playing an important role in the 'Black Front'. The manouevre was too obvious and the report was not followed up.[40]

Cases of individual rather than organized dissent were more frequent, but the causes were more of a personal than of an ideological nature. One quarrelsome Hitler Youth leader with a reputation for turning any difference of opinion into something of a personal feud was no respecter of authorities either, and he had most of his feuds with Gruber. Not surprisingly he was eventually expelled. He wasted no time in creating his own youth group and interfered with Hitler Youth activity personally and through the courts where and whenever he could. This gained him a notoriety which, as he persisted, earned him the nickname *Reichsjugendnarr* – the *Reichs* Youth Fool.[41] Alfred Bach, the editor of the *Hitler-Jugend-Zeitung*, the chief press organ of the Hitler Youth, was expelled in July 1930 for opposing the aims of the movement, while the actual reason for his conflict with Gruber was a difference of opinion over the layout of the paper.[42] Disobedience, personal differences, friction between a Hitler Youth leader and the local *Gauleiter*, as for example between the Hitler Youth *Gauführer* of Baden Felix Wankel and the *Gauleiter* Robert Wagner,[43] often led to personal vendettas, expulsion, and the creation of a rival youth group or the joining of another political party such as the SPD. One of the most unsavoury affairs involved the *Gebietsführer* of Hochland (Upper Bavaria), Emil Klein. He was a 'residue' of the Gruber era and was known because of his strongly developed sense of loyalty still to lament the departure of the first *Reichsführer*. He considered Schirach's advent as the beginning of the end of the social revolutionary ethos of the Hitler Youth. But instead of leaving the Hitler Youth he believed that he could serve his cause better from within, and appears to have joined the *Roland-Kreis*. At first rumours started in the *Reichsjugendführung* which threw doubt on his 'Aryan' ancestry, because Klein was a name also possessed by many German Jews.[44] When this rumour could not be substantiated, allegations of the misappropriation by Klein of 3,000 *Reichsmark* suddenly arose.[45] Again these proved to be unfounded, but when attention then turned to his fiancée, who, it was claimed, was Jewish, the situation exploded into a full-scale row which ended with Klein's expulsion.[46] But by getting rid of Klein another problem had unwittingly been created because his successor Kurt Haller von Hallerstein held quite different ideas as to what the Hitler Youth should be. For one thing he considered the political character of the Hitler Youth morally corrupting because it educated its members simply to support a political party while in his view the educational aim should be to train German citizens. 'It is completely false to consider the Hitler Youth as a younger version of the NSDAP. The Hitler Youth's immediate task is to liberate it from all party political influences and to educate German youth to be citizens of the state. Our aim is to educate the citizens of the coming *Reich*. The political struggle is in the main the concern of the NSDAP and the SA. Only in exceptional cases has the Hitler Youth to participate in it.'[47]

He opposed any form of para-military training, and challenged the pseudo-military features that characterized the Hitler Youth as well as most other youth movements. In place of propaganda there should be education, and much to the horror of the NSDAP leadership and the militant opposition of the other Hitler Youth leaders of *Hochland* he tried to implement his policy.[48] His inevitable dismissal came in November 1932. What was surprising was that his successor was none other than Emil Klein, who in the meantime had been investigated and cleared by the *Untersuchungs und Schlichtungsausschuss (Uschla)*, the investigation and arbitration committee of the NSDAP.[49]

In the in-fighting among Hitler Youth leaders it was fairly common whenever personal differences degenerated into vendettas for two charges apart from 'ideological divergences' to predominate: one, that of not being of pure Aryan descent, the other, of misappropriation and embezzlement of Hitler Youth funds. What happened to Klein also happened to Robert Gadewolz, HJ *Gauführer* for Berlin-Brandenburg-Ostmark, less than six months after his declaration of loyalty to Hitler in 1931.[50] Innuendoes implying that his real name was Gadewolsky and his origins were in the ghettoes of Eastern Europe began to circulate in Berlin, but his dismissal finally came about on a charge of financial incompetence.[51] The same fate met Joachim Walter, erstwhile *Gauführer* of Berlin and then *Reichs* Education Leader and head of the *NS-Jugend-Verlag*, the Nazi Youth Publishing House.[52] It is impossible to ascertain to what extent, if at all, charges of misappropriation or financial incompetence were true. Certainly financial incompetence was possible among youths and young men devoid of any sound commercial training and experience of business administration, managing as it were hand-to-mouth with an overwhelming reliance on improvization. To run a political youth movement or just a small part of it and lead it in the massive political activity and turmoil of the early 1930s as well as to prove a sound financial administrator was asking too much. Hence disorderly or insufficient book-keeping was the Achilles heel of most Hitler Youth leaders, and if they became inconvenient for whatever reasons the first official step was to check their books, which in the majority of cases yielded the desired results. The discovery of widespread administrative incompetence at the *Gebiets* and lower level did not make way for greater efficiency however; it remained a problem for the duration of the life of the Hitler Youth.

The year 1933 was a watershed for Germany's youth, for the Hitler

Youth as well as for the dissenters. The latter, from then on, acted, if they did so, against more than the Hitler Youth – they acted against the National Socialist state: dissent was identified with treason. The problem created by the identification of party with state gave rise to deep soul-searching in many quarters; whereas previously a political opponent had acted against another opponent within the pluralism of a democratic structure, the denial of this pluralism, its complete elimination by the National Socialist government, now turned the political opponent into a traitor. Yet the majority of those who opposed Hitler would have been as fervent in their assertion of true German patriotism as would have been the followers of Hitler, old and young. They would have confessed to as deep a love for their Fatherland as those whom they opposed. Perhaps they loved Germany even more. But now consciously to make the decision to be 'traitors' to National Socialism for the sake of Germany was bound to involve deep personal agonies fed by endemic doubts and conflicts of loyalties. That opposition groups managed to form themselves at all, that for shorter and longer periods they could become active, again illustrates the discrepancy between the totalitarian claims of National Socialist youth education and actual reality. That this opposition in whatever form did not succeed in becoming anything more than a beacon of youth, a moral torch which on occasions shone brilliantly in the darkness of Hitler's dictatorship only to be rapidly and drastically extinguished, that in fact it failed to become more than just a beacon, that each of its attempts ended in failure, is no reason to dismiss it and relegate its role to a footnote. History is not only the chronicle of victors and successes, it is also the chronicle of failure and of the vanquished. Perhaps a 'balance sheet' of history would show that man's failures grossly outnumber his successes.

The origins of the opposition groups in Nazi Germany were as diverse as their tactics were different, but in them the same feature became manifest as in the later war-time opposition movement built up around Goerdeler, Beck, and Stauffenberg: namely the breaking down, for the time being at least, of party-political and religious boundaries and the prominence of social revolutionary influences. The experience of the last few years of the Weimar Republic, when party-political fragmentation ensured the success of Hitler and his movement, was a warning to most people. Individual members of the youth movements of the parties, the churches, the trade unions, and the youth leagues turned to one another, conscious that if opposition was to bear any fruit at all co-operation had to transcend narrow divisions. Disappointment with the leadership of the German youth movements too helped to break down existing barriers, for many spoke 'of the unforgettable disappointment that in 1933 a large part of the leadership of the youth movement humiliatingly capitulated before the

National Socialists, adapting themselves to the new situation and donning new positions, offices, titles, and uniforms, leaving us younger ones not only lonely and helpless but even exhorting us to abandon our fruitless and dangerous opposition . . . and instead to adapt as they did. We were meant to be confused about everything that was for us great, inalienable, and holy: freedom, humanitarianism, cleanliness, the law, and the true socialism which we practised. I shall never forget those years and the feelings when we and a few faithful friends swam against the current of the all-engulfing brown stream and when frequently, particularly in the light of the example given by our former leaders, doubts arose and we wondered whether the few of us or the many of the others were right. And some of us who were not up to this unbearable tension also capitulated though not without rupturing their whole inner being.'[53]

They were all small groups who like the Hitler Youth in its early years felt that they represented the *verlorenen Haufen* (the 'lost horde').

> We are a small, defiant force
> The last of the last
> No bright bugle wakens us
> Nor sombre drums the hunted.[54]

Among the youth leagues – the militant youth organizations of such parties as the KPD and the SPD apart – dissent made its first appearance.[55] Although the rank and file and a great number of their leaders changed over to the Hitler Youth, the strict regimentation and tighter discipline of the HJ made the period of transition difficult.[56] The leaders were in a vulnerable position because the change of uniform did not place them beyond suspicion by the Hitler Youth leadership; on the contrary it may have increased it. In many cases the suspicion was justified because under the guise of the brown shirt the former leaders of the youth leagues tried to salvage as much as possible.[57] Those who before the Hitler Youth Law still tried to operate outside in the form of music or lay theatre groups found obstacle after obstacle placed in their way. In one case a music group which had organized a visit to Great Britain where it was to perform and which had the support of Goebbels' Ministry of Popular Enlightenment and Propaganda was stopped by the official intervention of the *NS-Kultusgemeinde* who accused the leaders of being freemasons, and the whole circle of belonging to the 'political reaction'.[58] In another case the *Gauführerin* of the BDM in Lower Silesia, Inge Knoke, together with forty other BDM leaders resigned her office and concluded her letter of resignation with the telling paragraph: 'Those of us who have been in the youth movement before the Hitler Youth, before salaried Hitler Youth positions existed, are now systematically being eliminated . . . The reason for this may be known to you.

But precisely because the [former] youth league leader works neither for honours nor for payment, she cannot watch the current development of youth leadership silently. It is only a question of time: either the youth leagues are allowed a decisive word within the youth leadership or we give the world abroad an example, causing the collapse of the Hitler Youth Movement and with it that of Germany's future.'[59] In retrospect the last sentence was an immense overestimation of the political weight of the former youth league leaders, but in June 1934 the position of the National Socialist government could still be judged by many as precarious.

Since at that time the Hitler Youth was not the only youth movement, nor for that matter the only youth organization within the NSDAP – Ley's youth groups of young workers and Tschammer und Osten's sports youth had not yet been subordinated – and Schirach's position was still not fully consolidated, some youth leaders thought they could exploit the existing rivalries within the NSDAP and join with their formations other inno-cuous-sounding National Socialist organizations such as the *NS-Luftschutz-Bund*, the air-raid protection league. Friedrich Hielscher, a man of some prominence in the opposition to Hitler, hoped to escape the proletarian influences of the SA in the Hitler Youth by putting his youth group under the protection of the more élitist and aristocratic SS. He had told his members: 'We must be fully in the picture about what is going on. We have to have a man who will cover us. Otherwise we need not even begin our underground work.'[60]

Robert Ley, the head of the KDF, the Strength through Joy Movement, and the *Arbeitsfront*, at that stage still engaged in active rivalry with Schi-rach, welcomed virtually anyone into his ranks, which provided the op-portunity for members of Strasser's 'Black Front' to join and under Ley's protection even to edit their own newspaper.[61] During the early years of Hitler's régime it was still possible to transfer to one of the National Social-ist movements in the hope that either National Socialism would shed those features which were particularly repellent or that it was no more than a temporary accommodation with a spook that would soon disappear. But as Hitler consolidated his position, the question of just how far National Socialism could be combated from within, how far tactical co-operation on the surface could continue without putting at stake or even sacrificing fundamental issues of principle and involving individual participation in National Socialist crimes, could no longer be ignored.

Schirach himself forced the issue by simply adopting the attitude 'he that is not for me is against me'. By labelling every youth activity outside the Hitler Youth as a 'conspiracy of the youth leagues' he invoked the assist-ance of the *Gestapo*, the SA and the SS to eliminate his rivals.[62] The *HJ-Streifendienst* (the internal Hitler Youth 'police') was put to good use to

infiltrate other groups. One of the first to be arrested was Eberhard Köbel —
more widely known under the name he gave himself: 'Tusk' — who was one
of the most prominent (if also most eccentric) members of the German
Youth Movement.[63] He and his subsequently-arrested associates received
their first dose of SS brutality in the cellars of the infamous *Columbia-Haus*
in Berlin.[64] A suicide attempt may have saved his life; he was released but
was still subjected to continuous police surveillance.[65] He left Germany first
for Czechoslovakia in July 1934, prompted by the execution of several
former youth leaders in the course of the Röhm purge. Later he moved on to
Sweden and from there to Great Britain.[66]

Some of those who were the victims of Schirach's initial round-up
regained their liberty but remained under *Gestapo* surveillance. During the
Röhm purge Adalbert Probst, one of the leaders of the Catholic Youth
Movement, was killed 'whilst trying to escape'.[67] The same fate met a Hitler
Youth leader from Plauen, Ernst Lämmermann.[68] The persecution of
former youth leaders was supplemented within the Hitler Youth by the persecution of leaders who had originally been members of the youth leagues.[69]
The majority were systematically expelled on charges ranging from 'illegal
youth league activity' to 'immorality' and 'embezzlement'. As is fairly usual
in all kinds of persecutions, the most fervent persecutors were the converts.
Most fanatical in this respect was the former youth league member and
later *HJ-Obergebietsführer* Gotthart Ammerlahn.[70] Those former youth
leaders who like Koebel, Hans Ebeling, Fritz Borinski, and Karl O. Paetel
left Germany, lost their citizenship. Others spent years in concentration
camps, such as Dachau, where many of them perished.

Simultaneously with the actions against the leaders of the German youth
leagues, legal proceedings started against the two leading publishing houses
of the youth leagues. However, the German judiciary turned down applications for investigations.[71] The *Ludwig-Voggenreiter-Verlag* in Potsdam
interpreted the signs of the times correctly[72] and one of its editors, a locally
prominent SA leader Arthur Ehrhardt, soon adjusted its publishing programme to Schirach's Hitler Youth orientated requirements.[73] The other
prominent youth publisher, Günther Wolff from Plauen, proved much
harder to break. In his case too the German judiciary refused to become the
tool of the Hitler Youth, and sheer naked terror failed to break him. Re-
peatedly arrested and assaulted, fetched out of bed at night by a Hitler
Youth 'commando' and severely beaten, he refused to give in and continued
to publish the literary products of former members of the youth leagues, including poems and songs by Eberhard Köbel, going as far as stating in a
1935 edition of a song book edited by Köbel that no National Socialist fighting song had been included.[74] Since terror could not break the man and the
judiciary failed to co-operate, all that Schirach could do was to forbid any

public reference to the publishing house: 'The *Günther Wolff-Verlag* stands in direct contact with the Communist youth leader Köbel, called Tusk. Furthermore it publishes books, periodicals etc. which not only do not correspond with the character and style of the Hitler Youth but, worse, in their tendency are directed against the new state. The formations of the HJ, the *Jungvolk*, and the BDM are forbidden to subscribe to publications and issues which in their tendency are anti-National Socialist.'[75]

In spite of almost insurmountable difficulties Günther Wolff managed to keep in business until finally early in 1938 he was expelled from 'NS-Writers-Chamber' and from the 'Publishing Association' which, at long last, provided the legal lever which prohibited any further publishing activity.[76]

The bulk of those former youth leaders who emigrated initially moved into countries immediately adjoining Germany in the hope that they could carry on illegal youth activity from across the border.[77] Karl O. Paetel, leader of the former 'Social Revolutionary Nationalists', moved to Paris; others went to Sweden, Austria, and Czechoslovakia.[78] Sweden and Austria proved to be disappointing for there the authorities firmly discouraged open political activity. Austria especially, under the Dollfus and Schuschnigg régimes, severely clamped down on the illegal activities of German emigrants, not necessarily because of a desire to placate Hitler but because of the predominantly left-wing leanings of former German youth group leaders.[79] In a country where the Social Democrats had just been suppressed with violence and bloodshed the political activity of émigrés suspected of left-wing sympathies was not tolerated.

The greatest activity emanated from Czechoslovakia, where in Eger and Prague former youth movement leaders continued publishing their propaganda brochures and leaflets which were then smuggled into Germany.[80] Attempts at co-ordinating the activities of the youth league leaders abroad resulted first in the creation of a 'Working Party of the Youth Leagues' in Brussels in July 1937, which then formed the *Deutsche Jugendfront*.[81] This was mainly the work of Hans Ebeling, the founder of the former *Deutsche Jungenschaft*, who established contact with Karl O. Paetel in Paris, and the Socialist Fritz Borinski who had emigrated to London. However, the attempt to found a common anti-Fascist front of the former youth leagues failed because of the intransigence of the Communist deputies who demanded that their programme be accepted without change as the sole directive of future action.[82] The *Jugendfront* published regular circulars as well as the periodical *Kameradschaft*, which was smuggled into Germany in sufficient quantity apparently to cause its official proscription.[83] After the German invasion of the Netherlands Ebeling managed to escape to Great Britain, but his close collaborator Theodor Hespers, a former boy scout leader, was caught by the Gestapo and taken to Germany where he was executed in 1943.[84] But he was far from being the first victim. Helmut Hirsch, an associate of Otto Strasser and Eberhard Köbel, ventured back into Germany illegally where he was arrested and charged with attempting to prepare Hitler's assassination. He was found guilty and executed in 1937.[85]

Of the former youth leagues the most influential inside Germany seems to have been Köbel's *d.j.1.11* an abbreviation for *Deutsche Jungenschaft, 1 November (1929)*, the date of its foundation. Köbel, before his arrest and subsequent emigration, had apparently hoped to infiltrate the *Jungvolk* with it, but failed.[86] It continued to exist illegally, certainly up to the war, though its members were subjected to severe persecution and punishment when caught. One branch was infiltrated by a member of the *HJ-Streifendienst*, who in his official report writes: 'The organization of the individual groups is very tight. Their leadership lies in the hands of a central office unknown to the leaders. Even a signature in the course of official business is not customary. In its place a rune is used, meaningless to the outsider. Even the use of proper names is not customary. Members are addressed by nicknames. Thus it happens that the leaders know their comrades not by their ordinary names, which makes it difficult to ascertain the latter, since questions always cause great stir and one has to wait for a favourable opportunity. From the indications given by the leaders I understand that the old *d.j.1.11* boys now serve as leaders, which ensures the continuance in the groups of the *d.j.1.11* spirit and that their people occupy high positions in the Hitler Youth.'[87] The files of the prosecution office of the *Volksgerichtshof* of 1938 reveal the existence of *d.j.1.11* groups in Hamburg, Hanover, Leipzig, Dessau, Haynau in Silesia, Breslau, and Bonn. What Köbel had failed to achieve in 1933 and 1934, the former leader of the German Boy Scouts League, Gerhard Tessmer, accomplished in Haynau, namely the complete infiltration of the *Jungvolk* there, until in late 1937 the arrest of one Silesian *d.j.1.11* member led to the discovery of the whole Silesian network and its contacts in France and Czechoslovakia. Fortunately for the accused they were sentenced only to varying terms of imprisonment, causing disappointment in some quarters of the *Reichsjugendführung*.[88]

The *d.j.1.11* in particular, and the former German youth leagues generally, continued to be a matter of concern for Schirach until the outbreak of war. Nor, as already indicated, did he always find an ally in the German judiciary if a former youth leader was caught for violating Paragraph 4 of the Presidential decree of 28 February 1933 (the decree suspending civil liberties which was passed in the immediate wake of the *Reichstag* fire). At first he managed to obtain some convictions, until a court pointed out that the paragraph invoked had nothing to do with youth activity at all and did not proscribe the youth leagues and their work.[89] Even proscription of *d.j.1.11* literature, of the *d.j.1.11* and other youth leagues themselves could not always ensure the conviction of illegal members, because the decrees promulgating their proscription were known only to official bodies and the *Gestapo* and not publicly.[90] Therefore the German courts argued that the leaders who founded them anew and their members were bound to have acted in ignorance of the law, for which they were not to blame.[91] Only as late as May 1937, under the pressure of the *Gestapo* headquarters, were the decrees officially published.[92] In the meantime the *Reichsjugendführung* tried more or less unsuccessfully to apply the same methods as within the Hitler Youth, such as using charges of immorality and financial, especially currency, offences. But the legalization of the totalitarian claims of the Hitler Youth had by the end of 1939 destroyed the remnants of the pre-1933 German youth movement as an effective force and influence in the life of German youth. In southern Germany the youth league groups seem to have played a less prominent role to begin with – at least the police records have not much to report about them – though several members of the opposition group *Weisse Rose* had formerly been members of illegal youth groups.[93]

However, southern and south-western Germany was a stronghold of denominational youth groups which enjoyed a longer span of life than the youth leagues. While in practice the Protestant youth groups had been eroded from within and without by the National Socialists, the Concordat, theoretically at least, had ensured the continuance of the Catholic Youth Movement.[94] But, as already mentioned, the Concordat was not without its ambiguities, particularly in Article 31.[95] When the Catholic Church refused to integrate its youth movement into the Hitler Youth, Schirach reacted by declaring simultaneous membership in the Hitler Youth and the Catholic Youth to be incompatible, though in practice even after Hitler Youth membership had become compulsory Schirach's ruling was not really enforceable. Since court cases on this issue did not usually vindicate the attitude adopted by the *Reichsjugendführung*, methods of harassment were resorted to. Catholic youth literature was confiscated on various pretexts and until these had been legally tested months passed by before it was released again. Catholic civil servants were threatened unofficially with a promotion stop or even with dismissal if their children did not belong to the Hitler Youth.[96] Public appearances of closed formations of uniformed Catholic youth groups were forbidden on grounds of causing public uproar or being offensive to the 'predominantly National Socialist consciousness of the local population'.[97] Uniforms were forbidden, and individual Catholic Youth homes were attacked and ransacked by Hitler Youth formations.

However, in spite of the harassment, Catholic youth groups and boy scouts numbering about 2,000 boys managed to undertake a well-organized pilgrimage to Rome at Easter 1935 where they were received by Pope Pius XI, and up to 1937 they successfully organized summer camps abroad in the Balkans, Italy, and Lapland.[98]

After the Hitler Youth had officially become the state youth organization the measures applied against the Catholic Youth organization became more direct and severe. In April 1937, before the *Volksgerichtshof* in Berlin, a trial was staged against some of its leading members. Apparently because some of the accused, like Chaplain Joseph Roussaint, were also members of the Catholic Peace Union which had allegedly enjoyed Communist support, they were convicted of high treason and sentenced to several years hard labour.[99] In March 1939, as a consequence of the implications of the 'Youth Service Law',[100] the Catholic Youth movement as a national as well as regional organization was forbidden, and any Catholic youth activity was restricted to the parish level.[101] This did not mean the end of harassment; raids by local Hitler Youth groups were frequent and even before that date meetings had to be held in secret at places which had to be changed each time. In Munich, for example, Catholic youth groups met at night in the cellar of the municipal electricity administration at the *Blumenstrasse* or in the midst of one of its largest cemeteries, the *Waldfriedhof*.[102]

The outbreak of war posed a question of conscience for many Catholic youths. No categoric statement can be made as to how it was resolved, but it seems that most, now that their country was at war, felt their first duty to be to their Fatherland. To quote one example, late in October 1939 various members of Catholic youth groups in Munich met at the Franciscan Monastery of St Anna – the very place which had provided room for an arms dump for Hitler's SA on the eve of the 1923 putsch – and dissolved their groups until the end of the war.[103]

The Protestant Church and the Protestant youth groups suffered very much from the attitude of their church leadership. Only the '*Reichs*church' under Müller and youth associations for those over the age of eighteen were allowed to continue functioning, and this practically meant continuation within the ranks of the Hitler Youth anyway.[104] The Confessing Church, which rejected Müller, and the Lutheran churches of Württemberg and Bavaria faced difficulties similar to those of the Catholics. Since the majority of Protestant youth groups before 1937 were required to be integrated into the Hitler Youth, several youth leaders deliberately released the members of their youth groups, thus preventing them from automatically becoming members of the Hitler Youth. Martin Niemöller, Hermann Ehlers, the future president of the parliament of the Federal Republic, and others on their own personal initiative, without support from their superiors, ran a recruiting campaign to have Protestant youths join the ranks of the Confessing Church. For tactical reasons the Confessing Church decided not to create one centralized youth organization, but instead operated its youth activities at regional levels under different names. The only centrally issued item was the periodical *Jugendwacht*, which continued publication until April 1938. The public appearances of the Confessing Youth, however, were subjected to the same tactics of intimidation as the Catholic Youth and of course the Protestants were always vulnerable to the charge that they deliberately deviated from agreements concluded officially between the Protestant Church and the National Socialist government.[105] Even some of those Protestant youth leaders who had initially believed in the possibility of fruitful co-operation with the Hitler Youth, such as Karl Friedrich Zahn, a Protestant pastor who had become the *Reichs* Church Youth leader and was at first a convinced National Socialist, realized within two years of Hitler's advent to power that Schirach had merely made use of Protestant supporters. In a document drawn up by him in October 1935 for use by the *Reichs* Church Committee he mentioned among other things that Schirach personally attended only those weddings of higher Hitler Youth leaders which were not held in church, that Hitler Youth leaders in various regions made it their business to interfere with church attendance, and that Schirach would not be likely to adhere to the letter of the agreement of 1933 unless compelled to sign a supplementary agreement which would specifically refer to the infringements listed. For that purpose Zahn had drawn up a draft, but, needless to say, his *Reichsbischof*, Müller, took no action. Zahn himself was killed in the war.[106]

Quite another kind of opposition which the Hitler Youth faced in increasing numbers after 1936 came from gangs of hostile young men. They were not necessarily members of former youth movements, nor were they necessarily politically motivated or, as the BBC put it, infected 'by the spirit of revolt against the Nazis'.[107] Their common denominator, if indeed they had one, was the rejection of compulsory Hitler Youth service. Mostly they were of necessity Hitler Youth members already who banded together in gangs with exotic names such as the *Edelweiss*-Pirates, the Navajos, the Black Gang, the *Lechler Landsturm*, and others.[108] Little is known about their internal structure and it is fairly safe to assume that they were nothing more than voluntary gatherings of youths who met in 'cafés or pubs, dressed in what for those days was extravagant *Stenzen* (spiv) attire such as checked shirts, battered hats, and gruesome signet rings very often adorned with skull and crossbones. They were mainly a phenomenon of urban centres and industrialized regions.[109] Both the *Gestapo* and the *Reichsjugendführung*, against the background of a general rise of juvenile delinquency, considered them a serious danger since naturally they also harboured criminal elements, and during the war cases increased in which these gangs teamed up to attack Hitler Youth leaders in the black-out.[110] The first major action against them was carried out in Leipzig in 1937 where allegedly 1,500 youths had banded together in 'secret gangs' who actually had it as their declared aim to gain more members in this city than the Hitler Youth. From Leipzig the gang network spread not only throughout Saxony but extended to Berlin and Cologne. The leaders, Helmut Hess and Horst Lippert were caught; these two, aged seventeen, were sentenced to three years' hard labour and another leader, Kurt Hoppe, aged sixteen, to one year's imprisonment.[111] Hitler Youth judges, such as *Hauptbannführer* and *Landgerichtsrat* Dr Walter Tetzlaff, interpreted all forms of youth associations outside the Hitler Youth as treason against the German people.[112] Unless really criminal offences against persons and property had been committed the first body to mete out punishment to these youths was the Hitler Youth itself. It used such judiciary right as it possessed as a result of the executive instructions to the Hitler Youth Law and the 'Disciplinary Decree' of 1940 to issue formal warnings, reprimands, promotion withdrawal, degradation, and arrest (to be executed at weekends with a diet of bread and water).[113] But such punishment could be administered only to youths up to the age of fourteen.[114] The growing chaos of war reduced the probability of ever effectively coping with the problem of adolescent criminality, and public opinion samples regularly collected by the *SS Sicherheitsdienst* indicate growing public concern at the increasing 'vagabonding' and the phenomenon of 'neglected' youth; they also point to one of the major causes (the war apart) — reaction by the Hitler Youth against their regimentation.[115] The sentences by civil judges against some of these youths were considered too mild and the result of judges being unaware 'that here was a serious symptom of a danger confronting youth' and not just a few isolated cases.[116] Generally the highest quota of juvenile delinquency during the war came from the blacked-out cities of western and central Germany.

As we have noted, it was not uncommon for gangs to form within Hitler Youth units, especially in those which were daily confronted by the realities of war as were, for example, the anti-aircraft helpers.[117] For a member of the Hitler Youth 'leadership corps' to show himself in their bunkers, or among Hitler Youths directly involved in the multifarious activities which sprang up after major air-raids, was to invite demonstrations of a kind which no other sector of the German population could risk unless it wanted to ensure its transfer into a concentration camp. For example, in April 1944, shortly after a major air-raid on Munich, a large Hitler Youth rally was called in one of the cinemas of the city. It was attended by large numbers of youths who had come directly from salvage work among the ruins, and they were severely reprimanded by a 'spit-and-polish' HJ-leader from 'Prussia'[118] for their slovenly appearance. Grumbles became audible from the audience, then whistles, and a spontaneous and enthusiastic rendering of the last verses of one of the Peasant Rebellion songs:

> *'Dem Ritter fuhr ein Schlag ins Gesicht*
> *Und der Spaten zwischen die Rippen.*
> *Er brachte das Schwert aus der Scheide nicht*
> *Und nicht den Fluch von den Lippen.* . . .
>
> *Ja Gnade dir Gott du Ritterschaft*
> *Der Bauer steht auf im Lande*
> *Und tausendjährige Bauernkraft*
> *Macht Schild und Schärpe zur Schande.*

> The knight received a slap in his face
> And a spade between his ribs.
> He could not pull the sword from its sheath
> Nor utter the curse on his lips.

> May God have mercy with you knights;
> The peasant is rising in the land
> And a thousand years of peasants' strength
> Turns shield and sash into nothing.

When the HJ-leader thought it wise to step down from the stage he was accompanied by the tune of the notorious song *Es zittern die morschen Knochen* ('The rotten bones are trembling'), which in its 'internal' Hitler Youth rendering had vital parts of the words changed, beginning with *Es zittern im Arsch die Knochen* ('The rotten bones are trembling in the arse'). A few more ribald sing-songs followed and the rally ended, fortunately for all, on a decidedly good-humoured note.[119]

Dissent and resistance from the youth movements of the former organized political parties of the Left showed features similar to the attitude of the remaining activists of the former youth leagues. With the complete destruction of the Communist and Socialist party apparatus and their fighting organizations like the *Rote Frontkämpferbund* or the *Reichsbanner Schwarz-Rot-Gold*, these parties had been deprived of their leaders, who were either prisoners or émigrés. What the threat of Hitler coming to power was unable to achieve – the working together of SPD and KPD – seems in part to have been achieved by one of the first illegal Socialist youth organizations, the *Rote Stosstrupp* founded by Rudolf Küstermeier from members of Socialist and Communist student and young workers' organizations.[120] It proclaimed itself a movement 'without membership book and without membership badge' and managed also to attract German

Jews as well as Catholics.[121] With its centre in Berlin from which it issued an illegal weekly, the *Roter Stosstrupp*, it maintained branches in all the major cities of northern and central Germany, though how numerous these branches were cannot be ascertained. In any event, Küstermann's organization was discovered by the *Gestapo* in November 1933 and he was charged with high treason and sentenced in August 1934 to ten years' hard labour.[122] Other attempts to continue left-wing youth work continued, but besides remaining always so small as to be politically insignificant, youth groups of the Left were most vulnerable to discovery for they had not only the National Socialists against them but the bulk of the German bourgeoisie – many of whom might have been loath to denounce members of the former youth leagues or Protestants and Catholics, but felt no compunction regarding what they considered as the 'common enemy'. The predominant number of those youthful opponents of Hitler who were executed between 1933 and 1945 were Social Democrats or Communists or members of their former youth organizations.[123] In fact between 1940 and 1945 in the *Zuchthaus* of Brandenburg 1,807 inmates were executed for political reasons. Seventy-five of them were under twenty years old, twenty-two were pupils and students, one had just reached the age of sixteen.[124] The execution of one of them, the Communist youth official Ernst Knaack, is recorded in the dry soulless language of civil service jargon:

'The condemned with his arms tied to his back was brought in by two prison officials at 12.36. The executioner Röttger from Berlin was ready with his three assistants. Also present was the prison doctor Reg. Med. Rat. Dr. Müller.

'After confirming the identity of the person brought in as the condemned the supervisor of the execution ordered the executioner to proceed. The condemned, quiet and concentrated, without resisting was put under the guillotine whereupon the executioner carried out the decapitation and thereupon announced that the sentence had been carried out.

'The execution, from the moment of bringing in of the condemned to the announcement that the sentence had been executed, lasted 7 seconds.'[125]

Knaacke, in his last letter to his brother, had written: 'My life is now finished. My life is not completed, because I still consciously wanted to live. I was full of plans and still hoping to achieve and reach so much. My life has not found completion in the sum of its achievements, but was suddenly broken off by force. It is completion in death, because I could not live differently. . . .'[126]

The group which caught the imagination of most and about which the German government was unable to prevent news from spreading throughout and beyond Germany was that led by Hans and Sophie Scholl. In its *Bericht aus dem Inland* dated 15 March 1943 the SD (Security Service) public opinion samples report:

'Also according to our information rumours concerning the activities of oppositional circles are spreading and disturb the population. Thus in many parts of the Reich talk goes on about 'large demonstrations of Munich students', furthermore one talks of handbills and posters of Marxist content on public buildings in Berlin and other cities. Some sources of our information stress the point that the population apparently no longer meets such manifestations as before, by for instance the prompt removal of the inflammatory writings or the handing over of leaflets, but instead reads the contents and hands them on . . . a sharp rejection of this punishable action can be observed only very rarely.'[127]

The SD reported that the police in Düsseldorf alone had confiscated thirty different 'Communist' brochures and leaflets and arrested sixty-one persons for distributing them. Arrests for similar activities had been carried out in Dortmund, Stettin, Magdeburg, Görlitz, Chemnitz, Nuremberg, Saarbrücken, and Weimar.[128] Stalingrad was reverberating throughout Germany but nowhere more so than in Munich, where in bold white letters the walls of the Ludwig-Maximilian-University displayed the slogan *Nieder mit Hitler* ('Down with Hitler'), which in spite of the frantic endeavours of Ukrainian women to scrape them off remained legible for several days. Something was clearly afoot and had been afoot for the citizens of Munich ever since 1941 and more regularly since the autumn of 1942. In the spring and summer of 1941 duplicated leaflets had been dropped into many Munich letter boxes containing nothing more than excerpts from the sermons of leading Catholic clergymen against the euthanasia programme.[129] In 1942 they contained the clergy's denunciation of the state expropriation of several Catholic monasteries and convents,[130] and this was followed by leaflets of purely political content:

Appeal to all Germans.

The war is approaching its certain end. As in 1918 the German Government tries to direct attention to the growing U-boat danger, while in the East the armies stream backwards incessantly and in the West the invasion is expected. America's armaments production has not yet reached its highpoint, but even today it surpasses everything so far witnessed by history. Hitler leads the German people with mathematical certainty into the abyss. *Hitler can no longer win the war, he can only prolong it!* His guilt and that of his aides has infinitely surpassed any measure. Just punishment comes closer and closer.

But what does the German people do? It sees nothing and hears nothing. It blindly follows its seducers into ruin. Victory at any price is written in its banners. I fight to the last man, says Hitler – while the war is lost already.

Germans. Do you and your children want to suffer the same fate as that suffered by the Jews? Do you want to be measured with the same yardstick as your seducers? Shall we forever be the most hated people in the world? No. Therefore part company with the National Socialist subhumans. Prove by your action that you think differently. A new war of liberation is beginning. The better part of the people fights on our side. Tear off the cover of indifference which you have put around your hearts. Make your decision before it is too late. Do not believe National Socialist propaganda which is frightening you to the core with the Bolshevik terror. Do not believe that Germany's future is associated for better or worse with the victory of National Socialism. Criminal actions cannot obtain a German victory. Separate yourselves *in good time* from everything connected with National Socialism. Afterwards there will be a terrible but just reckoning with those who, cowardly and undecidedly, kept quiet.

What does the outcome of this war teach us, a war that has never been a national one? The imperialistic concept of power, irrespective of the source from which it emanates, must be abolished once and for all. A one-sided Prussian militarism must never be allowed to come to power again. Only with the generous co-operation of all European peoples can those foundations be created upon which reconstruction is possible. Any centralizing force such as the Prussian state attempted to exercise over Germany and Europe must be nipped in the bud. The coming Germany can only be a federal one. Only a healthy federal state-system can infuse new life into a weakened Europe. By means of a reasonable socialism the workers must be liberated from their condition of lowest enslavement. The deceptive image of autarchy in the economy of Europe must disappear. Every people, every individual has a right to the wealth of the world.

Freedom of speech, freedom of religion, protection of the individual citizens from the arbitrary actions of criminal terror-states, those are the foundations for a new Europe. Support the resistance movement and hand on the leaflets.[131]

It was one of the most widespread leaflets of those distributed by a group of Munich university students composed of Hans and Sophie Scholl, Christoph Probst, Willi Graf, Alexander Schmorell, which was inspired as well as actively supported by Dr Kurt Huber, Professor of Psychology and Philosophy at the Ludwigs-Maximilian-University. The Scholls came from Swabia and, like their three other brothers and sisters had been enthusiastic members of the Hitler Youth, Hans Scholl reaching the rank of *Fähnleinsführer* in the *Jungvolk*.[132] The enthusiasm soon evaporated after 1936 when, after a series of irritating incidents, he joined a Catholic youth group, was rounded up by the police and spent a few days in prison, though without serious consequences to himself. Before war broke out he had become a student of medicine, was drafted into the army and participated in the Western campaign as a medical orderly. After that, though not demobilized, he was permitted to continue his studies, and by comparison with others of his age group lived a rather priviliged existence. At the university he made the acquaintance of Alexander Schmorell, a Baltic German who, with his parents, had left Russia in the wake of the Bolshevik revolution and whose father had succeeded in establishing himself comfortably as a doctor in Munich.[133] They were joined by Christoph Probst, a native Bavarian and the only one of the group to be married, having two small sons.[134] Later came Willi Graf, a native of Saarbrücken, and the last one to join them was Hans Scholl's sister Sophie who, unlike the others, began to read philosophy rather than medicine in Munich in 1942.[135] The first introductory philosophy lectures were given by Professor Huber, who 'in the style of Fichte' preached an ethical and religious idealism which left a profound impression on his listeners, including students from other disciplines.[136] Leaflets had already begun to circulate before Sophie Scholl joined the university, but when she saw the first one she had no idea that it was her brother and his friends who duplicated and distributed them, or that it was Professor Huber who actually wrote some of them. She discovered the originator by chance and from then on was one of the group, which had adopted the name 'The White Rose' as the symbol of purity. In the spring and early summer, using a studio that a painter had put at their disposal before leaving for Russia, they duplicated leaflets, at first distributing them within the university, then, as they gained more courage, dropping them into letter boxes in Munich and other southern German towns and cities until finally they took them by suitcase and distributed them in Frankfurt, Stuttgart, Vienna, Freiburg, Saarbrücken, Mannheim, and Karlsruhe – a rather hazardous undertaking considering that, especially on long-distance trains, police and *Gestapo* checks on the contents of suitcases were a regular occurrence.[137] During the summer vacation the 'Medical Company' of the university was transferred to Russia to gain personal experience. During that time also the leaflet actions of the 'White Rose' ceased. But what they could see in Russia deepened their convictions and ensured the resumption of the campaign after their return to Munich in the early autumn of 1942.[138]

At that time grievances were coming to a head. Many Munich citizens took exception to what appeared to be the carefree and extrovert life of the 'students' while other men were serving at the front and women were being increasingly drafted into the munitions factory. *Gauleiter* Giesler, intent upon winning the support of the bulk of Munich's population, personally appeared at the university and addressed the students with a speech in which he expressed his disgust with the low standard of their morale and, turning to the female students, said that in war-time they had no business to play about in universities and that their talents would be better put to use if they presented the *Führer* with a child.[139] Giesler had overstepped the mark. The male students shouted him down and he had to leave the university humiliated. The Scholls and their friends immediately exploited the open dissatisfaction among the students and with a new leaflet campaign agitated against a régime which, as they argued, had lost any moral right to lead Germany. The spectre of disaster could already be seen in North Africa and even more impressively, and psychologically more oppressively, at Stalingrad.

Less than a fortnight after the fall of Stalingrad, on the morning of 16 February 1943, citizens of Munich who were walking along the *Ludwigstrasse* towards the *Siegestor* saw in bold white letters 'Freedom' and 'Down with Hitler' painted on the walls of a public building.[140] Two days after the slogan-painting action, on Thursday 18 February, Hans and Sophie Scholl started another leaflet action, this time again inside the university. Early in the morning, before lectures began, they distributed leaflets in the lecture theatres and when some were left over they emptied the suitcase from the top floor of the main entrance hall of the university. The university caretaker saw them and immediately called the police. All exits of the university were closed, the police arrived and took the Scholls to the *Wittelsbach Palais*, now the *Gestapo* headquarters. A search of their flat revealed the names of other members of the 'White Rose'. Roland Freisler, the notorious president of the 'People's Court', arrived in Munich and the trial was held on 22 February 1943. Christoph Probst was also accused. The trial was brief and the sentence was death by decapitation. On the afternoon of the same day the condemned were allowed to see their closest relatives for the last time. Sophie was the first to die, 'free, fearless and with a smile on her face'. Hans Scholl, before putting his head under the guillotine, shouted so that it resounded through the bleak corridors of the prison of Munich-Stadelheim, 'Long live Liberty'. Probst followed.[142] Himmler apparently did not want any martyrs and demanded a stay of the execution – several hours too late.[143]

Schmorell, Graf, and Professor Huber were arrested a few weeks later and executed on 13 August. Their death was in vain: the hope that it would cause repercussions throughout Germany proved futile. The memory of the 'White Rose' group and of the many other youths who went the same lonesome path was to be merely resurrected by a guilt-ridden generation of elders as a kind of atonement.

XI War

The outbreak of war saw the Hitler Youth prepared: the invocation of the myth of Langemarck, the demand for unselfish self-sacrifice, had played its part and would continue to do so for the next six years. As one of the leading functionaries of the *Reichsjugendführung* wrote:

'From the experience of the world war was born the idea of National Socialism; out of its armies came the unknown frontline soldier, Adolf Hitler, as its leader. The myth of the sacrifice in the World War of Germany's youth has given to the post-war youth a new faith and a new strength to unfold the ideals of National Socialism. One of the historic examples provided for us shows that Germany's youth sacrificed their lives for Germany and that Herbert Norkus and all the others who gave their lives did so for a new Germany. This sacrifice has been the most decisive precondition for a revolutionary educational idea and its youth movement.'[1]

Self-sacrifice or no, the *Reichsjugendführer*, Baldur von Schirach, certainly received preferential treatment. He received Hitler's personal permission to join the army towards the end of 1939, and by way of 'special training' completed his career from simple private to full lieutenant in less than six months. His military career ended on 2 August 1940 when he was appointed *Reichsstatthalter* of Vienna.[2] In his place, Arthur Axmann, so far head of the Hitler Youth's Social Affairs Department, was appointed as *Reichsjugendführer*. He proved to be a reliable and efficient organizer who at least during the first few years of the war, commanded the respect of his subordinates. In order to rationalize the administrative structure of the Hitler Youth he immediately completed the adjustment of its regional organization to those of the party by making the *Bann* area correspond with that of an NSDAP *Kreis*, which incidentally in 1940 also increased the total number of *Banne* to 223. Furthermore the initially strict division between *Jungvolk* and HJ which had already been crumbling in the last years before the war was officially eliminated.[3] Between June and December 1941

Above Hitler Youths prepare for
action on the Eastern Front

Left Jungvolk members salvage
property after an air raid

Above left 'The rifle is the bride of the German soldier': an HJ leader explains how to clean a carbine
Above right A signalling unit of the Berlin HJ rehearsing – six months before Berlin itself became a battleground
Below HJ military training camp in the Alps

Above Three Hitler Youths decorated for valour during the air raids on Hamburg in July 1943
Below Hans and Sophie Scholl (left and centre), with Christoph Probst – leaders of the 'White Rose' group in Munich which agitated for the fall of Hitler. All were arrested and decapitated in August 1943

Above The end draws near: with the Reichs Chancellery already coming under fire Hitler decorates members of the Hitler Youth with the Iron Cross a few days before his death
Below Boys dressed as soldiers captured by American forces near Remagen

Axmann served with the army in Russia, where he lost his right arm.

The Hitler Youth could immediately draw on a reservoir of youths that had been trained in diverse para-military skills. Most useful of course were the boys who served in the special formations of the Hitler Youth. These had had their origin in the continuous pressure of the *Reichsjugendführung* to extend its area of influence. But these particular extensions were also dictated by necessity. During 1936 and 1937 internal Hitler Youth reports highly critical of the generally low standards of appearance, training, and morale within Hitler Youth units began to multiply, and laxity of training, lack of discipline, and a general failure of the Hitler Youth to provide stimulating activities were listed among the factors responsible for this development. The Hitler Youth had ceased to be a challenge; it had become just another part of the weekly routine, and a compulsory one at that. As one way of counteracting this, and of inducing new enthusiasm, the Hitler Youth began to cater for the special interests of its members.[4]

Gliding, of course, was the major sport pioneered in Germany before 1933 and already in 1934 the German Airsport Association had begun to enrol schoolboys into its formations. Within the Hitler Youth, aviation enthusiasts formed themselves into separate groups, building model gliders. At the annual model gliding competition held in Germany in 1936, 1,500 Hitler Youths participated. A year later, for those over eighteen years of age within the SA, the *NS-Flieger-Korps* (NSFK) was founded, which was led by a body of skilled gliding instructors as well as instructors for piston-engined aircraft. Yet while trying to stimulate the interest of the youth in air training, the German government was loath to allocate additional funds which would have allowed the purchase of the amount of equipment necessary. The NSFK's endemic financial shortage brought about rather an undesirable development: the bulk of its members consisted of those who could actually afford to purchase their own gliders.[5]

Shortly after the foundation of the *NSFK*, provisions were made for developing Hitler Youth air-training by the foundation of the *Flieger-HJ*. Initially, the last two years of service with the *Jungvolk* were to serve as a preparatory stage for the *Flieger-HJ*, but by 1941 it had become standard practice for aviation enthusiasts to pass two or three months in the general Hitler Youth and then transfer to the *Flieger-HJ*. What distinguished them from the former was the *Luftwaffe*-blue uniforms with light blue piping and the armlet of the HJ. In its early days a distinction was maintained between the 'model-building' *Jungvolk* members and those of the HJ, but these were soon blurred and this branch of the *Jungvolk* merged into the HJ.[6]

Basically the purpose of membership in the *Flieger-HJ*, which reached an eventual total of 78,000, was to give a rudimentary knowledge of the theoretical and practical aspects of aviation. Members started by building model gliders and acted as 'work horses' for the older ones who had to be catapulted up into the air for their first gliding test. Between the ages of fourteen and eighteen a member of the *Flieger-HJ* would try to obtain his 'wings': the A, B, and C certificates in gliding.[7] Another exciting aspect was the close contact that existed with the *Luftwaffe* at whose bases *Flieger-HJ* members were frequent and always welcome visitors, often being taken up in bombers or two-seat fighters.[8]

Another special formation of the Hitler Youth was the *Motor-HJ* which by 1933 had 3,000 members. After 1936 a period of further but forced expansion began. The storm troopers had their own motorized branch, the *Nationalsozialistisches Kraftfahr Korps* (NSKK), led by Major Konrad Hühnlein. Schirach was not slow to realize the possibilities inherent in the NSKK for the Hitler Youth. He approached Hühnlein and they agreed on co-operation and jointly formed the *Reichsmotorschule*. Every Hitler Youth could be a member from the age of sixteen onwards – the age when a German youth could officially obtain his first driving licence for a motor cycle – and at the age of eighteen he could transfer to the NSKK. Membership figures for the *Motor-HJ* rapidly rose and estimates range from 90,000 to 102,000 in 1938. However, in spite of this high number of members, the *Motor-HJ* was afflicted by the same problem as the *Flieger-HJ* – shortage of funds and equipment. In 1938 it possessed a total of 300 motor cycles, the remainder being the private property of its members. Yet in 1937 *Motor-HJ* members obtained 10,000 driving licences and in 1938 28,000. But driving was only part of the exercise; training included a thorough mechanical knowledge and a sound knowledge of the traffic code, international as well as German. The ultimate purpose of this training is mentioned in an internal memorandum of the *Reichsjugendführung*: 'It is self-evident that members of the *Motor-HJ* will later serve in the motorized units of the *Wehrmacht*.'[9]

Consequently the demands made upon the members were high. Besides all the other usual activities of the general Hitler Youth, a member of the *Motor-HJ* had to have annually a minimum of eighty hours driving and 105 hours service as a mechanic.[10]

Very popular, particularly in northern Germany, was the *Marine-HJ* – the naval Hitler Youth – which reached a membership of 62,000 boys. In 1935 the first *Reichsseesportschule* was founded in Brandenburg, later followed by one at the opposite end of Germany on the shores of Lake Constance. As in the case of the other special formations of the Hitler Youth, so in the *Marine-HJ* – demands made upon the individual boy both in terms of time and actual physical and mental accomplishment were rather higher

than those of the general Hitler Youth. Within the ranks of *Marine-HJ* all
the necessary sailing certificates could be obtained and before the war the
most exciting experience of any member was an exercise in the Baltic on one
of the two sailing vessels used by the German Navy for the training of its
naval cadets, the *Gorch Fock* and the *Horst Wessel*. Inland exercises included river navigation, as in 1940 when units of the *Marine-HJ* sailed in a
convoy of vessels down the Danube from Passau in Lower Bavaria to
Vienna and Budapest. The conclusion of this exercise was an official reception of the *Marine-HJ* by the Hungarian government followed by a public
parade of the *Marine-HJ*.[11]

There were also smaller special formations, one of them a signalling unit
which in 1943 was absorbed by both the *Flieger-HJ* and the *Flakhelfer*, the
anti-aircraft helpers. Another catered for future medics, a unit absorbed by
the general Hitler Youth in 1939, while yet another was the *Reiter-HJ*, a
cavalry unit designed to attract mainly the youth of rural regions.[12] At the
outbreak of war a special unit was created for Hitler Youth air-raid war-
dens, but such training as they received had by 1942 become part of the general training of every member of the *Jungvolk*, the HJ, and the BDM.

One kind of 'special service' required of every member of the Hitler
Youth, male or female, irrespective of whether or not he or she belonged to a
special formation, was the land service. It was also the only service which
made some provisions in the predominantly male-orientated Hitler Youth
for the talents of the female members. In a Hitler Youth circular of 8 January 1940 the 'blood-and-soil' motivation found explicit expression:

'Land service is a political task of National Socialism. Its purpose is to
bring back boys and girls from the cities to the land, to create new recruits
for the agricultural occupations and thus secure their continuous existence.
The best of them should be given an opportunity to settle. The Hitler Youth
is the sole executor of the land service'.[13]

In 1934 the first forty-five land service groups were founded. At first
these were distinctly separate units, but the war blurred the division between them and the general land and harvest service which every Hitler
Youth member was expected to perform. In 1939 11,752 boys and 14,264
girls helped to bring in the harvest. Because of the lack of adult manpower
during the war the total figure had increased to 38,522 in 1943 and by that
time it had become virtually impossible to distinguish between what had
formerly been a land service group and a Hitler Youth unit carrying out its
land service in the 'battle for agricultural production'.[14]

Thus the war did not find the German youth, the Youth of Adolf Hitler,
unprepared. The entire set of traditions inherited from the German Youth
Movement, the youth literature of the period, the sombre yet exhilarating
ceremonial had steeped a generation in the spirit of sacrifice, a willingness

immediately exploited by a régime which was only too aware of how much selfless enthusiasm existed among the youth of Germany. Constantly throughout the war incidents occurred of boys appearing at their local Hitler Youth headquarters complaining that they had been overlooked in their call-up to the Hitler Youth, backing up their claims with their birth certificates. With a shrug of the shoulder and a derogatory remark about some bureaucracy which had yet again failed to do its work properly, they were immediately enrolled in the *Jungvolk*. That the birth certificates had been faked was in most cases only discovered afterwards or when the erasure of the last digit of the year of birth had been carried out too clumsily.[15] Mostly in these cases father or brother had been called up into the army and now the sons too 'wanted to do their bit'. They were usually allowed to stay.

The Hitler Youth found its first active deployment in the areas most immediately affected by the war, such as Germany's eastern provinces and a few months later those of the west. While schools – much to the pleasure of the regular incumbents – were cleared and turned into army quarters, Hitler Youths acted in a variety of functions from couriers to guides as well as 'transport managers' for the bulk of the local population who were evacuated out of the immediate war zone. Members of the BDM and the *Jungmädel* assisted in looking after the young children. In point of fact the Hitler Youth throughout Germany had already begun to play their part during the week before the war broke out, for it was they and not the ordinary postmen who delivered the individual call-up papers, and it was they who then, as well as for the entire duration of the war, delivered the ration cards once a month to each household.[16]

All physically-fit sixth-formers were immediately drafted for the summer on to the farms to bring in the harvest. For the majority of them this was the end of school life forever because from the farms they were immediately taken over by the Labour Service and from there, after completing their service, were transferred into the army.[17] For all these actions the 'Youth Service Law' represented the legal foundation. Sometimes of course the duties demanded under this law came into conflict with newly issued instructions, such as that given by Schirach on 18 September 1939 which in view of the blackout ordered all members of the *Jungvolk* and the *Jungmädel* to be at home before the onset of darkness. Practically-speaking, this was impossible, and this and similar instructions were tacitly ignored.[18] One concerted Hitler Youth action throughout Germany during the first weeks of the war was also associated with the blackout. In order to facilitate an easier crossing of the streets in the darkness the curbs at each street corner were painted white, a task carried out by the Hitler Youth and repeated annually. It was a highly popular activity because it was one of the very few activities for which the Hitler Youths were actually paid.[19] Whether the youths or the curbs were whiter remained a matter of dispute between painters and parents. During the first months of the war alone 1,091,000 Hitler Youths were actively deployed for the war effort.[20]

At the outbreak of war the Hitler Youth numbered a total of 8,870,000 boys and girls aged between ten and eighteen.[21] They were commanded by 765,000 leaders of all ranks, of which 8,018 were professional youth leaders, but the figure does not include between 20,000 and 30,000 older leaders who held a leadership office on an honorary basis.[22] The bulk of the latter as well as more than a quarter of the professional youth leaders were called up into the army. Endemically short of leaders this immediately produced a new leadership crisis which could only be met in the first place by pushing the age level of Hitler Youth leaders down, so that sixteen- and seventeen-year-old boys found themselves in *Unterbannführer* positions responsible for anything between 500 and 600 boys.[23] Secondly, the *Reichsjugendführung* was reorganized because out of its 424 full-time leaders, 273 volunteered or were called up into the army. In their place stepped students, teachers, and party members with previous experience in youth affairs.[24] The organization of the *Reichsjugendführung* was drastically rationalized, cutting its vast proliferation of fourteen different offices down to six main offices, ultimately organized into three groups: deployment, training, and ideological orientation.[25]

The continuous pronounced activism of the Hitler Youth, which between 1936 and 1940 had so often been devoid of sense and purpose and had simply represented activity for activity's sake, now had a new and apparently meaningful point of focus. The government called for the collection of brass, copper, scrap metal, razor blades, paper, and bottles, and the Hitler Youth collected them, climbing innumerable stairs, knocking on innumerable doors, ringing innumerable bells, each time saluting smartly and asking whether any of the articles required were available.[26] *Fähnlein*, *Jungzug*, and *Jungenschaft* were divided up by districts, roads, and blocks of houses, and rarely was a flat left out. If there was no reply the youth came back later, and later again, and if there was no luck one day, it would always be worth trying the next. And while one group collected another stood in the backyard and sang, as persuasively as the rough and hoarse voices of boys can, German folk songs and those of the Youth Movement. Strident NS party songs were seldom sung on occasions when the object of the exercise was to obtain the help of the public, for they were simply not popular.[27]

No doubt most of those who participated were involved in the collection drives with heart and soul:

'H. . . . is collecting bottles. I see him before me as he is running from door to door begging patiently for his bottles.

'And then the moment when it came to take them to the collection centre. In his uniform, on the back a satchel stuffed with bottles, in the left hand a basket full of them, balanced only by a massive net in the right hand, also full of bottles. And all that beneath a face looking as though through him and his bottles the war would be won.'[28]

Anything that 'the Fatherland' asked for was obtained; even when during the first winter of the Russian campaign the government asked for such sacred articles as skis, the youngsters of the Hitler Youth talked their owners into parting with them in such quantities that the supply eventually exceeded the demand. And whatever they could not get they simply 'organized'. And organizing in those years of endemic shortage became a fine art as well as a craft which in the end differed very little from actual stealing except that the ends were thought to be unselfish.

Groups of the BDM were despatched to field hospitals to entertain and care for the wounded. They helped in state kindergartens and stood waiting on the platforms of railway stations ready to ply troops in transit with drink and food. In 1940 alone members of the BDM assisted in 318,782 households, 64,106 in the Red Cross, 60,263 in army hospitals and 107,185 at railway stations.[29] Between party offices and later also between those of the armed forces Hitler Youths established a regular messenger service which was later extended to the military barracks of the garrisons of the armed forces.[30] For the Hitler Youth total war came at a considerably earlier stage than for the rest of Germany's civilian population.

As before the war so each of the war years was given a particular slogan for the Hitler Youth:

> 1940   The Year of Trial
> 1941   Our Life, a Road to the *Führer*
> 1942   Service in the East and on the Land
> 1943   War Service of the German Youth
> 1944   The year of the War Volunteers[31]

Each slogan is indicative of the direction in which the fortunes of war were turning. Nevertheless, in spite of the growing preoccupation with the changing fortunes of war the Hitler Youth also continued a generally outward-directed policy which received a particularly strong impetus with the beginning of the 'Crusade against Bolshevism' in 1941. It had begun in 1937 with Schirach's visit to Italy and was extended in 1938 ('The Year of Understanding'), which was specially devoted to developing contacts with kindred movements throughout Europe.[32] Activities were supervised by the *Auslandsamt* of the *Reichsjugendführung* which organized exchanges of youth groups with Italy and the Balkan countries and also supported the Hitler Youth groups of German minorities throughout the world.[33] In Slovakia, for instance, the Hitler Youth numbered 17,400 members and Luxemburg had all but 400 fewer.[34] Estonia with its 20,000 Germans contained 5,000 Hitler Youths and before the outbreak of war the free City of Danzig had 43,400 members. Within days of the German occupation of Strasbourg the Hitler Youth organized itself there, having already existed as a clandestine movement since the early 1930s. Regular situation reports about Hitler Youth activities in the German border regions and in occupied territories were issued by the *Reichsjugendführung* throughout the war. Local response to them was judged as good in the *Warthegau*, rather more difficult in Lorraine, good in the Eupen-Malmedy region of Belgium (an area that had come to Belgium as a result of the Versailles peace treaty), very good in Luxemburg, and good in Holland and Norway.[35]

On 14 September 1942, at the zenith of the expansion of the Third *Reich*, Arthur Axmann and Baldur von Schirach, the latter of whom, besides being the *Gauleiter* of Vienna, had also been appointed to a basically meaningless office as 'Reichsleader for Education of the NSDAP', jointly called a 'European Rally' in Vienna to found the 'European Youth League'. It included Italy's Fascist Youth Movement, the Youth Movement of the Spanish *Falange*, the Flemish National Socialist Youth, the Walloon Rexist Youth, the Danish and Dutch National Socialist Youth, the Norwegian *Nasjional-Samling-Youth*, the Finnish Youth movement, the Bulgarian Brannik-Youth, the Rumanian State Youth, the Great Ustashi Youth, the Slovak Hlinka Youth, the Hungarian Levente Youth as well as observers from youth groups in Holland and France. Japanese youth leaders were also present. In spite of the 'international flavour' of the gathering the German press gave it very little coverage, while in Axis countries and those occupied by Germany it received the treatment of a major news item.[37] Probably the official German attitude is best illustrated by the standpoint taken during one of Goebbels' secret conferences with German journalists, in which they received instructions as to what line to take on specific issues. On 16 September 1942:

'The Minister polemicized very sharply against the talk of a "new Europe". He did not consider it advisable for our side to make so much noise about this subject at present. No one in the world would believe that we would fight for a new Europe without pursuing our own material interests. One would believe it possible that the Germans generally might fight for an idea, but the Nazis are known to be conducting a fight for oil and wheat in order to bring about a material improvement of our people, not chasing phantoms.'[38]

Less than five months later, however, in his total war speech, the disaster of Stalingrad was sufficient for the Bolshevik threat to Europe to be invoked: 'Here is a threat to the *Reich* and the European continent, which overshadows all previous dangers that have confronted the Occident. If we would fail in this struggle, then we will have gambled away our entire historic mission.'[39] And again four months later: 'Almost the whole of Europe is working for our war effort; one day it will also enjoy the fruits of our common struggle. After victory one part of the world will form a powerful continental community, composed of free peoples dedicated to a common great cause. Only in that way can Europe expect to continue to function. . . .'[40]

From October 1939 the para-military training of the Hitler Youth was intensified, carried out mainly at weekends and, as the war continued, increasingly supervised by former Hitler Youth leaders who as soldiers had been highly decorated for valour.[41] The delegation of frontline officers to units of the *Jungvolk* and the HJ became a permanent feature from the summer of 1941 onwards, but their stays were shorter and the rotation quicker. Usually they were officers who had been wounded and were recovering in their home or in garrison cities.[42]

The new burst of activity produced by the war led in practice to a general reduction of the amount of 'political' and 'ideological' instruction. But the *practice* of National Socialist ideology was something which many Hitler Youths of both sexes were confronted with, especially with the extension of Germany's 'living space' in the east, to which many members of HJ and the BDM were despatched to assist in the 'resettlement programmes'.[43] These meant, of course, the expulsion of the native Polish populations from the *Warthegau* – that region of Poland annexed by Germany as distinct from German-occupied Poland, the *Général Gouvernement* – and their replacement by racial Germans who had been and still were throughout the course of the war brought back into Germany from the German minority groups in eastern Central Europe and from the Southern Tyrol. It was the task of the Hitler Youth to assist in these programmes and most of them did so very willingly:

'During the war we dreamt of the foundation of a German Empire. By and by, without noticing it, we slipped into an attitude according to which the ends justify the means. There was no one among us who was not repelled by the situation. . . . But were soldiers being asked whether or not they would like to make an attack? We thought of ourselves as soldiers on the home front. Innumerable men, although basically sensitive, considerate, and helpful, had had to learn in the war to kill members of the enemy in cold blood. And they had learned it because they believed in doing their duty to Germany and because it is easier to do so in a group than as an individual.

'Today I know that this deployment of the girls in the resettlement villages was harmful. They were a particularly activist selection, but they were not without heart. The task with which they were confronted compelled them by force of circumstances to play a warlike male role. It required a different psychological constitution from ours, to watch without feeling entire families being driven from their ancestral homes. And in addition to that, to intervene if these unfortunate people furtively tried to take some of their beloved possessions with them. . . . Before the girls went to the farms, I told them: '"What is demanded of us is difficult, but bear in mind that after the last war, the German farmers had to leave their homes."

'When we asked one of the SS-leaders where the Poles whose expulsion we were witnessing were going to, the reply was that they would be settled on farms that had become free through the resettlement of German farmers, or that they were being settled within the *Général Gouvernement*. And these answers were enough to satisfy us . . . we had developed a great ability to avoid delicate questions. As a rule our subconscious directed us not even to enter into dangerous discussions. If we had realized that it was impossible for a sufficiently great number of farms to be available in the *Général Gouvernement* to take the number of those expelled and driven into homelessness and poverty, then this realization, too, would not have worried us unduly: The Poles were our enemies. We had to use the moment in which we were more powerful than they to weaken their "racial substance". Such arguments we described as "Realpolitik". I have never admitted to myself that basically we planned "genocide".'[44]

In 1942, the 'Year of Service in the East and on the Land', 18,000 Hitler Youth leaders from Germany were serving in the occupied territories of Poland and the western Ukraine, and the *Reichsjugendführer's* report for that year mentions the creation of ten leadership schools and camps as well as hostels, while a total of 30,000 boys and girls carried out their land service in the east.[45] During that same year the Hitler Youth there was joined by the 'Eastern Volunteers of the Germanic Youth', predominantly Dutch, Norwegians, Danes, and Flemings. The dispatch of the Hitler Youth and the 'Germanic Volunteers' to these areas was not solely to make up manpower at harvesting time, but also to provide inspiration as well as training for future settlers in the east.[46] As early as February 1940 an office to train future settlers, the *Siedlernachwuchsstelle Ost*, had been called into being by the *Reichsjugendführung* in co-operation with the *Reichsführer-SS* Himmler.[47]

The Hitler Youth was also deployed in making up for the shortage of teachers among the newly-arrived groups of racial Germans.[48] These racial German children automatically became subject to the Hitler Youth law, which also applied to children where only the father was of German extraction. HJ and BDM leaders, in the main devoid of any real training in teaching, ran schools in isolated areas of Poland teaching racial German children. They were only German by name and neither they nor their parents knew more than a few words of what was supposed to be their native language.[49] The preparation of the teachers consisted of nothing more than a rapid three-month teacher training course at best and three weeks practice in agricultural work. Their main assets were enthusiasm and a gift for improvization.[50] But their task was not restricted to running schools. Often it was their responsibility to assist in the reintegration of the racial Germans into the German 'racial community'. This meant a full-time occupation in which those concerned had to run German lessons for the adult population, organize community evenings for whole villages with music and songs, advise on matters of 'good taste' where furnishings and clothes were concerned, standards being supplied according to what was alleged to exist in the *Reich*: after all the Germans had to look distinct from and superior to the Polish farm hands. The fact that at the time of their initial arrival on their new farms there was nothing apparent that separated the racial Germans from the Polish farmers was one of the first revelations for those Hitler Youths in the east who had believed that there existed an innate German superiority which would manifest itself in outward appearance also. Needless to say, the task overwhelmed those entrusted with it.[51]

The youngsters who had joined the Hitler Youth before or during the early 1930s were veteran soldiers by 1941, and many of those who followed them into the front-lines during the war were determined to meet Hitler's demand of his youth to be 'quick like greyhounds, tough like leather, and hard like Krupp steel'.[52] Existing para-military training was further extended by the creation of *Wehrertüchtigungslager*, special camps where HJ members from the age of fifteen received three weeks of basic infantry training.[53] In the *Wehrertüchtigungslager* military training was not restricted to German Hitler Youths but included 'Germanic Youths' from northern and western Europe who might find themselves in the hands of non-German instructors, such as members of the Latvian or Dutch *Waffen-SS*. Their inspector was *HJ-Oberbannführer* Gerhard Hein who had been decorated with the Knight's Cross and Oakleaves.[54] The behaviour of these young soldiers revealed the nature of NS education and training in a way that made older observers rather uncomfortable. The German expressionist poet and lyricist, Gottfried Benn, a doctor in the regular army, noted as late as 1944. 'The German army is carried essentially by two commissioned ranks, the morbid field-marshals forever listening to Hitler, and the young lieutenants. The lieutenants emerged from the Hitler Youth and therefore have an education behind them the essence of which was the elimination of the intellectual and moral content of literature and its replacement by Gothic princes and daggers – and for whom marching exercises and bed-

The Regional Organisation of the Hitler Youth in 1943

ding down in hay lofts became a way of life. Already in peace-time they were far removed from those still educated in the old traditions, from parents, educators, clergymen, and humanistic circles. With their sights set they are well equipped for the task of deliberately destroying part of the globe in the name of the Aryan mission.'[55] Despite a certain degree of exaggeration, it adequately reflects the impression Germany's youth now made upon the older generation.

Under the pressure of events and the insatiable needs of the German war machine all forms of basic training whether carried out by army recruits or within the Hitler Youth were progressively reduced from 1943 onwards. From 26 January of that year anti-aircraft batteries were manned by Hitler Youths, officially by grammar-school pupils from the age of fifteen onwards.[56] But since the administrative work for the call-up of *Luftwaffen-helfer* was carried out by the offices of the NSDAP errors concerning the interpretation of HJ crept in. For example officially the *Flieger-HJ* was a formation of the HJ and not of the *Jungvolk*. Since it also included the age groups which normally would serve in the *Jungvolk*, they had taken to wearing HJ insignias and considered themselves to be HJ members. In some parts of Germany, the call-up of Hitler Youths to anti-aircraft duties was interpreted to include the entire *Flieger-HJ*. The older ones manned the guns, the younger ones served in the communication network of the flak, at searchlight batteries and as despatch riders, all apparently in accordance with the clause in their call-up papers: 'The boys will only be used for duties corresponding with their age group.'[57] Only when early in October 1943 a searchlight position manned entirely by boys of fourteen and younger was hit and the entire crew were killed, was the order clarified to exclude the younger age groups from service as *Luftwaffenhelfer*.[58] But service as despatch riders during air raids continued. Once a raid was over it was up to the older men and women of the party organizations and the Hitler Youth to feed and rehouse those who had been bombed out.[59] There must have been many a Hitler Youth who achieved local notoriety for efficiency demonstrated in successfully ferreting out large unoccupied flats whose owners had moved into the safer countryside, or flats occupied by just one person, and who only with reluctance and in the face of police enforcement would open his or her doors to accommodate those who had lost their homes. As the bombing offensive increased in intensity, boys and girls who were really mere children spent days and nights dishing out meals to the victims and guarding their salvaged property – usually stacked under the open sky – against looters.

Hitler Youth *Luftwaffenhelfer* were expected to continue their schooling in their flak positions but the practical aspects of service life made this impossible.[60] At first it was intended that they should serve only within the vicinity of their home, but it soon became established practice to transfer them all over Germany as the war situation required. Four and more transfers in less than twelve months were not uncommon: 'Because we changed position fourteen times within the period of one year, every form of school education lapsed since the summer of 1943. In the summer of 1944 we received our reports transferring us immediately into the seventh form.'[61] Though this may be an exceptional case the routine was hardly conducive to the continuation of grammar-school instruction. The boys, with only one adult, the chief gunner, lived in the positions and while originally schooling had been envisaged as taking place in the morning hours, day and night bombing of Germany made this impossible and ultimately there was nothing that distinguished the children from the rest of the soldiers, not even death:

'In a suburb of Berlin I saw a row of dead *Flakhelfer* lying side by side. An air raid had just ended. The flak position in which these schoolboys served had received several direct hits. I entered a barrack room in which the survivors had gathered. They sat along the wall on the floor turning their white faces distorted by terror towards me. Many cried.

'In another room lay the wounded. One of them, a boy with a soft round child's face, tried to come to attention when an officer in whose company I was asked him whether he suffered any pain: "Yes, but this is not important. Germany must be victorious".[62]

The KLV camps were meant to house the grammar-school pupils of the exposed cities of Germany for the duration of the war.[63] Furthermore, of course, it was expected that having removed the youths from the influence of the home, ideological indoctrination could be carried out unhampered by countervailing influences.[64] Entire grammar-school forms were transferred to rural regions of eastern and southern Germany. The *Reichsjugendführung* published a special lavishly illustrated volume in which the KLV programme was praised as 'the greatest social action of the war'.[65] Pictures showed boys or girls doing their school work and enjoying all the natural advantages provided by the countryside.[66] The *Reichsjugendführer* Arthur Axmann alleged that the children's nourishment in the KLV camps was twenty per cent superior to the food they received at home and that in fact the camps were housed in hotels and pensions taken over by the state for this purpose. However, he complained that the unreasonable attitude adopted by many parents was one of the main obstacles.[67]

In fact, other than persuasion there was nothing the government, the NSDAP, or anybody else could do to compel a parent to send its child to a KLV camp. In 1943, for example, Gauleiter Giesler sent a facsimile of his personally handwritten letter to all Munich parents advising them to do two things. First, he asked those adults whose livelihood did not necessitate their staying in Munich to move into the Bavarian countryside where accommodation would be ready for them, and secondly, he advised parents to send their children into the KLV camps.[68] The response to the latter request was not over-enthusiastic. True the camps were in the main reasonably comfortable, but they were frequently too far removed to be easily accessible to the parent. The one pressure that could be brought to bear upon parents was the absence of grammar schools, many of which were evacuated and rehoused in KLV camps. This meant that pupils ready to enter the first form of the grammar school in 1943 and 1944 could in effect not do so unless they entered a KLV camp. The alternatives consisted of continuing attendance of the *Volksschule*, the primary school until such times when schools could function normally again, whenever that might be, or of attending publicly-recognized private schools, which were not slow in recognizing the commercial advantages – some of them lowering their fees to attract greater numbers. In their locations grammar schools might be split up into two or more camps, since no camp was designed originally to house more than fifty youths. On many occasions the shortage of qualified teachers compelled two or more grammar schools to fuse temporarily and pool their teaching resources.[69]

The psychological burden was considerable, weighing heavily on both parents and children. After each air raid every child was bound to ask itself whether anyone at home was still alive – the temporary breakdown of communication services inevitably increased anxiety. Those parents, in the main mothers, who could afford it had themselves evacuated to a location near their child or children. Axmann accused them of having a disruptive influence on camp life, an accusation not without foundation; as these parents were very much in the minority, their presence caused feelings of envy among those separated from their parents. And of course there was also that type of parent who deliberately equipped their children with the absolute minimum or less in order to let the state (*Vater Staat*) redress the balance free of charge.[70]

KLV camps were supervised not by the local education authorities but by special inspectors of 'NS Teachers' League'. Each camp was led jointly by a teacher and a Hitler Youth leader. Their immediate superior was a *Hauptlagerleiter* who was in charge of several camps and who in turn was responsible to the Inspector. Official NSDAP reports were laudatory about the exemplary co-operation between teachers and Hitler Youth leaders.[71] But the intellectual poverty of National Socialist 'ideology' which made a skilled political ideologue incapable of indoctrinating young minds at any depth ensured that on the ideological level the KLV experiment in National Socialist education remained a hope unfulfilled.

Since the German east had always been considered unendangered territory, approximately 500,000 youngsters had been evacuated into KLV camps in eastern Prussia, the *Warthegau*, Upper Silesia, and Slovakia. The failure during the winter of 1944–45 to pull them out quickly enough dragged many of them as well as the local civilian population into the vortex of disaster. At a time when the whole of Germany was disintegrating, hundreds of thousands of children and parents worried about each other's fate. After the war the missing persons offices of the German Red Cross were besieged by children who had survived and who made their way west asking what had become of their mothers and fathers, and by parents asking for news of their children, thousands of whom had become the victims of the passions and misfortunes of war.

The KLV programme also affected the Hitler Youth adversely, since it broke up existing units in the cities, where a sufficient number of boys and girls always remained to form new though under-strength units,[72] while those in rural regions became inflated while still suffering from a lack of experienced leaders – another factor which made for easy and early promotion.[73]

Sometimes war service could come to a Hitler Youth unexpectedly as happened in July and August 1944 to a *Flieger-HJ* unit from Munich, whose members' ages ranged from ten to fifteen. They had left for Pomerania on a gliding holiday in the dunes of the Baltic near Zoppot. In the middle of their holiday they received orders from the local NSDAP headquarters to proceed to Allenstein in East Prussia and from there to Bischofsburg. Near to this town the local population was engaged in building anti-tank traps, mainly digging anti-tank ditches. It was feared after the German Army Group Centre had completely disintegrated under the impact of the Russian summer offensive that the Russian army would break through the German front. The older boys of the Hitler Youth unit joined those civilians digging the anti-tank ditch; the younger ones were detailed for less strenuous work, such as bringing supplies on horse carts from Bischofsburg. One member of this group recalls poignantly the paradox inherent in the situation arising from their task on the one hand and from their age on the other:

'We put up our tents and cooked some macaroni while the sun cast its last rays across the fields. Too tired to sing we went to sleep.

'In the middle of the night I woke up, scared out of my sleep by a distant rumbling. I pushed Gerd who slept next to me. "What is the matter?" he asked dozily.

"Can you hear the rumbling?"

'"What rumbling?"

'"Listen". It sounded like an endless column of heavy lorries driving thunderously across a steel bridge. We crawled out of our tents. The night was cool and dew glistened dimly in the calm light of the moon. Our guard, wrapped in blankets, sat beside the embers of the camp fire. He was awake.

'"Can you see it?" he asked.

'In the east the horizon formed a long red line, broken at intervals in different parts by fireflashes. In parts the line became feeble for seconds and at times extinguished completely. A little later, the flashes which caused this line returned and so restored its continuity – all accompanied by incessant rumbling and grumbling of the earth.

'"I hope it never gets as far as down here," said Gerd. "My father is in Russia and he said if they should ever get into Germany we should kill ourselves, for what we could expect from the Russians would be even worse."

'"Oh, they will never get so far, we will beat them to the devil. All the same I should be glad if we get back soon," I said.

'"I hope so too," said our guard, who was a boy from the second squad. "My mother will give me a mighty good thrashing. She will never believe me when I tell her that they sent us to dig trenches."'[74]

With the growing influence of the SS in all spheres of life in Germany during the war years, the recruiting drives of the *Waffen*-SS were heavily concentrated on the HJ. Under the impact of 'total war' the idea was born of creating a special division of the Hitler Youth within the *Waffen*-SS, which ultimately was to be 12th SS-*Panzer Division Hitlerjugend*.[75] Goebbels at the time objected to the name of the division on the grounds that it might provide the enemy with propaganda ammunition.[76] But he was overruled by Hitler. Orders were issued and on 16 February 1943 the first talks took place between the *Reichsjugendführung* and Himmler's *SS-Führungshauptant*. The formal order to set up the division was issued finally on 24 June 1943.[77]

It was intended that recruits were to be drawn from the *HJ-Wehrertüchtigungslager*, from youths aged between seventeen and eighteen, but in practice it was not uncommon to find sixteen-year-olds and even younger boys in the division.[78] The Hitler Youth motto for 1943, 'War Service of the German Youth', was put to the test because the *Hitlerjugend* Division, if it acquitted itself well, was meant to create a precedent for other German divisions, (notably the *Wehrmacht* élite division *Grossdeutschland*) which were considered suitable for integrating sizeable numbers of youths within their ranks.[79] This particular plan was, however, abandoned and subsequently the place for Hitler Youth volunteers, other than in the *SS*, proved to be the *Volksgrenadier* divisions.

The first problem encountered was an acute shortage of experienced personnel. This was drawn from the depleted ranks of the 1. SS-*Panzerdivision Leibstandarte SS Adolf Hitler (LAH)* which together with the *Hitlerjugend Panzergrenadier* Division was originally intended to form the I. SS-*Panzer Korps*.[80] The LAH had been decimated in the winter of 1942–43 during which it fought on the southern wing in Russia. Against Hitler's explicit orders it had abandoned Charkov to the Russians in February, but then it had reconquered it in March 1943. It had been pulled out of action for refitting and training replacements in order to play a vital role in *Operation Zitadelle*, the abortive German attempt in July 1943 to remove the Russian salient at Kursk and regain the initiative in the East.[81]

The LAH was to provide the nucleus of the *Hitlerjugend* Division but since the most serious shortage was that of experienced company, platoon, and squad commanders, expediency dictated the step of rapidly promoting platoon commanders to company commanders.[82] Furthermore 50 *Wehrmacht* officers who had at one time or another been Hitler Youth leaders were transferred to the *Hitlerjugend* Division.[83] To obtain the necessary numbers of squad and section leaders HJ members who at their previous military training in the *Wehrertüchtigungslager* had demonstrated a 'special aptitude for military leadership' were after their basic training sent to the *Waffen-SS* NCO school at Lauenburg for a three months training course for NCOs.[84] They lacked the reality of battle experience just as much as those whom they were to lead, a lack which they later tried to compensate for with a death-defying recklessness at great cost to themselves.

The first commander of the *Hitlerjugend* Division was the 34-year-old Major General Fritz Witt, himself a product of the German Youth Movement as well as of the pre-1933 Hitler Youth.[85] In 1933 Witt was one of the first 120 volunteers of the LAH and two years later he was company commander.[86] During the campaign in France he received the Knight's Cross and for his part in the reconquest of Charkov, the Oakleaves.[87] Instead of a *Parteisoldat* he was very much a soldier's soldier enjoying a very high reputation among the *Waffen*-SS and the *Wehrmacht* alike and in many respects represented an ideal choice for a commander who had to transform boys into men.

During July and August 1943 the first batches of recruits arrived at the training camp Beverloo in Belgium, a total of approximately 10,000 boys, many of whom had not yet reached their seventeenth birthday.[88] Nor for that matter were they all volunteers. Many had previously volunteered for other branches of the armed services, mainly the *Luftwaffe* and the U-Boat branch of the Navy, but when they were called up they found themselves in *Waffen*-SS barracks; others, like *Jungvolk* leaders, had been subjected to various degrees of moral blackmail or simply talked into volunteering.[89] It is indicative of the high quality of the leadership that it succeeded very quickly in overcoming the initial misgivings created by this kind of 'persuasion' and infusing the young division with a strongly developed *esprit de corps* and an aggressive enthusiasm which was not found wanting when put to the real test in Normandy a year later.

Although there were not enough uniforms to go round, basic training began immediately, as did the organization of the division into two infantry regiments, one panzer regiment, one artillery regiment, one engineer battalion, and a detachment each of reconnaisance, anti-tank, anti-aircraft, and signalling groups.[90] In October 1943 the *Hitlerjugend* Division was formally renamed the 12th *SS-Panzer Division Hitlerjugend* but armour then was as scarce as the uniforms had been in the summer.[91] The *panzer* regiment which was being formed near Reims had only four 'up-gunned' Mark IVs and four Panthers and even these had been brought back unofficially from the Eastern Front against OKH orders.[92] The artillery regiment had only a few light howitzers while general transport vehicles like cars, lorries, and traction vehicles were almost non-existent.[93] As a first stop-gap measure the division received vehicles requisitioned from the Italian army, now split into a pro-Ally and a smaller pro-German contingent.[94] The absence of spares soon caused the surroundings of Beverloo to be littered with these abandoned, useless vehicles.[95] During November and December 1943 and the early months of 1944 the equipment situation improved radically, and when in the early spring of 1944 the division's armour was transferred to Hasselt in Belgium, the division could embark on divisional exercises as a *panzer* division. Both *Generaloberst* Guderian and Field Marshall von Rundstedt, the Commander-in-Chief West, attended exercises of the division and paid tribute both to the enthusiasm of the boys and the high degree of efficiency reached in so short a time.[96]

Compared with other *Waffen*-SS and *Wehrmacht* units, the *Hitler-jugend* Division knew no 'square-bashing' or goose-stepping exercises. Given the youth of the recruits it was rightly assumed that such forms of training, apart from being quite irrelevant to the military situation and conditions which would be encountered in combat would only undermine their morale. Great emphasis was placed upon a good informal relationship between officers and men and a divisional order issued on Witt's personal initiative asked all company commanders to establish contact with the parents of their recruits.[97]

Witt's successor, Kurt Meyer, actually writes that 'many old-fashioned principles of military training had to be replaced by new ones which in their final analysis had their origins in the German Youth Movement', which ignored the traditional relationship between officers and ranks.[98] Orders, in so far as the situation allowed it, were phrased to indicate the reasoning behind them, on the assumption that the soldiers' efforts could be maximalized if they understood the purpose.[99] The emphasis of training lay on conditions likely to be experienced in battle, and therefore combat conditions were simulated as closely as possible, including the use of live ammunition. Upon Guderian's suggestion rifle practice at the shooting range was abandoned and instead carried out during exercises in the field, so to speak. The lessons learnt from the Russian infantry and armour of the importance of effective camouflage were driven home to the boys, as was the importance of monitoring the enemy's as well as camouflaging one's own radio signals.[100] Because of their age, the boys received special rations and up to the age of eighteen received a sweet ration in lieu of cigarettes – a regulation very much resented and of course violated by those affected.[101] Too young to smoke, yet old enough to die.

On 6 June 1944 the division moved into battle, but already on its seventy-mile march from its base to the Caen sector it had been heavily mauled by the strafing attacks of Allied fighter bombers. But in their first attack against the Canadians they knocked out twenty-eight Canadian tanks at a loss of six of their own.[102] They fought the rest of the Normandy campaign in this area, and, as Chester Wilmot records, 'the troops of the 12th SS, who were holding this sector, fought with a tenacity and ferocity seldom equalled and never excelled during the whole campaign'.[103] They sprang at Allied tanks 'like wolves', as a British tank commander recalls, 'until we were forced to kill them against our will'.[104] It was the Allies' first

encounter with the Hitler Youth generation, a generation whose development had in the main taken place in Hitler's Germany. Whether they were
'fanatical Nazis' is something impossible to determine; however, one must
not forget that they were a generation whose attitudes, particularly towards
the enemy, had been influenced by the experience of the Allied air offensive
over Germany. To a generation fed by Goebbels' propaganda that the intention of the Allies was not just to defeat Germany but to destroy it and to
exterminate its citizens, the Allied area bombardment of Germany's cities
seemed to be ample confirmation.

Within a month the *Hitlerjugend* Division had lost 20% of men killed,
40% missing and wounded, and 50% of its tanks and armoured vehicles.[105]
On 16 June 1944 Kurt Witt had been killed and was replaced by Major
General Kurt Meyer, *Panzermeyer*, at the age of thirty-three the youngest
divisional commander in the German army.[106] The son of a worker, himself
an ex-miner, police officer, and then one of the early members of the
SS-*Verfügungstruppe*, he typified the 'political soldier', but he possessed
considerable gifts of personal leadership and was a good tactician.[107] Frequently described in immediate post-war literature as an 'unrepentant Nazi
fanatic',[108] it ought to be added that it was primarily due to his influence in
the late 1950s and the early 1960s before his death that the *Waffen*-SS's ex-
servicemen organization broke such ties as existed with Neo-Nazi organizations and became a body dominated by political moderates.

In July the Division was pulled out of the Normandy front, but the
respite was to last only six days, for as the German positions between Maltot
and Vendes threatened to collapse the *Hitlerjugend* Division was thrown
back into the fire, into the heart of the Falaise pocket from which it managed to break out with only a fraction of its original strength.[109] Normandy
was not only the testing ground of the *Hitlerjugend* Division, it was also its
grave. When on 4 September 1944 the Division in the course of its retreat
crossed the Meuse near Yvoir, it consisted of 600 men, with all its tanks
gone and no ammunition for the artillery.[110] 'It is a pity that this faithful
youth is sacrificed in a hopeless situation,' commented Field Marshal von
Rundstedt.[111]

After Normandy the *Hitlerjugend* Division continued to exist in name,
but its recruits were like those of most other German divisions, scraped
from the bottom of the barrel of Germany's manpower reserves. By the
middle of September the division was back in Germany for refitting so that
it could participate in the Ardennes offensive, during which it fought in the
Bastogne area.[112] Transferred in February 1945 to Hungary to take part in
the German offensive east of Lake Baloton aimed at the recapture of Budapest, it took part in the general retreat of Axis forces in South-eastern
Europe and on 8 May 1945, numbering 455 men and one tank, it crossed

the demarcation line at the river Enns and surrendered to forces of the American 7th Army.[113]

Hitler Youths were found in other military formations during the war. The creation of the *Volkssturm* in October 1944 officially introduced compulsory military service in home guard units for every male from the ages of sixteen to sixty.[114] In the event the recruits were often both younger as well as older. After all even eleven-year-olds could fire the recoiless anti-tank weapon the *Panzerfaust*. Girls too found their way into the war effort. Alleged to be physically incapable of loading a Luger pistol or a machine gun, they 'manned' anti-aircraft batteries as in the 6th battery of the flak reserve unit 61 at Vienna-Kagran. During a daylight raid on Vienna one of their 88mm guns shot down a Liberator bomber, but shortly afterwards the unit received a direct hit which killed three girls and wounded two.[115] The same unit, still manned by girls, was deployed in an anti-tank role when the Russians under Malinovsky attacked Vienna.[116]

There were occasions when objections were raised at the highest level of the German army against this irresponsible destruction of the young generation, but to have any chance of success such objections had to be grounded on purely practical reasons. General Westphal, Field Marshal Rundstedt's Chief of Staff, offers a good example of the practical objections put up against the 'front deployment of the Hitler Youth', behind which, in his case, there were far more fundamental moral objections. In a memorandum to the OKW he argued that the Hitler Youth would be of little military value and – Westphal made no attempt here to hide his sarcasm – 'the combative enthusiasm of youth' would hardly be maintained if they were used in staffs and other rear eschelons of the armed forces. Any premature deployment of the Hitler Youth would for future years endanger the reservoir of recruitment to the German armed forces.[117]

Needless to say, the memorandum remained without effect. *Reichsjugendführer* Axmann as late as 28 March 1945 declared: 'From the Hitler Youth has emerged a movement of young tank busters', and he emphasized yet again the slogans which had become commonplace since the beginning of the war. 'There is only victory or annihilation. Know no bounds in your love to your people; equally, know no bounds in your hatred of the enemy. It is your duty to watch when others are tired; to stand when others weaken. Your greatest honour, however, is your unshakeable faithfulness to Adolf Hitler.'[118]

Encounters with fanatical Hitler Youths were often horrifying. In the Ruhr pocket the Germans would let the American armour through and then wait for the slower-moving American infantry units who combed through the depths of the *Teutoburger Wald*. Here the German units contained a high proportion of Hitler Youths of all age groups who would ambush American troops and after inflicting severe casualities disappear in the forest.[119] When cornered they frequently fought to the last child. Lieutenant-Colonel Roland Rolb of the US 84th Division noted one case where his men were opposed by an artillery unit manned by children of twelve and under: 'Rather than surrender, the boys fought until killed.'[120]

To the last moment Germany's youth was exhorted to mount and assist on the defence of the *Reich* against the 'Bolshevik hordes' and the 'Anglo-American gangsters'. And more often than not they followed the call. 'They had been fed with heroes' legends ever since they could remember. For them the *'Appell* to the last *Einsatz'* ['call to the last battle'] was no phrase but appealed to their innermost feelings. They felt that the hour had come, the moment in which they counted, in which they would no longer be pushed aside because they were too young. They could be found everywhere; they shovelled day and night on the *Ostwall* or on the *Westwall*. They fed the refugees, they helped the wounded. In the air raids they fought the flames and helped to rescue the sick and the injured. And finally they confronted the Russians with the *Panzerfaust*.'[121] The major recorded encounters took place in Breslau and in Berlin. In Breslau, surrounded by the Russian forces since March 1945, *Gebietsführer* Herbert Hirsch formed a Hitler Youth regiment well equipped and led by experienced army NCOs. Time and again their counter-attacks managed to retrieve vital positions from the Russians, and the local population soon nicknamed their position as the 'Hitler Youth corner'. They fought on until the city's surrender on 9 May 1945.[122]

A diary entry of 13 April 1945 records: 'The colonel is swearing in young women and girls as combatants. They have to repeat the standard oath formula and are then deployed as gun crews in the northern sector. The flak-gun before the wall of the seminar building is manned by boys aged thirteen to fifteen dressed in uniforms too wide and covered by helmets too big for them.'[123]

Upon Axmann's personal order on 23 April 1945 battalions of Hitler Youths were raised to defend the Pichelsdorf bridges across the river Havel in Berlin to keep the way open for Wenck's phantom army, Hitler's last hope of relief.[124] As the *Armee Wenck* in the form in which Hitler imagined it did not exist, the Hitler Youth fought in vain.

'In the shallow trenches before the Pichelsdorf bridge on both sides of the *Heerstrasse* separated by smaller or greater distances lay Hitler Youths with *Panzerfaust*s alone or in twos. Dawn had already progressed sufficiently to see against the darker background the dark outlines of heavy Russian tanks near the *Heerstrasse* railway station. Their guns were directed towards the bridge. We found the leader of the defending battle group ... from whose mouth we heard the fate of his people. "When the fighting started here five days ago," he told us, "there were roughly 5,000 Hitler Youths and a few soldiers available to take on the desperate struggle against the overwhelming odds. Insufficiently equipped with only rifles and *Panzerfaust* the boys had suffered terribly by the effects of the Russian artillery barrage. Of the 5,000 boys only 500 could still be used for combat.'[125] This was by no means an isolated incident. A Wehrmacht officer gives an account of meeting the youngsters: 'We asked him how at his age of thirteen he comes to be involved in the fighting. And he points to his comrades who partly come from Oranienburg: "Our leader *Hauptbannführer* Frischefsky and the police fetched us from our homes and we had to assemble in the SS barracks and on the *Schlossplatz*. There we were divided up into our *Fähnleins* and were attached to the SS and the *Volkssturm*. We first saw action in the north and east of the city. Most of us were killed by infantry fire because we had to attack across the open fields. Then the fighting in the city. Two days of it. In two days and two nights Oranienburg changed hands four times. That finished another part of us. Then the Russians started bombarding the city with the *Stalinorgel*. And when we wanted to finish and go home we were stopped and had to join the escape across the canal in the direction of Eden. My *Jungzugführer* who refused was strung up on the nearest tree by a few SS men and an SA man. But then he was already fifteen years old. . . . This morning we have been collected together again for our next *Einsatz*." '[126]

They were sacrificed in front of the bridges and they were sacrificed outside Hitler's bunker. On his last public appearance in the garden of the *Reichs* Chancellory Hitler on his 56th birthday awarded decorations to some of the defenders of Berlin, including the Iron Cross 2nd Class to several twelve-year-old Hitler Youths,[127] who were simply thrown into the cauldron of destruction. The boys of the Hitler Youth Division had at least received sound military training; those coming after them had little preparation other than the myth of Langemarck and the legends of 'the heroes of the National Socialist movement'. They were frightened little boys caught between the heroic clap-trap with which their imagination had been fed and the bloody brutality of war.

One such group of terrified little boys manned the barricade erected from street cars across Munich's Maximilian bridge. The youngest was about ten, the oldest not quite fourteen years old. Dressed in a motley of Hitler Youth, *Luftwaffe*, and *Waffen*-SS uniforms too big for them they were too frightened to fire their *Panzerfausts* against a seemingly endless column of Sherman tanks that came rumbling down Munich's *Maximilianstrasse*. It was Monday, 30 April 1945. At about the same time that their Führer committed suicide these Hitler Youths were taken prisoners of war. The following day they were taken to a place of which they had only so far heard in whispers and in macabre political jokes: the liberated concentration camp of Dachau.

'To our left and right soldiers mingled with concentration camp inmates, the latter wearing the vertically blue-striped suits which hung on figures so thin that it was impossible to believe that these people could still speak, let alone walk. Their heads were either shaven or otherwise covered by a beret of the same material as the suits. The gate was flanked by two Sherman tanks, their crews sitting on the turrets and hulls feeding the surrounding men with chewing gum and chocolate and handing out cigarettes. . . . During the first few minutes after entering the compound I thought the inmates were going to tear us to pieces. Astonishingly enough, they just flanked the way wherever we went, but never a word was uttered, not a hand raised against us. First we were taken to a railway siding that branched off from the SS main camp. An American soldier selected a few of us (apparently the strongest-looking ones) and in perfect German ordered us to open one of the freight carriages on the siding. With metal bars and a good deal of effort we pushed back the doors.

'The first thing that fell out was the skeleton of a woman. After that nothing more fell out, for the dead bodies were standing so close to one another, like sardines, that one supported the other. . . . Next we were taken to a red brick building enveloped by an acrid smell. We entered a hall and, for a moment, we thought we were in a boiler room with a number of big furnaces. That idea was immediately dispelled when we saw before each furnace a stretcher of metal with iron clamps. Some of these were still half-way in the furnace, covered by the remnants of burnt bodies. That night was a sleepless one. The impact of what we had seen was too great to be immediately digested. I could not help but cry.'[128]

For this Hitler Youth a world had collapsed. He was but one of millions of a generation characterized by a neutral observer as follows: 'Since these boys had begun to live their lives with any degree of consciousness, there existed for them only shortage and deprivation, the rationing of foodstuffs, of clothes, and all the little things which children still love even when a hard education has taken from them the fear of death. Since this youth began to go through life with open eyes he knew of the worries of a heavily working mother who had also to carry the burden of knowing her husband to be in the war; this youth knows only work, work, and yet again work. For more than two years now he has had to live under the bombs of the enemy. No one need therefore be surprised if this youth has become hard, hard on the outside, hard in his heart and thought. There is scarcely a tear any more when the news of the hero's death of the father or the brother is received; they were barely known anyway; only his mother's talk and their letters had drawn the contours of their personalities. . . . They embody in a very literal sense the offspring of the dead of the Third *Reich*.'[129]

Hitler, the Third *Reich*, and the Hitler Youth had come to an end. So for that matter had the German Youth Movement as a militantly organized mass movement. Some of its members may now and again think back to the time when they were all thrown together by crisis, by stark naked fear, and by belief in their country. And in such introspective moments they may cherish the sense of comradeship of the past and be tempted to look with mild and benevolent contempt upon those excluded from that spirit of comradeship for which in the free-for-all of an industrial competitive society there is little or no room. But that temptation towards nostalgia is cruelly and abruptly halted by the memories of the victims, of the innocent, and of the appalling misuse made of idealism and the willingness for personal sacrifice. These were worthy of a better cause than that which the man whose name they once bore had to offer. The Hitler Youth illustrates one of the most terrifying aspects of National Socialism: the basic idealism that was used as its driving force, and that rationalised its distortions.

XII Aftermath

'After Auschwitz there can be no more poetry.'[1] The last dream of the Germans, the idea of the *Volk* and the *Volksgemeinschaft* had dissolved and become part of that cloud whose acrid stench surrounded those efficient death factories which were dedicated to guaranteeing the purification of the German race. Another revolt, hopefully the last in Europe, against machines and the age of steam had failed, leaving behind destruction and suffering on a scale impossible to convey within the full range of the vocabulary of any language.

And there, prostrate among the debris, was Germany's young generation, a youth surrounded by broken symbols and discredited ideals whose perversion made the largest part of this generation at least immune in the future to ideologies and apathetic to political radicalism. The twenty-year sentence passed on Schirach at the Trial of Major War Criminals in Nuremberg was hardly commented upon. Axmann's expressions of regret at having sacrificed his Hitler Youths at the Battle of Berlin were noted and forgotten. The problems of the present, pre-occupation with actual survival, were too great to allow much time to be spent pondering on questions of responsibility.

In 1945 there was an acute shortage of food: only 40% of the food needed in Germany was available, though the full impact of this was not to be felt until 1946 and 1947. The rubble of destruction in Germany alone amounted to 400 million cubic metres; of nineteen million dwellings, $2\frac{3}{4}$ million had been completely destroyed and $1\frac{1}{4}$ million severely damaged. Hamburg lost 53% of its homes, Cologne 70%, Dortmund 66%, Berlin 37%, Munich 33%, Magdeburg 50%, Dresden 60%.[2] Shacks, barns, the cellars of ruins: these were to be the homes of many for years to come. More than sixteen million Germans were refugees from the East, twelve million of whom found refuge in the Western zones. The productive capacity of German industry had declined almost to zero; that of its textile industry, for instance, was such that at its early post-war level every German would have received an overcoat only once every forty years and a shirt only once every ten years.[3] Allied restrictions on the movement of individuals made it almost impossible to venture from one zone to another. Public transport, especially the railways, was utterly disrupted. Whatever money existed was worth very little; consequently the black market flourished throughout Germany, and one could obtain twenty American cigarettes for 150 Marks, two pounds of coffee for 600 Marks and a pound of butter for 250 Marks.[4]

It is against this background of destruction, destitution, and starvation that one must view the numbness of many, if not most, Germans especially youths, when confronted in the press and films with the atrocities of the concentration camps. Only those confronted with them face-to-face were not likely to forget so quickly. But for most the war was over; to survive its consequences was now of paramount importance.

Germany's post-war youth grew up among the ruins, lived in them, queued among them and indeed received its education in them. It was an environment that produced that new pragmatism towards most questions which became so typical of the first two decades of Germany's post-war history. Together with their mothers they cleared the streets of rubble, they stripped the ruins of their wood for fuel, and whole gangs of boys and girls were posted along points of the railway lines where coal trains had to slow down, to board the wagons and in a matter of seconds throw down enough coal to fill a few bags. They raided vehicles – preferably belonging to Americans – for food and cigarettes and funneled them into the black markets of the cities.

The reintroduction of compulsory education in October 1945 was perhaps the beginning of a return to normal life. But it was hardly noticeable at the time. Lack of schoolrooms in many cases caused two or more schools to have to be accommodated in one. Lessons were given on a shift basis and in the early years school forms were as much a black market as the streets outside. Membership of a particular form no longer represented a reliable indicator of the age group of pupils; the dislocations produced by the war in the German educational process were so great that in forms where one would normally expect thirteen-year-old boys, many of the seventeen- to eighteen-year-old age group could be found,[5] a problem which affected grammar schools for boys more than those for girls, since it had been the boys who had been more directly exposed to the war.

Problems were equally as serious at university level, where one of the entry requirements was one, sometimes two, semesters of unskilled manual work to reconstruct the lecture halls. Yet the students were impressive. Haggard, starved, and clad in all shades of field grey, they approached their studies with a seriousness and a sense of purpose which to a university teacher of the late sixties and early seventies must sound almost legendary.

As one American visiting professor at the University of Marburg recorded in 1946:

'I have hardly ever had better students than those at Marburg. To me and my colleagues these young men and women displayed unusual intellectual earnestness, characterized by a deep understanding of the problems of the time and by a burning desire to acquire reliable knowledge and instruction and information about the methods of scientific work. It may be true that very few of these students could have been described as convinced democrats. However, I do not consider this attitude in any way as a negative factor; rather it appears to me as the manifestation of a cautious attitude, suitable for any serious human being who is reluctant to jump from one ideology to the other of which he knows little and which as yet he has not seen at work.'[6]

Whereas in 1918 a large part of Germany's youth had found it difficult to adjust to civilian life, there was no similar problem in 1945. The overwhelming majority of those who returned became civilians with a vengeance and when as early as 1948 demands increased for a German contribution to the defence of the West, their reaction was spontaneous: '*Ohne uns!*' ['Without us!']. The call for rearmament met almost unequivocal rejection, not least because the formal rearmament of one part of Germany would cement its division into two parts. This does not mean that the young rejected any form of political engagement. After all, German youth groups had themselves ferried across the German Bight to the island of Heligoland in the summer of 1951 in protest against this island being used for target practice by the Royal Air Force, with the ultimate objective of making it completely uninhabitable; and in this protest they were successful. Approaching RAF squadrons about to bomb the island circled over it and then returned to base, their bomb bays still shut. In the autumn of 1949 and the summer of 1950 German youths joined the workers of the Salzgitter steel works when these were to be blown up by the occupying powers in the process of dismantling the German steel industry. And Salzgitter was not blown up.[7] They protested against the division of Berlin, that burning symbol of the division of their country, and did not shun Russian fire when they climbed the Brandenburg Gate to haul down the red flag and replace it with the colours of black, red, and gold, just as they faced Russian T-34s in 1953 in Berlin, Magdeburg, and Leipzig – with nothing more in their hands than bricks. And when Europe as a political concept re-emerged they thought that they could give the development a little more push by dismantling the frontier gates at Kehl and elsewhere and publicly burning them.[8]

The fact that German youths in one part of Germany were in a position to protest in public underlined the fact that their contemporaries in that part of Germany occupied by Soviet Russia had not been in any position to speak out openly against the policies of the occupying power, including the process of gradual rearmament that had been taking place since 1946. Unlike in the western zones, youth in the Soviet zone had, on the surface at least, experienced little break in their continuity. The Russians and their German assistants made a point of organizing youth quickly. What once had been the HJ now became the FDJ, the Free German Youth, uniformed in blue instead of brown shirts, and under Erich Honnecker's able leadership was rapidly fused with the SED (Socialist Unity Party) apparatus. Young Germans in the west could if they so desired protest; in the east where, as in Hitler's Germany, the party was identified with the state, they could not, unless they were prepared to face life in a concentration camp, now adapted to the needs of the SED and their Russian masters, or, worse, life in Siberia. When utter despair drove them into the streets, the overwhelming presence of the Russian army ensured that the protest would be quelled. The only vote left, that with their feet, was exercised as long as it was possible.

Yet the question was often asked whether in spite of massive oppression in the east and the watchful eyes of the Western Allies, right-wing radicalism in German youth movements had really altogether disappeared. In fact the subject of 'Neo-Nazism' in general and Neo-Nazi youth organizations seems to have belonged to the general editorial stand-bys of newspapers and magazines until the subject was utterly discredited by the methods deployed by *Paris-Match* in 1966.[9] However, sensationalized as the various treatments may have been, the reports were rarely without some substance, as the two major occasions when the subject was raised – in 1953 and in 1959 – demonstrate.

The first occasion when the sensational news exploded upon the world was on 14 January 1953 when the British High Commission in Bonn and the British Foreign Office in London published a communiqué informing the public that British authorities had had a group of former leading members of the NSDAP under surveillance who apparently planned at some time in the future to seize power in Western Germany. The main centre of activity was in the British zone of occupation and in order to subject the group to closer investigation the British High Commissioner, Sir Brian Robertson, had decided to arrest its leading members. These included Dr Werner Naumann, a former Secretary of state of Goebbels' ministry who in Hitler's 'Last Testament' had been appointed as Minister of Propaganda. Several other members were either former *Gauleiters* or party functionaries, as well as including several former leaders of the Hitler Youth. For weeks the Naumann group occupied the front pages of the newspapers until gradually public interest faded. When finally towards the end of 1954 the news came that all members in custody had been released and no further legal proceedings would be taken it hardly caused a stir.[10]

The British authorities, however, had had genuine cause for concern. The arrests had been preceded by a development in North-Rhine-Westphalia and Lower Saxony which was potentially dangerous. The FDP there, the Free Democrats, contained a rather higher than normal representation of former NSDAP functionaries in its ranks. The leader of the FDP in the diet of North-Rhine-Westphalia, Wilke, was a former member of the *Reichsjugendführung* whose political ability led him rapidly along the path of political promotion. Wilke was believed to have aimed at infiltrating the FDP with former National Socialists, something he had apparently already tried before in the CDU (Christian Democrats) where he had been unsuccessful. Associates of his achieved greater success in the SPD (the Social Democratic Party), where an entire group of former Hitler Youth leaders established contact with one of the SPD's leaders, Professor Carlo Schmid.[12] Wilke established his position in the FDP in North-Rhine-Westphalia in 1947 and six years later the party's leadership in this region included fifteen former prominent members of the NSDAP, including seven former SS leaders and four Hitler Youth leaders. In Lower Saxony the situation was very similar. This, of course, says very little about the political attitudes of the individual personalities concerned, but considering their concentration the presence of former, though young, NSDAP members was bound to alarm outsiders, especially since similar developments could be observed in the conservative DP (the German Party), and the BHE (a party dominated by refugees from Eastern Germany).[13]

There was very little that could be done at the party level, where within the FDP this development was readily admitted: 'We declare openly that in the regional association (of the FDP in North-Rhine-Westphalia) a number of people are active who in their youth had joined the HJ and occupied leading positions within it. Also former members of the *Waffen*-SS are working in the regional centre, the districts, and the wards. It is self-evident that we have looked at these colleagues very closely, before we entrusted them with any responsibility. Our experience has been that they have dedicated themselves to the task given to them by the party leadership and that with all their strength they have worked for the Free Democratic Party. Time and again in the course of numerous checks the party leadership has been able to note that negative tendencies have never made an appearance.'[14]

The Chairman of the FDP in North-Rhine-Westphalia, Dr Middelhauve, emphasized his own personal attitude in the matter as follows: 'As regards this point I should like to summarize my opinion by saying that it would be objectively unjust to consider every political activity [of former members of the NSDAP] from the beginning with mistrust and to suspect that their intention is to undermine the party. Particularly in the interest of democracy the FDP's endeavours ought to be rated very highly, endeavours devoid of selfish ends and guided only by legal considerations. These endeavours represent pioneering work which has prevented the rise of irremediable bitterness and a dangerous drift away of elements of goodwill into the radical camp.'[15]

That Dr Middelhauve was no doubt correct in his assessment has been borne out by the subsequent history of the German Federal Republic. At the time, however, it was asking more than could be expected for the occupying powers and public opinion abroad to take the same view. From the point of view of the British High Commission these developments were serious enough, but when it became quite obvious that connections existed between the FDP and the Naumann circle the spectre of a conspiracy grew too large to be ignored and British action followed. In the light of the actual supporting evidence the charge that Naumann and his circle endangered the security of the British forces of occupation because his aim was the resurrection of National Socialist rule was somewhat extravagant, not to say ludicrous, but against the background of the time perhaps understandable.

It seems that when the affair became politically embarrassing the entire case was handed over to the Federal German constitutional court which, like the occupying powers, was equally unable to produce further evidence and ultimately had to release the prisoners without preferring charges. However, the action did not remotely affect the presence of former NSDAP and Hitler Youth members in the FDP, some of whom, like the former *HJ-Gebietsführer* Siegfried Zoglmann, advanced to become members of the Federal parliament in Bonn or to ministerial posts.

The issue of Neo-Nazism, and especially that of Neo-Nazi groups, arose again late in 1959 when two youths were caught daubing swastikas on a synagogue in Cologne. Immediate connections with, and responsibility of, extreme right-wing parties were alleged, though none was proved. What followed was a wave of swastika-daubing throughout the world. In the Federal Republic, of 234 cases subject to prosecution, only 8% had been committed out of political conviction, while, for instance, 48% were acts of rowdyism and 15% children's scrawling.[16] It would have been extremely unwise for the German authorities to ignore these incidents, but the international coverage they received was certainly excessive. Even newspapers with claims to being 'quality papers' reported such fictions as that 50,000 German youths were organized in extreme right-wing movements and using as their manual Hitler's *Mein Kampf*.[17] It seems that many foreign correspondents in Bonn became the victims of two factors: first, the vast number of nationalist youth groups in Western Germany, a number, however, which in no way indicated their actual membership; secondly, the claims made by the leaders of these youth groups concerning their membership, which in every case had not been merely exaggerated but had actually lapsed into the realm of fantasy.[18]

The *Bundesjugendring*, an organization in which the majority of German youth organizations are represented, has grouped the 'national youth leagues' into four broad categories. First, there are those of a pronounced political character which ideologically or organizationally are affiliated with nationalist parties or other similar adult bodies. Secondly, youth leagues as those before 1933; thirdly, military youth groups which enjoy the support of ex-servicemen's organizations; and fourthly, political student groups which co-operate very closely with extreme right-wing parties.[19] Of these, the first group started very early in the history of the Federal Republic when Herbert Münchow, former *HJ-Gebietsführer*, founded the *Reichsjugend* which co-operated closely with the DRP, the German *Reichs* Party, though that party's official youth group was the *Junge Kameradschaft*. Although both groups were spread over the entire Federal Republic its membership never reached that of the DRP, which in its heyday did not exceed 30,000 and which since its merger with the NPD in 1965 has ceased to exist. So has the *Reichsjugend* and the *Junge Kameradschaft*. Moreover their entire history, as with the history of every German post-war right-wing radical movement, has been marked by internal rivalries which in turn led to the splitting of youth groups and their multiplicity. Another right-wing party of the 1950s was the *Deutsche Gemeinschaft* whose youth organization was the *Junge Deutsche Germeinschaft* from which after internal quarrels the *Jungdeutsche Bewegung* emerged, while another splinter group adopted the name *Wiking Jugend* and enjoyed the support of Mathilde Ludendorff.[20]

The strongest group numerically in the 1950s was the *Jugendbund Adler* led by Richard Etzel, one of the early members of the Hitler Youth in Munich, who had been fined for his political activities in 1932. Etzel described the task of his *Jugendbund* as follows:

'Our work endeavours to burn the consciousness into every heart that the failure of the young generation of our *Volk* does not only mean its own downfall, but it means also the death of one of the most valuable members of the community of peoples.

'In our activity, which serves the training of young human beings, we work for the body so that it will become and stay tough, strong, hard, and quick; we train the spirit to enlarge knowledge and stimulate ability. Wherever in a healthy body lives an active spirit, there is room for a soul capable of great emotion, and which is conducive to that attitude of cleanliness and honour which we in our most recent past as well as in the present have been painfully missing or are still missing.'[21]

Attempts to consolidate national youth groups by the creation in 1954 of a *Kameradschaftsring Nationaler Jugendbünde* soon faltered. A significant point about this organization, however, was that its activities reached into Austria and the German-speaking southern Tyrol of Italy. The Austrian influence was considerable and when the KNJ was disintegrating because of the incompatibility of its members, the Austrian *Bund Heimattreuer Jugend* replaced it. That body was headed by Konrad Windisch, a Viennese whose contacts ranged across Western Europe where he was in close touch with right-wing radical movements in France, Belgium, and Holland.[22]

The youth league groups tried in many respects to assume the heritage of the youth leagues, of the *Bündische Jugend* of the Weimar Republic. Thus the *Deutsch-Wandervögel* claimed to strive for the unification of a 'racially conscious' German youth. Another one, the *Schiller-Jugend* founded in 1955, received the enthusiastic support of Dr Herbert Böhme, the lyricist of Hitler's storm troopers. Through his organization, the *Deutsches Kulturwerk Eruopäischen Geistes*, he attempted to infiltrate the grammar schools using the *Schiller Jugend* as one of his instruments. He was stopped by the authorities and this official intervention led to an exodus of members from the youth groups, many of whom had initially become members believing they were joining a purely cultural-orientated organization.[23]

The military youth leagues were in terms of membership the strongest in the decade between 1950 and 1960. The most prominent of these were the *Deutsche Jugendbund Kyffhäuser*, the youth branch of the ex-servicemen's league *Kyffhauserbund*. Others were the *Deutsche Jugend im Verband Deutscher Soldaten* and the *Marinejugend*, but as in the other two categories the membership here too dwindled from the late 1960s to such an extent that most of them, in so far as they still exist, consist of the leader and a handful of followers.[24] Thus for instance when the right-wing monthly *Nation Europa* in August 1961 called for an international youth congress at Coburg, Richard Etzel, an active contributor to the journal, arrived with one member on the back seat of his motor cycle. Incidentally, the only other youth group present – which mustered five members – was a Belgian youth group. Apart from that, youth was not present at all, nor for that matter were there any Neo-Nazis, only old ones.

The fourth category, that of the student groups, was most prominently represented in the late 1950s and early 1960s by the *Bund Nationaler Studenten*. In contrast to the majority of youth groups contained in the three previous categories, the BNS did not have among its leaders anyone who had been directly associated with any of the organizations of the NSDAP, a fact on which they placed considerable emphasis. It collaborated closely with the DRP and especially up to 1960 appeared to attract a considerable number of students into its ranks. In Bonn the BNS's impression must have been at first a positive one for the monthly journal of the league *Student im Volk* managed to obtain a full-page advertisement from the Federal Ministry of Defence for officer recruitment into the *Bundeswehr*. Apparent success induced over-confidence; the BNS, believing as it did in riding on the crest of a 'national wave', dropped its moderate cover; former NSDAP functionaries addressed its meetings in increasing numbers, and when finally the clamour of public opinion could no longer be ignored, the BNS was proscribed by court action.[25] In its place appeared a host of other organizations many of which operated in the fold of Adolf von Thadden's DRP, and were to become a source of embarrassment to him once the NPD had been launched by him and when he was at great pains to give his party a respectable and democratic middle-class image. The NPD's successes in local elections in 1965, 1966, and early 1967 were to a very large extent due to the support gained from the age group of those under thirty. However, this support was very much a protest vote against the grand coalition between the CDU/CSU and the SPD. Deprived of a genuine alternative many young Germans cast their vote for what for a short time appeared to be the only genuine party of opposition. As soon as the two-party dichotomy once again reappeared young voters returned to the fold of the established parties, as the Federal elections of 1969 demonstrate.[26]

In the meantime several changes had taken place which were to transform the youth scene in Western Germany. For one thing there was a change of generations. In post-war Germany one can distinguish three main age groups; first, the sceptical generation, consisting in the main of those who had returned from the war and who were the students of the universities until the mid-1950s. They were succeeded by an age group who were once again the recipients of an orderly education and who enjoyed the fruits of the economic miracle that their fathers had produced. But the conditions existing in the late-1940s were still vivid in their memories and they readily accepted the material yields of the miracle. And they, at least at university level, were replaced in the mid-1960s by an age group whose historical consciousness was no longer branded by the experiences of the past, who therefore were once again prepared to aspire towards utopia, and whose aim was not so much a totalitarian *state* as a totalitarian *society*.

As late as 1964 public opinion surveys conducted among the youth in Western Germany produced a picture in which there were no fundamental objections to their nation's political, social, and economic structure. Traditional authorities, though at times cumbersome, were still accepted as valid, and by-products of economic prosperity such as social conformism and social prestige were seen as inevitable and unavoidable if one wished to achieve material success. A year later changes in attitude, especially among university students, became more pronounced. Taking their style, even their slogans, from the student protest movement in the United States, notably from Berkeley, students directed their first protests against the hierarchic structure of German universities, clamouring for educational reforms and debunking the customary excess of ceremonial. At that stage the student movement still enjoyed a considerable amount of support from the academic staff, but practical issues were soon replaced by issues of politics, some of which were of a less direct practical relevance, like the demonstrations against the Shah of Persia on the occasion of his visit to Berlin in June 1967. The death of a student who was actually not one of the demonstrators but an innocent bystander was the signal for student demonstrations throughout Western Germany. Once that cause had been exhausted a new one was found in the campaign against the 'monopoly press' as personified by Axel Springer and his publishing ventures. The campaign directed itself against the size of his combine which threatened the variety of opinion, as well as against Springer's political attitude which one could describe as democratic conservative. That the problem of over-concentration of the press is a very serious one few would doubt – whether Molotov cocktails and mass fanaticism are the right answer for it is rather more doubtful. Vietnam, too, as in other Western countries became a good leading issue for student politicians in Germany.[27]

University reform, Springer, and Vietnam kept West Germany's university students on the streets throughout 1967 and early 1968, a wave of protest which reached its high point with the attempted assassination of one of the radical left-wing leaders of the German student movement, Rudi Dutschke. For days Dutschke's life was in balance and the event triggered off the biggest wave of militant protest among university students the Federal Republic had ever experienced. From Good Friday 1968 onwards, for four days, students dominated the scene in the cities of Western Germany. The 'Days of May 1968' in Paris lent further glamour to student demonstrators. The Extra Parliamentary Opposition, the APO as it called itself, was on the march clamouring against the 'Emergency Law Legislation' by means of which the German Federal government was obtaining policing powers hitherto retained in the hands of the Allies. Heroes long forgotten were resurrected – Kurt Eisner, Erich Mühsam, Ernst Toller. Some were more familiar, such as Rosa Luxemburg and Karl Liebknecht, and some were new like Ho Chi-Minh, Fidel Castro, and Che Guevara. And, of course, the historical leaders of international Communism – Marx, Lenin, Trotsky – all received their due.

Like the German youth movements of old, the APO knew very well what it did not like in contemporary society. The philosopher Herbert Marcuse and his criticism of modern industrial society provided the most trenchant weapons. But when asked to supply the model of a workable alternative to a liberal democratic society answers have remained remarkably vague or naive, ranging from a system of soviets to utopian and anarchist daydreams. This failure was one of the reasons, perhaps, why after 1968 the APO lost much of its élan, breaking up in countless Trotskyist, Maoist, and Spartacist factions. The other reason can be seen in the election result of September 1969 which, with the election of the Socialist Willy Brandt as chancellor, fulfilled the hopes of many of the young and deprived the APO of both its *raison d'être* and its mass support. What remained was a hard core divided into two main groups, one believing that only by means of violent revolution could society be changed, the other convinced that only the long march through the institutions would achieve this: the policy of 'Adolphe Légalité' under different auspices.

The former opinion crystallized in the form of the Baader-Meinhof group whose intellectual head was Ulrike Meinhof, once editor of the student magazine *konkret*. Describing themselves as the 'Red Army Faction' it was their declared aim 'to carry the war into the residential districts of the ruling classes. . . . Through suitable actions it must be demonstrated that the attacks are in principle directed against all institutions of the class enemy, all administrative centres and police posts, against the centres of the economic combines, against the functionaries of these institutions, against leading civil servants, judges, and directors.'

In small commando troops, no fewer than three, no more than ten, urban guerrilla warfare was to be carried into the cities of Western Germany, because 'the large city possesses a mass of targets. . . . In the large city the entire flank of the enemy is exposed. He never knows which objective is being attacked.'[28] The cases of arson attributed to political left-wing radicals increased from 48 in 1949 to 117 in 1970 and culminated two years later in a series of bomb attacks against American army headquarters in Frankfurt and Heidelberg, against a Federal judge, the Criminal Investigation Centre in Munich, and against the offices of the Springer publishing concern. The net result was four people killed and forty-one injured.[29]

Three months later Ulrike Meinhof, Andreas Baader, the son of a renowned historian, Gudrun Esslin, daughter of a Protestant clergyman, and their associates had been arrested. But the hunt had cost the lives of several policemen and of at least one innocent member of the public, a Scotsman living in Stuttgart. Criminality in the pursuit of perfection, in the quest for utopia, was nothing new in history, but it was new on the West German political scene since 1945. It marks the extreme position of that large group of young Germans who no longer look for the solution of conflicts by rational answers but instead turn to irrationalism in search of a new Jerusalem, or a Langemarck with a different omen.

How much this is also true of the second group, the *Jusos*, the Young Socialists, only time will tell. But the threat of Chancellor Willy Brandt on the eve of the 1973 SPD congress to give up his office as party chairman if the radical influences attempted to compromise the promises he had made to the German electorate in 1972 is indicative that the danger from the extreme Left is felt and that instead of decreasing it is increasing. At all levels of the Social Democratic Party, but especially at the ward level, the *Jusos* have been active, and by subtly clever tactics managed to infiltrate many of their members, thus hoping eventually to change the entire *basis* of the SPD membership. And, as it has been put, once this has been achieved who needs to worry about the party leaders?

Thus, in one way or another, youth has not abandoned political activism; the only difference is that whereas half a century ago it was engaged in a variety of right-wing causes, engagement now is principally on the extreme Left, a development which has also affected the Christian Democrats and the Liberals in Germany. The resurgence of militant nationalist youth movements in post-war Germany was at the best of times no more than a spectre which vanished when confronted with reality. Concern is expressed by the Bonn government that perhaps the development has gone too far, for conscientious objection to military service is nowhere as high as in the Federal Republic, reaching a record 33,792 in 1972 with a continuing upward trend.[30]

But all this, of course, is only half the truth – if for no other reason than that one is talking only about one half of Germany. And student unrest, student demonstrations, open opposition to the party in power, open objection to military service, all these belong to the category of 'strictly forbidden' in the DDR. There para-military training from the age of six when a child enters the 'Young Pioneers' continues in the FDJ to which the Young Pioneer is transferred at the age of fifteen, and is especially emphasized by the GST, the *Gesellschaft für Sport und Technik* run by a Major-General of the National People's Army, which organizes the DDR equivalents of what was once known as *Wehrertüchtigungslager*, all of course in service of the defence of socialism against the aggressive imperialism of its western neighbour.

'A few minutes after the alert is sounded the youths march out to their exercise in the Tromper Wieck area. March security is being exercised, "Water courses" and "deep ravines" have to be crossed by narrow planks or handling on ropes. As the hours advance so the temperature rises. Marching through knee-deep sand pulls on the muscles. And then we speed up the advance by running, followed by hand-grenade throwing. The best manage fifty metres, others find it difficult to reach the thirty-metre mark. The next station is the rifle range. The small calibre sub-machine gun must rest firmly in the hands. Or else nothing will come of hitting the target in the black.

'This exercise lasts four hours. In those four hours the boys display fitness, endurance, and toughness.'[31]

This could well represent a report of a Hitler Youth exercise in a *Wehrertüchtigungslager*: in fact it is a 1971 report of one of the camps of the GST whose author also makes the point that their achievement is not merely the product of GST training but also of their *Wehrerziehung* at school. Seven-year-old children at school are confronted with the following kind of problems: 'Describe the uniform of the soldier illustrated' or 'Which tasks have the soldiers of our *Volksarmee* to fulfil? Write what you have read about it, listened to or seen.'[32] Things get a little more complicated when mathematical problems at school include such a one as: 'An enemy guided missile with a speed of 3,000 metres per second approaches the territory of the Socialist countries and is located by the radar system 600 km before crossing the frontier. How much time is available to destroy the rocket at the latest when crossing the frontier?'[33]

History lessons too are deployed to familiarize pupils with 'the development of the historical motives of military preparedness'. And the methods recommended are:

Analysis of the effective class forces in wars, revolutions, revolutionary national movements of a military character and uprisings. Examination of the characters of wars. Evaluation of historical events from a military-political perspective. Precise application of military concepts. Military examples of historical and revolutionary personalities. Maintenance of historical military tradition.[34]

It is impossible to gauge how the German youth in the DDR responds to this in a society that curbs any free and spontaneous expression of opinion. In comparison the situation is perhaps healthier though unpredictable in the Federal Republic where as a result of the youth protest movement much that had been fossilized has been transformed back into a state of flux from which, for better or worse, much can be reshaped and remoulded.

Nietzsche once asserted that it is the fate of youth to deliver the final blow to a pseudo-culture that is in the process of collapse. Perhaps the consumption-orientated conformism of a capitalist society needs to be overthrown as much as the conformism enforced by the rigidity of ideological dogma in the East. Whether either of them is in the process of collapse is open to debate. What seems clear though is that the ties that held most of Germany's youth in bondage for a century and a half have been completely destroyed but in the process of destruction have been replaced by others.

But then bondage is an unalterable condition, a fact of life, compared with which the claim to the *right* of the pursuit of happiness as a self-evident truth is no more than a piece of high-minded eighteenth-century nonsense. Man in bondage – a bondage of one kind or another – is as natural as it would be unnatural for youth not to question the validity of this condition, or in fact rebel against it and to fashion and follow its own ideals. In the past youth has succeeded at times in changing and ameliorating this condition – not, however, in abolishing it. But never, in German history at least, has there been a time in which German youth paid a higher price for such an attempt, a price of personal sacrifice and physical as well as mental injuries sustained, than in the era dominated by the symbol of the rune and the swastika.

Glossary
Abbreviations
Hitler Youth Ranks
Diagrams

Glossary and Abbreviations

In general, only those terms the meaning of which has not been explained in the text are here translated.

Arbeitsfront — See DAF.
AHS — Adolf Hitler Schools.
Anschluss — Union of Germany with German Austria.
Auslandsamt — Foreign Department of the RJF.
BDAJ — *Bund Deutscher Arbeiter Jugend*, League of German Workers' Youth.
BDM — *Bund Deutscher Mädchen*, League of German Girls within the Hitler Youth.
BHE — *Bund der Heimatlosen und Entrechteten*, League of Expellees and Expropriated, party political grouping in West Germany.
Bund der Artamanen — Organization during the 1920s and early 1930s aiming at settlement on land in the east, seeking a reinvigoration of the race by a return to pre-industrial modes of life.
Bündische Jugend — Youth Leagues representing a wide spectrum of political and social attitudes.
DAF — *Deutsche Arbeitsfront*, German Workers' Front, NS organization replacing Trade Unions.
DAP — *Deutsche Arbeiter Partei*, German Workers' Party; see NSDAP.
DP — *Deutsche Partei*, West German Party.
Deutsches Jugendwerk e.V. — Organization founded by Schirach to enter the Reichs-committee of German Youth associations.
DJV — *Deutsches Jungvolk*, Hitler Youth formation for boys aged between 10 and 14.
DJM — *Deutsche Jungmädel*, Hitler Youth formation for girls aged between 10 and 14.
FDJ — *Freie Deutsche Jugend*, Free German Youth, SED youth organization in East Germany.
FDP — *Freie Demokratische Partei Deutschlands*, Free Democrats, West German party.
Freikorps — Free Corps; volunteer troops recruited after the armistice by the German government for use to secure 'law and order' within and her eastern frontiers without.
Frontjugend — Literally translated, Front Youth.
Führerbefehl — Order directly originating from Hitler.
Führerprinzip — Leadership principle.
Gau — An old German term for province or district used by the NSDAP to describe a party (not state) administrative district.
Gauverband — BDM administrative area as well as unit; see diagram p.271.
Gauführer — Gauleader, pre-1933 HJ rank.
Gauleiter — NSDAP head of a Gau.

269

Gleichschaltung   – centralization and co-ordination at both administrative and ideological levels.

Grenzlandamt   – HJ department for border regions.

Gruppenführer   – Storm trooper rank, but prior to 1933 also Hitler Youth rank.

GST   – *Gesellschaft für Sport und Technik*, Society for Sports and Technical Affairs, East German organization responsible among other things for the paramilitary training of the FDJ.

Hauptamt   – Main Office.

Hauptlagerleiter   – Main Camp Leader.

HJ   – *Hitler-Jugend*, Hitler Youth formation for boys aged 14–18.

Hitler-Jugend, Bund der Deutschen Arbeiterjugend   – Hitler Youth, League of German Workers' Youth.

HJ im Dienst   – HJ on Duty.

HJ-Streifendienst   – Hitler Youth unit established for investigatory and disciplinary purposes within the Hitler Youth.

Jugendführer   – Youth Leader.

Jungmann   – Form of address for NPEA pupil.

Jungmannschaft   – Literally translated, young crew or team.

Jungsturm   – Literally translated, young assault group.

Junker   – Form of address for an Ordensburg student.

Kadettenvorschule   – Preparatory schools for officer cadets in Imperial Germany.

KLV   – *Kinderlandverschickung*; initially a programme to send deprived children on holiday into the countryside, after 1942 it became a programme to evacuate all children from cities threatened by air raids.

KPD   – *Kommunistische Partei Deutschlands*, Communist Party of Germany.

Kreis   – Administrative district of medieval Germany, a term which has remained in use to the present day.

Landjugendamt   – HJ department for youths of rural regions.

Landschaftskultur   – Cult of the landscape.

Lebensraum   – Living space.

Lektorat   – Usually a publishers' editorial office.

NPEA   – *Nationalpolitische Erziehungsanstalt*, National Political Education Institute.

NSB   – *National-Socialistische Beweging*, Dutch NS movement.

NSDAP   – *Nationalsozialistische Arbeiterpartei Deutschlands*, National Socialist Work Party of Germany.

Nationalsozialistische Freiheitsbewegung   – National Socialist Liberty Movement.

NS-Kultusgemeinde   – NS supervisory organ for cultural activities at local level.

NSKK   – NS *Kraftfahrkorps*, NS Driver Corps.

NSFK   – NS *Fliegerkorps*, NS Aviation Corps.

NSLB   – *Nationalsozialistischer Lehrerbund*, NS Teachers' League.

NSP   – National Socialist Party in Poland.

NSSB   – *Nationalsozialistischer Schülerbund*, NS Pupils' League.

NSS   – See NSSB.

NSStB   – *Nationalsozialistischer Studentenbund*, NS Students' League.

Obergebiet   – Largest single HJ administrative unit.

Oberpräsident   – State administrative head of a province or region.

OKW   – *Oberkommando der Wehrmacht*, High Command of the Armed Forces.

Ortsgruppe   – A term used, though not invented, by the NSDAP applied to the smallest administrative NSDAP unit, a village or depending on size, a group of villages. Towns and cities too were divided into *Ortsgruppen*.

Ortsgruppenleiter   – NSDAP head of *Ortsgruppe*.

Panzerfaust   – The 'first against armour', a recoilless anti-tank projectile.

Parteisoldat   – Party soldier, derogatory term applied to officers whose career was furthered by close adherence to the NSDAP rather than by military talents, though of course the combination of both existed as well.

Parteitag — Party Rally or Party Day.

RAD — *Reichsarbeitsdienst*, Labour Service, compulsory prior to military service.

Reichsappell — Reichs roll-call or inspection.

Reichsauschuss der Deutschen Jugendverbände — Reichs Committee of German Youth Associations.

Reichsführung — Reichs leadership of the Hitler Youth during Gruber's tenure of office.

Reichsführer — Reichsleader.

RFSS — *Reichsführer* SS.

RJF — *Reichsjugendführung, Reichsjugendführer*, Reichs Youth leader as well as office.

Reichsjugendtag — Reichs Youth rally or day.

Reichsjugendbücherei — Reichs Youth Library.

Reichsleitung — In a Hitler Youth context, a term identical to that of *Reichsführung*.

Reichstag — German parliament.

Reichsstelle für Jugendschrifttum — Reichs Office for Youth Literature.

Reichswehr — Name of the German army 1919–35.

Der Rote Sturmtrupp — The Red Assault Troop.

SA — Storm troopers.

Schlamperei — Untidiness.

SED — *Sozialistische Einheitspartei Deutschlands*, Socialist Unity Party created from the compulsory fusion of SPD and KPD in East Germany.

SD — *Sicherheitsdienst*, SS Security Service.

Siedlernachwuchsstelle — Youth Settlers Training Office.

SPD — Social Democratic Party of Germany.

Spartakus Bewegung — Movement which was a precursor of the Communist Party in Germany.

Spiessbürger — Philistine.

SS-Junkerschulen — SS officer schools.

Volksgenosse — NS form of address, meaning in effect fellow racial member.

Volksgerichtshof — People's Court.

Volksherzog — The Duke of the People.

Volksschule — Basic school attended from the age of 6 to 15 unless after the fourth year the pupil changed to a grammar school.

Volksstaat — Racial state. In the NS terminology the concept of the Volk was equivalent to that of race, hence terms like *volkisch*, for instance, mean racial.

Volkssturm — Home guard.

Wandervogel — Migratory or roving bird.

Weltanschauung — Ideology.

Wehrertüchtigungslager — HJ military training camps supervised by the *Wehrmacht* or *Waffen*-SS.

Wehrmacht — Name of the German Army 1935–45.

Zuchthaus — Penitentiary.

Hitler Youth Ranks

In the course of the short history of the Hitler Youth the ranks changed frequently. Those shown below were the greatly simplified ones in use in 1943. For the strength of the units commanded see diagram p.271.

Jugendführer des Deutschen Reiches: Baldur v. Schirach
Reichsjugendführer: Arthur Axmann

HJ	DJV
Stabsführer	—
Obergebietsführer	—
Gebietsführer	—
Oberbannführer	—
Bannführer	*Jungbannführer*
Stammführer	*Unterbannführer*
Gefolgschaftsführer	*Fähnleinführer*
Scharführer	*Jungzugführer*
Kameradschaftsführer	*Jungenschaftsführer*
Hitlerjunge	*Pimpf*

BDM	DJM
Reichsreferentin	—
—	—
Obergauführerin	—
Hauptmädelführerin	—
Untergauführerin	*JM-Untergauführerin*
Mädelringführen	*JM-Ringführerin*
Mädelgruppenführerin	*JM-Gruppenführerin*
Mädelscharführerin	*JM-Scharführerin*
Mädelschaftsführerin	*Jungmädelschaftsführerin*
Mädel	*Jungmädel (JM)*

Diagrams

I Regional Organization of the Hitler Youth in 1943

There were a total of six *Obergebiete*, each containing a minimum of six *Gebiete* and a maximum of eight. Since 1940 a *Gebiet* corresponded with a NSDAP *Gau*. Each *Gebiet*, depending on size, contained several HJ *Banne*, DJ *Unterbanne*, *Jungmädeluntergaue* and *Untergaue*. There were 42 *Gebiete* and 223 *Banne* (with corresponding DJV, DJM and BDM formations) as well as RJF command centres in Bohemia-Moravia (CSR), the General-Gouvernement (Poland), Ost (Baltic countries, Russia, Ukraine, Balkans) and the Netherlands.

One *Bann* had five *Unterbanne*, each *Unterbann* four *Gefolgschaften*, each *Gefolgschaft* three *Scharen* and each *Schar* three *Kameradschaften*. This applies equally to the equivalent DJV, DJM and BDM formations.

HITLER YOUTH ORGANIZATIONAL STRUCTURE: *Obergebiet* AND BELOW

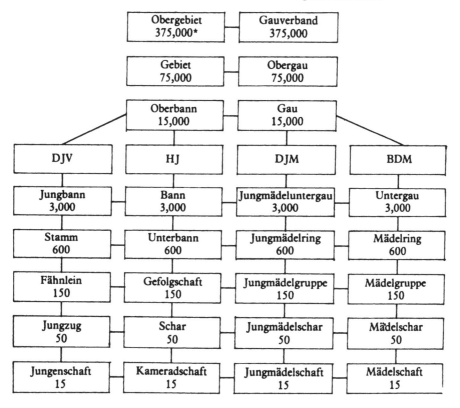

Obergebiet 375,000*	Gauverband 375,000		
Gebiet 75,000	Obergau 75,000		
Oberbann 15,000	Gau 15,000		
DJV	HJ	DJM	BDM
Jungbann 3,000	Bann 3,000	Jungmädeluntergau 3,000	Untergau 3,000
Stamm 600	Unterbann 600	Jungmädelring 600	Mädelring 600
Fähnlein 150	Gefolgschaft 150	Jungmädelgruppe 150	Mädelgruppe 150
Jungzug 50	Schar 50	Jungmädelschar 50	Mädelschar 50
Jungenschaft 15	Kameradschaft 15	Jungmädelschaft 15	Mädelschaft 15

* Figures comprise approximate number of Hitler Youths in area or unit respectively.

NAMES AND NUMBERS OF *Obergebiete* AND *Gebiete*

OBERGEBIET OST
Ostpreussen (1)
Mark Brandenburg (2)
Niederschlesien (4)
Sudetenland (35)
Danzig-Westpreussen (37)
Wartheland (38)
Oberschlesien (40)

OBERGEBIET MITTE
Kurhessen (14)
Mittelland (15)
Sachsen (16)
Thüringen (17)
Mittelelbe (23)
Mainfranken (39)

OBERGEBIET WEST
Westfalen-Nord (9)
Ruhr-Niederrhein (10)
Köln-Aachen (11)
Moselland (12)
Hessen-Nassau (13)
Westmark (25)
Düsseldorf (34)
Westfalen-Süd (42)

OBERGEBIET SÜD
Franken (18)
Hochland (19)
Württemberg (20)
Baden (21)
Schwaben (36)
Bayreuth (22)
Tirol-Vorarlberg (33)

OBERGEBIET NORD
Berlin (3)
Pommern (5)
Nordmark (6)
Nordsee (7)
Niedersachsen (8)
Mecklenburg (24)
Hamburg (26)
Osthannover (41)

OBERGEBIET SÜDOST
Wien (27)
Niederdonau (28)
Oberdonau (29)
Steiermark (30)
Kärnten (31)
Salzburg (32)

II *Reichsjugendführung* in 1933

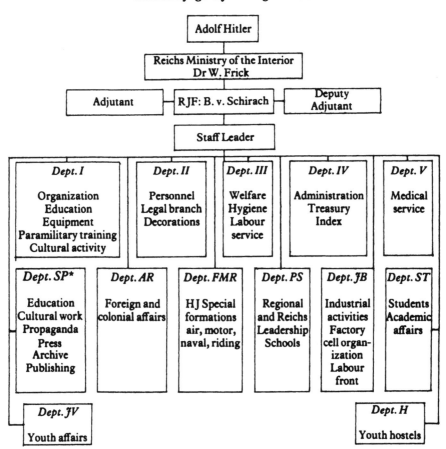

* Letters after departments are simply abbreviations of their functions

III *Reichsjugendführung* in 1942

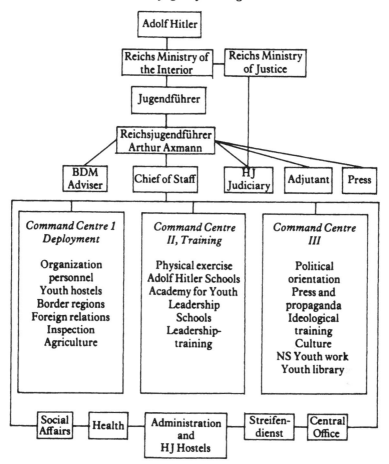

IV Model of the Educational Pattern of the NS-State

A child would enter school (*Volksschule*) at the age of six and leave at the age of fifteen. At the age of ten the child would join the DJV or DJM; this would also be the first opportunity to enter grammar school. NPEA selections also took place at this age. At twelve a second opportunity arose to enter grammar school, and at this age AHS selections were also made. At fourteen the child changed from the DJV and DJM to the HJ and BDM respectively. Those who remained at the *Volksschule* would now leave to enter either a three-year commercial school or to begin an apprenticeship in a trade. At eighteen HJ and BDM membership ceased and Hitler Youth members transferred to the NSDAP. Pupils in grammar schools, NPEAs or AHSs would now matriculate. For male as well as female youths six to twelve months of labour service followed, which in the case of young men would be succeeded by a two-year period of military service. This was followed by further professional training, university study, etc. Both NPEA and AHS pupils, by way of active service within the NSDAP, could enter the *Ordensburg* for three years, an opportunity also open for a suitable candidate who had not enjoyed the benefits of any higher education. At the *Ordensburg* as well as in the course of subsequent NSDAP service, qualifications for the last and 'highest' NS educational institution, the *Hohe Schule*, could be obtained, and from there access to the highest offices of the NSDAP.

In practice this model was never fully implemented except at NPEA and AHS level. Moreover there were numerous *ad hoc* 'training courses' which allowed such stages as the AHS and *Ordensburg* (indicated below) to be by-passed.

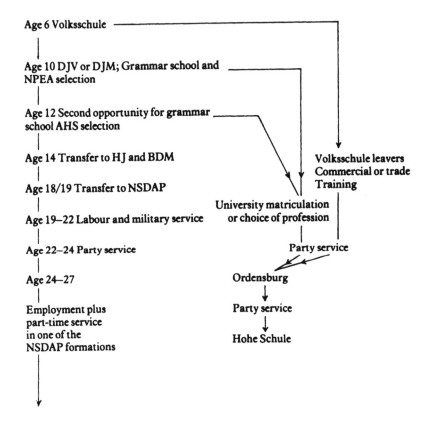

Reference Notes and Sources

Reference Notes and Sources

Abbreviations

BHSA Abt.1	Bayrisches Hauptstaatsarchiv, Abteilung 1, Allgemeines Staatarchiv, Munich NSDAP Hauptarchiv Ministerium fuer Kultus und Erziehung Ministerium des Inneren Finanzministerium
BHSA Abt. II	Bayrisches Hauptstaatsarchiv, Geheimes Staatsarchiv, Munich Innere Verwaltung: Monatsberichte und Lageberichte Protokoll des parlamentarischen Untersuchungsauschusses über Vorgänge vom 1.5.1923 Protokolle uber die Sitzungen des Ausschusses zur Untersuchung der Vorgänge vom 1. Mai 1923 und der gegen Reichs- und Landesverfassung gerichteten Bestrebungen vom 26.9.1923 bis 9. Nov. 1923 Ministerratssitzungen Lageberichte des Reichskommisars für Überwachung der offentlichen Ordnung
BHSA Abt. IV	Bayrisches Hauptstaatsarchiv, Abteilung IV, Kriegsarchiv Munich Personalakten
BHSA Abt. V	Bayrisches Haupstaatsarchiv, Abteilung V, Stadtarchiv München
BA	Bundesarchiv Koblenz NSDAP Hauptarchiv Akten der Reichskanzlei Reichsjustizministerium
BA S.Sch.	Bundesarchiv Koblenz, Sammlung Schumacher
BA ZSg	Bundesarchiv Koblenz, Zeitgeschichliche Sammlung, now dissolved and recatalogued under Nationalsozialistische Drucksachen (NDS).
WKT	Wolfgang Koch Tagebuch
IfZ	Institut für Zeitgeschichte München, Akten des Volksgerichtshofes Akten des Oberreichsanwaltes beim Volksgerichtshof.

Chapter I: Traditions

1 Harry Pross, *Jugend, Eros, Politik*, Munich 1964, p.22; the account of Langemarck is based on the diary of H. Dane, then aged 17, Reserve Infantrie Regiment 214.

2 G. Forster, *Sämtliche Schriften, Die Glückseligkeit der Wilden*, vol. I, Leipzig 1843, pp.296–7.

3 E. Adler, *Herder i Oświecenie niemieckie*, Warsaw 1965; E. Lemberg, *Nationalismus, Psychologie und Geschichte*, Reinbeck bei Hamburg 1964, pp.102–65.

4 G. W. F. Hegel, *Die Vernunft in der Geschichte. Einleitung in die Philosophie der Weltgeschichte*, Leipzig 1930, p.49.

5 Herder's views on the concept of the *Volk* are spread virtually over his entire work. The edition consulted here is *Sämtliche Werke*, ed. by B. Suphan, vols. 1–33, Berlin 1877–1913.

6 Herder, *op. cit.*, vol. XVIII, p.204.

7 cf. Herder's poem *Germanien* in F. Sehrwald, *Deutsche Dichter und Denker*, Altenburg 1880, vol. II, p.332.

8 Herder, *op. cit.*, vol. XXIX, p.329.

9 *ibid.*, vol. XIV, p.52; vol. XIII, p.384.

10 *ibid.*, vol. V, p.554; 528–9, 546, 555; vol. XIII, p.255.

11 *ibid.*, vol. V, pp.565, 585, 512; vol. VII, p.458.

12 *ibid.*, vol. I, p.152; vol. XVII, p.288.

13 *ibid.*, vol. XVIII, p.284, 271.

14 *ibid.*, vol. XXIX, p.411.

15 F. Schnabel, *Deutsche Geschichte im 19. Jahrhundert*, vol. II, p.42.

16 E. M. Arndt, *Geist der Zeit*, vol. II, p.197.

17 *ibid.*, p.212.

18 W. Killy (ed.), *Deutsches Lesebuch*, vol. II, Frankfurt 1960, p.40.

19 F. L. Jahn, *Das deutsche Volksthum*, Lübeck 1810, p.325.

20 F. Schleiermacher, *Sämtliche Werke*, Abt. 2, vol. I, pp.224, 230–1, 237; vol. IV, p.439.

21 Herder, *op. cit.*, vol. I, p.23.

22 H. Steffens, *Über die Ideen der Universitäten*, Berlin 1809, pp.46, 62, 68.

23 H. v. Kleist, 'Katechismus der Deutschen' in *Sämtliche Werke*, Munich 1954, p.856 ff.

24 Klopstock, *Werke*, 1. Teil, *Der Messias*, vol. I, Stuttgart 1883.

25 G. Kaiser, *Pietismus und Patriotismus im Literarischen Deutschland*, Wiesbaden 1961, p.124 ff.

26 E. M. Arndt, *Lieder für Teutsche*, 1813, p.13.

27 Schleiermacher, *op. cit.*, p.406.

28 J. G. Fichte, *Reden an die deutsche Nation*, Rede 1, Goldmann Taschenbuch, Munich (without date).

29 *ibid.*, pp.56, 60, 64–5, 69–70.

30 Herder, *op. cit.*, vol. I, p.400; vol. XVIII, p.137.

31 *ibid.*, vol. XVII, p.59.

32 Schleiermacher, *op. cit.*, p.233.

33 Fichte, *op. cit.*, p.78.

34 Novalis, *Sämtliche Schriften*, ed. by K. C. E. Ehmann, vol. III, p.228.

35 Fichte, *Reden an die deutsche Nation*, p.78.

36 Schleiermacher, *op. cit.*, p.43.

37 Arndt, *Lieder fur Teutsche*, p.62.

38 Jahn, *op. cit.*, p.21.

39 *ibid.*

40 Fichte, *Reden an die deutsche Nation*, p.85; Arndt, *Geist der Zeit*, part III, p.396.

41 H. v. Kleist, *op. cit.*

42 cf. J. Hirn, *Tirols Erhebung im Jahre 1809*, Innsbruck 1909.

43 H. Rössler, *Graf Johann Philipp Stadion*, vol. I, p.277 ff.

44 H. Heitzer, *Insurrectionen zwischen Weser und Elbe*, (East) Berlin 1959, p.166 ff.

45 R. Ibbeken, *Preussen 1807–1813*, Berlin 1970, p.443 ff.

46 *ibid.*
47 E. Zechlin, *Die deutsche Einheitsbewegung*, Berlin 1969, p.33 ff.
48 *ibid.*
49 G. Linne, *Jugend in Deutschland*, Gütersloh 1970, p.42.
50 *ibid.*, pp.45–7.
51 *ibid.*, p. 47.
52 *ibid.*
53 F. Schnabel, *op. cit.*, vol. II, p.53.
54 W. Conze and D. Groh, *Die Arbeiterbewegung in der nationalen Bewegung*, Stuttgart 1966, pp.13–41.
55 P. J. Siebenpfeiffer, *Von Hambacher Fest 1832*, Munich 1910.
56 Zechlin, *op. cit.*, p.93.
57 V. Valentin, *Geschichte der deutschen Revolution 1848–49*, 2 vols., Cologne 1969, vol. II, p.1 ff; F. Eyck, *The Frankfurt Parliament 1848–49*, London 1968, p.57 ff.

Chapter II: Beginnings

1 V. Engelhardt, *Die deutsche Jugendbewegung als kulturhistorisches Phänomen*, Berlin 1923, Hans Kohn, 'Youth Movements' in *Encyclopaedia of Social Sciences*, vol. XV.
2 E. Friedell, *Kulturgeschichte der Neuzeit*, vol. 3, Munich 1931, p.79.
3 Conze, *op. cit.*, p.41.
4 G. A. Rein, *Die Revolution in der Politik Bismarcks*, Göttingen 1957, p.117 ff.
5 G. Ritter, *The Sword and the Sceptre*, Coral Gables 1970, vol. I, p.167 ff.
6 Linne, *op. cit.*, pp.76–80.
7 H. Rosenberg, *Die Entstehung der Weimarer Republik*, Frankfurt 1961, Chapter I.
8 cf. R. Pascal, *The German Novel*, Manchester 1956; E. K. Bramsted, *Aristocracy and the Middle Classes in Germany*, London 1964.
9 cf. K. M. Bolte, *Sozialer Aufstieg und Abstieg*, Stuttgart 1959; G. Kath, *Das soziale Bild der Studentenschaft*, Bonn 1964.
10 cf. F. Stern, *The Politics of Cultural Despair*, New York 1961.
11 H. W. Koch, *Der Sozialdarwinismus. Seine Genese und sein Einfluss auf das imperialistische Denken*, Munich 1973, p.74 ff.
12 V. Engelhardt, *op. cit.*
13 A comparative analysis of the impact of industrialization in Europe and the U.S.A. is still outstanding. For some pertinent remarks on the subject see Ernst Nolte, *Der Faschismus in seiner Epoche*, Munich 1963, p.343 ff.
14 Th. Veblen, *Imperial Germany and the Industrial Revolution*, New York 1965; Ritter, *op. cit.*; E. Kehr 'Zur Genesis des Königlich-Preussischen Reserve Offiziers' in *Der Primat der Innenpolitik*, ed. by H.-U. Wehler, Berlin 1965.
15 Stern, *op. cit.*, p.153 ff.
16 *ibid.*
17 Max Weber, *Jugendbriefe*, Tübingen (without date).
18 Stern, *op. cit.*, p.131 ff.
19 G. Masur, *Propheten von Gestern*, Frankfurt 1961, p.375.
20 Stern, *op. cit.*, p.154.
21 E. Nolte, *op. cit.*, p.351.
22 G. Wyneken, *Der Kampf für die Jugend. Gesammelte Aufsätze*, Jena 1919.
23 P. de Lagarde, 'Über die Klage, dass der deutschen Jugend der Idealismus fehle' in *Deutsche Schriften*, 1885, pp.412–13.
24 Koch, *op. cit.*, p.157 ff.
25 F. Nietzsche, *Unzeitgemässe Betrachtungen*, 1873.

26 Stern, *op. cit.*, p.52 ff.

27 Lagarde, *op. cit.*

28 P. de Lagarde, 'Zum Unterrichtsgesetze' in *Deutsche Schriften, op. cit.*, p.237, p.322. See also K. Löwith, *Von Hegel zu Nietzsche. Der revolutionäre Bruch im Denken des Neunzehnten Jahrhunderts*, Stuttgart 1950, pp.312–26.

29 Lagarde, 'Die Religion der Zukunft' in *Deutsche Schriften, op. cit.*, p.267; *ibid.* 'Über das Verhaltnis des deutschen Staates zu Theologie, Kirche und Religion', p.69.

30 V. Engelhardt, *op. cit.*; Masur, *op. cit.*, p.374 ff.

31 cf. Hans Heinrich Muchow, *Sexualreife und Sozialstruktur der Jugend*, Hamburg 1962, *Jugendgenerationen im Wandel der Zeit*, Vienna 1964, summarized also in *Zeitgeist im Wandel. Zeitgeist der Weimarer Republik*, ed. by Hans Joachim Schoeps, Stuttgart 1968.

32 E. Busse-Wilson, *Stufen der Jugendbewegung*, Jena 1925, p.81, p.87.

33 For a relatively brief but incisive treatment see W. Laqueur, *Young Germany*, London 1962; V. Engelhardt, *op. cit.*

34 Laqueur, *op. cit.*, pp.16–22; H. Blüher, *Wandervogel. Geschichte einer Jugendbewegung*, vol. I., Celle 1912, p.1.

35 H. Becker, *German Youth: Bond or Free*, London 1946, p.99.

36 Ch. Lütkens, *Die deutsche Jugendbewegung. Ein soziologischer Versuch*, Frankfurt 1925, p.24 ff.

37 Wynecken, *op. cit.*, p.123 f.

38 Laqueur, *op. cit.*, p.11; furthermore the slogan 'youth should be led by youth' is frequently attributed to Hitler. Indeed he used it,, but it was often used in the pamphlets of the pre-First World War youth movement.

39 *ibid.*, pp.15–25.

40 J. Schult, *Aufbruch einer Jugend*, Bonn 1956, p.22.

41 K. Bondy, *Die proletarische Jugendbewegung*, Lauenburg 1922, p.54.

42 Schult, *op. cit.*, p.33.

43 Masur, *op. cit.*, p.385.

44 W. Stählin, *Fieber und Heil in der deutschen Jugendbewegung*, Hamburg 1923, p.25.

45 F. W. Förster, *Jugendseele, Jugendbewegung, Jugendziele*, Munich 1923, p.252 ff.

46 O. Piper, *Jugendbewegung und Protestantismus*, Rudolfstadt 1923, p.33.

47 Laqueur, *op. cit.*, p.73.

48 Th. Herrle, *Die deutsche Jugendbewegung*, Gotha 1921, p.103.

49 Masur, *op. cit.*, p.384.

50 *ibid.*

51 Laqueur, *op. cit.*, pp. 25–32; see also H. Fallada, *Damals bei uns Zuhaus* Rowolth, Hamburg 1956.

52 Blüher, *Wandervogel . . .*, *op. cit.*, p.112; Laqueur, *op. cit.*, p.32.

53 cf. F. Fischer, *Krieg der Illusionen*, Düsseldorf 1969, p.311 ff.; K. Wernecke, *Der Wille zur Weltgeltung*, Düsseldorf 1970, p.220 ff.

54 A. Messer, *Die Freideutsche Jugendbewegung*, Langensalza 1920, p.12; H. Buddensieg, *Vom Geist und Beruf der deutschen Jugendbewegung*, Lauenburg 1924, p.46.

55 A. Messer, *op. cit.*, p.19.

56 Laqueur, *op. cit.*, p.36.

57 Messer, *op. cit.*, p.13.

58 Bondy, *op. cit.*, p.78.

Chapter III: Re-Formation

1 E. v. Salomon, *Die Geächteten*, Berlin 1930, pp.30–3.

2 *ibid.*, p.42; Reichskriegsministerium (ed.), *Darstellungen aus den Nachkriegskämpfen deutscher Truppen und Freikorps*, Berlin 1936–40, vol. VI. pp.21–7, 58.; L.F.R. Maercker, *Vom Kaiserheer zur Reichswehr*, Leipzig 1921, p.64.

3 For a more detailed discussion of this point see Karl Seidelmann, *Bund und Gruppe als Lebensform deutscher Jugend*, Munich 1955, and Th. Wilhelm 'Der geschichtliche Ort der deutschen Jugendbewegung' in *Grundschriften der deutschen Jugendbewegung*, Düsseldorf 1963.

4 H. C. Brandenburg, 'Nachkriegsgeneration 1918 – Nachkriegsgeneration 1945' in *Europäische Begegnungen*, 1962.

5 G. Gründel, *Die Sendung der Jungen Generation*, Munich 1932, p.15.

6 Apart from R. C. L. Waite's *Vanguard of Nazism: The Free Corps Movement in Postwar Germany 1918–23* Cambridge, Mass, 1952 (a somewhat tendentious treatment) no analysis based on the vast source materials available has so far been published.

7 Nolte, *op. cit.*, p.381.

8 W. Gerhart, *Um des Reiches Zukunft*, Freiburg 1932, p. 137.

9 Salomon, *op. cit.*, p.121.

10 *ibid.*, pp.338–53.

11 E. v. Salomon, *Der Fragebogen*, Hamburg 1951, p.328 ff.

12 H.-C. Brandenburg, *Die Geschichte der HJ*, Cologne 1968, p.16.

13 Walter Flex, *op. cit.*, p.22.

14 Brandenburg, *Die Geschichte*, *op. cit.*, p.18.

15 Salomon, *Die Geächteten*, *op. cit.*, p.38.

16 *ibid.*, pp.256–69.

17 H. J. Gordon, *The Reichswehr and the German Republic*, Princeton 1957, pp.226–8. H. W. Koch, 'The Freikorps' in *History of the First World War* ed. by B. Pitt, London 1969–72, vol. VIII, p.3181 ff.

18 For a pertinent and hitherto unsurpassed analysis of the structural problems of the Weimar Republic see K. D. Bracher, *Die Auflösung der Weimarer Republik*, Villingen 1955; Kurt Sontheimer, *Anti-demokratisches Denken in der Weimarer Republik* (new ed.), Munich 1962.

19 H. Stelter, *Eine Geschichte deutscher Jugendbewegung, zugleich Handbuch und Richtlinien der deutschen Jugendbewegung*, Berlin (undated).

20 Seidelmann, *op. cit.*

21 Laqueur, *op. cit.*, pp.157–66.

22 Linne, *op. cit.*, quoting Robert Oelbermann, p. '39; Pross, *op. cit.*, p.286 ff.

23 Linne, *op. cit.*, p.140.

24 Pross, *op. cit.*, p.265 ff.

25 cf. J. Schult, *Das Weimar der arbeitenden Jugend*, Weimar 1920.

26 Linne *op. cit.*, p.148.

27 cf. Chapter I.

28 E. Nolte, *op. cit.*, p.343 ff.

29 Sontheimer, *op. cit.*, Chapters 6, 9, 10.

30 Matzke, *Jugend bekennt: So sind wir!*, Leipzig 1930, p.83.

31 G. Franz-Willing, *Die Hitlerbewegung*, Hamburg 1962, p.126.

32 *ibid.*, p.129.

33 For the origin and the early history of the NSDAP see Franz-Willing *op. cit.* and Ernst Deuerlein, 'Hitlers Eintritt in die Politik', in *Vierteljahrshefte für Zeitgeschichte*, 7, Stuttgart 1959, p.182.

34 Nolte, *op. cit.*, p.387 ff.

35 Franz-Willing, *op. cit.*, p.21 ff.; W. Hoegner, *Der schwierige Aussenseiter*, Munich 1959; E. Müller-Meiningen, *Aus Bayerns schwersten Tagen*, Munich 1923; E. Röhm *Geschichte eines Hochverräters*, Munich 1928; W. Benz (ed.), *Politik in Bayern 1919–33. Berichte des württembergischen Gesandten Moser v. Filseck*, Stuttgart 1971.

36 H. Heiber, *Die Republik von Weimar*, Munich 1966, p.126 ff.
37 *ibid.*
38 Franz-Willing, *op. cit.*, p.137 ff.; Maser, *op. cit.*, p.307 ff.
39 BA NS 26/332, 26/333.
40 *ibid.*
41 *ibid.*
42 *HJ kämpft und siegt, Die Jungenschaft, Blätter für Heimabendgestaltung im Deutschen Jungvolk*, Issue 10, Berlin 1938.
43 *ibid.*
44 BA NS 26/331.
45 *ibid.*
46 *ibid.*
47 BA NS 26/336.
48 *ibid.*
49 See also report contained in the *Völkischer Beobachter*, Issue 39, 17 May 1922.
50 BA NS 26/336. Provisions for a girls' section were also made. In practice, however, several years were to pass before any NSDAP youth organization for girls was set up. BHSA, Abt. I, NS 1483.
51 There had been a previous public appearance in Coburg together with other right-wing formations on 14–15 October 1922. The party day in Munich was the first purely NSDAP rally. BA NS 26/333, NS 26/336.
52 BA NS 26/336.
53 BA NS 26/333.
54 *ibid.*; Brandenburg, *op. cit.*, p.23 ff.
55 K. Heiden, *Geschichte des Nationalsozialismus Hamburg* 1932, p. 33; Franz-Willing *op. cit.*, p.76 ff.; R. Jung, *Der nationale Sozialismus – Seine Grundlagen, seine Werdegang und seine Ziele*, Munich 1922.
56 *Völkischer Beobachter*, Issue 59, 27 June 1920.
57 A. Schilling, *Dr Walter Riehl und die Geschichte des Nationalsozialismus*, Leipzig 1933, p.67.
58 W. Maser, *Die Frühgeschichte der NSDAP*, Frankfurt 1965, p.245 ff.; also 'Der Hitlerpunkt auf der Landkarte' in *Münchner Post*, Issue 28, 3 February 1922.
59 A. Ciller, *Deutscher Sozialismus in den Sudetenländern und in der Ostmark*, Hamburg 1944, p.151.
60 Reported by Jung's secretary, cf. Franz-Willing, *op. cit.*, p.95.
61 Brandenburg, *op. cit.*, p.24.
62 Schilling, *op. cit.*, p.271 f.; Jung, *op. cit.*, p.81; Franz-Willing, *op. cit.*, p.96.
63 Schilling, *op. cit.*, p.271 f.; Franz-Willing, *op. cit.*, p.96.
64 *ibid.*, p.252; Franz-Willing, *op. cit.*, p.96.
65 *ibid.*
66 Jung, *op. cit.*, pp.81–3.
67 A. Hitler, *Mein Kampf*, Dünndruckausgabe, Munich 1937, p.384.
68 BA NS 26/333; Brandenburg, *op. cit.*, p.22.
69 *ibid.*
70 *ibid.*
71 Hofmann, *op. cit.*, pp.17–123; H. Bennecke, *Hitler und die SA*, Munich 1962, pp.47–92.
72 BHSA, Abt. I, NS 1485, NS 1487; *Münchner Neueste Nachrichten*, Issue 108, 22 April 1923.
73 Hermann Esser quoted in Maser *Frühgeschichte*, *op. cit.*, p.389.
74 *ibid.*
75 Otto Strasser, *Hitler und Ich*, Konstanz 1948, p.47.
76 BHSA, Abt. II, MA 99 521.
77 Maser, *op. cit.*, p.389.

78 *ibid.*
79 BHSA, Abt. II, MA 103 476, MA 106669–106699, MA 99 521.
80 BHSA, Abt. I, NS 1817.
81 BA NS 26/104; BHSA Abt. I, NS 1493.
82 Bennecke, *op. cit.*, p.94.
83 cf. ref. 81.
84 BHSA Abt. IV, HSI V, EE7, Endres manuscript.
85 *ibid.*
86 BA NS 26/331.
87 BHSA Abt. II, MA 103 476; Bennecke, *op. cit.*, p.69.
88 *ibid.*; Hofmann, *op. cit.*, pp.95–137.
89 Hofmann, *ibid.*
90 *ibid.*
91 The member was Kurt Neubauer, BA NS 26/336; 26/333; BHSA, Abt. I, NS 1492.
92 Information provided by Herr Heinrich Puls and by the late Pater Stefan Bachmaier of the Franciscan monastery of St Anna Munich where the SA and other right-wing formations maintained an arms dump. A member of the *Jungsturm Adolf Hitler* acted as a messenger between the monastery and SA units posted at the Wittelsbach bridge.

Chapter IV: Birth

1 Ernst Deuerlein, *Der Hitler Putsch. Bayrische Dokumente zum 8./9. November 1923*, Stuttgart 1962. The protocol of the court proceedings is available on microfilm at the Institut für Zeitgeschichte, Munich; see also Hofmann, *op. cit.*, p.241 ff.
2 BHSA, Abt. V, Staatsanwaltschaft München I, 3098; Bennecke, *op. cit.*, p.106.
3 Bennecke, *op. cit.*, p.107.
4 W. Horn, *Führerideologie und Parteiorganisation in der NSDAP*, Düsseldorf 1972, pp.154–208.
5 cf. G. Rossbach, *Mein Weg durch die Zeit*, Weilburg/Lahn 1950.
6 BHSA Abt. I, NS 1805; BA NS 26/331.
7 BA NS 26/336.
8 Brandenburg, *op. cit.*, p.24.
9 BA NS 26/336.
10 BA NS 26/332.
11 *Der Hitlerprozess vor dem Volksgericht München*, 2 vols, Munich 1924, vol. II, p.8.
12 BHSA Abt. II, MA 101249.
13 This entire complex has received a thoroughly documented analysis in Horn, *op. cit.*, Chapter IV.
14 Hitler's proclamation is contained in the *Völkischer Beobachter*, 26 February 1925; also Hitler's speech of 27 February 1925 in *Reden des Führers, Politik und Propaganda Adolf Hitlers 1922–1945*, ed. by Erhard Klöss, dtv Munich 1967, p.52 ff.
15 *Völkischer Beobachter*, Hitler's proclamation, *op. cit.*, 26 February 1925.
16 BHSA Abt. II, MA 1943, 101249; *Völkischer Beobachter* 14 March 1925.
17 BA NS 26/332; BHSA, Abt. I. NS 1541, NS 1805.
18 *ibid.*; BA S.Sch. G. VIII Nr. 239.
19 *ibid.*; BA NS 26/364.
20 BA NS 26/332.
21 cf. ref. 17.
22 *ibid.*
23 BA NS 26/336.

24 *ibid.*
25 cf. ref. 17; Staatsarchiv Bremen 4/65-II. E.3.a.13 (HJ-Grossch-Jugend) vol. I and 4, 14,b-II.E.3.a.13. vol I.
26 Brandenburg, *op. cit.*, p.26.
27 BA NS 26/332.
28 *Völkischer Beobachter*, 26 February 1925; Hitler, *Mein Kampf*, p.103.
29 Röhm, *op. cit.*, p.313.
30 K. O. Paetel, *Handbuch der deutschen Jugendbewegung*, Flarchheim 1930, pp.17–18.
31 BA NS 26/332.
32 cf. ref. 25.
33 Hitler, *Mein Kampf*, pp.348, 451 ff., 611 ff.
34 *Völkischer Beobachter*, 13 May 1925; BA NS 26/332, BA S.Sch. G. VIII Nr. 239.
35 *Die Kommenden* vol. I Issue 1, December 1926, p.557 f.; Brandenburg, *op. cit.*, p.29 ff.
36 BA NS 26/335.
37 *ibid.*; BA S.Sch. G. VIII Nr. 239.
38 *ibid.*
39 cf. Horn, *op. cit.*, Chapter IV.
40 *ibid.*
41 *ibid.*
42 Bennecke, *op. cit.*, p.128.
43 *ibid.*; also H. Heiber (ed.) *Das Tagebuch des Joseph Goebbels, 1925–26*, Stuttgart 1960 entry 30 July 1926.
44 Bennecke, *op. cit.*, p.127 ff; Horn, *op. cit.*, p.231 ff.
45 Horn, *op. cit.*, p.243.
46 *ibid.*
47 SABE (SA Befehle) 1 November 1926, printed in Bennecke, *op. cit.*, p.237 ff.
48 *ibid.*
49 *ibid.*
50 BA NS 26/389, 26/335. BHSA Abt. I, NS 1541, NS 1542, NS 1544, NS 1804. The name *Hitler Jugend* had previously been carried by the Thuringian (Gera) branch of the 'Greater German Youth Movement'.
51 BA NS 26/335.
52 Brandenburg, *op. cit.*, p.29.
53 BHSA Abt. I, NS/1541.
54 *ibid.*
55 *ibid.*
56 BA NS 26/360.
57 BHSA Abt. I, NS/1542.
58 *ibid.*
59 cf. ref. 57; Brandenburg, *op. cit.*, p.244 ff.
60 *ibid.*
61 *ibid.*
62 *ibid.*
63 G. Wehner, *Die rechtliche Stellung der HJ*, Doctoral Thesis, University of Leipzig 1939; Brandenburg, *op. cit.*, p.31.
64 A. Klönne, *Hitlerjugend. Die Jugend und ihre Organisation im Dritten Reich*, Marburg, Lahn 1960, p.9.
65 H. Bolm, *Hitler-Jugend in einem Jahrzehnt*, Hamburg 1938, p.52; see also Chapter X below.
66 *ibid.*
67 BHSA Abt. I, MInn/71799; R. Ruder in 'Die Hitlerjugend' in *Deutsche Jugend*, p.196, estimates the figure at 500.

68 BA S.Sch. G. VIII, Nr. 239.
69 Brandenburg, *op. cit.*, p.33.
70 cf. ref. 64.
71 Klönne, *op. cit.*, p.10; Brandenburg, *op. cit.*, p.33 ff.
72 BA S.Sch. G. VIII, Nr. 239; Brandenburg, *ibid.*; Hitler on 9 November 1927 stipulated that suitable Hitler Youth leaders could stay on even after completing their 18th birthday.
73 *ibid.*
74 BHSA Abt. I, NS/1776; see Schirach's answer at the Nuremberg Trial, *Trial of Major War Criminals*, vol. XIV, p.373.
75 cf. ref. 25.
76 BHSA Abt. I, NS/1542.
77 BHSA Abt. I, NS/1541.
78 *ibid.*
79 BA NS 26/390.
80 *Wille und Macht. Führerorgan der Nationalsozialistischen Jugend*, September 1937; Burden, *op. cit.*, p.38 ff.
81 *Nationalsozialistische Monatshefte*, vol. 1930, Issue 1.
82 BA NS 26/362; F. W. Hymmen '10 Jahre HJ' in *Die Junge Kameradschaft. Jahrbuch der HJ 1935* ed. by E. Fischer, p.12.
83 Thus for instance the tune of the *Horst-Wessel-Lied* was that of a popular Communist song, while the song *Brüder in Ketten und Banden* was pirated from the Communists with only a few minor changes to the text.
84 BA S.Sch. G. VIII Nr. 239.
85 *ibid.*
86 *ibid.*
87 Hymmen, *op. cit.*, p.14.
88 *Statistisches Jahrbuch 1928* pp.580–1.
89 Bennecke, *op. cit.*, p.137 ff.
90 cf. ref. 84.
91 BHSA Abt. I NS/1542.
92 Staatsarchiv Bremen 4, 65-IV. 25 (Politische Berichte, München).
93 *ibid.*
94 See Gruber's own address in 'Die HJ kämpft und siegt' in *Die Kameradschaft*, 1935; Brandenburg, *op. cit.*, p.246 ff.
95 *ibid.*
96 *ibid.*
97 cf. ref. 25.
98 BA NS 26/370.
99 BA NS 26/354.
100 BA NS 26/360, 26/1366B, 26/1264; *Das Deutsche Führerlexikon 1935*, p.415; *Wer Ist's* 1935, p.415; J. C. Fest, *The Face of the Third Reich*, London 1969, p.343 ff.
101 BHSA Abt. I, NS/1542; *Der Jungvolkführer*, 24 March 1932; Fest, *ibid.*
102 BA NS 26/354.
103 BA NS 26/370; Brandenburg, *op. cit.*, p.37.
104 *ibid.*
105 BA S.Sch. G. VIII Nr. 239.
106 BHSA Abt. I, NS/1541.
107 cf. ref. 114.
108 BA NS 26/327.
109 Brandenburg, *op. cit.*, p.37.
110 *ibid.*
111 Burden, *op. cit.*, p.54.
112 BA NS 26/336.

113 *ibid.*
114 *ibid.*
115 *ibid.*
116 *ibid.*
117 BA S.Sch. G. VIII Nr. 239.
118 *ibid.*; BHSA Abt. I NS/1541.
119 K. O. Paetel, *Jugend in der Entscheidung. 1913–33–45*, Bad Godesberg 1963, p.63.
120 Brandenburg, *op. cit.*, p.39.
121 *ibid.*
122 BHSA Abt. I, NS/1544.
123 *ibid.*; also NS/1555.
124 BHSA Abt. I, MInn 71799 225365.
125 *ibid.*
126 cf. ref. 117.
127 Baldur v. Schirach, *Die Hitlerjugend, Idee und Gestalt*, Leipzig 1934, p.21;
    Bennecke, *op. cit.*, p.144 ff; Horn, *op. cit.*, p.287 ff.
128 Bennecke, *op. cit.*, p.147 ff.
129 *ibid.*
130 *ibid.*; see also Pfeffer von Salomon's farewell message reprinted in Bennecke, p.251.
131 *ibid.*, p.149 ff.
132 BHSA Abt. I, NS/1557.
133 *Verordnungsblatt der Obersten SA Führung*, 23 October 1932.
134 Brandenburg, *op. cit.*, p.40.
135 BHSA, R. Ko. In. Nr. 128; Hertha Siemering, *Die deutschen Jugendverbände*, Berlin
    1931, p.251; Brandenburg, *op. cit.*, p.40.
136 *ibid.*
137 BA NS 26/366.
138 BHSA Abt. I, NS/1555.
139 BA ZSg. 3/1473.
140 Schirach, *Hitlerjugend, op. cit.*, p.25.
141 BHSA Abt. I, NS/1544.
142 Brandenburg, *op. cit.*, p.40.
143 BHSA Abt. I,NS/1544, 1555.
144 BHSA Abt. I, NS/1555.
145 BA S.Sch. G. VII Nr. 199A.
146 BHSA Abt. I, NS/1544.
147 BHSA Abt. I, NS/1541.
148 *ibid.*
149 Brandenburg, *op. cit.*, p.55; W. Klose, *Generation im Gleichschritt*, Oldenburg 1964,
    p.16 ff.
150 cf. Bracher, *op. cit.*, p.287 ff.
151 *ibid.*
152 For a good description of this type of electioneering, cf. Salomon, *Der Fragebogen,
    op. cit.*, p.348 ff.
153 BHSA Abt. I, NS/1541.
154 BA NS 26/370. That Schirach's influence was instrumental in Gruber's fall is a
    conviction expressed by two former members of Schirach's staff whose accounts are
    in the possession of the author. The comment of Gruber's immediate successor
    Renteln concerning the organizational disarray resemble too much the kind of
    allegations usually made within the Hitler Youth in cases of resignations to be taken
    at face value.
155 BA NS 26/357.
156 BA NS 26/364; BA NS 26/361; BHSA Abt. I, MInn. 71799 225361.
157 *ibid.*

158 BA NS 26/370, 26/335, 26/357; BHSA Abt. I. NS/1555. The documents reflect the bitterness of Gruber's quarrels but not necessarily the real substance of the charges and counter charges.

159 cf. ref. 25.

160 BA NS 26/337.

161 BHSA Abt. I. NS/1849.

162 Forschungsstelle für die Geschichte des Nationalsozialismus Hamburg, Dokument 102: Hauptarchiv/NSDAP/306.

163 BA NS 26/364; BHSA, Abt. I, NS/1544. Harald Scholtz, *Nationalsozialistische Ausleseschulen*, Göttingen 1973, pp.51–2.

164 Schirach, *Hitlerjugend, op. cit.*, p.21.

165 BA NS 26/364; BHSA Abt. I, NS 1543 Klonne *op. cit.*, dates Gruber's 'resignation' in error one year earlier.

166 BA NS 26/364.

167 BA NS 26/338; NS 26/370.

168 BHSA Abt. I, NS/1542 Brandenburg, *op. cit.*, p.49 ff.

169 *ibid.*, BHSA NS/1555; BA NS 26/332.

170 This figure, which may be exaggerated, is given by Günter Kaufmann, *Das kommende Deutschland*, Berlin 1940, p.33.

171 BA NS 26/339.

172 BHSA Abt. I, MInn 71799/225363/14; NS/1544 Siemering, *op. cit.*, p.99.

173 BA NS 26/339, Brandenburg, *op. cit.*, p.55 ff.

174 *ibid.*

175 Bracher, *op. cit.*, p.481 ff.

176 BHSA Abt. I, NS/1542; MInn 71799/225362 BA NS 26/339.

177 BA S.Sch. G. VIII Nr. 239; all figures given are approximate conversions based on the then existing exchange rate of 20 *Rentenmark* to £1.

178 BHSA Abt. I, NS/1544.

179 *ibid.*

180 BA NS 26/337; BHSA Abt. I, NS/1542.

181 H. Bolm, *op. cit.*, p.168.

182 BA NS 26/337.

183 Schirach, *Hitlerjugend, op. cit.*, p.29.

184 BA NS 26/369; Klose, *op. cit.*, p.10.

185 *Münchner Neueste Nachrichten*, Nr. 212, 6 August 1932; F. Friedenburg, *Die Weimarer Republik*, Berlin 1946, p.217.

186 Lothar Danner, *Ordnungspolizei Hamburg*, Hamburg 1958, p.233 ff.

187 BA NS 26/369; BHSA Abt. I, NS/1544, NS/1555; Joseph Goebbels, *Vom Kaiserhof zur Reichskanzlei*, Munich 1934, entries for 26 January 1932 and 29 January 1932; Klose, *op. cit.*, p.8 ff.

188 *ibid.* The *Münchner Post* of 27–8 February 1932 alleged that the murder had been committed by storm troopers. The *Völkischer Beobachter* of 21 May 1932 reported the arrest of six Communists and four former SA members for the murder.

189 Becker, *op. cit.*, p.160, p.204; Fest, *op. cit.*, pp.302, 314.

Chapter V: Dominance

1 BHSA Abt. I, NS/1555; BA S.Sch. G. VIII Nr. 239; for a detailed breakdown of the Hitler Youth membership in 1932 see P. Strachura, *Development and Organization of the Hitler Youth 1930–33*, unpublished Ph.D thesis, East Anglia, Chapter 7 and 'Epilogue'.

2 Klönne, *op. cit.*, p.11.

3 BA S.Sch. G. VIII Nr. 239.

4 *ibid.*

5 *ibid.*

6 *ibid.*

7 BHSA Abt. I, NS/1542. Information supplied to the author by Herr Helmut Sündermann, August 1961.

8 *ibid.*

9 cf. ref. 3.

10 M. Vandray, *Der politische Witz im Dritten Reich*, Munich 1967, p.61.

11 BA NS 26/337; BHSA Abt. I, NS/1555.

12 cf. Breakdown of Hitler Youth social composition in *Gau Rheinland-Pfalz* BHSA Abt. I, NS/1776; Klose, *op. cit.*, p.17.

13 *ibid.*

14 BHSA Abt. I, NS/1555.

15 G. Kaufmann, *op. cit.*, p.19.

16 G. Hempel, *Die Kieler Hitlerjugend*, Kiel 1938, p.21.

17 BHSA Abt. I, NS/1555.

18 Hempel, *op. cit.*

19 *ibid.*

20 *ibid.*

21 *ibid.*; Klose, *op. cit.*, p.19.

22 Bracher, *op. cit.*, p.168.

23 cf. G. Stoltenberg, *Das Schlesw. Holst. Landvolk 1918–33*, Düsseldorf 1962; Salomon, *Der Fragebogen, op. cit.*, pp.221–40; E. v. Salomon, *Die Stadt*, Reinbeck bei Hamburg 1934; also see Hans Fallada, *Bauern, Bonzen, Bomben*, ro-ro-ro reprint Hamburg 1964.

24 Hempel, *op. cit.*

25 Salomon, *Der Fragebogen, ibid.*; *Die Stadt, op. cit.*

26 BHSA Abt. I, NS/1535, NS/1544, MInn Nr. III 31436; Klose, *op. cit.*, p.21.

27 H. Müller, *Katholische Kirche und Nationalsozialismus: Dokumente 1930–1935*, dtv Munich 1965, p.5.

28 J. Conway, *The Nazi Persecution of the Churches 1933–45*, London 1968, p.7.

29 Sontheimer, *op. cit.*, pp.221–43.

30 cf. Othmar Spann, *Der wahre Staat*, Leipzig 1921; *Hauptpunkte der unversalistischen Staatsauffassung*, Berlin 1930; Müller, *op. cit.*, p.38.

31 On the relationship between NSDAP and the Roman Catholic Church, see Conway *op. cit.*

32 Brandenburg, *op. cit.*, p.97.

33 Quoted in H. Köhler, *Arbeitsdienst in Deutschland*, Berlin 1967, p.224.

34 cf. *Werkhefte katholischer Laien*, 1958; Brandenburg, *op. cit.*, p.97.

35 The author remembers clearly receiving in April 1943 the order to emphasize the correct wording to his unit, a *Jungenschaft* at the time. The order was subsequently repeated at *Jungzug* and at *Fähnlein* level. It originated from the *Gebietsführung*, *Gebiet Hochland*, but was said to have originally come from the *Reichsjugend-führung*. Incidentally, the order also included the prohibition of the 'Western Campaign' song *Kamerad wir marschieren im Westen* as being offensive to French susceptibilities in view of the presence of large numbers of French, Belgian and Dutch workers.

36 Brandenburg, *op. cit.*, p.97 ff.

37 *ibid.*

38 M. Priepke, *Die Evangelische Jugend im Dritten Reich 1933–36*, Frankfurt 1960, p.

39 Kaufmann, *op. cit.*, p.42.

40 BHSA Abt. I, NS/1776, NS/1542, NS/1543, NS/1544. The proscription was issued to arrest the rapidly mounting wave of political violence in the streets. The new name adopted by the Hitler Youth was *National-Sozialistischer Jugend Bund*.

41 BHSA Abt. I, NS/1544.
42 *ibid.*
43 *ibid.*
44 B. v. Schirach, *Ich glaubte an Hitler*, Hamburg 1967, p.133.
45 *ibid.*, p.134.
46 *ibid.*
47 BA NS 26/337.
48 BHSA Abt. I, NS/1541; Brandenburg, *op. cit.*, p.119.
49 F. v. Papen, *Memoirs*, London 1952, p.163 ff.
50 BA NS 26/337, NS 26/345; Köhler, *op. cit.*, p.222; Th. Vogelsang, *Die Reichswehr, Staat und NSDAP*, Stuttgart 1962, pp.231, 348. The secret training of youth formations by the *Reichswehr* goes back to 1922/3.
51 *ibid.*; BHSA Abt. I, MK 13852, MF 68510.
52 BA NS 26/345, NS 26/354.
53 Brandenburg, *op. cit.*, p.122.
54 BA NS 26/333, 26/339; BHSA Abt. I, NS/1536.
55 Bracher, *op. cit.*, p.609.
56 BHSA Abt. I, NS/1541, NS/1845.
57 M. Schwarz, *Biographisches Handbuch der Deutschen Reichstage*, 1965, p.334.
58 BHSA Abt. I, NS/1542.
59 Schirach, *Ich glaubte*, p.153.
60 *ibid.*
61 BHSA Abt. I, NS/1544; Klönne, *op. cit.*, p.10; Klose, *op. cit.*, p.10.
62 BA NS 26/337.
63 BA NS 26/367.
64 Author's personal information.
65 BA NS 26/367.
66 BA 26/367, Klose, *op. cit.*, p.22.
67 *ibid.*
68 *ibid.*
69 *Wille und Werk. Pressedienst der deutschen Jugendbewegung*, ed. by W. Kind, vol. 1932.
70 BA NS 26/367; BHSA Abt. I, NS/1544.
71 Schirach *Hitlerjugend*, *op. cit.*, pp.183–6.
72 *ibid.*
73 cf. ref. 69.
74 Schirach, *Hitlerjugend*, *op. cit.*, pp.183–6.
75 BHSA Abt. I, NS/1544. BA NS 26/367; *Vorwärts, Zentralorgan der SPD* Nr. 469a 299, vol. 49, 5 October 1932.
76 BA NS 26/367.
77 Bracher, *op. cit.*, p.645 ff.
78 *ibid.*, p.677 ff; H. Heiber, *Die Republik von Weimar*, dtv Munich 1966, p.266 ff.
79 *ibid.*; Goebbels, *Vom Kaiserhof*, *op. cit.*, entry for 28 December 1932.
80 *ibid.*; E. Forsthoff, *Deutsche Verfassungsgeschichte der Neuzeit*, Stuttgart 1961, p.192.
81 *ibid.*
82 W. S. Churchill, *Great Contemporaries*, London 1941, p.227.
83 W. S. Allen, *The Nazi Seizure of Power*, London 1966, p.73.
84 M. Maschmann, *Fazit*, Stuttgart 1964, p. ´8.
85 *ibid.*, p.19.
86 Schirach, *Hitlerjugend*, *op. cit.*, p.31.
87 Fest, *op. cit.*, p.302.
88 *ibid.*, p.300.
89 Schirach, *Hitlerjugend*, *op. cit.*, p.180.

90 H. J. Schoeps, *Die letzten Dreissig Jahre: Rückblicke*, Berlin 1963, p.98. It was not unknown for Jewish pupils to be accepted by the Hitler Youth as propagandists, though full membership was denied to them. cf. BHSA Abt. I, NS/1535.

91 Theodor Heuss, 'Fragmente' in *Vierteljahrshefte für Zeitgeschichte*, Stuttgart 1967, p.2.

92 For the best analysis of all stages of this process see Bracher, Sauer, Schulz, *Die national-sozialistische Machtergreifung*, Cologne 1962.

93 R. Dahrendorf, *Democracy and Society in Germany*, London 1967, p.402 ff.

94 Klönne, *op. cit.*, p.28.

95 H-H. Dietze, *Die Rechtsgestalt der HJ*, Berlin 1939, p.88.

96 *Das Junge Deutschland*, Amtliches Organ der Jugendführer des Deutschen Reiches, May–April 1933, p.97.

97 Klose, *op. cit.*, p.28.

98 *Wille und Werk*, *op. cit.*, April 1933.

99 cf. F. Tobias, *Der Reichstagsbrand*, Berlin 1961.

100 Brandenburg, *op. cit.*, p.135.

101 *ibid.*

102 *ibid.*; R. Höhne, *Kennwort Direktor*, Fischer Taschenbuch, Frankfurt 1970, p.135 ff.

103 *ibid.*

104 See also Eberhard Köbel's attitude in *Die Kiefer*, issue 3, May 1933, p.16.

105 Proscription at the national level was often preceded at the *Land* level; cf. *Das Junge Deutschland*, May–April 1933.

106 Brandenburg, *op. cit.*, p.144.

107 BA NS 26/334.

108 BA NS 26/337.

109 BA NS 26/334.

110 K. O. Paetel, *Jugend in der Entscheidung*, *op. cit.*, p.155; Brandenburg *op. cit.*, p.138.

111 cf. Erich Mathias and Rudolf Morsey, *Das Ende der Parteien*, Düsseldorf 1960.

112 BA NS 26/334.

113 Pross, *op. cit.*, p.420; Brandenburg *op. cit.*, p.149.

114 *ibid.*; BA NS 26/334; Schirach *Hitlerjugend*, p.36.

115 BA NS 26/334.

116 Schirach, *Hitlerjugend*, *op. cit.*, p.36.

117 BA NS 26/366.

118 *ibid.*; Schirach is actually quoting Hitler.

119 *ibid.*; BHSA Abt. I, NS/1544.

120 *Das Junge Deutschland*, *op. cit.*, July 1933.

121 BA NS 26/366, *Das Junge Deutschland*, *op. cit.*, July 1933.

122 *Das Junge Deutschland*, *op. cit.* August 1933, Verfügung des Reichsinnenministers vom 8 Juli 1933, BA ZSg 3/499 (now NS Drucksachensammlung).

123 *ibid.*; Richtlinien des Reichsministers des Inneren für die Jugendführer des Deutschen Reiches vom 8 Juli 1933.

124 Schirach, *Ich glaubte*, *op. cit.*, p.177, pp.185–8; Brandenburg, *op. cit.*, p.146.

125 *Das Junge Deutschland*, *op. cit.*, July 1933.

126 *ibid.*

127 Pross, *op. cit.*, p.420.

128 Kaufmann, *op. cit.*, p.41; see also ref. 111.

129 *ibid.*, p.42.

130 Schirach, *Ich glaubte*, p.169, p.189.

131 cf. ref. 122.

132 cf. ref. 123.

133 BA NS 26/339.

134 *Das Schwarze Korps*, 19 July 1935.
135 *Reichsjugendführung. Aufbau, Gliederung, Anschriften der Hitler-Jugend*, p. 12 ff.
136 *ibid.*
137 *ibid.*
138 *Reichsjugendführung. HJ im Dienst*, p.11.
139 cf. ref. 135.
140 Brandenburg, *op. cit.*, p.151 ff.
141 *ibid.*
142 *ibid.*
143 Schirach, *Ich glaubte, op. cit.*, p.233; see also Chapter XI below.
144 BA NS 26/339; see also Chapter XI below.
145 B. v. Schirach, *Revolution der Erziehung*, Munich 1938, pp.8, 43; A. Axmann,
    'Hitler-Jugend 1933–43. Die Chronik eines Jahrzehnts' in *Das Junge Deutschland*
    Issue 1/2, vol. 37, February 1943.
146 *ibid.*; see also Chapter X below.
147 R. Kneip, *Jugend zwischen den Kriegen*, Heidenheim 1967, p.169 ff.
148 *ibid.*
149 *Wer Ist's* 1935, p.866; *Das Deutsche Führerlexikon* 1934/5, p.251.
150 *Das Deutsche Führerlexikon* 1934/35, p.417.
151 A. Klönne, *Gegen den Strom. Ein Bericht über die Jugendopposition im Dritten
    Reich*, Hanover 1958, p.52.
152 Schirach, *Hitlerjugend, op. cit.*, p.135.
153 Axmann, *op. cit.*
154 cf. ref. 152.
155 cf. ref. 153.
156 Information supplied by Herr H. Sündermann to the author.
157 Klönne, *Hitlerjugend, op. cit.*, p.15; Brandenburg, *op. cit.*, p.161 ff, Klose, *op. cit.*
    p.67.
158 Schirach, *Hitlerjugend, op. cit.*, p.130.
159 *Völkischer Beobachter*, 25 January 1934 and 26 January 1934.
160 BA NS 26/360.
161 A. Axmann, *Der Reichsberufswettkampf*, Berlin 1938, p.313.
162 *ibid.*; also Klönne, *Hitlerjugend, op. cit.*, p.16.
163 *ibid.*
164 Klönne, *Hitlerjugend, op. cit.*, p.16.
165 Brandenburg, *op. cit.*, p.164.
166 *Dokumente der deutschen Politik*, vol. II, Berlin 1936, p.287 ff.
167 Klose, *op. cit.*, p.68.
168 Schirach, *Hitlerjugend, op. cit.*, p.135 ff.
169 *ibid.*
170 Burden, *op. cit.*, p.86 ff.
171 *ibid.*
172 *Völkischer Beobachter*, 10 September 1934.
173 *ibid.*
174 Kaufmann, *op. cit.*, p.243.
175 *ibid.*
176 *ibid.*
177 'Ausbildungsverordnung für das Führerkorps der Hitler-Jugend vom 23 Februar
    1938' in *Das Dritte Reich* ed. by G. Rühle, Berlin 1938, p.132 ff.
178 *ibid.*
179 R 43II/515 *Jugendführer;* R43II/515a K. O. Paetel, *Handbuch der deutschen
    Jugendbewegung*, Flarchheim 1930, p.89.
180 N. J. Ryschkowsky, *Die Hitlerjugend* quoted in Klönne, *Hitlerjugend, op. cit.*, p.42.
181 Kaufmann, *op. cit.*, p.45.

182 Klönne, *op. cit.*, p.42.
183 See the figures quoted by Kaufmann, *op. cit.*, p.45.
184 A very good analysis of the social origins of the Hitler Youth is provided by Strachura, *op. cit.*, Chapter II.
185 R43II/515; R43II/515a See also Melita Maschmann's observations, *op. cit.*, p.148.
186 A. Möller, *Wesen und Forderung der Hitler-Jugend*, Breslau 1935, p.71; Klose *op. cit.*, pp.152, 157.
187 *ibid.* cf. BHSA Abt. I, MK 14858 VIII 15728 A III.
188 BHSA Abt. I, MK 14858 Nr. VII 42669 Brandenburg, *op. cit.*, p.165.
189 *Führerdienst*, May/June 1933 quoted by Brandenburg, *op. cit.*, p.131.
190 Printed in Brandenburg, pp.153–4. The origin and cause of the order were Hitler Youth actions at local level against Catholic as well as Protestant youth groups.
191 Priepke, *op. cit.*, p.194 ff.
192 BA NS 26/339; for Müller's role see Conway, *op. cit.*, Chapter II.
193 *ibid.*
194 *ibid.*; also Klaus Scholder, 'Die evangelische Kirche in der Sicht der nationalsozialistischen Führung' in *Vierteljahrshefte für Zeitgeschichte*, Stuttgart 1966, pp.15–35.
195 Priepke, *op. cit.*, p.181.
196 Reprinted in full in Brandenburg, *op. cit.*, p.158–9.
197 *ibid.*
198 *ibid.*
199 *Dokumente der deutschen Politik*, ed. by Hohlfeld, Berlin 1954, vol. IV, p.30.
200 For details see Conway, *op. cit.*, Chapter I.
201 *ibid.*
202 *ibid.*
203 BA NS 26/339.
204 Müller, *op. cit.* Doc. Nr. 59.
205 *ibid.*; also Doc. Nr. 328; BA NS 26/339.
206 G. Lewy, *The Catholic Church and Nazi Germany*, New York 1964, p.43.
207 R. d'Harcourt, 'National-Socialism and the Catholic Church in Germany' in *The Third Reich* published by the International Council for Philosophy and Humanistic Studies London 1954, p.807. For rather early complications over the interpretation of article 31 cf. BHSA Abt. I, MK 13984, Nr. III 3482.
208 *ibid.*, clause quoted in full in Brandenburg, *op. cit.*, p.322.
209 cf. Conway, *op. cit.*; Lewy, *op. cit.*, p.84.
210 BA NS 26/357.
211 BHSA Abt. I MK 14858 Nr. VIII 582694 III: this file contains highly interesting correspondence on the relations between Hitler Youth and the Roman Catholic Church in southern and south-western Germany between 1935 and 1940; J. B. Neuhäusler, *Kreuz und Hakenkreuz*, Munich 1946, vol. I, p.213.
212 *ibid.*
213 BHSA Abt. I, MK 13984 Nr. III 3482; MK 14858 Nr. VIII 51420 A III; 8638 A III.
214 BA NS 26/339, BA R 22/4103 (I am indebted to Dr Lothar Gruchmann for drawing my attention to this document.)
215 *ibid.*
216 *Durchführungsverordnung vom 29 März zum Gesetz zur Sicherung der Einheit von Partei und Staat vom 1 Dezember 1933.*
217 BA NS 26/338.
218 BA S.Sch. G. VIII Nr. 239, *Abkommen zwischen dem Reichsjugendführer und dem Reichsführer-SS vom 7 Oktober 1938.*
219 *ibid.*
220 BA NS 26/357; also see below, Chapter X.
221 Brandenburg, *op. cit.*, p.178 ff.

222 *ibid.*
223 *ibid.* BHSA Abt. I, MK 14858, Nr. VIII 50200; Klose, *op. cit.*, p.66 ff.
224 *ibid.*
225 Author's own recollection; Klose, *op. cit.*, p.71.
226 Very specific and exacting requirements were set out for each test but at least after the outbreak of war were rarely enforced. For the requirements see Kaufmann, *op. cit.*, p.57 f.
227 *Gesetz über die Hitler-Jugend vom 1 Dezember 1936* in Reichsgesetzblatt I, Nr. 113, 3 December 1936, p.993.
228 *ibid.*
229 For an eye-witness account see Salomon, *Der Fragebogen, op. cit.*, p.322 ff.
230 Fest, *op. cit.*, p.310.
231 Axmann, *op. cit.*, p.34.
232 H. Stellrecht quoted by Fest, *op. cit.*, p.315; also Stellrecht 'Jugenderziehung und Wehrmacht' in *Die Wehrmacht*, vol. I, issue Nr 7, Berlin 1937.
233 *ibid.*
234 cf. ref. 231.
235 *Erste Durchführungsverordnung zum Gesetz der Hitler-Jugend vom 25 März 1939* reprinted in Brandenburg, *op. cit.*, p.306 ff.
236 *Zweite Durchführungsverordnung zum Gesetz der Hitler-Jugend vom 25 März 1939* reprinted in Brandenburg, *op. cit.*, p.308 ff.
237 *ibid.*; in order to distinguish between the original Hitler Youth volunteers and the compulsory members the distinctions of *Stamm-HJ* for the former and *Allgemeine-HJ* for the latter were introduced. In practice, however, these distinctions very quickly disappeared.

Chapter VI: Ideology

1 Ludwig Hemm, *Die unteren Führer in der Hitler-Jugend*, Doctoral Thesis (unpubl.). University of Würzburg 1940, p.187.
2 cf. P. G. J. Pulzer, *The Rise of Political Anti-Semitism in Germany and Austria*, New York 1964.
3 cf. Nolte, *op. cit.*, pp.343–55, 445–51, 486–91.
4 See Chapters II and III above.
5 cf. E. Sandvoss, *Hitler und Nietzsche*, Göttingen 1969.
6 See Chapter I above.
7 *ibid.*
8 H. W. Koch, *Der Sozialdarwinismus, op. cit.*, p.151 ff.
9 H. v. Treitschke, *Politik*, 2 vols.
10 Paetel quoted by Fest, *op. cit.*, p.305.
11 Bracher, *op. cit.*, pp.37–47.
12 *ibid.*, pp.129–34 ff.
13 See Chapter VII below.
14 John H. E. Fried, 'Fascist Militarisation and Education for War' in *The Third Reich, op. cit.*, p.775.
15 E. Jünger (ed.), *Krieg und Krieger*, Berlin 1930, p.15.
16 Quoted by Fest, *op. cit.*, p.311.
17 Klönne, *op. cit.*, p.77.
18 See Chapter IV above.
19 It was primarily due to the pressure and agitation exerted by the Hitler Youth that the exclusive student corporations were abolished: cf. *Führerblätter der HJ*, August 1935, p.14. Whether of course the Hitler Youth was an NSDAP formation in which

the Socialist ideological component was more genuine than in any other of its branches as Klönne (*op. cit.*, p.77) maintains remains, irrespective of the support of Willi Münzenberg, an assertion for which as yet there is no proof. Evidently this points to a gap in our knowledge for no comparative analysis of the role of the 'socialist' ideology in the various NSDAP formations exists as yet.

20 See Chapters VIII and IX.

21 A recollection of the author dating back approximately to the autumn of 1943.

22 Schirach, *Hitlerjugend, op. cit.*, p.76; also Gruber's speech of December 1928, BHSA Abt. I, NS/1541.

23 cf. F. W. v. Oertzen, *Die deutschen Freikorps 1918–1923*, Munich 1938; F. Schauwecker, *Aufbruch der Nation*, Berlin 1930, p.403.

24 cf. ref. 22.

25 *ibid.*

26 *ibid.*

27 E. Hanfstängl, *Hitler – The Missing Years*, London 1957, p.75 ff.

28 This mood is consistently reflected in the reports of the Württemberg envoy in *Politik in Bayern, op. cit.*

29 E. v. Salomon, *Das Schicksal des A.D.* Hamburg 1960, p.24 ff.

30 See note 19 and also Stachura, *op. cit.*, who provides an otherwise very illuminating chapter on the ideological aspects of the Hitler Youth.

31 Oswald Spengler, *Preussentum und Sozialismus*, Munich (n.d.), pp.98–9.

32 B. v. Schirach, *Revolution der Erziehung*, Munich 1938, p.45.

33 Schirach, *Hitlerjugend, op. cit.*, pp.77–8.

34 *ibid.*

35 Maschmann, *op. cit.*, p.150.

36 *ibid.*, p.41.

37 BA S.Sch. G. VIII Nr. 239.

38 *Gesetz über Kinderarbeit und über die Arbeitszeit der Jugendlichen vom 30 April 1938* (Jugendschutzgesetz) in *Das Dritte Reich* vol. VI ed. by G. Rühle, Berlin 1939, p.108.

39 BA NS 26/360; see for example any issue of *Die Hitler-Jugend, Die Jungenschaft, Die Mädelschaft*, as well as the *Führerdienst der HJ*.

40 Maschmann, *op. cit.*, p.25.

41 Author's personal recollection.

42 Maschmann, *op. cit.*, p.27.

43 Speech in Reichenberg, 2 December 1938 quoted by Fest, *op. cit.*, p.312.

44 Becker, *op. cit.*, pp.175–6.

45 Schirach, *Revolution, op. cit.*, p.49 ff.

46 Maschmann, *op. cit.*, p.27.

47 That this approach may yield very positive results when contrasted with an excessive glorification of individualism, as is customary in western countries, a recent study of child upbringing in the USA and the USSR underlines. See Urie Bronfenbrenner, *Two Worlds of Childhood. USA and USSR*, London 1971, pp.51–69; p.95 ff.

48 Maschmann, *op. cit.*, p.144.

49 *ibid.*

50 Klose, *op. cit.*, p.78.

51 *ibid.*

52 *ibid.*

53 *ibid.*

54 *ibid.*

55 *ibid.*, p.10.

56 *Trial of the German Major War Criminals*, London 1947, part XIV, p.373.

57 BA S.Sch. G. VIII Nr. 239.

58 Pross, *op. cit.*, p.441.

59 Dahrendorf, *op. cit.*, p.441.
60 *ibid.*, p.442.
61 This was, for instance, the situation in *Gebiet Hochland* in 1944–5.
62 BA NS 26/366.
63 *ibid.*
64 A fragment of this film identified by the author is in possession of the Film Archive of the Imperial War Museum, London.
65 The exception was the film *Soldaten von Morgen*, which, from the point of view of propaganda as well as technical execution, is far superior to any other film made by the *Reichsjugendführung*. A 16-mm copy of the film is held by the Imperial War Museum and available on loan to educational institutions.
66 Special performances were arranged on Sunday mornings. The younger members of the Hitler Youth frequently had to visit the homes of the members of their unit to bring them personally to the meeting place.
67 See Chapter V., ref. 122.
68 Letter of H. H. John, head of the Organization Department of the RJF to Kurt Gruber, shortly before the latter's death, 1 December 1943 (copy in author's archive).
69 As was the case in *Fähnlein 8*, Munich 22.
70 See Chapter VII.
71 Conway, *op. cit.*, p.283.
72 *ibid.*, p.443 fn. 64.
73 *ibid.*, p.127 ff.
74 *ibid.*
75 Telegram of the *Gestapo-Leitstelle* Nürnberg-Fürth of 24 July 1938 reproduced by Bracher, Sauer, Schulz, *op. cit.*, pp.347–8.
76 Hans-Günter Zmarzlick, *Wieviel Zukunft hat unsere Vergangenheit?*, excerpt reprinted in DIE ZEIT Nr. 44, 1969.
77 BHSA Abt. II, Epp Nachlass file 450; Conway, *op. cit.*, p.151.
78 *ibid.*, p.151–2.
79 *The Trial of German Major War Criminals*, London 1947, part 14, p.395.
80 Conway, *op. cit.*, p.160, quoting Nuremberg Document NG-1392 and NG-1755, BA NS 26/357.
81 *Hitler's Secret Conversations 1941–44*, New York 1953, pp.516–20.
82 WKT entry for 24 September 1939.

Chapter VII: Literature

1 This chapter is heavily indebted to Peter Aley's *Jugendliteratur im Dritten Reich*, still the best monograph on this subject. Hamburg 1967, p.5.
2 Berhard Payr and Hans-Georg Otto (ed.), *Das Deutsche Jugendbuch*, Munich 1942, p.3.
3 *ibid.*
4 *ibid.*
5 *ibid.*
6 *ibid.*
7 Aley, *op. cit.*, p.19.
8 *Die Schulbücherei*, ed. by Reichsverwaltung des NSLB, Leipzig 1939, p.12.
9 Aley, *op. cit.*, p.12.
10 *ibid.*
11 *ibid.*, p.25.
12 *NS Frauenwarte* 1936, Nr. 6, p.170, also quoted by Aley, *op. cit.*, p.26.

13 *ibid.*
14 *ibid.*
15 Gottfried Neesse, 'Reichjugendführung' in H.-H. Lammers and H. Pfundtner (eds.), *Grundlagen, Aufbau und Wirtschaftsordnung des nationalsozialistischen Staates*, Berlin 1938, vol. I, p.30.
16 *Jugenschriften-Warte*, vol. 47, issue 7/8, Stuttgart 1942, p.64.
17 Fritz Helke 'Kritik am Jugendbuch durch die Jugend' in *Jugendschriften-Warte*, vol. 40, issue 5, 1935, p.6.
18 Aley, *op. cit.*, p.30 ff.
19 Fritz Helke, 'HJ-Arbeit am Schrifttum' in *Der Deutsche Schriftsteller*, 1936, issue 1, p.8.
20 *Börsenblatt für den Deutschen Buchhandel*, Nr. 283, December 1936, pp.1063–6.
21 *Die Schulbücherei*, *op. cit.*, p.20 ff.
22 *ibid.*
23 Aley, *op. cit.*, p.96.
24 D. Klagges, 'Die Märchenstunde als Vorstufe des Geschichtsunterrichts' in *Jugendschriften-Warte*, vol. 45, issue 7/8 Stuttgart 1940, p.40 ff.
25 *ibid.*
26 *ibid.*
27 K. v. Spiess, 'Was ist ein Volksmärchen' in *Jugendschriften-Warte*, vol. 43, issue 6/7, Stuttgart 1938, p.37.
28 G. Grenz, 'Vom Märchenerzählen' in *Die Neue Gemeinschaft. Parteiarchiv für nationalsozialistische Feier-und Freizeitgestaltung*, Munich 1943, p.548 f.; Aley, *op. cit.*, p.102.
29 Georg Schott, *Weissagung und Erfüllung im Deutschen Volksmärchen*, Munich 1936, p.199.
30 Gunter Harmut, *Deutsche Weihnachten, Brauchtum und Feiergestaltung*, Halle 1937, p.29.
31 Herman Lorch, *Germanische Heldendichtung*, Leipzig 1934, p.iii.
32 Erich Beier-Lindhardt, *Das Buch vom Führer für die deutsche Jugend*, Oldenburg 1933; Hitler's speech is also quoted in this book, p.77; see also Chapter V above.
33 Lorch, *op. cit.*
34 A. Rosenberg, *Der Mythus des 20. Jahrhunderts*, Munich 1935, p.614.
35 E. Loewy, *Literatur untern Hakenkreuz. Das Dritte Reich und seine Dichtung*, Fischer Bücherei, Frankfurt 1969, p.290.
36 *Deutsche Heldsagen. Neuerzählt von Hans Friedrich Blunck*, Stuttgart 1958.
37 See the specific interpretation quoted by Aley *op. cit.*, p.111.
38 Felix Dahn, *Ein Kampf um Rohm*, Stuttgart 1954.
39 *Die Schulbücherei*, *op. cit.*, p.38.
40 Aley, *op. cit.*, p.115.
41 Rosenberg, *op. cit.*, p.306.
42 *ibid.*, p.158.
43 E. Rothemund, 'Das Jugendbuch in der deutschen Schule' in *Das Deutsche Jugendbuch*, *op. cit.*, p.54.
44 Josef Prestel, 'Wandel des Heldenbildes' in *Jugendschriften-Warte*, vol. 40, issue 7, Stuttgart 1935, p.45; Aley, *op. cit.*, p.116.
45 Aley, *op. cit.*, p.117.
46 M. Führer, *Nordgermanische Götterüberlieferung und deutsches Volksmärchen. 80 Märchen der Brüder Grimm vom Mythus her beleuchtet*. Munich 1938, p.3.
47 *ibid.*, p.4.
48 S. Ott, *Die altnordische Dichtung in der Schule*, Esslingen 1940, p.5.
49 Hitler, *Mein Kampf*, *op. cit.*, p.474.
50 Rosenberg, *op. cit.*, p.629.
51 Speech of the Minister of the Interior Dr Frick, 9 May 1933, in *Dokumente der*

deutschen Politik, vol. I 1933, ed. by P. Meyer-Benneckenstein, Berlin 1936, pp.300–11.

52 *Deutsches Wesen und Schicksal*, ed. by the Reichswaltung des NSLB, Bayreuth 1936.

53 W. Frenzel, 'Jugendbuch und Vorgeschichte' in *Jugendschriften-Warte* vol. 43, issue 10, Stuttgart 1938, p.65 f.; Aley, *op. cit.*, p.123.

54 E. Weisser, 'Schulausgaben über Friedrich den Grossen' in *Jugendschriften-Warte* vol. 41, issue 9, Stuttgart 1936, p.65.

55 *Das Deutsche Jugendbuch*, *op. cit.*, p.57.

56 *ibid.*, p.56.

57 *ibid.*

58 Loewy, *op. cit.*, p.312.

59 R. Schneider-Neustadt, *Deutsche Grösse*, Stuttgart 1934, p.40 f.

60 *ibid.*

61 *ibid.*, p.302.

62 Hans Grimm, *Volk ohne Raum*, Munich 1926, new. ed. Lippoldsberg 1956.

63 G. Stark, *Völkisches Erbgut in den Schuldramen unserer Klassiker*, Bamberg 1935, p.7.

64 *Die Schulbücherei*, *op. cit.*, p.41.

65 A. Schwarzlose, 'Der Weltkrieg im Spiegel des deutschen Schrifttums' in *Jugendschriften-Warte*, vol. 40, issue 8, Stuttgart 1935, p.49; Aley, *op. cit.*, p.131.

66 Th. Lüddecke, 'Der heroische Auftrieb in der Literatur', *ibid.*, issue 7, p.48.

67 Prestel, 'Volkhafte Dichtung' in *Völkisches Lehrgut*, ed. by K. Higelke, Leipzig 1935, p.19; Aley, *op. cit.*, p.133.

68 *ibid.*, p.20.

69 *ibid.*

70 General von Cochenhausen quoted by Rothenmund, *op. cit.*, p.60.

71 Aley, *op. cit.*, p.137 ff.

72 Author's personal recollection.

73 Aley, *op. cit.*, p.137 ff.

74 E. Neugebauer, 'Schülerbücherei und Jugendschrifttum im Dienst der Wehrerziehung' in *Jugendschriften-Warte*, vol. 45, issue 3/4 Stuttgart 1940, p.34 ff.

75 *Jungen im Einsatz. Kriegsjahrbuch der Hitler-Jugend*, Munich 1944.

76 Aley, *op. cit.*, p.142 ff.

77 H. Mohr, 'Zur Frage der politischen Jugendschrift' in *Jugendschriften-Warte*, vol. 39, issue 6, Stuttgart 1934, p.41.

78 Ph. Bouhler, *Kampf um Deutschland*, Munich 1939, preface.

79 Hitler, *Mein Kampf*, p.476.

80 cf. *Das Schwarze Korps*, 12 December 1935, p.10.

81 *Pimpf im Dienst*, *op. cit.*

82 B. v. Schirach, *Die Fahne der Verfolgten*, Berlin 1933, *Das Lied der Getreuen*, Berlin 1938.

83 E. Gritzbach, *Hermann Göring*, Munich 1940.

84 B. Eichinger, 'Das deutsche Jugendbuch im Auslande' in *Jugendschriften-Warte*, vol. 41, issue 6, Stuttgart 1936, p.48.

85 Aley, *op. cit.*, p.164 ff.

86 *ibid.*, p.166 ff.

87 Rothemund, *op. cit.*, p.61.

88 Relevant works here are Count Bossi Fedrigotti's *Standschütze Bruggler*, and Karl Springenschmied's work.

89 *Die Schulbücherei*, *op. cit.*, p.22.

90 Lüddecke, *op. cit.*, p.47.

91 *ibid.*

92 *Die Schulbücherei*, *op. cit.*, p.22.

93 Prestel, *op. cit.*, p.24.
94 R. Sprockhoff, 'Das Fremdwort im Jugendbuch' in *Jugendschriften-Warte*, vol. 41, issue 3, Stuttgart 1936, p.21; Aley, *op. cit.*, p.169 ff.
95 Rothemund, *op. cit.*, p.64.
96 'Wer war uns Old Shatterhand' in *Das Schwarze Korps*, 1 April 1937, p.16.
97 Rothemund, *op. cit.*, p.64.
98 *Völkischer Beobachter*, 21 April 1940.
99 Aley, *op. cit.*, p.173.
100 *ibid.*
101 W. Vesper (ed.), *Die Neue Literatur*, Leipzig 1939, pp.101–2.
102 Wittek's reply to Vesper quoted in Aley, *op. cit.*, p.174.
103 Aley, *op. cit.*, p.175.
104 *ibid.*, p.176.
105 *ibid.*
106 H. Wollschläger, *Karl May* ro-ro-monographie, Hamburg 1965.
107 *ibid.*
108 And only to reverse its attitude; cf. ref. 96.
109 Aley, *op. cit.*, pp.177, 178.
110 See Chapter VI.
111 Aley, *op. cit.*, quoting librarian in 1943.
112 *ibid.*
113 I. Dyrenfurth-Graebsch, *Geschichte des deutschen Jugendbuches*, Hamburg 1951, p.262.
114 Dahrendorf, *op. cit.*, p.327 ff., 415 ff.

Chapter VIII: Education

 1 Hitler, *Mein Kampf*, *op. cit.*, *p.457 ff.*
 2 *Hitler's Secret Conversations*, *op. cit.*, pp.376, 406–7, 647–8.
 3 *Mein Kampf*, p.452.
 4 *ibid.*, p.453.
 5 *ibid.*, p.454–5.
 6 *ibid.*
 7 *ibid.*
 8 *ibid.*, p.456.
 9 *ibid.*
10 *ibid.*, p.460 ff.
11 *ibid.*, p.464 ff.
12 *ibid.*, p.467 ff.
13 *ibid.*
14 *ibid.*, p.468.
15 *ibid.*, p.470.
16 *ibid.*, p.474.
17 *ibid.*
18 *ibid.*, p.475.
19 *ibid.*, p.476.
20 BA NS 22/739. For an excellent documentation of most aspects of National Socialist education see Hans-Jochen Gamm, *Führung und Verführte*, Munich 1964.
21 Quoted in Kurt Zentner, *Geschichte des Dritten Reiches*, Munich 1965, p.347; also see Gamm, *op. cit.*, p.312.
22 Zentner, *ibid.*
23 See Chapter VII above, ref. 51.

24 See Schirach's speech of 7 December 1936 in *Dokumente der Deutschen Politik, op. cit.*, vol. 4, Berlin 1938, pp.331–5.
25 G. Pein, 'Der deutsche Lehrer und Erzieher als pädagogischer Offizier' in *Nationalsozialistisches Bildungswesen*, Nr. 5, 1940, p.145 ff.
26 *ibid.*; also Schirach, *Revolution, op. cit.*, p.125.
27 *ibid.*
28 Klose, *op. cit.*, p.189.
29 See Chapters IV and V above.
30 Klose, *op. cit.*, p.190.
31 *ibid.*
32 *ibid.*, p.191.
33 cf. Rolf Eilers, *Die nationalsozialistische Schulpolitik*, Cologne 1963.
34 Klose, *op. cit.*, p.191; for further incidents cf. BHSA Abt. I, MK 14858.
35 *ibid.*
36 *ibid.*
37 *ibid.*
38 *Leitgedanken zur Schulordnung 1934–5*, BA NS 22/739.
39 *ibid.*
40 Gamm, *op. cit.*
41 A. Kluger (ed.), *Die deutsche Volksschule im Grossdeutschen Reich*, Breslau 1940, p.387.
42 Conflicting demands between school and Hitler Youth emerged in the main as a result of the war and were in practice decided in favour of the latter.
43 BHSA Abt. I, MK 14858 Nr VIII 13820 A III; Eilers, *op. cit.*
44 Gamm, *op. cit.*, p.26–7.
45 See note 24.
46 Fest, *op. cit.* p.308
47 Desmond Young, *Rommel*, London 1950, pp.56–7; B. v. Schirach, *Ich glaubte, op. cit.*, pp.64–5. For further aspects of paramilitary training see BHSA Abt. I, MK 13985 Nr. 1501 Adj.
48 cf. Eilers, *op. cit.*
49 Klose, *op. cit.*, p.203.
50 *ibid.*
51 cf. H. Stellrecht, *Neue Erziehung*, Berlin 1944.
52 Klose, *op. cit.*, p.203.
53 Stellrecht, *op. cit.*
54 Eilers, *op. cit.*, p.86.
55 A survey made by the author in 1970.
56 Zentner, *op. cit.*, p.347.
57 BA R 43 II/9566.
58 cf. Adolf Viernow, *Zur Theorie und Praxis des nationalsozialistischen Geschichtsunrichts*, Halle 1935.
59 BA NS 22/739; cf. P. Brohmer, *Biologieunterricht und völkische Erziehung*, Frankfurt 1936.
60 cf. A. Dorner (ed.), *Mathematik im Dienst der nationalpolitischen Erziehung*, Frankfurt 1936; Zentner, *op. cit.*, p.348.
61 cf. ref. 55.
62 Eilers, *op. cit.*, p.38.
63 BHSA Abt. I, MK 14858 Nr. 1557/40 Adj.; cf. Albert Müller, *Sozialpolitische Erziehung*, Berlin 1943. In 1942 Himmler too received a report compiled by his staff giving much the same picture; cf. BA NS 19/1531.
64 cf. Bleuel/Klinner, *Deutsche Studenten auf dem Weg ins Dritte Reich*, Gütersloh 1967.
65 Brandenburg, *op. cit.*, p.107.

66 cf. B. v. Schirach, *Wille und Weg des Nationalsozialistischen Deutschen Studentenbundes*, Munich 1929.

67 W. Kunkel, 'Der Professor im Dritten Reich' in *Die deutsche Universität und das Dritte Reich*, Munich 1966, p.103 ff.

68 *ibid.*

69 *Deutsches Geistesleben und Nationalsozialismus – Eine Vortragsreihe der Universität Tübingen*, Tübingen 1965, pp.25–46.

70 H. Seier, 'Der Rektor als Führer' in *Vierteljahrshefte für Zeitgeschichte*, Stuttgart 1964, pp.105–46.

71 *ibid.*

72 W. Hagemann, *Publizistik im Dritten Reich*, Hamburg 1948, p.99.

73 K.-D. Bracher, *Die deutsche Diktatur*, Cologne 1969, p.294.

74 *ibid.*, p.295.

75 *Die deutsche Universität*, op. cit., p.154.

76 *ibid.*

Chapter IX: Elites

1 Horst Ueberhorst, *Elite für die Diktatur. Die Nationalpolitischen Erziehungsanstalten 1933–45*. The best and most incisive analysis of the entire spectrum of National Socialist 'élite' education has been provided by Harald Scholtz, *Nationalsozialistische Ausleseschulen. Internatsschulen als Herrschaftsmittel des Führerstaates*, Göttingen 1973. Ueberhorst had been a pupil of an NPEA, Scholtz of an *AHS*. The latter goes to considerable lengths to salvage whatever there is to save of the intellectual reputation of the *AHS*, sometimes successfully. Unfortunately Scholtz's book became available too late to make other than purely cursory use. G. A. Rowan-Robinson, 'Training the Nazi Leaders of the Future' in *International Affairs*, vol. 17, 1938, p.233–51; Gamm, *op. cit.*, pp.401–14; Klose, *op. cit.*, pp.203–7.

2 Dietrich Orlow, 'Die Adolf-Hitler-Schulen' in *Vierteljahrshefte für Zeitgeschichte*, Stuttgart 1965, pp.272–85; Scholtz, *Ausleseschulen*, op. cit., pp.162–254; Gamm, *op. cit.*, pp.422–38; Klose *ibid.*

3 Harald Scholtz 'Die NS-Ordensburgen' in *Vierteljahrshefte für Zeitgeschichte*, Stuttgart 1967, pp.269–98; Gamm, *op. cit.*, pp.414–21; 'Führers of the Future' in *Manchester Guardian* 17 November 1937.

4 H. P. Rothfeder, *A Study of Alfred Rosenberg's Organization* (unpubl. dissertation). Ann Arbour, Michigan 1963; Orlow, *op. cit.*, footnote 1a, p.272.

5 Robert Ley, *Wir alle helfen dem Führer*, Munich 1937, p.137 ff; R. Ley, 'Der Erziehungswert bei der nationalsozialistischen Führerauslese' in *Völkischer Beobachter*, 24 November 1937; Scholtz, *Ordensburgen*, op. cit., p.271.

6 Scholtz, *ibid.*; Ueberhorst, *op. cit.*, pp.36–7.

7 *Deutsche Schulerziehung. Jahrbuch des Deutschen Zentralinstituts für Erziehung und Unterricht*, ed. by R. Benze, Berlin 1940, pp. 248–57.

8 cf. Ernst von Salomon, *Die Kadetten*, Hamburg 1957 (reprint), p.6 ff.

9 J. Haupt, 'Neuordnung im Schulwesen und Hochschulwesen' in *Das Recht der nationalen Revolution*, Berlin 1933, issue 5, p.24 ff.

10 B. Rust, 'Erziehung zur Tat' in Deutsche Schulerziehung, *op. cit.*, vol. 1943, p.6; Ueberhorst, *op. cit.*, pp.64 ff., 103 ff.; *Der Jungmann*, 6. Kriegsnummer p.5.

11 Ueberhorst, *op. cit.*, p.437 ff.

12 *ibid.*

13 BA S.Sch. G. III Nr. 270; R. Benze, *Erziehung im Grossdeutschen Reich. Eine Überschau über ihre Ziele, Wege und Richtungen*, Frankfurt 1939, p.42 ff.

14 BA S.Sch. G. III Nr. 270; sworn affidavit by Dr Albert Holfelder, Head of the Office

of Education in the Ministry of Science and Education, printed in Ueberhorst, *op. cit.*, p.60 f.

15 *Merkblatt für die Aufnahme in Nationalpolitische Erziehungsanstalten.*

16 See Chapter V above, refs. 227, 235, 236.

17 *Der Jungmann*, vol. IV (1938), issue 6/7, p.68; *Nationalpolitische Erziehungsanstalt Stuhm im Aufbau. Festschrift*, Königsberg 1938, p.89 f.

18 Holfelder affidavit, *op. cit.*

19 H. Heuer, 'Englische und deutsche Jugenderziehung' in *Zeitschrift für neusprachlichen Unterricht*, vol. 36, Berlin 1937, p.215 ff.

20 A. Heissmeyer, 'Über die Nationalpolitischen Erziehungsanstalten' in *Der Altherrenbund Amtl. Organ der deutschen Studenten*, vol. 1, 1939, issue 3, p.202; Rust, *op. cit.*; Der Jungmann, vol. IV (1938) issue 6/7, p.67.

21 J. Haupt, *Nationalerziehung*, Langensalza 1933, p.7; Scholtz *Ausleseschulen*, *op. cit.*, p.82, maintains that high fees prevented the establishment of any social egalitarianism. But he provides no supporting evidence, which, such as it is, would seem to contradict his assertion.

22 Ueberhorst, *op. cit.*, p.41.

23 *ibid.* also pp.428–9; A. Baeumler/A. Heissmeyer *Weltanschauung und Schule*, vol. I, issue 2, December 1936, p.106.

24 cf. ref. 18; Gamm, *op. cit.*, p. 381.

25 Ueberhorst, *op. cit.*, p.38 ff.

26 H. Heuer, *op. cit.*

27 BA R 43 II/956b.

28 Scholtz, *Ausleseschulen, op. cit.*, p.155.

29 cf. ref. 18.

30 *ibid.*, BA NS 26/354.

31 *ibid.*

32 BA S.Sch. G. III Nr. 270.

33 *ibid.*

34 Ueberhorst, *op. cit.*, p.428.

35 Ueberhorst's remark that the Hitler Youth 'never forgave' Haupt is something of an understatement.

36 cf. Ueberhorst, *op. cit.*, p.56 footnote 3.

37 *Erlass des Reichministeriums für Wissenschaft, Erziehung und Volkserziehung vom 7.10.1937.*

38 cf. ref. 15.

39 cf. ref. 20.

40 cf. ref. 15.

41 Ueberhorst, *op. cit.*, p.78.

42 Author's personal recollection.

43 *ibid.*

44 *ibid.*; also Ueberhorst, *op. cit.*, pp.78–9.

45 BA R 43 II/956b; *Der Jungmann*, vol IV (1938), issue 6/7, p. 64.

46 BA R 43 II/956b.

47 *ibid.*

48 *Merkblatt, op. cit.*

49 Letter of a former teacher at Bensberg in author's possession.

50 BA R 43 II/956b.

51 *Merkblatt, op. cit.*

52 cf. ref. 17.

53 *ibid.*, p.24 f.; Scholtz, *Ausleseschulen, op. cit.*, p.151.

54 O. Calliebe, 'Die Nationalpolitischen Erziehungsanstalten' in *Deutsche Schulerziehung, op. cit.*, p.253; *Der Jungmann*, vol. IV (1938), issue 6/7, pp.74 f., 76 f.; vol. I (1936), issue 3/4, pp.18 f., 19 f., 23 f.

55 BA R 43 II/956b; Rust, *Erziehung, op. cit.*, p. 10; *Der Jungmann*, vol. III (1937), issue 5, p.20 f.
56 cf. note 17, p.68; *Der Jungmann*, vol. I (1936), issue 2, p.22 ff; *Der Jungmann*, vol. I (1936), issue 2, p.22 ff.; *Der Jungmann* 1. Kriegsnummer, p.29; *ibid.* 8 Kriegsnummer, p.3.
57 Rust, *Erziehung, op. cit.*, p.10; Calliebe, *op. cit.*, p.253; Scholtz, *Ausleseschulen, op. cit.*, pp.146–7.
58 *Der Jungmann*, vol. I (1936), issue 3/4, p.47.
59 Scholtz, *Ausleseschulen, op. cit.*, p.146.
60 *Der Jungmann*, vol. IV (1938), issue 6/7, p.60; *ibid.*, vol. I (1936), issue 3/4, pp.48 ff., 83 f.
61 *ibid.*, vol. I (1936), issue 3/4, pp.47–8 ff; vol. IV (1938), p.62.
62 *ibid.*, vol. I (1936), issue 3/4, p.83 f.
63 *ibid.*, p.48 ff.
64 *ibid.*, vol. IV (1938), issue 6/7, p.62.
65 cf. ref. 62, p.76 f.
66 G. A. Rowan-Robinson, *op. cit.*, ref. 1.
67 Scholtz, *Ausleseschulen, op. cit.*, p.143.
68 *Merkblatt, op. cit.*
69 BA NS 19/1560.
70 *ibid.*
71 Scholtz, *Ausleseschulen, op. cit.*, p.157.
72 BA S.Sch. G. III Nr. 270.
73 cf. ref. 27.
74 *ibid.*
75 *ibid.*
76 *ibid.*
77 *ibid.*
78 *ibid.*
79 *ibid.*
80 Author's archive.
81 In Ph. Bouhler (ed.), *Der Grossdeutsche Freiheitskampf. Reden Adolf Hitlers*, Munich 1941, p.350 ff. This crucial part of the speech has been omitted by Max Domarus, *Hitlers Reden*, vol. II, Würzburg 1963.
82 G. Skroblin, 'Die nationalpolitischen Erziehungsanstalten' in *Die höhere Schule*, 1941, p.211 f.
83 cf. H. Höhne, *The Order of the Death's Head*, London 1970.
84 *Hitler's Secret Conversations, op. cit.*, p.381 f.; Eberhard Jäckel, *Frankreich in Hitlers Europa. Die deutsche Frankreichpolitik im Zweiten Weltkrieg*, Stuttgart 1966, p.302.
85 *Hitler's Secret Conversations, op. cit.*, p.382.
86 *ibid.*
87 *ibid.*
88 *ibid.*
89 G. H. Stein, *The Waffen SS*, London 1966, p.153 ff.
90 BA S.Sch. G. III Nr. 270; Himmler's memorandum concerning the treatment of the eastern races in *Vierteljahrshefte für Zeitgeschichte*, Stuttgart 1957, pp. 194–8.
91 *Der Jungmann*, 6. Kriegsnummer, p.14.
92 Heissmeyer to *SS-Standartenführer*, Dr Brandt, letter reprinted in Ueberhorst, *op. cit.*, p.113 ff.
93 *Das Schwarze Korps*, 16 June 1938; *ibid.*, 8 June 1939; Eugen Kogon, *Der SS-Staat*, Frankfurt 1960 (new ed.) p.20, English translation *The Theory and Practice of Hell*.
94 Ueberhorst, *op. cit.*, p.135 ff.; *ibid.*, p.432.
95 *ibid.*

96 BA NS 19/1560.
97 *ibid.*
98 BA R 43 II/956b.
99 Ueberhorst, *op. cit.*, p.137.
100 cf. affidavit by Kurt Petter, former inspector of the *AHS*, Ueberhorst, *op. cit.*, p.179.
101 BA S.Sch. G. III Nr. 270; BA NS 19/1531.
102 *ibid.*
103 *ibid.*
104 *SS-Gruppenführer* Berger to Himmler 14 February 1942, Ueberhorst, *op. cit.*, p. 156 ff.
105 BA S.Sch. G. III Nr. 270.
106 In the light of this development, which seemingly assured the predominance of the *SS* in all spheres of German life, one must interpret Heissmeyer's suggestion that all *NPEA* teaching staff should carry ranks of the general *SS*. cf. also ref. 105.
107 Hitler's order dated 7 December 1944 in Ueberhorst, *op. cit.*, p.177.
108 cf. Chapter XI above.
109 *Der Jungmann*, 7. Kriegsnummer, p.38 ff.
110 cf. Chapter XI above.
111 Account of Bensberg pupil in author's archive.
112 BA S.Sch. G. III Nr. 270.
113 Heissmeyer's testimony in Ueberhorst, *op. cit.*, p.434.
114 cf. Dietrich Orlow, *op. cit.; Verfügung des Führers und Reichskanzlers vom 15.1.1937* in G. Rühle (ed.), *Das Dritte Reich. Das fünfte Jahr 1937*, p.117; Joint declaration of Schirach and Ley in *ibid.* p.117 ff.; Eilers, *op. cit.*, pp.46, 117–19.
115 Scholtz, *NS-Ordensburgen, op. cit.*, p.271 footnote 7a; Scholtz, *Ausleseschulen, op. cit.*, p.191.
116 cf. ref. 98 and also Ley's letter in reply to Rust of 22 January 1937 in Gamm, *op. cit.*, pp.133–4; Scholtz, *NS-Ordensburgen, op. cit.*, p.271.
117 Scholtz, *NS-Ordensburgen, op. cit.*, p.273.
118 *Organisationsbuch der NSDAP*, Munich 1938, p.443.
119 *ibid.; Vorschriftenhandbuch der Hitlerjugend*, Berlin 1942, vol. 3, p.1862.
120 *Junges Deutschland*, Berlin 1937, p.49.
121 Orlow, *op. cit.*, p.273.
122 *Auslese und Ausmusterung der Schüler für die Adolf-Hitler-Schulen, Jahrgang 1938. 15 November 1937* cited in Orlow, *op. cit.*, p.275.
123 *ibid.; Vorschriftenhandbuch, op. cit.*, pp.1865–7.
124 Orlow, *op. cit.*, p.276; Eilers, *op. cit.*, p.47.
125 *Vorschriftenhandbuch, op. cit.*, pp.1871–2.
126 Author's archive.
127 Orlow, *op. cit.*, p.277.
128 *ibid.*
129 *ibid.*, p.278.
130 Scholtz, *Ausleseschulen, op. cit.*, p.210.
131 Orlow, *op. cit.*, p.279.
132 cf. O. W. von Vacano, *Sparta, der Lebenskampf einer nordischen Herrenschicht*, Bücherei der Adolf-Hitler-Schulen, 1942.
133 *ibid.*
134 Orlow, Adolf-Hitler-Schulen, *op. cit.*, p.281.
135 cf. George L. Mosse, *The Crisis of German Ideology*, New York 1964.
136 Orlow, Adolf-Hitler-Schulen, *op. cit.*, p.282.
137 *ibid.*
138 Eilers, *op. cit.*, p.14; Scholtz, *Ausleseschulen, op. cit.*, as a former AHS pupil sees this in rather a different light. Perhaps a case in which distance lends a little enchantment.
139 Orlow, *Adolf-Hitler-Schulen, op. cit.*, p. 282.

140 *ibid.*
141 *ibid.*, p.283; Ley, *Wir alle helfen dem Führer*, *op. cit.*, p.130.
142 Orlow, Adolf-Hitler-Schulen, *op. cit.*, p.283.
143 *ibid.*
144 H. Rhein, 'In Lothringen' in *Jungenblatt der Adolf-Hitler-Schulen*, I, 1941.
145 cf. ref. 107.
146 Orlow, Adolf-Hitler-Schulen, *op. cit.*, p.284.
147 cf. U. Bronfenbrenner, *Two Worlds of Childhood*, *op. cit.*, which outlines and brings out very clearly the importance of this early stage of the educational process.
148 Their precise function was never clearly defined other than that they were an educational institution under the control of Ley's *Reichsorganisationsleitung der NSDAP.*
149 Scholtz, NS-Ordenburgen, *op. cit.*
150 R. Benze and G. Gräfer, *Erziehungsmächte und Erziehungshoheit im Grossdeutschen Reich*, Leipzig 1940, p.225.
151 Ley, *Wir alle . . . op. cit.*, pp.166, 173.
152 *ibid.*, p.172.
153 *Völkischer Beobachter*, 27 May 1938.
154 Scholtz, NS-Ordensburgen, *op. cit.*, p.275 ff; *Der Angriff* 5 May 1936, p.10.
155 Scholtz, NS-Ordensburgen, *op. cit.*, p.275.
156 *ibid.*
157 Ley, *Wir alle . . .* p.117 ff.
158 Scholtz, NS-Ordensburgen, *op. cit.*, p.275.
159 *ibid.*; *Der Hoheitsträger*, issue 9, 1943, p.17 ff.
160 Scholtz, *ibid.*
161 *ibid.*, p.276.
162 *ibid.*
163 *Gauschulungsleiter* Kölker of the *Gau* Cologne Aachen with specific reference to his experiences at the Ordensburg Vogelsang quoted in Scholtz NS-Ordensburgen, *op. cit.*, p.284.
164 *ibid.*
165 *ibid.*
166 BA NS 22/604.
167 Ley, *Wir alle . . . op. cit.*, p.159 ff.
168 Scholtz, NS-Ordensburgen, *op. cit.*, p.279.
169 *ibid.*, p.285.
170 *Der Hoheitsträger*, *op. cit.*, p.19.
171 BA NS 22/739.
172 Scholtz, NS-Ordensburgen, *op. cit.*, p.286.
173 BA NS 22/739.
174 *Völkischer Beobachter*, 24 November 1937; Poliakov and Wulf, *Das Dritte Reich und seine Denker*, Berlin 1959, pp.124–64.
175 Poliakov and Wulf, *Das Dritte Reich . . . ibid.*, p.146.
176 *ibid.*

Chapter X: Dissent

1 cf. Bennecke, *op. cit.*; Horn, *op. cit.*; Strachura, *op. cit.* Chapter VI.
2 *ibid.*
3 *ibid.*
4 Horn, *op. cit.*, p.238 ff; G. Schildt, *Die Arbeitsgemeinschaft Nord-West. Untersuchungen zur Geschichte der NSDAP 1925–26* Doctoral diss. Freiburg 1964.
5 *ibid.*

6 BHSA Abt. I, NS/1804.
7 *ibid.*
8 Bennecke, *op. cit.*, p.129 ff; Chapter IV above, p.108 ff.
9 cf. Chapter IV above, p.108 ff; H. Bolm, *Hitler-Jugend in einem Jahrzehnt: ein Glaubensweg der Niedersächsischen Jugend*, Braunschweig 1938, p.52.
10 Horn, *op. cit.*, p.260 ff.; K. O. Paetel, *Versuchung oder Chance*, Berlin 1965, p.160; R. Kühnl, *Die nationalsozialistische Linke 1925–30*, Meisenheim 1966, pp.225 ff, 243 f.
11 Kühnl, *op. cit.*, p.234.
12 The phenomenon of 'national-Bolshevism' is analysed by O. E. Schüddekopf, *Linke Leute von Rechts*, Stuttgart 1960.
13 Paetel, *Versuchung, op. cit.*, p.210.
14 Kühnl, *op. cit.*, p.252.
15 *ibid.*; Brandenburg, *op. cit.*, p.40.
16 Bennecke, *op. cit.*, p.142 ff; Horn, *op. cit.*, pp.261–5.
17 BA S.Sch. G. VIII Nr. 239.
18 Kühnl, *op. cit.*, p.376.
19 BHSA Abt. I, NS/1508; Strachura, *op. cit.*, Chapter VI.
20 *ibid.*
21 *ibid.*
22 *ibid.*
23 Schüddekopf, *op. cit.*, p.335.
24 Paetel, *Versuchung, op. cit.*, p.159.
25 BHSA Abt. I, NS/1541.
26 BHSA Abt. I, NS/1834.
27 Strachura, *op. cit.*, Chapter VI.
28 BHSA Abt. I, NS/1508.
29 *ibid.*
30 Strachura, *op. cit.*
31 *ibid.*
32 *ibid.*
33 BA S.Sch. G. VIII Nr. 205.
34 *ibid.*
35 Strachura, *op. cit.*
36 BHSA Abt. I, NS/1542.
37 Brandenburg, *op. cit.*, p.201.
38 Bennecke, *op. cit.*, p.165.
39 BA NS 26/362.
40 BA NS 26/370.
41 BHSA Abt. I, NS/1555.
42 Staatsarchiv Bremen 4.65-II.E.3.a.13.
43 BA NS 26/340.
44 BHSA Abt. I, NS/1544; NS/1535; NS/1542.
45 *ibid.*
46 *ibid.*
47 BHSA Abt. I, NS/1541.
48 *ibid.*
49 BA NS 26/337; BHSA Abt. I, NS/1542.
50 BA NS 26/362.
51 *ibid.*; BA S.Sch. G. III Nr. 241.
52 Strachura, *op. cit.*, Chapter VII.
53 J. Georgi, 'Die geistige Überwindung des Nationalsozialismus und die Freideutsche Bewegung' in *Freideutscher Rundbrief*, issue 3, Hamburg 1948. BA S.Sch. G. VII Nr. 205; BHSA Abt. I, NS/1544.

54 Karl Heinz Meyer quoted by Brandenburg, *op. cit.*, p.193.
55 cf. Arno Klönne, *Gegen den Strom. Ein Bericht über die Jugendopposition im Dritten Reich*, Hanover 1958.
56 Brandenburg, *op. cit.*, p.194.
57 *ibid.*
58 Letter of the *NS-Kulturgemeinde* to the *Aussenpolitisches Amt der NSDAP* 18 June 1936 in *Jugend zwischen den Kriegen. Eine Sammlung von Aussagen und Dokumenten*, Heidenheim 1967.
59 Brandenburg, *op. cit.*, p.313.
60 F. Hielscher, *Fünfzig Jahre unter Deutschen*, Hamburg 1954, p.173.
61 BA NS 26/357.
62 *ibid*; R43 II/515.
63 Laqueur, *op. cit.*, p.175 f.
64 *ibid.*
65 Brandenburg, *op. cit.*, p.196.
66 The background and the nature of Köbel's emigration and the route he took have still not been unequivocally verified. cf. Laqueur, *op. cit.*, p.175, and Brandenburg, *op. cit.*, p.196.
67 *Jugend zwischen den Kriegen*, *op. cit.*, p.170.
68 BA R 22/4103.
69 cf. ref. 67, p.171.
70 Brandenburg, *op. cit.*, p.197.
71 *ibid.*
72 *ibid.*
73 Arthur Ehrhardt during the Second World War, upon his own request, transferred from the *Wehrmacht* to the *Waffen-SS*. Holding the rank of a Major he was directly responsible to Himmler for compiling a history of German anti-partisan warfare. After the war he went underground until 1950 and from 1951 until his death in 1971 he edited the European – rather than German – extreme right-wing monthly *Nation Europa* in Coburg.
74 Institut für Zeitgeschichte, Akten des Oberreichsanwalts beim Volksgerichtshof Nr. 8 J 419/37g.
75 *ibid.*
76 *ibid.*
77 *ibid.*
78 *ibid.*
79 *ibid.*
80 *ibid.*
81 *ibid.*
82 *ibid.*
83 *Deutscher Reichs- und Preussicher Staatsanzeiger*, issue 212, 12 September 1938.
84 Brandenburg, *op. cit.*, p.218.
85 cf. ref. 74.
86 *ibid.*
87 *Geheimschrift Nr. 21 der Reichsjugendführung der NSDAP – Amt für Jugendverbände* 1 February 1936; Brandenburg, *op. cit.*, pp.204–5.
88 cf. ref. 74.
89 *ibid.*
90 *ibid.*
91 *ibid.*
92 *ibid.*
93 Klönne, *Gegen den Strom*, *op. cit.*, p.66; G. Weissenborn, *Der lautlose Aufstand*, Hamburg 1954, p.344.
94 cf. Chapter V above.

95 *ibid.*
96 BHSA Abt. I, MK 14858 Nr. VIII 58269 III; H. J. Cron (ed.), *Dreissig Jahre Bund Neudeutschland*, Cologne 1949, p.98.
97 Brandenburg, *op. cit.*, p.222.
98 BHSA MK 13984 Nr. VI 101296; MInn 71799, 22536 15. Klönne, *Gegenden Strom, op. cit.*, p.66.
99 Brandenburg, *op. cit.*, p.223; Roussaint's sentence was eleven years hard labour. He survived the war and is now President of the VVN, the association of the persecutees of the Nazi regime.
100 cf. Chapter V, refs. 236 and 237.
101 Brandenburg, *op. cit.*, p.223.
102 WKT entries on several dates during 1938 and 1939.
103 WKT entry for 30 October 1939.
104 cf. Chapter V.
105 Priepke, *op. cit.*
106 For a summary see Brandenburg, *op. cit.*, pp.224–5.
107 BBC broadcast from 1945 quoted *ibid.*, p.213.
108 BA R 43 II/956b.
109 *ibid.*; Klönne, *Hitlerjugend, op. cit.*, p.96.
110 BA R 22/4003; *Informationsdienst des Reichsministers der Justiz.*
111 Institut für Zeitgeschichte, Akten des Volksgerichtshofes 8 J 330/38.
112 W. Tetzlaff, *Das Diszplinarrecht der Hitler-Jugend*, Berlin 1944, p.53.
113 *Dienststrafordnung der Hitler-Jugend*, 4 October 1940; Klönne, *Hitlerjugend, op. cit.*, p.21.
114 *ibid.*; Klose, *op. cit.*, p.219.
115 H. Bobrach (ed.), *Meldungen aus dem Reich. Lageberichte des Sicherheitsdienstes der SS 1939–44*, Neuwied 1965, p.403.
116 *ibid.*
117 Brandenburg, *op. cit.*, p.212.
118 For a traditional Bavarian anyone not speaking a South German dialect is perforce a 'Prussian'.
119 The incident took place on Wednesday 26 April 1944 at the Türken-Film-Theater in Munich.
120 A. Leber (ed.), *Das Gewissen entscheidet*, Berlin 1956, p.32.
121 · *ibid.*
122 *ibid.*
123 See the list of Germans up to the age of 30 executed between February 1933 and May 1945 in K.-H. Jahnke, *Entscheidungen, Jugend im Widerstand 1933–45*, Frankfurt 1970. This includes also the members of the youth group organized by Dr J. Rittmeister, which became associated with the Russian spy network, the 'Red Orchestra'. For details see H. Höhne, *Kennwort Direktor*, Fischer-Taschenbuch, Frankfurt 1972.
124 Klose, *op. cit.*, p.235.
125 Facsimile reproduction in Jahnke, *op. cit.*, p.111.
126 *ibid.*, p.109.
127 Boberach, *op. cit.*, p.372.
128 *ibid.*
129 WKT entry for 8 October 1941.
130 *ibid.*
131 Reprinted in Inge Scholl, *Die weisse Rose*, Fischer Taschenbuch, reprint, Frankfurt 1971, p.119 ff.
132 *ibid.*
133 *ibid.*
134 *ibid.*

135 *ibid.*
136 G. Ritter, *Carl Goerdeler und die deutsche Widerstandsbewegung*, dtv, Munich 1964, p.366.
137 Scholl, *op. cit.*, p.63.
138 *ibid.*, p.59.
139 *ibid.*, p.124.
140 *ibid.*, p.71 ff.
141 *ibid.*, p.74 ff.
142 *ibid.*, p.85 ff.
143 U. v. Hassel, *Vom anderen Deutschland*, Fischer-Taschenbuch, Frankfurt 1964, p.270 (English translation: *The Hassel Diaries*).

Chapter XI: War

1 G. Kaufmann, *op. cit.*, p.207.
2 R43 II/515 Jugendführer.
3 *ibid.*; BA S.Sch. G. VIII Nr. 239.
4 BA NS 26/364.
5 BA NS 26/382; A. Axmann, *Hitlerjugend, op. cit.*, p.35 ff.; Klose, *op. cit.*, p.95 ff.
6 *ibid.*; BA NS 26/360, NS 26/382.
7 *ibid.*
8 BA NS 26/382.
9 *Jungen im Einsatz, op. cit.*, p.23; also Axmann, *Hitlerjugend, op. cit.*, p.35, cf. ref. 8.
10 *ibid.*
11 *ibid.*; BA 26/382; BHSA Abt. I, NS/1541; about the additional demands imposed upon members of the special formations of the Hitler Youth see G. Kaufmann, *Das kommende Deutschland, op. cit.*, p.217 ff. Incidentally the idea for specialized formations first occurred to Lenk, who set up a sailing unit: cf. BA NS 26/333.
12 Klose, *op. cit.*, p.95 ff.
13 *ibid.*, p.103.
14 R 43 II/515a, Klose *op. cit.*, p.104; however, Klose's distinction between *Landdienstgruppen* and the general *Ernteeinsatz* was at least during the war far less rigid than he suggests.
15 Author's personal recollection.
16 Kaufmann, *op. cit.*, p.210 ff; Klönne, *op. cit.*, p.21; Klose, *op. cit.*, p.238.
17 *ibid.*
18 *ibid.*
19 WKT entry for 2 October 1939.
20 Kaufmann, *op. cit.*, p.211.
21 Axmann, *op. cit.*, p.34 ff; Klose, *op. cit.*, p.238.
22 *ibid.*
23 *ibid.*
24 *ibid.*; Brandenburg, *op. cit.*, p.229.
25 *ibid.*; Brandenburg, *op. cit.*, p.230; *Kriegsdienstvorschrift der HJ 20 September 1939.*
26 Kaufmann, *op. cit.*, p.211.
27 cf. ref. 15.
28 WKT entry for 8 November 1941.
29 Klose, *op. cit.*, p.249.
30 BA NS 26/370.
31 BA NS 26/370; Klose, *op. cit.*, p.249.
32 *ibid.*, p.243.
33 *ibid.*
34 *ibid.*

35 *ibid*; BA S. Sch. GVIII, Nr. 239
36 BA NS 26/375; Axmann, *op. cit.*, p.48; Klose, *op. cit.*, p.248.
37 *Der Wanderer*, 19 November 1942; see also P. Kluke, 'NS Europaideologie' in *Vierteljahrshefte für Zeitgeschichte*, Stuttgart 1955, p.247 ff.
38 W. A. Boelke (ed.), *Wollt Ihr den totalen Krieg, Die geheimen Goebbels-Konferenzen 1939–1943*, dtv Munich 1969, p.318.
39 H. Heiber (ed.), *Goebbels Reden 1939–1945*, vol. II, Düsseldorf 1972, Goebbels' speech of 18 February 1943, p.176.
40 *ibid.*, speech of 5 June 1943, p.237.
41 Axmann, *op. cit.*, p.35 ff., *Jugend im Einsatz, op. cit.*
42 BA S.Sch. G. VIII Nr. 239.
43 Klose, *op. cit.*, p.246 f.
44 Maschmann, *op. cit.*, pp.123–4.
45 Axmann, *op. cit.*
46 Klose, *op. cit.*, p.247.
47 *ibid.*
48 *ibid.*
49 *ibid.*
50 Maschmann, *op. cit.*, p.124.
51 *ibid.*
52 Hitler, *Mein Kampf*, p.392.
53 Kaufmann, *op. cit.*, p.217; Klönne, *op. cit.*, p.22.
54 Brandenburg, *op. cit.*, p.230.
55 Gottfried Benn quoted by Klose, *op. cit.*, p.251.
56 *Jugend im Einsatz, op. cit.*; cf. BHSA Abt. II, Epp Nachlass file 451.
57 Brandenburg, *op. cit.*, p.231.
58 cf. ref. 15.
59 *ibid.*
60 Klose, *op. cit.*, p.252 ff.; Brandenburg, *op. cit.*, p.231.
61 Klose, *op. cit.*, p.252.
62 Maschmann, *op. cit.*, p.159.
63 cf. Chapters VIII and IX above.
64 Gamm, *op. cit.*, p.26 f.
65 Axmann, quoted by Klose, *op. cit.*, p.254.
66 A. Schmidt, *Jugend im Reich*, Berlin 1943, p.34.
67 cf. ref. 65.
68 Copy of letter in author's archive.
69 Brandenburg, *op. cit.*, p.231.
70 Klose, *op. cit.*, p.254.
71 Brandenburg, *op. cit.*, p.231.
72 *ibid.*
73 cf. ref. 15.
74 Account in author's archive.
75 K. G. Klietmann, *Die Waffen-SS. Eine Dokumentation*, Osnabrück 1965, p.181 ff.
76 L. P. Lochner (ed.), *The Goebbels Diaries*, London 1948, p.263.
77 Klietmann, *op. cit.*, p.181.
78 *Panzermeyer* (Kurt Meyer) *Grenadiere*, Munich 1957, p.204.
79 *ibid.*
80 Klietmann, *op. cit.*, p.181.
81 Panzermeyer, *op. cit.*, p.205.
82 *ibid.*
83 Klietmann, *op. cit.*, p.181.
84 Panzermeyer, *op. cit.*, p.205.
85 *ibid.*, p.207.

86 E. G. Krätschmer, *Die Ritterkreuzträger der Waffen-SS*, Göttingen 1957, p.22 f.
87 *ibid.*
88 Panzermeyer, *op. cit.*, p.207.
89 *ibid.*
90 *ibid.*, p.205; Klietmann, *op. cit.*, p.183 ff.
91 Klietmann, *op. cit.*, p.182.
92 Panzermeyer, *op. cit.*, p.206.
93 *ibid.*
94 *ibid.*
95 cf. ref. 74.
96 Panzermeyer, *op. cit.*, p.206.
97 *ibid.*, p.207.
98 *ibid.*
99 *ibid.*
100 *ibid.*; Meyer's account has been borne out by numerous conversations the author has
    had with former members of the HJ division, irrespective of their present political
    attitudes, which have ranged from NPD to SPD support.
101 *ibid.*, p.208.
102 *ibid.*, p.208 ff.
103 Chester Wilmot, *Struggle for Europe*, London 1952, p.377.
104 D. Young, *op. cit.*, p.56.
105 Klietmann, *op. cit.*, p.182.
106 Panzermeyer, *op. cit.*, p.236.
107 M. Shulman, *Defeat in the West*, London 1947, p.104.
108 *ibid.*
109 Panzermeyer, *op. cit.*, p.304 f.; Klietmann, *op. cit.*, p.1822.
110 Panzermeyer, *op. cit.*, p.313.
111 *ibid.*, p.271.
112 Klietmann, *op. cit.*, p.183.
113 *ibid.*; Stein, *op. cit.*, p.249.
114 BA NS 26/382; *Völkischer Beobachter*, 19 October 1944.
115 Klose, *op. cit.*, p.261.
116 Th. Rosiwall, *Die letzten Tage*, Vienna 1969, p.233.
117 Reprinted in K. Zentner, *Illustrierte Geschichte des Zweiten Weltkrieges*, Munich
    1963, p.454.
118 *Völkischer Beobachter*, 28 March 1945.
119 C. Ryan, *The Last Battle*, London 1966, p.226.
120 *ibid.*; Ch. Whiting, *The Battle of the Ruhrpocket*, New York 1970, p.86.
121 Maschmann, *op. cit.*, p.262.
122 v. Alfen and Niehoff, *So kämpfte Breslau*, Munich 1961, p.126; Klose, *op. cit.*, p.264.
123 H. Altmer quoted by E. Kuby, *Das Ende des Schreckens*, Munich 1955, p.140 ff.
124 Maschmann, *op. cit.*, p.270.
125 G. Boldt, *Die letzten Tage der Reichskanzlei*, Hamburg 1962, p.197 ff.
126 Diary of Hugo Hartung quoted by Kuby, *op. cit.*, p.116.
127 This was the occasion on which Hitler's last public photograph was taken.
128 cf. ref. 74.
129 *Die Tat* reprinted in Zentner, *op. cit.*, p.523.

Chapter XII: Aftermath

1 This quote was impossible to pin down. It is attributed to several German writers
   including Heinrich Böll and Peter Weiss.

2 E. Klöss, *Der Luftkrieg über Deutschland*, dtv Munich 1963, p.270.
3 H. W. Koch, 'German and Austria: a Question of Survival' in *History of the Second World War*, vol. VII, London 1966–9, p.2755 ff.
4 *ibid.*
5 This situation, although based on the author's own experience, was by no means unique.
6 *Die Neue Zeitung*, Munich, 11 October 1946.
7 *Süddeutsche Zeitung*; 12.10. 1950; 15.1.1951.
8 *Süddeutsche Zeitung*; 9.6.1950.
9 *Der Spiegel*, 1966; 14.6.1966. cf. also H. Schelsky: *Die Skeptische Generation*, Cologne 1957.
10 M. Jenke, *Verschwörung von Rechts?*, Berlin 1961, p.161 ff.
11 'Bericht über die Lage im Landesverband Nordrhein-Westfalen der FDP' quoted by Jenke, *op. cit.*, p.158 f.
12 *ibid.*
13 *ibid.*
14 'Antwort der FDP – Behauptungen und Tatsachen zu der Verhaftungsaktion des britischen Hochkommisars', *ibid.*, p.159 f.
15 *ibid.*
16 *Die nazistischen und antisemitischen Vorfälle*, Memorandum of the Federal Ministry of the Interior, February 1960.
17 cf. Antony Terry in the *Sunday Times*, 3 January 1960.
18 H.-H. Knütter, *Ideologien des Rechtsradikalismus im Nachkriegsdeutschland*, Bonn 1961, p.33.
19 *Unsere Auseinandersetzung mit nationalistischen Tendenzen in der Jugendarbeit*, Deutscher Bundesjugendring, Frankfurt 1960.
20 For details see Jenke, *op. cit.*, p.326 ff.; Knütter, *op. cit.*, p.35.
21 *ibid.*, p.328.
22 *ibid.*
23 *ibid.*, p.330.
24 *ibid.*, p.331.
25 *ibid.*, p.334.
26 H. W. Koch, 'Bavaria Again' in *New Society*, 24 November 1966, London; and 'Germany 20 Years After' in *New Society*, 25 September 1969.
27 For details see *Der Spiegel*; volumes for 1965 to 1968.
28 *Der Spiegel*, Nr. 23, 29 May 1972.
29 *ibid.*
30 *The Times*, 16 April 1973.
31 *Neues Deutschland*, (East) Berlin, 14 July 1971.
32 *Unsere Fiebel: Volk und Wissen*, (East) Berlin 1969.
33 *Mathematik in der Schule*, Issue 6, (East) Berlin 1970, p.416.
34 *Pläne für den fakultativen gesellschaftswissenschaftlichen Unterricht in der erweiterten Oberschule*, (East) Berlin 1970, p.217.

Bibliography

Bibliography

ADLER, E. *Herder i Oświecenie niemieckie*, Warsaw 1965.

AHRENS, H. *Die deutsche Wandervogelbewegung von den Anfängen bis zum Weltkrieg*, Hamburg 1939.

ALFEN and NIEHOFF. *So kämpfte Breslau*, Munich 1961.

ALEY, P. *Jugendliteratur im Dritten Reich*, Hamburg 1967.

ALLEN, W. S. *The Nazi Seizure of Power*, London 1966.

ALTRICHTER, F. *Das Wesen der soldatischen Erziehung*, Oldenburg 1938.

ARENDT, H. *The Origins of Totalitarianism*, Cleveland 1964.

ARIS, R. *History of Political Thought in Germany*, London 1936.

ARNDT, E. M. *Der Rhein. Deutschlands Strom aber nicht Deutschlands Grenze*, Berlin 1813.

ARNDT, E. M. *Geist der Zeit*, 4 vols. Berlin 1807–18.

ARNDT, E. M. *Lieder für Teutsche*, 1813.

ARNDT, R. *Mit 15 Jahren an die Front. Als kriegsfreiwilliger Jäger durch Frankreich die Karpathen u. Italien, 1914–18*. Leipzig 1933.

AXMANN, A. *Der Reichsberufswettkapf*, Berlin 1938.

AXMANN, A. *Hitlerjugend 1933–43*, Berlin 1943.

AXTMANN, H. *Kinder werden Pimpfe, Erzählung aus dem Leben des Jungvolks*, Reutlingen 1937.

BACH, S. 'Gestaltung und Zielsetzung der Hitler-Jugend' in *Nationalsozialistische Monatshefte*, January 1930.

BARTELMAS, E. F. *Unser Weg: Vom werden einer Hitlerjugend Schar*, 1933 Stuttgart. (ed.): *Das Junge Reich: Vom Leben und Wollen der neuen Deutschen Jugend*, Stuttgart 1935.

BARTSCH, M. *Erbgut, Rasse und Volk. Ein Lese-u. Arbeitsbogen für den Schulgebrauch*, Breslau 1934.

BAUMANN, H. *Trommel der Rebellen. (Neue Lieder u. Sprechchöre.)*, Potsdam 1935. *Unser Trommelbube. Neue Lieder in Wort u. Weise*, Potsdam 1934. *Der grosse Sturm. (Chor Spiel)*, Potsdam 1935.

BAYNES, R. H. (ed.) *The Speeches of Adolf Hitler, 1922–39*. London 1942.

BECK, F. A. *Geistige Grundlagen der neuen Erziehung, dargestellt aus der nationsozialistischen Idee*, Osterwieck 1933.

BECKER, H. *German Youth: Bond or Free*, London 1946.

BECKER, H. 'Interpretive Sociology and Constructive Typology,' in *Twentieth century Sociology*, Gurvitch, G., and Moore, W. E., eds., New York 1945.
'Peoples of Germany', in *Problems of the Post-War World*, McCormick, T. C. T., ed. New York 1945.
'Changing Societies as Family Contexts', in *Marriage and the Family*, Becker and Hill, eds., Boston 1942.

Systematic Sociology on the Basis of the Beziehungslehre and Gebildelehre of Leopold von Wiese, New York 1932.
The Student Challenge, Chicago 1924–5.
BECKER and GILDEMEISTER. *Förderung der Jugendpflege durch Reich, Länder, Gemeiden und Gemeinderverbände*, Berlin 1932.
BECKER, J. 'Zentrum and Ermächtigungsgesetz' in *Vierteljahrshefte für Zeitgeschichte (VfZG)*, Stuttgart 1961.
BEIER-LINDHARDT, E. *Das Buch vom Führer für die deutsche Jugend*. Mit einem Geleitwort des Reichsjugendführers Baldur von Schirach, Oldenburg 1933.
BENNECKE, H. *Hitler und die SA*, Munich 1962.
BENZ, W. (ed.) *Politik in Bayern 1919–33. Berichte des württembergischen Gesandten Moser v. Filseck*, Stuttgart 1971.
BENZE, R.-Gräfer, G. *Erziehungsmächte und Erziehungshoheit im Grossdeutschen Reich*, Leipzig 1940.
BENZE, R. (ed.) *Deutsche Schulerziehung. Jahrbuch des Deutschen Zentralinstituts für Erziehung Unterricht*, Berlin 1940.
BENZE, R. *Erziehung im Grossdeutschen Reich*, Frankfurt 1943.
BERGER, G. *Verwaltungs- und Dienstvorschriften für die NSDAP-HJ*; Bd. 1–11, Berlin 1935.
BERGHAHN, V. R. *Der Stahlhelm. Bund der Frontsoldaten, 1918–35*, Düsseldorf 1966.
BERGHÄUSER, E. *Von Wandervogels Art und Fahrt*, Rudolstadt 1912
Pachantenmären, Leipzig 1915.
Wandervogels Sturzflug, Rudolstadt 1922.
BERGMANN, R. 'Die Reichswehr', in *Das Buch der Hitlerjugend. Die Jugend im Dritten Reich*, Munich 1934.
BETHGE, E. *Dietrich Bonhoeffer. Eine Biographie*, Munich 1967.
BEYER, H. *Von der Novemberrevolution zur Räterepublik in München*, Berlin 1957.
BLEUEL, H. P. and Klinnert, E., *Deutsche Studenten auf dem Weg ins Dritte Reich, Ideologien – Programme – Aktionen 1918–35*, Gütersloh 1967.
BESSON, W. *Württemberg und die Deutsche Staatskrise, 1928–33*, Stuttgart 1959.
BLUNCK, H. F. *Deutsche Heldensagen. Neuerzählt von Hans Friedrich Blunck*, Stuttgart 1958.
BLÜHER, H. *Wandervogel. Geschichte einer Jugendbewegung*, Celle 1912.
BLÜHER, H. *Die deutsche Wandervogelbewegung als erotisches Phänomen*, Berlin 1921.
BOBRACH, H. (ed.) *Meldungen aus dem Reich. Lageberichte des Sicherheitsdienstes der SS 1939–44*, Neuwied 1965.
BOEHM, M. H. *Das eigenständige Volk. Volkstheoretische Grundlagen der Ethnopolitik und Geisteswissenschaften*, Göttingen 1932.
Volkstheorie als politische Wissenschaft, Jena 1934.
BOELKE, W. A. (ed.) *Wollt Ihr den totalen Krieg, Die geheimen Goebbels-Konferenzen 1939–43*, dtv Munich 1969.
BOLDT, G. *Hitler's Last Days*, London 1973.
BOLM, H. *Hitler-Jugend in einem Jahrzehnt*, Braunschweig-Berlin-Leipzig-Hamburg 1938.
BONDY, K. *Die proletarische Jugendbewegung*, Lauenburg 1922.
BOLTE, K. M. *Sozialer Aufstieg und Abstieg*, Stuttgart 1959.
BORGWARDT, K. *Die sozialistische Jugendbewegung*, Rostock 1924.
BORINSKI, F. and MILCH, W. *Jugendbewegung*, London 1945.
BOSSE, R. *Aus der Jugendzeit*, Leipzig 1904.
BOUHLER, Ph. *Kampf um Deutschland*, Munich 1939.
(ed.) *Der Grossdeutsche Freiheitskampf. Reden Adolf Hitlers*, Munich 1941.
BRACHER, K. D. *Die Auflösung der Weimarer Republik*, Villingen 1955.
'Stufen totalitärer Gleichschaltung: Die Befestigung der NS Herrschaft 1933/34' in *VfZG*, Stuttgart 1956.

Die deutsche Diktatur, Cologne 1969.
BRACHER, SAUER, SCHULZ. *Die national-sozialistische Machtergreifung*, Cologne 1962.
BRADY, R. A. *The Spirit and Structure of German Fascism*, New York 1937.
BRAMSTED, E. K. *Aristocracy and the Middle Classes in Germany*, London 1964.
BRANDENBURG, H. C. *Die Geschichte der HJ*, Cologne 1968.
'Nachkriegsgeneration 1918 – Nachkriegsgeneration 1945' in *Europäische Begegnungen*, 1962.
BRANDT, L. *Warum? Nationalsozialistischer Schülerbund!*, Munich 1931.
BRAUN, O. *Von Weimar zu Hitler*, Hamburg 1949.
BRENNECKE, F. *Vom Deutschen Volk und seinem Lebensraum. Handbuch für die Schulungsarbeit in der HJ*, Munich 1938.
BREUER, H. *Der Zupfgeigenhansl*, 26th ed., Leipzig 1915.
BROCKMEIER, W. *Du Deutschland wirst bleiben*, Berlin 1943.
BROHMER, P. *Biologieunterricht und völkische Erziehung*, Frankfurt 1936.
BROOK-SHEPERD, G. *Dollfuss*, London 1961.
BROSZAT, M. 'Die Anfänge der Berliner NSDAP 1926/27'. *VfZG*. Stuttgart 1960.
Der Nationalsozialismus, Hanover 1960.
Der Staat Hitlers, Munich 1969.
'Soziale Motivation und Führer-Bindung des Nationalsozialismus', *VfZG*. Stuttgart 1970.
BRONFENBRENNER, U. *Two Worlds of Childhood, USA and USSR*, London 1971.
BRÜNING, H. *Memoiren 1918–34*, Stuttgart 1970.
BRUFORD, W. H. *Germany in the Eighteenth Century*, Cambridge 1965.
BUCHHEIM, K. *Die Weimarer Republik*, Munich 1960.
BUCHHEIM, H. *Glaubenskrise im Dritten Reich, Drei Kapitel nationalsozialistischer Religionspolitik*, Stuttgart 1953.
BUDDENSIEG, H. *Vom Geist und Beruf der deutschen Jugendbewegung*, Lauenburg 1924.
BULLOCK, A. *Hitler, A Study in Tyranny*, London 1962.
BÜRKNER, T. *Der Bund Deutscher Mädel in der Hitler-Jugend*, Berlin 1937.
BURDEN, H. T. *The Nuremberg Party Rallies, 1923–39*, London 1967.
BURMANN, H. and MÖLDERS, C. *Handbuch des gesamten Jugendrechts*, Berlin 1933.
BUSSE-WILSON, E. *Stufen der Jugendbewegung*, Jena 1925.
BUTLER, R. *The Roots of National Socialism. 1783–1933*, London 1941.
CANTRIL, H. *The Psychology of Social Movements*, New York 1941.
CARSTEN, F. L. *The Reichswehr and Politics: 1918 to 1933*, Oxford 1966.
The Rise of Fascism, London 1967.
Revolution in Central Europe, London 1972.
CASSELS, A. 'Mussolini and German Nationalism, 1922–25' in *The Journal of Modern History*, June 1963.
CASSIRER, E. *The Philosophy of the Enlightenment*, Princeton 1951.
CERFF, K. 'Die Hitlerjugend gestaltet den Rundfunk', in *Wille und Macht*, vol. 1935, issue 1.
CHITAROW, R. *Unser Kampf gegen Faschismus und Kriegsgefahr!* Berlin 1931.
CHURCHILL, W. S. *Great Contemporaries*, London 1941.
CILLER, A. *Deutscher Sozialismus in den Sudetenländern und in der Ostmark*, Hamburg 1944.
CLEMENS, J. (ed.) *Ruf von Trier*, Düsseldorf 1931.
CONZE, W. 'Zum Sturz Brünings', *VfZG*, Stuttgart 1953.
'Brünings Politik unter dem Druck der Grossen Krise' in *Historische Zeitschrift*, 1964.
'Die Politischen Entscheidungen in Deutschland 1929–33' in *Die Staats-und Wirtschaftskrise des Deutschen Reiches. 1929/33*, Stuttgart 1967.
CONZE, W. and GROH, D. *Die Arbeiterbewegung in der nationalen Bewegung*,

Stuttgart 1966.

CONWAY, J. S. *The Nazi Persecution of the Churches, 1933–45*, London 1968.

CRON, H. J. (ed.) *Dreissig Jahre Bund Neudeutschland*, Cologne 1949.

CUNNINGHAM, C. *Germany: Today and Tomorrow*, 1936.

CURTIUS, E. R. *Die geistigen Wegbereiter des modernen Frankreich*, Bonn 1919.

CZECH-JOCHBERG, E. *Adolf Hitler und sein Stab*, Oldenburg 1933.

DÄHNHARDT, H. 'Wandlungen in der bürgerlichen Jugend' in *Das Junge Deutschland. Amtliches Organ der Reichsausschuss der deutschen Jugendverbände*. Issue 8, August, 1930.

DAS DEUTSCHE FÜHRERLEXIKON 1934/5.

Die Antifaschistische Aktion, Dokumentation und Chronik Mai 1932 bis Januar 1933, ed. and introduced by Heinz Karl and Erika Kücklich, Berlin 1965.

DAHN, F. *Ein Kampf um Rom*, Stuttgart 1954.

DAHRENDORF, R. *Democracy and Society in Germany*, London 1967.

DANNER, L. *Ordnungspolizei Hamburg*, Hamburg 1958.

DARGEL, M. (ed.) *Mädel im Kampf*, Berlin 1941.

DEGENER, H. A. L. (ed.) *Wer Ist's 1935*
Der Dienst in der Allgemeinen Hitler-Jugend.
Pflichtjahrgang 1923, Berlin 1941.
Der Tag von Potsdam, Munich 1933.
Reichsjugendtag der HJ, October 1932.

DEUERLEIN, E. 'Hitlers Eintritt in die Politik' in *VfZG*, Stuttgart 1959. (ed.) *Der Hitler Putsch. Bayrische Dokumente zum 8./9. November 1923*, Stuttgart 1962.
Deutsches Geistesleben und Nationalsozialismus – Eine Vortragsreihe der Universität Tübingen, Tübingen 1965.
Deutscher Jugenddienst, Potsdam 1933.

DIETRICH, A. *Die Schule im Gefüge der nationalen Ordnung*, Berlin 1940.

DIETRICH, O. *Mit Hitler in die Macht. Persönliche Erlebnisse mit meinem Führer.* Munich 1935.

DIETZE, H. H. 'Verfassungsrechtliche Stellung der HJ' in *Deutsches Recht*, 1939, Issue 13/14.

DINGRÄVE, L. *Wo Steht die Junge Generation?* Jena 1931.

DONOHOE, J. *Hitler's Conservative Opponents in Bavaria, 1930–45*, Leiden 1961.

DORNER, A. (ed.) *Mathematik im Dienst der nationalpolitischen Erziehung*, Frankfurt 1936.

DÖRNER, C. *Freude, Zucht, Glaube, Handbuch für die kulturelle Arbeit im Lager*, Potsdam 1937.

DORPALEN, A. *Hindenburg in der Geschichte der Weimarer Republik*, Berlin 1966.

DROZ, J. *L'Allemagne et la Revolution française*, Paris 1949.

DUDERSTADT, H. *Vom Reichsbanner zum Hakenkreuz*, Leipzig 1934.

DÜNING, H.-J. *Der SA-Student im Kampf um die Hochschule*, Weimar 1936.

DYRENFURTH-GRAEBSCH, I. *Geschichte des deutschen Jugendbuches*, Hamburg 1951.

EBELING, H. *The German Youth Movement*, London 1945.

EHRENTHAL, G. *Die Deutschen Jugendbünde*, Berlin 1929.

EHRING, H. *Bauern, Kumpels, Kameraden*, Berlin 1938.

EILERS, R. *Die nationalsozialistische Schulpolitik*, Cologne 1963.

ENGELHARDT, V. *Die deutsche Jugendbewegung als kulturhistorisches Phänomen*, Berlin 1923.

ESCHENBURG, T. 'Die Rolle der Persönlichkeit in der Krise der Weimarer Republik' in *VfZG*, Stuttgart 1961.
et al, *The Road to Dictatorship: Germany 1918–33*, London 1962.

ESPE, W. M. *Das Buch der NSDAP*, Munich 1934.

EYCK, E. *Geschichte der Weimarer Republik*, Zurich 1954–56.

EYCK, F. *The Frankfurt Parliament 1848–49*, London 1968.

FABIAN, A./MOSLEHNER, O. *Heldengeist im Heldenliedd. Eine Einführung* in die Edda und andere altdeutsche Dichtungen *für* die Jugend des 3. Reiches, Breslau 1934.

FANDRERL, W. (ed.) *HJ Marschiert! Das neue Hitler-Jugend Buch*, Berlin 1933.

FALLADA, H. *Bauern, Bonzen, Bomben, ro-ro-ro* reprint, Hamburg 1964.

FEDRIGOTTI, Count Bossi. *Standschütze Bruggler*, new ed. Oldenburg 1973.

FICHTE, J. G. *Reden an die deutsche Nation, Goldman Taschenbuch*, Munich n.d.

FISCHER, H. 'Der Aufstieg der NSDAP und die Nationalsozialistiche Machtergreifung 1933/34' in *Geschichte in Wissenschaft und Unterricht*. Issue 6, 1969.

FEST, J. C. *The Face of the Third Reich*, London 1969.

Adolf Hitler, Frankfurt 1973.

FICK, L. *Die Deutsche Jugendbewegung*, Jena 1939.

FISCHER, E. (ed.) *Die Junge Kamaradschaft*, Berlin 1935.

FISCHER, F. *Krieg der Illusionen*, Düsseldorf 1969.

FISCHER, J. 'Entwicklung und Wandlungen in den Jugendverbänden im Jahre 1929' in *Das Junge Deutschland. Amtliches Organ der Reichsausschuss der deutschen Jugendverbände*. Issue 1, January 1930.

'Entwicklungen und Wandlungen in den Jugendverbänden im Jahre 1931' in *Das Junge Deutschland. Amtliches Organ der Reichsausschuss der deutschen Jugendverbände*. Issue 2, February 1932.

'Die Nationalsozialistische Bewegung in der Jugend' in *Das Junge Deutschland. Amtliches Organ der Reichsausschuss der Deutschen Jugendverbände*. Issue 8, August 1930.

FLECHTHEIM, O. K. *Die KPD in der Weimarer Republik*, Offenbach 1948.

FLEX, W. *Der Wanderer zwischen beiden Welten*, Munich 1918.

FORSTHOFF, E. *Deutsche Verfassungsgeschichte der Neuzeit*, Stuttgart 1961.

FÖRSTER, F. W. *Jugendseele, Jugendbewegung, Jugendziele*, Munich 1923.

FOURET, L. A. 'Pedagogie Hitlerienne' in *Revue des Deux Mondes, 8me Periode XXIV*, 1934.

FRANKE, V. *Anti-Nazi development among German Youth*, New York 1945.

FRANZ, G. *Die Politischen Wahlen in Niedersachsen, 1867 bis 1949*, Bremen 1957.

FRANZ, H. *Die Strasse frei-dem Jungvolk*, Berlin 1934.

FRANZ-WILLING, G. *Die Hitler Bewegung: Der Ursprung 1919–22*, Hamburg 1962.

FRASCHKA, G. *Das Letzte Aufgebot: Vom Sterben der Deutschen Jugend*, Rastatt 1960.

FRIEDENBURG, F. *Die Weimarer Republik*, Berlin 1946.

FRIEDELL, E. *Kulturgeschichte der Neuzeit, vol. 3*, Munich 1931.

FÜHRER, M. *Nordgermanische Götterüberlieferung und deutsches Volksmärchen. 80 Märchen der Brüder Grimm vom Mythus her beleuchtet. Band III der Beiträge zur Volkstumsforschung*, Munich 1938.

GALERA, K. S. V. *Das Junge Deutschland und das Dritte Reich*, Leipzig 1932.

GAMM, H. J. *Der braune Kult, Das Dritte Reich und seine Ersatzreligion*, Hamburg 1962.

GAY, P. *Weimar Culture*, London 1969.

GEHL, J. *Austria, Germany and the Anschluss 1931–38*, Oxford 1963.

GERLACH, E. 'Westdeutsche Jugend 1943. Leserkundliche Beobachtungen einer Volksbibliothekarin' in *Die Bücherei, Zeitschrift der Reichsstelle für* das Büchereiwesen, Leipzig, 11. Jg. Heft 1–3, 1944.

GERLACH, H. v. *Von Rechts nach Links*, Zürich 1937.

GILBERT, G. M. *The Psychology of Dictatorship*, New York 1950.

GOEBBELS, J. *Vom Kaiserhof zur Reichskanzlei*, Munich 1934.

GORDON, H. J. *The Reichswehr and the German Republic*, Princeton 1957.

GLONDAJEWSKI, G. and SCHUMANN, H. *Die Neubauer-Poser-Gruppe, Dokumente und Materialien des illegalen antifaschistischen Kampfes*, Berlin 1959.

GOOCH, G. P. *Studies in German History*, London 1948.

GÖRZ, H. — WREDE, F. O. *Unsterbliche Gefolgschaft*, Berlin 1936.

GRANZOW, K. *Tagebuch eines Hitlerjungen 1943–45*, Bremen 1966.

GRASS, G. *Die Blechtrommel*, Frankfurt 1962.

GREGOR, M. *Die Brücke*, Munich 1964.

GRENZ, G. 'Vom Märchenerzählen' in *Die Neue Gemeinschaft. Parteiarchiv für nationalsozialistische Feier-und Freizeitgestaltung*, Munich 1943.

GRETZ, H. 'Der Kampf um die Hitlerjugend' in *Nationalsozialistische Monatshefte*, January 1930.

GRIESMAYER, G. *Wir Hitlerjungen: Unsere Weltanschauung in Frage und Antwort*, Berlin 1936.

GRIMM, H. *Volk ohne Raum*, Munich 1926, new ed. Lippoldsberg 1956.

GRITZBACH, E. *Hermann Göring*, Munich 1940.

GROSSE, A. 'Die Hitlerjugend. Bund deutscher Arbeiterjugend' in *Handbuch der Deutschen Jugendbewegung* edited by K. O. Paetel, Flarchheim 1930.

GRUBE, K. *Zur Charakterologie der deutschen Jugendbewegung*, Magdeburg 1930.

GRUBER, K. *Der Gau Sachsen. Ein Buch der Grenzlandheimat*, Dresden 1938.

GRUBER, K. 'Die gegenwärtige Hitlerjugend' in *Die Junge Front*, Vol. 1929.

GRÜNDEL, G. *Die Sendung der jungen Generation*, Munich 1932.

GÜNTHER, A. *Geist der Jungmannschaft*, Hamburg 1934.

GÜNTHER, K. *Neues Deutschland: Ein Erinnerungsbuch für die Jugend an das Erwachsen des Deutschen Volkes 1933*, Breslau 1935.

HAARER, J. *Mutter, erzähl von Adolf Hitler! Ein Buch zum Vorlesen, Nacherzählen und Selbstlesen für kleinere und grössere Kinder*, Munich 1940.

HAGEMANN, W. *Publizistik im Dritten Reich*, Hamburg 1948.

HAGENER, C. *Deutschland unter der Diktatur, 1933–45*, Braunschweig 1966.

HALPERIN, S. W. *Germany tried Democracy*. Rev. ed., New York 1965.

HANFSTÄNGL, E. *Hitler – The Missing Years*, London 1957.

d'HARCOURT, R. 'Jeunesse Hitlerienne' in *Revue des Deux Mondes, 8me Periode, XVIII*, 1933.

L'Evangile de la Force, Paris 1936.

HARTMUT, G. *Deutsche Weihnachten, Brauchtum und Feiergestaltung*, Halle 1937.

HARTSHORNE, E. Y. *The German Universities and National Socialism*, Cambridge 1937.

'German Youth and the Nazi Dream of Victory' in *America Faces the War*, No. 6, 1941.

HASS, K. *Jugend unterm Schicksal. Lebensberichte junger Deutscher 1946–49*, Hamburg 1950.

HASSELBACH, U. v. *Die Entstehung der nationalsozialistischen deutschen Arbeiterpartei*, Doctoral thesis, University of Leipzig 1931.

HASSEL, U. v. *The Von Hassell Diaries 1938–44*, London 1948.

HAUFER, H. *Kampf: geschichte einer Jugend*, Jena 1934.

HAUPT, J. *Nationalerziehung*, Langensalza 1933.

'Neuordnung im Schulwesen und Hochschulwesen' in *Das Recht der nationalen Revolution*, ed. by G. Kaisenberg und F. A. Medicus, Berlin 1933.

HAVERBECK, W. 'Aufbruch der Jungen Nation. Ziel und Weg der Nationalsozialistischen Volksjugendbewegung' in *Nationalsozialistische Monatshefte*, February 1933.

HEBERLE, R. *From Democracy to Nazism: a Regional Case Study on Political Parties in Germany*, Baton Rouge 1964.

Zur Soziologie der nationalsozialistischen Revolution, VfZG, Stuttgart 1965.

HEGEL, G. W. F. *Die Vernunft in der Geschichte. Einleitung in die Philosophie der Weltgeschichte*, Leipzig 1930.

HEIBER, H. (ed.) *Das Tagebuch des Joseph Goebbels 1925/26*, Stuttgart 1960.

Die Republik von Weimar, Munich 1966.

(ed.) *Goebbels Reden 1939–1945*, 2 vols., Düsseldorf 1971–72.
HEIDEGGER, M. *Die Selbstbehauptung der deutschen Universität*, Breslau 1933.
HEIDEN, K. *Die Geschichte des Nationalsozialismus*, Berlin 1933.
HEITZER, H. *Insurrectionen zwischen Weser und Elbe*, (East) Berlin 1959.
HELLER, H. *Sozialismus und Nation*, 1925.
HELWIG, W. *Die blaue Blume des Wandervogels*, Gütersloh 1960.
(ed.) tusk, *Gesammelte Schriften*, Heidenheim 1962.
HEMM, L. *Die unteren Führer in der Hitler-Jugend*, Doctoral thesis. University of Würzburg 1940.
HENNICKER *Die Jugendverbände in der Bundesrepublik*, Stuttgart 1959.
HEMPEL, G. *Die Kieler Hitlerjugend*, Kiel 1938.
HERDER, J. G. v. *Sämtliche Werke*, ed. by B. Suphan, vols. 1–33, Berlin 1877–1913.
HERRLE, Th. *Die deutsche Jugendbewegung*, Gotha 1921.
HERMENS, F. & SCHIEDER, T. *Staat, Wirtschaft und Politik in der Weimarer Republik*, Berlin 1967.
HERTZMANN, L. *DNVP: right-Wing Opposition in the Weimar Republic, 1918–24*, Lincoln 1963.
HEUER, H. 'Englische und deutsche Jugenderziehung' in *Zeitschrift für neusprachlichen Unterricht*, Berlin 1937.
HEUSS, T. *Hitlers Weg. Eine historisch-politische Studie über den Nationalsozialismus*, Stuttgart-Berlin-Leipzig 1932.
'Der Kampf um das deutsche Geschichtsbild' in *die Hilfe 40*, 1934.
Friedrich Naumann, Stuttgart 1937.
'Fragmente' in *VfZG*, Stuttgart 1967.
HEYEN, F. J. *Nationalsozialismus in Alltag*, Boppard 1967.
HIRN, J. *Tirols Erhebung im Jahre 1809*, Innsbruck 1909.
HIRSCH, E. 'Children's books for Germany' in *Junior Bookshelf*, 7 November 1943.
Der Hitlerprozess vor dem Volksgericht München, 2 vols, Munich 1924.
HITLER, A. *Mein Kampf*, Munich 1937.
Hitler's zweites Buch, Stuttgart 1961.
HJ erlebt Deutschland Die Grossfahrten der sächsischen Hitlerjugend, Leipzig 1935.
HOEGNER, W. *Die Verratene Republik*, Munich 1958.
Der Schwierige Aussenseiter, Munich 1959.
HÖHNE, R. *Kennwort Direktor*, Fischer Taschenbuch, Frankfurt 1970. *The Order of the Death's Head*, London 1970.
HONIG, G. (ed.) *JUNGMADELLEBEN. Ein Jahrbuch für 8–14 jahrige Mädel*, Leipzig 1936.
HOFER, W. *Der Nationalsozialismus, Dokumente 1933–1945*, Frankfurt/Main 1957.
HOFFMAN, H. and ZOGLMANN, S. *Jugend erlebt Deutschland*, Berlin 1935/36.
HOFMANN, H. H. *Der Hitlerputsch*, Munich 1961.
HOHLFELD, H. (ed.) *Dokumente der deutschen Politik*, Berlin 1936.
HOLBORN, H. 'Origins and Political Character of Nazi Ideology' in *Political Science Quarterly*, December 1964.
HOLZAPFEL, O. 'Politische Bildungsarbeit in den Jugendverbänden' in *Gesellschaft, Staat, Erziehung. Blätter für Politische Bildung und Erziehung*, vol. 1966.
HOMBURGER-ERIKSON, E. 'Hitler's Imagery and German Youth' in *Psychiatry*, vol. 1942.
HORN, W. *Führerideologie und Parteiorganisation in der NSDAP*, Düsseldorf 1972.
HUBBEN, W. *Die Deutsche Jugendbewegung*, New York 1937.
HÜTTENBERGER, P. *Die Gauleiter. Studie zum Wandel des Machtgefüges in der NSDAP*, Stuttgart 1969.
HYMMEN, F. W. '10 Jahre Hitler-Jugend' in *Die Junge Kameradschaft*, Berlin 1936.
IBBEKEN, R. *Preussen 1807–1813*, Berlin 1970.
INTERNATIONAL COUNCIL FOR PHILOSOPHY AND HUMANISTIC STUDIES

AND UNESCO (ed.) *The Third Reich*, London 1955.

IMT The Trials of the Major War Criminals before the International Military Tribunal at Nuremberg, 14 November 1945 to 1 October 1946. (Trial of Schirach of parts I, II, V, IX, XIV, XVIII, XIX, XXII.) London 1947.

JÄCKEL, E. *Frankreich in Hitlers Europe. Die deutsche Frankreichpolitik im Zweiten Weltkrieg*, Stuttgart 1966.

JAHN, F. L. *Das deutsche Volksthum*, Lübeck 1810.

JAHNKE, K-H. *Entscheidungen, Jugend im Widerstand 1933–1945*, Frankfurt 1970.

JAHR DER BEWÄHRUNG – der Dienst einer steirischen HJ-Einheit 1940, Graz 1940.

JANTZEN, W. 'Die Soziologische Herkunft der Führungsschicht in der Deutschen Jugendbewegung 1900–33' in *Führungsschicht und Eliteproblem Konferenz der Ranke-Gesellschaft*, Göttingen 1957.

JARMAN, T. L. *The Rise and Fall of Nazi Germany*, New York 1961.

JASPER, G. (ed.) *Von Weimar zu Hitler, 1930–33*, Cologne 1968.

JEDLICKA, L. *Ende und Anfang Österreichs*, 1918/19, Salzburg 1969.

JENKE, M. *Verschwörung von Rechts?*, Berlin 1961.

JOCHMANN, W. *Nationalsozialismus und Revolution: Ursprung und Geschichte der NSDAP in Hamburg, 1922–33*. Dokumente. Frankfurt/Main 1963.

JOEL, E. *Die Jugend vor der sozialen Frage*, Jena 1915.

JUGEND *Zwischen Den Kriegen. Eine Sammlung von Aussagen und Dokumenten*, Heidenheim 1967.

JUNG, R. *Der nationale Sozialismus – Seine Grundlagen, sine Werdegang und seine Ziele*, Munich 1922.

JUNG, W. *Deutsche Arbeiterjugend: Auslese, Förderung, Aufstieg*, Berlin 1940.

JÜNGER, E. *Der Kampf als inneres Erlebnis*, Berlin 1922.
Der Arbeiter, Herrschaft und Gestalt, Hamburg 1932.
In Stahlgewittern, Berlin 1926.
Krieg und Krieger, Berlin 1930.

KAISER, G. *Pietismus und Patriotismus im Literarischen Deutschland*, Wiesbaden 1961.

KATH, G. *Das soziale Bild der Studentenschaft*, Bonn 1964.

KAUFMANN, G. *Das kommende Deutschland*, Berlin 1940.

KAUFMANN, R. *Gebrannte Kinder: Die Jugend in der Nachkriegszeit*, Düsseldorf 1961.

KEMPKENS, K. 'Die Politische Bewegung in den Jugendverbänden' in *Das Junge Deutschland. Amtliches Organ der Reichsausschuss der deutschen Jugendverbände*. Issue VI, June 1930.

KILLY, W. (ed.) *Deutsches Lesebuch*, 4 vols. Frankfurt 1960.

KIEL, W. 'Der Weg der Jugendbünde zum Nationalsozialismus' in *Nationalsozialistische Monatshefte*, January 1930.

KINDERMANN, C. *Der Jungführer* im Deutschen Volksstaat, Leipzig 1930.

KINDT, W. 'Bund oder Partei in der Jugendbewegung' in *Das Junge Deutschland. Amtliches Organ der Reichsausschuss der Deutschen Jugendverbände*. Issue XII, December 1932.
(ed.) *Grundschriften der Deutschen Jugendbewegung*, Düsseldorf 1963.

KLEIST, H. v. *Sämtliche Werke*, Munich 1954.

KLEMER, G. *Jugendstrafrecht und Hitler-Jugend, Schriften zum Jugendrecht*, Berlin 1944.

KLIETMANN, K. G. *Die Waffen-SS, Eine Dokumentation*, Osnabrück 1965.

KLÖNNE, A. *Hitlerjugend. Die Jugend und ihre Organisation im Dritten Reich*, Marburg /Lahn 1960.
Gegen den Strom. Ein Bericht über die Jugendopposition im Dritten Reich, Hannover 1958.
'Die Hitlerjugend-Generation, Politische Folgen der Staatsjugenderziehung im Dritten Reich' in *Aus Politik und Zeitgeschichte, Beilage zur Wochenzeitung Das Parlament*, 24.2.1960.

KLOPSTOCK, F. G. *Werke*, Stuttgart 1883.
KLOSE, W. *Generation im Gleichschritt*, Oldenburg 1964.
KLÖSS, E. (ed.) *Reden des Führers, Politik und Propaganda Adolf Hitlers 1922–45*, Munich 1967.
Der Luftkrieg über Deutschland, Munich 1963.
KLOTZ, H. *Wir gestalten durch unser Führerkorps die Zukunft*, Berlin 1931.
KLUGER, A. (ed.) *Die Deutsche Volksschule im Grossdeutschen Reich*, Breslau 1940.
KLUKE, P. 'NS Europaideologie' in *VfZG*; Stuttgart 1955.
KNEIP, R. *Jugend zwischen den Kriegen*, Heidenheim 1967.
KNELLER, G. *The Educational Philosophy of National Socialism*, New Haven, Yale University Press, 1941.
KNIGHT, M. E. *The German Executive 1890–1933*, Stanford 1933.
KNOPP, W. 'Das Überwachungswesen der Hitler-Jugend/Bekämpfung der Jugendgefährdung und Jugendkriminalität' in *Das Junge Deutschland*, vol. 1944, issue 7.
KNÜTTER, H-H. *Ideologien des Rechtsradikalismus im Nachkriegsdeutschland*, Bonn 1961.
KÖBEL, E. *Fahrtbericht 29*, Potsdam 1929.
Der gespannte Bogen, Berlin 1931.
KOCH, H. W. *Der Sozialdarwinismus. Seine Genese und sein Einfluss auf das imperialistische Denken*, Munich 1973.
KOCHAN, L. *Pogrom, 10 November, 1938*, London 1957.
KÖHLER, H. *Arbeitsdienst in Deutschland*, Berlin 1967.
KÖNIGSWALD, H. v. *Preussisches Lesebuch*, Munich 1966.
KÖRBER, W. *Das ist die HJ*, Berlin 1935.
KOGON, E. *The Theory and Practice of Hell*, London 1950.
KOHN, H. *The Mind of Germany*, London 1962.
KOHN, H. *Prelude to Nation States*, New York 1967.
KORN, K. *Die Arbeiterjugendbewegung*, Berlin 1923.
KOTOWSKI, POLS, RITTER (eds.) *Das Wilhelminische Deutschland – Stimmen der Zeitgenossen*, Frankfurt 1965.
KRÄTSCHMER, E. G. *Die Ritterkreuzträger der Waffen-SS*, Göttingen 1957.
KREBS, A. *Wir Jungen tragen die Fahne*, Frankfurt 1939.
KRIEGER, L. *The German Idea of Freedom. History of a Political Tradition*, Boston 1957.
KRIEGER, L. and STERN, F. (eds.) *The Responsibility of Power*, London 1968.
KRIEGK, E. *Nationalpolitische Erziehung*, 22nd ed., Leipzig 1938.
Nationalsozialistische Erziehung, Osterwieck: Zickfeldt 1937.
Wissenschaft, Weltanschauung, Hochschulreform, Leipzig 1934.
KRÜGER, H. *Das Zerbrochene Haus*, Munich 1966.
KUBY, E. *Das Ende des Schreckens*, Munich 1955.
Die Russen in Berlin 1945, Hamburg 1965.
KÜHNL, R. *Die nationsozialistische Linke 1925–30*, Meisenheim/Glan 1966.
KUNKEL, V. 'Der Professor im Dritten Reich' in *Die deutsche Universität und das Dritte Reich*, Munich 1966.
KURELLA, A. *Die deutsche Volksgemeinschaft*, Jena 1918.
LADNER, G. *Seipel als Überwinder der Staatskrise vom Sommer 1922*, Vienna-Graz 1964.
LAGARDE, P. de. *Deutsche Schriften*, Göttingen 1878.
LANG, H. *Die Wissenkisse*, Leipzig 1936.
LANGE, M. G. *Totalitäre Erziehung. Das Erziehungssystem der Sowjetzone Deutschlands*, Frankfurt 1954.
LAMPRECHT, H. *Teenager und Manager*, Bremen 1960.
LAPPER, K. (ed.) and UTERMANN, U. *Jungen – Eure Welt! Das Jahrbuch der Hitler-*

Jugend, Munich, 1938, 1939, 1940, 1941, 1942, 1943.

LAQUEUR, W. *Young Germany*, London 1962.

LEBER, A. (ed.) *Das Gewissen entscheidet*, Berlin 1956.

LEMBERG, E. *Nationalismus, Psychologie und Geschichte*, 2 vols, Hamburg 1964.

LERNER, D. *The Nazi Elite*, Stanford 1951.

LERSNER, Frh. D. *Die evangelischen Jugendverbände Württembergs und die Hitlerjugend 1933/34*, Göttingen 1958.

LEWY, G. *The Catholic Church and Nazi Germany*, New York 1964.

LEY, R. *Wir alle helfen dem Führer*, Munich 1937.

LINNE, G. *Jugend in Deutschland*, Gütersloh 1970.

LITTMANN, A. *Herbert Norkus und die Hitlerjungen vom Beusselkietz*. Nach dem Tagebuch Gerd Mondt und nach Mitteilungen der Familie, Berlin 1934.

LOCHNER, L. P. (ed.) *The Goebbels Diaries*, London 1948.

LÖWITH, K. *Von Hegel zu Nietzsche. Der revolutionäre Bruch im Denken des Neunzehnten Jahrhunderts*, Stuttgart 1950.

LOEWY, E. *Literatur unterm Hakenkreuz. Das Dritte Reich und seine Dichtung*, Frankfurt 1969.

LORCH, H. *Germanische Heldendichtung*, Leipzig 1934.

LÜTKENS, Ch. *Die deutsche Jugendbewegung. Ein soziologischer Versuch*, Frankfurt 1925.

MAASS, H. *Geistige Formung der Jugend unserer Zeit*, Berlin 1931.

MAIKOWSKI, H. *Sturm 33. Geschrieben von Kameraden des Toten*, Berlin 1939.

MAERCKER, L. F. R. *Vom Kaiserheer zur Reichswehr*, Leipzig 1921.

MANN, G. *The History of Germany since 1789*, London 1968.

MANNHEIM, K. *Diagnosis of Our Time*, London 1943.

   Man and Society in an Age of Reconstruction, London 1940.

   'Mass Education and Group Analysis' in *Educating for Democracy*, ed. by Cohen, J. I., and Traver, R. M. W., London 1930.

MASCHMANN, M. *Fazit*, Stuttgart 1964.

MASER, W. *Die Frühgeschichte der NSDAP*, Frankfurt 1965.

   Adolf Hitler, Munich 1971.

MASSMANN, K. *Wir Jugend! Ein Bekanntnisbuch der Deutschen Nachkriegsgeneration*, Berlin 1933.

   Hitlerjugend – neue Jugend! Breslau 1938.

MASUR, G. *Propheten von Gestern*, Frankfurt 1961.

MATHIAS, E. and MORSEY, R. *Das Ende der Parteien*, Düsseldorf 1960.

MATTHIAS, E. 'Hindenburg zwischen den Fronten 1932' in *VfZG*. Stuttgart 1960.

MATZKE, F. *Jugend bekennt: So sind wir!*, Leipzig 1930.

MAU, H. 'Die deutsche Jugendbewegung' in *pädagogik*, Berlin 1947.

MAU, H. and KRAUSNICK, H. *Deutsche Geschichte der jüngsten Vergangenheit 1933–45*, Stuttgart 1956.

MAURER, H. *Jugend und Buch im neuen Reich*, Leipzig 1934.

McRANDLE, J. H. *The Track of the Wolf. Essays on National Socialism and its Leader, Adolf Hitler*, Evanston 1965.

MEINECKE, F. *The German Catastrophe*, New York 1950.

MESSER, A. *Die Freideutsche Jugendbewegung*, Langensalz 1920.

MEYER, K. *Grenadiere*, Munich 1957.

MILATZ, A. *Wähler und Wahlen in der Weimarer Republik*, Bonn 1968.

MILLAR, J.W. 'Youth in the Dictatorships' in *American Political Science Review*, vol.1938.

MITCHELL, A. *Revolution in Bavaria 1918–1919*, Princeton N. J. 1965.

MOHLER, A. *Die konservative Revolution*, Stuttgart 1950.

MÖLLER, A. *Wir werden das Volk. Wesen und Forderung der Hitlerjugend*, Breslau 1935.

MOELLER VAN DEN BRUCK, A. *Das Dritte Reich*, Berlin 1923.

MORSEY, R. 'Hitlers Verhandlungen mit der Zentrumsführung am 31 Januar 1933' in

VfZG, Stuttgart 1961.
Die Deutsche Zentrumspartei, 1917–23, Düsseldorf 1966.
MOSSE, G. L. *The Crisis of German Ideology*, New York 1964.
MOSSE, W. E. *Entscheidungsjahr, 1932 – Zur Judenfrage in der Endphase der Weimarer Republik*, Tübingen 1965.
MUCHOW, H. H. *Jugend und Zeitgeist, rowohlts deutsche enzyklopädie*, Hamburg 1962.
Sexualreife und Sozialstruktur, Hamburg 1962.
Jugendgeneration im Wandel der Zeit, Vienna 1964.
MÜLLER, A. *Sozialpolitische Erziehung*, Berlin 1943.
MÜLLER, H. (ed.) *Katholische Kirche und Nationalsozialismus: Dokumente 1930–35*, Munich 1965.
MÜLLER-HENNIG, E. *Wolgakinder*, Berlin 1935.
MÜLLER-MEININGEN, E. *Aus Bayerns schwersten Tagen*, Munich 1923.
MUNSKE, H. (ed.) *MÄDEL – EURE WELT! Das Jahrbuch der Deutschen Mädel*, Munich 1940–44.
MÜNZENBERG, W. *Die sozialistischen Jugendorganisationen während des Krieges*, Berlin 1919.
Die Dritte Front, Berlin 1930.
MUTH, H. 'Zum Sturz Brünings' in *Geschichte in Wissenschaft und Unterricht*, Vol. 1965.
NASARSKI, P. (Ed.) *Deutsche Jugendbewegung in Europa*, Cologne 1967.
Nationalpolitische Lehrgänge Für Schüler. Denkschrift des Oberpräsidenten der Rheinprovinz, Frankfurt 1935.
NAUMANN, F. *Werke*, Cologne 1964.
NEESSE, G. *Brevier eines jungen Nationalsozialisten*, Oldenburg 1933.
'Reichjugendführung' in *Grundlagen, Aufbau und Wirtschaftsordnung des nationalsozialistischen Staates*, Berlin 1938, ed. by H. H. Lammers and H. Pfundtner.
NEUHÄUSLER, J. *Kreuz und Hakenkreuz/Der Kampf des Nationalsozialismus gegen die katholische Kirche und der kirchliche Widerstand*, 2 vols, Munich 1946.
NEUMANN, F. *Behemoth: The Structure and Practice of National Socialism*, London 1942.
NEUMANN, S. *Die Parteien der Weimarer Republik*, Stuttgart 1965.
NOAKES, J. 'Conflict and Development in the NSDAP, 1924–27' in *Journal of Contemporary History*, Vol. 1966.
The NSDAP in Lower Saxony 1921–33: A Study of National Socialist Organisation and Propaganda, Oxford 1971.
NÖLDECKEN, W. *Die Deutsche Jugendbewegung*, Osnabrück 1953.
NOLTE, E. *The Three Faces of Fascism*, London 1965.
Die Krise des liberalen Systems und die faschistischen Bewegungen, Munich 1968.
(ed.) *Theorien über den Faschismus*, Cologne 1967.
NOVALIS, *Sämtliche Schriften*, ed. by K. C. E. Ehmann, 6 vols., Jena 1907.
NSDAP *Adolf Hitler und seine Kämpfer*, Munich 1933.
NSDAP *Das Deutsche Führerlexikon 1934–35*, Munich 1934.
NSDAP *Jugend hilft und dankt dem Bauern*, Munich 1939.
NSDAP Reichsleitung (ed.) *Nationalsozialistisches Jahrbuch 1934*.
NYOMARKAY, J. *Charisma and Factionalism in the Nazi Party*, Minneapolis 1967.
OERTZEN, F. W. v. *Die deutschen Freikorps 1918–1923*, Munich 1938.
O'NEILL, R. J. *The German Army and The Nazi Party 1933–39*, London 1966.
ORIENTALISCHE CIGARETTEN-COMPAGNIE, 'ROSMA' Album: *Männer im Dritten Reich*, Bremen 1934.
ORLOW, D. O. 'The Organisational History and Structure of the NSDAP, 1919–23' in *The Journal of Modern History*, June 1965.
'Die Adolf-Hitler-Schulen' in *Vierteljahrhefte für Zeitgeschichte*, Stuttgart 1965.

'The Conversion of Myths into Political Power: The Case of the Nazi Party, 1925–26' in *Amer. Hist. Review*, Vol. 72, 1967.

The History of the Nazi Party 1919–33, Vol. I, Pittsburg 1969. Vol. II, Newton Abbot 1973.

Organisationsbuch der NSDAP, Munich 1938.

PAETEL, K. O. 'Das Geistige Gesicht der nationalen Jugend' in *Das Junge Deutschland. Amtliches Organ der Reichsausschuss der deutschen Jugendverbände*. Issue 6, June 1929.

'Die heutige Struktur der nationalen Jugend' in *Das Junge Deutschland. Amtliches Organ der Reichsausschuss der deutschen Jugendverbände*. Issue 6, June 1929.

Handbuch der deutschen Jugendbewegung, Flarchheim 1930.

Das Bild vom Menschen in der deutschen Jugendführung, Bad Godesberg 1954.

'Die Deutsche Jugendbewegung als politisches Phänomen' in *Politische Studien*, Issue 86, July 1957.

Jugend in der Entscheidung 1913–1933–1945, Bad Godesberg 1963.

'Jugend von Gestern und Heute' in *Neue Politische Literatur*, 1964.

Versuchung oder Chance, Berlin 1965.

PAPEN, F. v. *Memoirs*, 1952.

PASCAL, R. *The German Novel*, Manchester 1956.

PASTENACI, K. *Volksgeschichte der Germanen*, Berlin 1936.

PAYR, B. and OTTO, H.-G. (ed.) *Das Deutsche Jugendbuch*, Munich 1942.

PEISER, W. 'Educational Failure of the Weimar Republic' in *School and Society*, vol. 1943.

PETERSON, E. N. 'The Bureaucracy and the Nazi Party' in *The Review of Politics*, vol. 1966.

The Limits of Hitler's Power, Princeton 1969.

PHELPHS, R. H. 'Hitler and the Deutsche Arbeiterpartei' in *American Hist. Review*, Vol. 1963.

PICHL, E. *Schoenerer*, 6 vols., Vienna 1913–38.

PINSON, K. P. *Modern Germany: Its History and Civilisation*, New York 1954.

PIPER, O. *Jugendbewegung und Protestantismus*, Rudolfstadt 1923.

PLESSNER, H. *Die verspätete Nation. Über die politische Verführbarkeit bürgerlichen Geistes*, Stuttgart 1959.

POLIAKOV and WULF *Das Dritte Reich und seine Denker*, Berlin 1959.

PRIDHAM, G. *Hitler's Rise to Power*, London 1973.

PRIEPKE, M. *Die Evangelische Jugend im Dritten Reich 1933–36*, Frankfurt 1960.

PROSS, H. *Die Zerstörung der deutschen Politik, Dokumente, 1871–1933*, Frankfurt 1959.

Jugend, Eros, Politik, Munich 1964.

PROSSE, E. H. *Die Politischen Kampfbünde Deutschlands*, Berlin 1931.

PULZER, P. G. J. *The Rise of Political Anti-Semitism in Germany and Austria*, New York 1964.

RAABE, F. *Die Bündische Jugend: Ein Beitrag zur Geschichte der Weimarer Republik*, Stuttgart 1961.

RAMLOW, R. *Herbert Norkus? – Hier! Opfer u. Sieg der Hitlerjugend*, Stuttgart 1939.

RANDEL, E. *Die Jugenddienstpflicht*, Berlin 1942.

RAUSCHNING, H. *Revolution des Nihilismus*, Zürich 1933.

Hitler Speaks, 1939.

REICHSKRIEGMINISTERIUM (ed.) *Darstellungen aus den Nachkriegskämpfen deutscher Truppen und Freikorps*, 8 vols., Berlin 1936–40.

REIN, G. A. *Die Revolution in der Politik Bismarcks*, Göttingen 1957.

REITLINGER, G. *The S.S.: Alibi of a Nation, 1922–45*, London 1956.

REMOLD; J. *Handbuch für die Hitler-Jugend*, Munich 1933.

RJF REICHSJUGENDFÜHRUNG (ed.) Adolf-Hitler-Marsh *Der deutschen Jugend*,

Munich 1939.
Das Buch der Jugend, 1934/35, 1935/36, 1937/38, 1940, 1941, 1942, Berlin, Stuttgart, Munich.
Jungen im Einsatz, Kriegsjahrbuch der Hitler-Jugend, Munich 1944.
HJ im Dienst, Handbuch für die Dienstgestaltung der HJ, Berlin 1934.
Aufbau, Gliederung und Anschriften der HJ, Berlin 1934.
Aufbaudienst (1. Der organisatorische Aufbau der HJ, 2. Der Dienst der Mannschaft und die Schulung der Führerschaft, 3. Die Leibeserziehung), Vienna 1939.
Aufbau und Abzeichen der HJ, (without date).
Bekleidung und Ausrüstung der HJ: Amtliche Bekleidungsvorschrift der Reichsjugendführung der NSDAP, Berlin 1934.
Die Uniformen der HJ, Hamburg 1934.
Die Kameradschaft, Blätter für Heimabendgestaltung der HJ, Berlin 1933.
HJ im Dienst: Ausbildungsvorschrift für die Ertüchtigung der deutschen Jugend, Berlin 1939.
Dienstvorschrift der HJ. (Rang und Dienstellungsordnung der HJ, Vorschrift über Bearbeitung von Personalangelegenheiten), Berlin 1940.
Jahrbuch der Hitlerjugend, Munich 1937–43.
Junge Welt, Monatszeitschrift der HJ, Berlin 1939.
Die Jungenschaft, Blätter für die Heimabendgestaltung im DJ (ed.): Amt für weltanschauliche Schulung, Berlin 1933 ff.
Jungvolk, Blätter deutscher Jungen, Munich 1933–34.
Jungvolk-Jahrbuch, Berlin 1937.
Jungvolk-Jahrbuch, Munich 1940.
Pimpf im Dienst, Berlin 1934.
Der Pimpf, (NS-Jugendblätter), Berlin 1937–41.
Die Jungmädelschaft, Blätter für die Heimabendgestaltung, Berlin.
Die Mädelschaft (Blätter für Heimabendgestaltung in BDM), Berlin.
Glaube und Schönheit, Munich 1933.
Kriminalität und Gefährdung der Jugend. Lagebericht bis zum Stande vom 1. Januar 1941, Berlin 1941.
Reichsjugendpressedienst (Amtlicher Pressedienst des Jugendführers des Deutschen Reiches), Berlin 1934.
Blut und Ehre: Liederbuch der Hitler-Jugend, Berlin 1933.
Unser Kriegs-Liederbuch, Munich 1939.
Unser Liederbuch, Lieder der Hitler-Jugend, Munich 1941.
Unser Dienst: Aufgabe für die neuen Einheiten der HJ, Berlin 1940.
Vorschriftenhandbuch der HJ, Berlin 1942.
Die Werkarbeit im Kriegseinsatz der HJ, Berlin 1942.
RITTEL, H. and STÄHLIN, W. 'Das Neue Reich' in *Das Junge Deutschland. Amtliches Organ der Reichsausschuss der deutschen Jugendverbande*, March 1930.
RITTER, G. *Carl Goerdeler und die deutsche Widerstandsbewegung*, dtv, Munich 1954.
RITTER, G. *The Sword and the Sceptre*, 4 vols, Coral Gables 1970–73.
ROBERTS, S. H. *The House that Hitler Built*, London 1937.
RÖGELS, F. R. *Der Marsch auf Berlin*, Berlin 1932.
ROGGER, H. and WEBER, E. *The European Right*, London 1965.
RÖHM, E. *Geschichte eines Hochverräters*, Munich 1928.
RÖSSLER, M. *Graf Johann Philipp Stadion*, 2 vols, Vienna 1969.
ROHE, K. *Das Reichsbanner Schwarz-Rot-Gold*, Düsseldorf 1966.
ROLOFF, E. A. *Bürgertum und Nationalsozialismus*, 1930–33, Hanover 1961.
ROLOFF, E. A. 'Wer wählte Hitler?' in *Politische Studien*, vol. 1964.
ROLOFF, E. A. *Braunschweig und der Staat von Weimar*, Braunschweig 1964.
ROSENBERG, A. 'Rebellion der Jugend' in *Nationalsozialistische Monatshefte*, January 1930.

330   *Bibliography*

ROSENBERG, A. *Der Mythus des 20. Jahrhunderts*, Munich 1935.
ROSENBERG, A. *Entstehung der Weimarer Republik*, Frankfurt 1961.
   Geschichte der Weimarer Republik, Frankfurt 1961.
ROSIWALL, Th. *Die Letzten Tage*, Vienna 1969.
ROSSBACH, G. *Mein Weg durch die Zeit: Erinnerungen und Bekenntnisse*, Weilberg
   /Lahn 1950.
ROWAN-ROBINSON, G. A. 'Training the Nazi Leaders of the Future' in *International
   Affairs*, vol. 17.
ROTH, H. *Psychologie der Jugendgruppe*, Berlin 1938.
ROTH, H. *Katholische Jugend in der NS-Zeit*, Düsseldorf 1959.
ROTHFELS, H. *Die Universitäten und der Schuldspruch von Versailles*, Königsberg
   1929.
RÜHLE, G. (ed.) *Das Dritte Reich, Dokumentarische Darstellung des Aufbaus der
   Nation*, Berlin 1935 ff.
RUST, B. 'Education in The Third Reich' in *Germany Speaks*, 1938.
RYAN, C. *The Last Battle*, London 1966.
SADILA-MANTAU, H. *German Political Profiles*, Berlin 1938.
   Unsere Reichsregierung, Berlin 1940.
SALOMON, E. v. *Die Kadetten*, Hamburg 1957 (reprint).
   Die Geächteten, Berlin 1930.
   Die Stadt, Berlin 1934.
   Nahe Geschichte, Berlin 1937.
   Der Fragebogen, Hamburg 1951.
   Das Schicksal des A. D., Hamburg 1960.
SAND, T. *Zickezacke Landjahr heil! Leben, Treiben, Taten u. Abenteuer d. Jungen u.
   Mädel im Landjahr. Von ihnen selber aufgeschrie ben und mit Zeichngn ungen
   versehen*, Stuttgart 1938.
SANDVOSS, E. *Hitler und Nietzsche*, Göttingen 1969.
SAUER, W. 'National Socialism: Totalitarianism or Fascism?' *American. Hist. Review*,
   Vol. 1967.
SAUTTER, R. *Hitlerjugend. Das Erlebnis einer grossen Kamaradschaft*, Munich 1942.
   Pimpf jetzt gilt's. Das Erlebnis der Jungbannfehden, Stuttgart 1937.
SCHÄFER, H. *Deutscher Jugendkalender, 1934/35*, Plauen 1935.
SCHÄFER, W. *NSDAP: Entwicklung und Struktur der Staatspartei des Dritten Reiches*,
   Hanover 1956.
SCHAIRER, R. *Not: Kampf: Ziel der Jugend in sieben Ländern*, Frankfurt 1935.
SCHEEL, G. A. *Die Reichsstudentenführung* – Arbeit und Organisation des deutschen
   Studententums, Berlin 1938.
SCHENZINGER, K. A. *Der Hitlerjunge Quex*, Berlin 1933.
   Der Herrgottsbacher Schülermarsch, Berlin 1935.
SCHELSKY, H. *Arbeiterjugend – gestern und heute*, Heidelberg 1955.
   Die Skeptische Generation, Cologne 1957.
SCHIERER, H. *Das Zeitschriftenwesen der Jugendbewegung*, Berlin, 1938.
SCHILLING, A. *Dr. Walter Riehl und die Geschichte des Nationalsozialismus*, Leipzig
   1933.
SCHIRACH, B. v. *Wille und Weg des Nationalsozialistischen Deutschen
   Studentenbundes*, Munich 1929.
   Die Fahne der Verfolgten, Berlin 1933.
   Die Hitler-Jugend: Idee und Gestalt, Leipzig 1934.
   Wesen und Aufbau der Hitler-Jugend: Dokumente der Deutschen Politik.
   Revolution der Erziehung, Munich 1938.
   Lied der Getreuen, Berlin 1938.
   Ich glaubte an Hitler, Hamburg 1967.
SCHLEIERMACHER, F. *Sämtliche Werke*, Berlin 1834–38.

SCHMIDT, U. 'Über das Verhältnis von Jugendbewegung und Hitlerjugend' in *Geschichte in Wissenschaft und Unterricht*, Vol. 1965.

SCHMIDT-PAULI, E. v. *Die Männer um Hitler*, Berlin 1932.

Geschichte der Freikorps 1918–1924, Stuttgart 1936.

SCHNABEL, F. *Deutsche Geschichte im 19. Jahrhundert*, 4 vols, Freiburg 1964.

SCHNABEL, R. *Das Führerschulungswerk der HJ*, Berlin 1938.

SCHNEIDER, B. *Daten zur Geschichte der Jugendbewegung*, Bad Godesberg 1965.

SCHNEIDER, E. A. *Ein Bildbuch der Hitlerjugend*, Berlin 1938.

SCHOENBAUM, D. *Hitler's Social Revolution: Class and Status in Nazi Germany 1933–39*, London 1966.

SCHOEPS, H-J. *Wir deutschen Juden*, Berlin 1934.

Die letzten Dreissig Jahre: Rückblicke, Berlin 1963.

(ed.) *Zeitgeist im Wandel. Zeitgeist der Weimarer Republik*, Stuttgart 1968.

SCHOLDER, K. 'Die evangelische Kirche in der Sicht der nationalsozialistischen Führung' in *VfZG*, Stuttgart 1966.

SCHOLL, I. *Die weisse Rose*, Fischer Taschenbuch, reprint, Frankfurt 1971.

SCHOLTZ, H. 'Die NS-Ordensburgen' in *VfZG*, Stuttgart 1967.

Nationalsozialistische Ausleseschulen. Internatsschulen als Herrschaftsmittel des Führerstaates, Göttingen 1973.

SCHOTT, G. *Weissagung und Erfüllung* im Deutschen Volksmärchen, Munich 1936.

SCHRAMM, H. *Das Hitlerbuch der Deutschen Jugend*, Hamburg 1933.

SCHÜDDEKOPF, O. E. *Linke Leute von Rechts*, Stuttgart 1960.

SCHULT, J. *Das Weimar der arbeitenden Jugend*, Weimar 1920.

SCHULT, J. *Aufbruch einer Jugend*, Bonn 1956.

SCHÜRER-STOLLE, L. *So sind wir. Jungmädel erzählen*, Berlin 1937.

SCHWARZ, M. *Biographisches Handbuch der Deutschen Reichstage*, 1965.

SCHWEND, K. *Bayern Zwischen Monarchie und Diktatur*, Munich 1954.

SEHRWALD, F. *Deutsche Dichter und Denker*, 2 vols, Altenburg 1880.

SEIDELMANN, K. *Bund und Gruppe als Lebensform deutscher Jugend*, Munich 1955.

SEIDL, E. *Kampfgenossen des Führers: Hitler und die Männer seiner Bewegung*, Linz 1933.

SEIER, H. 'Der Rektor als Führer' in *VfZG*, Stuttgart 1964.

SHULMAN, M. *Defeat in the West*, London 1947.

SIEBENPFEIFFER, P. J. *Vom Hambacher Fest 1832*, Munich 1910.

SIEFERT, H. *Der Bündische Aufbruch 1919–1933*, Bad Godesberg 1963.

SIEMERING, H. *Die deutschen Jugendverbände*, Berlin 1931.

Deutschlands Jugend in Bevölkerung und Wirtschaft, Berlin 1937.

SIMON, W. M. *Germany: A Brief History*, London 1967.

SONTHEIMER, K. *Anti-demokratisches Denken in der Weimarer Republik*, Munich 1962.

SPAHN, O. *Der wahre Staat*, Leipzig 1921.

Hauptpunkte der unversalistischen Staatsauffassung, Berlin 1930.

SPENGLER, O. *Preussentum und Sozialismus*, Munich (n.d.).

SPIESS, K. v. and MUDRAK, E. *Deutsche Märchen, deutsche Welt. Zeugnisse nordischer Weltanschauung in volkstümlicher Überlieferung*, Berlin 1939.

STÄHLIN, W. *Fieber und Heil in der deutschen Jugendbewegung*, Hamburg 1923.

STEFFENS, H. Über die Ideen der Universitäten, Berlin 1809.

STEIN, W. *The Waffen-SS at War*, Oxford 1966.

STELLRECHT, H. *Glauben und Handeln. Ein Bekenntnis der jungen Nation*, Berlin 1938.

Die Wehrerziehung der deutschen Jugend, Berlin 1936.

Neue Erziehung, 5 ed., Berlin 1944.

STELTER, H. *Eine Geschichte deutscher Jugendbewegung, zugleich Handbuch und Richtlinien der deutschen Jugendbewegung*, Berlin (without date).

STERN, F. *The Politics of Cultural Despair: A Study in the Rise of the Germanic Ideology*, New York 1965.

STIPPEL, F. *Die Zerstörung der Person/Kritische Studie zur nationalsozialistischen Pädagogik*, Donauworth 1957.

STOLTENBERG, G. *Das Schlesw.-Holst. Landvolk 1918–33*, Düsseldorf 1962.

STRACHURA, P. *Development and Organisation of the Hitler Youth 1930–33*, unpublished Ph.D. thesis, East Anglia 1972.

STRASSER, O. *Hitler und Ich*, Konstanz 1948.

STROHMANN, D. *Nationalsozialistische Literaturpolitik. Ein Beitrag zur Publizistik im Dritten Reich*, Bonn 1963.

TAUBER, K. P. *Beyond Eagle and Swastika: German Nationalism since 1945*, Connecticut 1967.

TETZLAFF, W. *Das Diszplinarrecht der Hitler-Jugend*, Berlin 1944.

TEUBNER, B. G. *HJ erlebt Deutschland*, Leipzig 1935.

TIMM, H. *Die Deutsche Sozialpolitik und der Bruch der Grossen Koalition im März, 1930*, Düsseldorf 1953.

TJADEN, K. *Rebellion der Jungen, Die Geschichte von tusk und von dj. 1.11*, Frankfurt 1958.

TOLAND, J. *The Last 100 Days*, London 1965.

TOBIAS, F. *Der Reichstagsbrand*, Berlin 1961.

TOMIN, V. and GRABOWSKI, S. *Die Helden der Berliner Illegalität*, Berlin 1967.

TONNIES, F. *Gemeinschaft und Gesellschaft*, Leipzig 1935.
    trans. by C. P. Loomis as *Fundamental Concepts of Sociology*, New York 1940.

TREVOR-ROPER, H. R. *Hitler's Secret Conversations 1941–44*, New York 1961.

TREVOR-ROPER, H. R. *The Last Days of Hitler*, London 1947.

UEBERHORST, H. *Elite für die Diktatur. Die Nationalpolitischen Erziehungsanstalten 1933–45*, Düsseldorf 1969.

UETRECHT, F. E. *Jugend im Sturm: Ein Bericht aus den schicksalsschweren Jahren, 1917–33*, Berlin 1936.

USADEL, G. *Die nationalsozialistische Jugendbewegung*, Bielefeld and Leipzig 1934.
    Zucht und Ordnung, Berlin 1935.

UWESON, U. and ZIERSCH, W. (eds.) *Das Buch der Hitlerjugend: Die Jugend im Dritten Reich*, Munich 1934.

VACANO, O. W. v. *Sparta, der Lebenskampf einer nordischen Herrenschicht*, Bücherei der Adolf-Hitler-Schulen, 1942.

VALENTIN, V. *Geschichte der deutschen Revolution 1848–49*, 2 vols, Cologne 1969.

VANDRAY, M. *Der politische Witz im Dritten Reich*, Munich 1967.

VEBLEN, Th. *Imperial Germany and the Industrial Revolution*, New York 1965.

VESPER, W. (ed.) *Deutsche Jugend*, Berlin 1934.

VIERA, J. *Utz kämpfte für Hitler*, Leipzig 1933.

VIERHAUS, R. 'Auswirkungen der Krise um 1930 in Deutschland' in *Die Staats-und Wirtschaftskrise des Deutschen Reichs 1929/33*, Stuttgart 1967.

VIERNOW, A. *Zur Theorie und Praxis des nationalsozialistischen Geschichtsunrichts*, Halle 1935.

VOGELSANG, T. 'Zur Politik Schleichers gegenüber der NSDAP' in *VfZG*, Stuttgart 1958.
    Reichswehr and NSDAP, Stuttgart 1962.

WAGNER, G. *Die Fahne ist mehr als der Tod*, Hamburg 1958.

WARD-PRICE, G. *I know these Dictators*, London 1937.

WEBER, E. *Varieties of Fascism*, Princeton 1964.

WEBER, M. *Jugendbriefe*, Tübingen (without date).

WEHNER, G. *Die rechtliche Stellung der HJ*, Doctoral thesis, University of Leipzig 1930.

WEISSENBORN, G. *Der lautlose Aufstand*, Hamburg 1954.

WERNER, K. *Mit Baldur von Schirach auf Fahrt*, Munich 1937.

WEYMAR, E. 'Ernst Moritz Arndt' in *Aus Politik und Zeitgeschehen, Beilage zur Wochenzeitung Das Parlament*, 18 May 1960.

WHITESIDE, A. G. 'The Nature and Origins of National Socialism' in *Journal of Central European Affairs*, vol. 1957.

WHITING, Ch. *The Battle of the Ruhrpocket*, New York 1970.

WILHELM, Th. 'Der geschichtliche Ort der deutschen Jugendbewegung' in *Grundschriften der deutschen Jugendbewegung*, Düsseldorf 1963.

WILMOT, Ch. *Struggle for Europe*, London 1952.

WIMMER, H. *Nationalismus und Jugenderziehung*, Hamburg 1936.

WITTRAM, R. *Nationalismus und Säkularisation*, Lüneburg 1949.

WOLFF, G. (ed.) *Die Deutschen Jugendbünde*, Planen 1931.

WOLLSCHLÄGER, H. *Karl May, ro-ro-monographie*, Hamburg 1965.

WOLTERS, F. 'Mensch und Gattung' in *Jahrbuch für* die geistige Bewegung, 1912.

WREDE, F. O. 'Eine Geschichte der Hitlerjugend' in *Nationalsozialistische Monatshefte*, September 1934.

WULF, J. *Literatur und Dichtung im Dritten Reich. Eine Dokumentation*, Gütersloh 1963.

WYNEKEN, G. *Der Kampf für* die Jugend, Jena 1919.
Der Gedankenkreis der freien Schulgemeinde, Jena 1919.
Schule und Jugendkultur, Jena 1919.
Eros, Lauenburg 1921.

YOUNG, D. *Rommel*, London 1950.

ZAHN, K. F. *Kirche und HJ*, Berlin 1934.

ZECHLIN, E. *Die deutsche Einheitsbewegung*, Berlin 1969.

ZEMAN, Z. A. B. *Nazi Propaganda*, Oxford 1964.

ZÖBERLEIN, H. *Der Glaube an Deutschland. Ein Kriegserleben von Verdun bis zum Umsturz*, Munich 1941.

ZORN, W. 'Student Politics in the Weimar Republic' in *Journal of Contem. History*, Vol. 1970.

Newspapers and Periodicals

Der Adler
Akademischer Beobachter, Kampfblatt des NSDStB
American Historical Review
American Political Science Review
Amtliches Nachrichtenblatt des Jugendführers des Deutschen Reiches
Der Aufmarsch, Monatszeitschrift des NSSB
Berliner Tagblatt
Börsenblatt für den deutschen Buchhandel
Das junge Deutschland. Amtliches Organ des Jugendführers des Deutschen Reiches
Deutsche Allgemeine Zeitung
Deutscher Reichs-und Preussischer Staatsanzeiger
Europäische Begegnung
Frankfurter Zeitung
Frankfurter Allgemeine Zeitung
Der Freiwillige
Die Junge Front. Führerblatt Der Hitler-Jugena
Führerblätter der HJ
Führerdienst der HJ
Führerinnendienst der HJ
Geschichte in Wissenschaft und Unterricht
Die HJ. Das Kampfblatt der Hitler-Jugend
Historische Zeitschrift
Der Hitler-Jugend Richter
Hitler-Jugend-Zeitung. Kampfblatt Schaffender Jugend
Der Hoheitsträger
Illustrierter Beobachter
Die Höhere Schule
Jugendschriften-Warte
Die Jungenschaft

Die Jungmädelschaft
Journal of Central European Affairs
Journal of Contemporary History
Journal of Modern History
Der Jungmann
Junge Nation. Bundesblatt Der Hitler-Jugend
Jugendblatt der Adolf-Hitler-Schulen
Die Kommenden
Die Neue Literatur
New Society
Mädel voran
Das deutsche Mädel
Die Mädelschaft
The Manchester Guardian
Münchner Neueste Nachrichten
Münchner Post
Niedersächsischer Beobachter
Der junge Nationalsozialist
Nationalsozialistische Bibliographie
Nationalsozialistische Monatshefte
Nationalsozialistisches Bildungswesen
Neues Deutschland
Der Pimpf. Nationalsozialistische Jungenblätter
Political Science Quarterly
Politische Studien
Politische Vierteljahresschrift
Das Reich
Reichsjugendpressedienst
Review of Politics
Das Schwarze Korps
Der Spiegel
Die Sturmfahne, Kampfblatt der HJ Österreichs
Sturmjugend. Kampfblatt Schaffender Jugend
Süddeutsche Zeitung
The Times
Verordnungsblatt des Reichsjugendführers
Vierteljahrshefte für Zeitgeschichte
Das Junge Volk
Völkischer Beobachter
Vorwärts
Wille und Werk. Pressedienst der Deutschen Jugendbewegung
Die Wehrmacht

Die Welt
Wille und Macht. Fuhrerorgan Der HJ
Die Zeit
Zeitschrift für neusprachlichen Unterricht
Zeitschrift für Politik
Die Deutsche Zukunft. Organ Der Nationalsozialistischen Jugend
*Der Zwiespruch. Amtliches Nachrichtenblatt der Deutschen
    Jugendbewegungsbünde*

Index

Index

Made in the USA
Coppell, TX
05 May 2020